with best wishes,

The Finger of the Scribe

The Finger of the Scribe

How Scribes Learned to Write the Bible

WILLIAM M. SCHNIEDEWIND

OXFORD
UNIVERSITY PRESS

Oxford University Press is a department of the University of Oxford. It furthers the University's objective of excellence in research, scholarship, and education by publishing worldwide. Oxford is a registered trade mark of Oxford University Press in the UK and certain other countries.

Published in the United States of America by Oxford University Press
198 Madison Avenue, New York, NY 10016, United States of America.

CIP data is on file at the Library of Congress
ISBN 978–0–19–005246–1

3 5 7 9 8 6 4 2

Printed by Sheridan Books, Inc., United States of America

Contents

Preface

According to the writer of Exodus, God gave Moses "two tablets of the covenant, tablets of stone, *written by the finger of God*." It is a glorious anthropomorphic image of divine inspiration. In contrast, I write about *the finger of the scribe*, which depended on education. Scribes depended on teachers and curriculum to learn how to write. Throughout the Bible, a variety of figures—scribes, prophets, priests, kings, and even a young boy—write various things, including both mundane and profound texts. The Hebrew Bible contains lists and letters but also liturgies and stories, all written by scribes. This book explores how the early alphabetic scribes began to learn how to write and, eventually, how they learned to write the Bible. In this book, I am particularly interested in scribal education—or, more specifically, scribal curriculum. What were scribes' textbooks? What did they practice? What did they memorize? And, how did this shape the Bible? I believe that I found the key to unlocking these questions in the scribal scribbles at Kuntillet ʿAjrud as well as in the cuneiform school texts used in Canaan at the end of the Late Bronze Age.

The project was many years in the making and was helped along the way by innumerable people. First of all, I want to thank my colleagues and students at UCLA, from whom I believe I learned and received more than I taught and gave. In particular, I wish to acknowledge Aaron Burke, Bob Cargill, Elizabeth Carter, Kara Cooney, Jacco Dieleman, Brian Donnelly-Lewis, Elizabeth VanDyke, Robert Englund, Tim Hogue, Moise Isaac, Alice Mandell, Roger Nam, Jason Price, Rahim Shayegan, Jeremy Smoak, Matt Suriano, Stephen Ward, and Jonathan Winnerman. I have a special appreciation for Elizabeth VanDyke, whose critical eye working as my Graduate Research Assistant improved this book immeasurably. I also received a great deal of support, encouragement, and critique along this journey from a variety of fellow travelers, including Susan Ackerman, Erhard Blum, David Carr, Aaron Demsky, Dan Fleming, Ron Hendel, Jan Joosten, Anat Mendel-Geberovich, Anson Rainey (z"l), Gary Rendsburg, Seth Sanders, Joachim Schaper, Mark Smith, Jeff Stackert, Steve Tinney, David Vanderhooft, Jackie Vayntrub, and Ed Wright. I have presented this material to a variety of audiences who have all shaped my thinking in a variety of ways. It began with the invitation by Gabrielle Boccacini to a conference on early Jewish education in Naples. There, I especially benefited from extended conversations with Steve Tinney about Mesopotamian education. I also wish to thank the Near Eastern Studies Department at Johns Hopkins University for the invitation to give the Samuel Iwry Lecture. I also presented parts of this book to the Biblical Colloquium and its members in the seminar organized by David Vanderhooft. Their interaction and comments were particularly stimulating. Finally, I need thank UCLA, which has given me the resources and support for this research. I appreciate the many people and places at UCLA that made this book possible, including Dean of Humanities David Schaberg, the Center for Jewish Studies, the Center for the Study of Religion and its director Carol Bakhos, and finally our Department chair Kara Cooney. Support for this research was also provided by the Reuben and Norma Kershaw Term Chair in Ancient Eastern Mediterranean Studies. Last but not least, I thank my family—my wife, Jeanne, and my daughters, Tori and Mikaela—and, a special shout-out for Tori, who discussed many things Egyptological with me and spurred my decipherment of the Lachish jar inscription. Nothing was here accomplished alone, but I take credit for all its shortcomings.

Abbreviations

ABD	Anchor Bible Dictionary
AOAT	*Alter Orient und Altes Testament*
BA	*Biblical Archaeologist*
BAR	*Biblical Archaeology Review*
BASOR	*Bulletin of the American Schools of Oriental Research*
BZAW	*Beihefte zur Zeitschrift für die alttestamentliche Wissenschaft*
COS	K. Lawson Younger and William W. Hallo, eds., *The Context of Scripture*, 3 volumes (Leiden: Brill, 2003).
EA	El-Amarna letters. See Anson F. Rainey, *The El-Amarna Correspondence: A New Edition of the Cuneiform Letters from the Site of El-Amarna Based on Collations of All Extant Tablets*, ed. William Schniedewind, vol. 1 (HdO 110; Leiden: Brill, 2015).
GKC	Gensenius-Kautzsch-Cowley, *Gensenius' Hebrew Grammar*, Wilhelm Gesenius, Emil Kautzsch, and Arthur Ernest Cowley (Oxford: Clarendon, 1910).
HALOT	*Hebrew and Aramaic Lexicon of the Old Testamen*t, Ludwig Kohler and Walter Baumgartner, 4 volumes (Leiden: Brill, 1994–2000).
HS	*Hebrew Studies*
HUCA	*Hebrew Union College Annual*
IEJ	*Israel Exploration Journal*
JANES	*Journal of Ancient Near Eastern History*
JAOS	*Journal of the American Oriental Society*
JBL	*Journal of Biblical Literature*
JEA	*Journal of Egyptian Archaeology*
JNES	*Journal of Near Eastern Studies*
JQR	*Jewish Quarterly Review*
JSOT	*Journal for the Study of the Old Testament*
JSOTSS	*Journal for the Study of the Old Testament Supplement Series*
JSS	*Journal of Semitic Studies*
KAI	*Kanaanäische und Aramäische Inschriften* (2nd edition), Herbert Donner and Wolfgang Röllig (Wiesbaden: Harrassowitz, 2002).
KTU	Dietrich Manfried, Oswald Loretz, and Joaquín Sanmartín, eds., *The Cuneiform Alphabetic Texts from Ugarit, Ras Ibn Hani and Other Places: From Ugarit, Ras Ibn Hani and Other Places* (Münster: Ugarit-Verlag, 1995).
NEA	*Near Eastern Archaeology*

OBO	*Orbis biblicus et orientalis*
RA	*Revue d'assyriologie et d'archaéologie orientale*
RB	*Revue Biblique*
RS	*Ras Shamra*
RSOu	*Ras Shamra–Ougarit*
SAA	*State Archives of Assyria*
SAOS	*Studies in Ancient Oriental Civilization*
SBL	*Society of Biblical Literature*
SBLMS	*Society of Biblical Literature Monograph Series*
SVT	*Supplements to Vetus Testamentum*
TB	*Tyndale Bulletin*
VT	*Vetus Testamentum*
ZA	*Zeitschrift für Assyriologie*
ZAW	*Zeitschrift für Alttestamentliche Wissenschaft*
ZDMG	*Zeitschrift der Deutschen Morgenländischen Gesellschaft*

1
The Emergence of Scribal Education in Ancient Israel

Where is the finger of the scribe in the Bible? Can we trace some tangible indications of how scribes learned to write? Can we tease out the way scribal education was reflected in the scrolls of the ancient parchment? And, in particular, how did scribes learn to write the Bible? In this book, I reconstruct some of the early scribal curriculum in ancient Israel, beginning with the material evidence of education—that is, ancient inscriptions and their historical contexts. I will reexamine scribal education from the context of recent archaeological finds and from the context of ancient Near Eastern educational paradigms. I will demonstrate that the early Israelite scribes borrowed and adapted from cuneiform curricular traditions in the early Iron Age in creating early Hebrew curriculum. And I will illustrate how this scribal curriculum influenced the writing of the Hebrew Bible.

The genetic code of early Hebrew education is broken. It is incomplete. It has suffered from the ravages of time, and it now has missing strands and connections. Can we reconstruct it? In ancient Hebrew inscriptions, I find traces of an array of different elementary scribal exercises used by Hebrew scribes. In cuneiform curriculum, I find parallels that fill out the missing code. The Hebrew inscriptions are like pieces of an incomplete puzzle. Now, however, it seems that early alphabetic scribes were closely related to their cuneiform forebearers. As a result, we can use cuneiform parallels to reconstruct some of the missing pieces of early Hebrew scribal curriculum. Using the educational DNA of curriculum from scribes who were working in Canaan as the Egyptian New Kingdom collapsed in the twelfth century BCE, we can re-create the genetic code for the education of the early Israelite scribes. Thereby, we can glimpse the fingerprint of scribes in the Bible.

The problem with the Bible itself as a testament to education is that it is a disembodied text. That is to say, we often have no concrete time or place for it. Scholars endlessly debate who wrote the Bible, when the Bible was written, etc. Answers are contested. The evidence is equivocal. I have not despaired on this account, but there is reason to be cautious in relating the Bible to scribal education. In this book, biblical literature is the (sometimes speculative) end of the discussion rather than the beginning. The beginning has to be an investigation into what we know from inscriptions and archaeology about the school curriculum of the early alphabetic scribes. The discipline of archaeology can give us some insight into the social, political, religious, and historical contexts of the texts. As for the inscriptions, this investigation searches far and wide for the fragments of school curriculum in the epigraphic record and tries to piece them together into a coherent narrative.

Scribal Curriculum and the Bible

Up until now, the scribal curriculum in ancient Israel has been a crux for biblical scholars. On the one hand, some scholars have envisioned a varied scribal curriculum with a considerable network of schools that included the biblical writings.[1] On the other hand, other scholars have argued that "our knowledge of the scribal curriculum in Israel is almost nil."[2] Even scholars such as Christopher Rollston who take an optimistic approach to our ability to reconstruct the scribal curriculum of ancient Israel offer almost no actual examples from the epigraphic record, apart from a few abecedaries.[3] Likewise, David Carr, in his influential book *Writing on the Tablet of the Heart: Origins of Scripture and Literature*, can offer only "faint clues that Israel was influenced by the textual-educational systems of ancient Mesopotamia and Egypt."[4] Carr suggests that "biblical literature came to serve as key parts of an indigenous curriculum for early Israelite scribes,"[5] but the tangible evidence for this use of biblical literature as part of the ancient scribal curriculum has been absent. The ancient Israelite scribal curriculum has been essentially unknown or unsubstantiated.

Understanding the scribal curriculum is important because it presages the canonization process. As Karel van der Toorn has pointed out, "Precisely because a curriculum is subject to closure, texts are in competition for a place. Unlike a place in a library, inclusion in a curriculum asserts the superiority of a written text over other texts. In this respect, the scribal curriculum could be viewed as a laboratory from which the canon was issued."[6] In Mesopotamia, scribes made an effort to put certain texts into the scribal curriculum. So, for example, in the conclusion to the Enuma Elish (the Babylonian Creation Epic), a scribal editor adds, "The wise and the learned should ponder them together, the teacher should repeat them and make the pupil learn by heart. . . . This is the revelation which an Ancient, to whom it was told, wrote down and established for posterity to hear."[7] Once a text became part of the scribal curriculum, it would be learned, studied, and passed on. In this way, it had lasting influence in ways that other literature would not have.

This book also begins with the premise that education shapes what we write and how we write it. In subtle ways, biblical literature has been shaped and influenced by the education and training of the scribes who wrote it. While a main focus of this book is reconstructing the educational curriculum of the early Israelite scribes, it also suggests a variety of ways in which this curriculum framed, influenced, and shaped biblical literature. The influence of scribal education touched on many spheres of scribal composition. Sometimes it involved mundane details like the language used in structuring devices to mark new paragraphs and ideas. Sometimes it was general, such as the adaptation of mundane literary genres into new literary genres. Sometimes the curriculum had a conceptual impact like the use and adaptation of memorized literary exercises. In small and large ways, education affected the composition of biblical literature. And the better we understand scribal education, the more clearly we can see how it influenced biblical literature.

The Late Bronze Age Context of the Israelite Scribal Curriculum

The first problem that we must solve is the fragmentary nature of our evidence. What was the "school" curriculum of the scribes who wrote the Bible, and when did it develop? To begin with, we should clarify what we mean by "school."[8] I do not use the term in an institutional sense but rather as an abstract noun relating to education—that is, as the process of learning under instruction. There is no evidence for formal "schools" in ancient Israel; rather, scribal education was done in an apprenticeship context. A master scribe took on "sons"—not necessarily a familial relationship, although we may assume that some scribal apprentices were the actual sons of the master. The apprenticeship system of scribal training is nicely laid out in documents from the Late Bronze Age city of Emar.[9] Hints of a similar system are evident in the administrative list of 1Kgs 4:3: "Elihoreph and Ahijah were sons of *Shisha*, scribes." The term *Shisha* was probably not a personal name but a corruption of the Egyptian title for a royal scribe, *sš*, "scribe."[10] In any case, the use of the expression "sons of" here already suggests a scribal apprentice system at work in early Israel similar to the model known from Emar. This cuneiform apprentice system utilized a standardized "school" curriculum.

The "Scribe" of the Lachish Jar Inscription

A recently published jar inscription from Lachish provides the first example of the title "Scribe" used in a linear alphabetic inscription. The inscription is also significant because it adapts Egyptian accounting symbols, making it the earliest example of the borrowing of hieratic accounting in alphabetic texts.[11] The inscription was excavated by a team led by Yosef Garfinkel at the site of Lachish, and it dates to the twelfth century BCE—that is, to the very end of the New Kingdom period in the southern Levant.[12] In Figure 1.1, we see a clearly and carefully inscribed, albeit fragmentary, inscription.

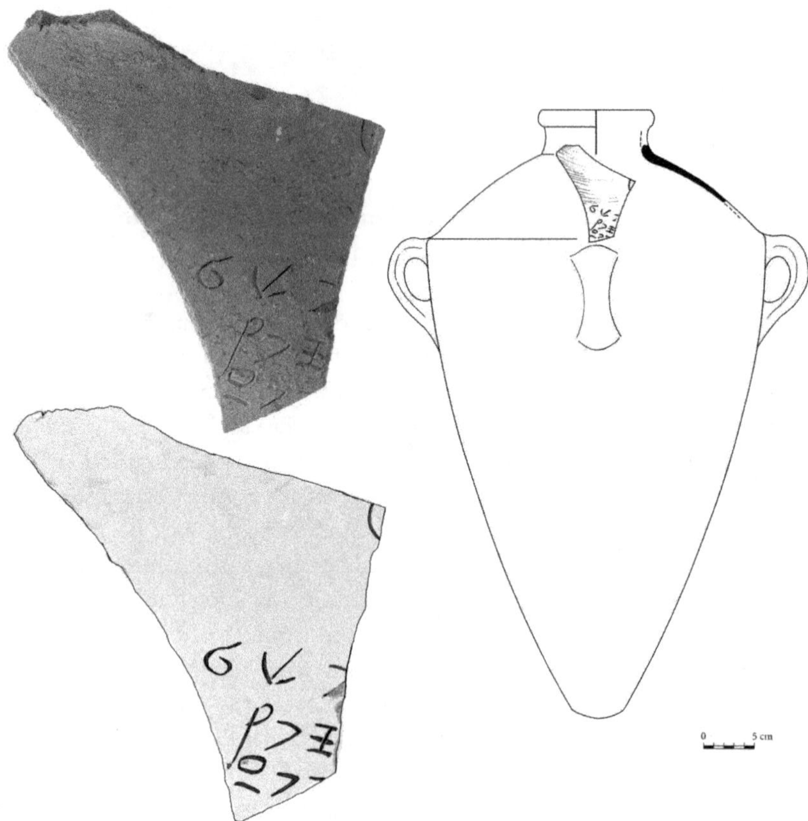

Figure 1.1 Lachish jar inscription with the title "Scribe." Courtesy of The Fourth Expedition to Lachish; photo by Tal Rogovsky; jar drawing by O. Dobovsky; inscription drawing by the author.

1)	[. . .] *p k l*	*Personal Name?*
2)	[. . .] *s p r*	[. . .] Scribe
3)	[. . .] X 5 ḥqꜣ.t	[. . .] 5 Hekat (of wheat)

The inscription was written on a large, common storage jar that typically held about 20–30 liters. The inscription was inscribed on the storage jar *before* firing—in other words, this is a planned inscription. And the letters are carefully and skillfully formed. This scribe knew what he was doing. Line 2 clearly reads *spr*, which is probably the title "Scribe." Although there are other ways of reading this,[13] jar inscriptions typically have personal names, titles, places, or commodities. Thus, the title "Scribe" is the most straightforward and logical reading of line 2. It follows, then, that line 1 was most likely the personal name of the scribe. Lemaire has suggested reconstructing the scribe's name as Pikol, a name known elsewhere in the Bible (see Gen 21:22; 26:26). Line 3 is the most difficult. The first grapheme is broken, and the second grapheme looks like the Hebrew letter *peh*, which is how the original publication has understood it. The third grapheme(s), however, are unusual: the oblong circle with a line under it is not otherwise known in the alphabetic corpus. However, the original editors correctly understood that it might "stand for a numeral or measure,"[14] but they offered no decipherment. If we suppose that this line refers to a commodity, interesting possibilities present themselves. First of all, a single line is sometimes used in Egyptian hieratic accounting texts for marking a plural.[15] Second, an oblong circle is used in hieratic as a simplified form of the hieroglyphic sign for *ḥqꜣ.t* ( ), that is, a measure of wheat.[16] Once we recognize this sign as deriving from Egyptian accounting symbols, everything becomes intelligible. The second sign on the third line should be read as the typical hieratic number "5."[17] Since the Egyptian *ḥqꜣt* was about four to five liters,[18] 5 *ḥqꜣt* would have been about 20–25 liters, which is the size of the storage jar upon which this inscription is written.[19] This final observation confirms the suggested reading.

In sum, we have a carefully planned and written inscription on a storage jar where an early alphabetic "scribe" borrows the symbols from the Egyptian accounting system. This inscription stands at a transition point when linear alphabetic is beginning to be used administratively and when the Egyptian hieratic tradition is being adopted by alphabetic scribes. The careful planning and writing, as well as the integration of a bureaucracy for accounting, suggests an alphabetic scribal curriculum underlines this fragmentary inscription.

The beginnings of an alphabetic curriculum presumably coincided with the emergence of alphabetic writing at the end of the Late Bronze Age and in the early Iron Age. We know that the alphabet developed and spread during the early Iron Age—at the end of the second millennium BCE. We must assume that a school curriculum developed with the emergence of the alphabet. But what was the basis of this school curriculum? One answer is implied in the older hypothesis that there was a major break between the end of the Late Bronze Age and the rise of early Israelite polities. Scholars like David Jamieson-Drake had argued that there was a gap between the end of the New Kingdom Egyptian administration of the Levant and the rise of early Israel.[20] Orly Goldwasser suggested that the hieratic accounting system (now seen above in the Lachish Jar Inscription) was borrowed during the administration of David and Solomon.[21] If this were true, then the early Israelite scribal curriculum developed in a vacuum. It could not have been influenced by either Egyptian or cuneiform traditions of the Late Bronze Age. It was created ex nihilo. But new data show this to be wrong. An alphabetic scribal curriculum in the southern Levant emerged from and was influenced by its Near Eastern context at the end of the Late Bronze Age.

The End of the New Kingdom

Our misunderstanding of early alphabetic scribalism is grounded in the dating of the end of the New Kingdom and the Late Bronze Age. It is now increasingly clear that the Late Bronze Age extended to the end of the twelfth century BCE.[22] And recent epigraphic discoveries make it clear that alphabetic writing was emerging and spreading already in the twelfth century—that is, on the heels of the collapse of the New Kingdom in the Levant. Moreover, the technologies and terminology for writing were taken directly from the Egyptian administration into early Hebrew alphabetic scribal culture. This includes the use of ink and papyrus, the adoption of hieratic accounting systems, and many loanwords from Egyptian relating to scribal practice.[23] It is hardly surprising in this respect that the administrative lists for early Judean kings have foreigners engaged as "scribes" and "recorders."[24] In other words, early alphabetic scribal education did not need to be invented ex nihilo. There were ready examples to adapt, and there were capable scribes and administrators that were "left behind" in the lands of Retjenu (as the Egyptians called ancient Canaan and Syria).

In this light, new alternatives present themselves. We must consider whether and how an early alphabetic scribal curriculum could have been influenced by its predecessors. The Egyptians certainly influenced the technologies of early alphabetic writing, such as the use of ink. The words for ink, papyrus, seals, scribal palettes, accounting and measuring, etc. were all taken from the Egyptian administration. However, the borrowing was strictly technological. Egyptians did not teach hieroglyphic writing to foreigners. "Hieroglyphic" means "sacred writing," and it was a sacred writing system for Egyptians alone. This is demonstrated by the fact that there are no Egyptian school texts found outside of Egypt. The Egyptians themselves actually used cuneiform for the administration of their empire in the Levant during the New Kingdom period (fifteenth through twelfth centuries BCE). The Canaanite Amarna letters—that is, letters from the servants of Pharaoh presiding over various cities under Egyptian hegemony—are written in cuneiform script and a Canaano-Akkadian dialect.[25] Egyptian scribes learned Akkadian for diplomatic communication and imperial administration. In this respect, the Egyptians participated in the use of Akkadian cuneiform as the lingua franca of the ancient Near East in the second millennium BCE. In other words, while Egyptian writing technology was borrowed in the Levant, their scribal curriculum does not seem to have been widely disseminated. The Egyptian literature that does influence biblical literature seems to have been preserved orally and by chance. In contrast, it was the cuneiform curriculum of Mesopotamia that was readily available to early alphabetic scribes.

Cuneiform School Curriculum in the Eastern Mediterranean

During the late second millennium BCE, cuneiform school texts were found throughout the ancient Near East, including the southern Levant and in Egypt. This contrasts sharply with the situation in the first millennium BCE as Dominique Charpin observes in *Reading and Writing in Babylon*, "In the first millennium, the geographical influence of cuneiform narrowed: only a few traces remained west of the Euphrates, directly linked to the political presence of the Assyrian and then the Babylonian kings. But there was no center reminiscent of Ebla in the third millennium."[26] This is borne out in the cuneiform record in Canaan. In the compendium *Cuneiform in Canaan*, there are fifty-five cuneiform texts dating to the second millennium from Israel, but only twenty-seven dating to the first millennium.[27] Even more instructive is the fact that the second millennium tablets from Canaan include a great variety of school texts; in striking contrast, no school texts dating to the first millennium BCE were found in Israel. More generally, there are few Akkadian school texts found outside of Mesopotamia in the first millennium. Akkadian was no longer a lingua franca in the first millennium, particularly in the West. Charpin suggests that the literary corpus in Assyria and Babylonia came to be ossified in the first millennium, and it was increasingly studied by a closed group of literati. The libraries of Nineveh, Sultanantepe, and Sippar contained almost all the same texts![28] They had a rigid canon to their curriculum, but these texts were not spread outside the confines of the empire. Outside of Assyria in the first millennium, we find royal inscriptions, administrative documents, letters, and cylinder seals.[29] These data are critical for assessing the possible points of contact during the Late Bronze Age, Iron Age, Babylonian period, and Persian period. In terms of cuneiform curriculum, the late second millennium provides the only strong evidence for the spread of cuneiform education and literary culture outside of Mesopotamia. In this book, I will trace how this cuneiform curriculum was adapted by early Israelite scribes.

Once we know some of the outlines of the early alphabetic scribal curriculum we may ask: How did it shape what is actually written in the Bible? As an entry into this question, I believe that we can reconstruct some examples of the ancient Israelite curriculum with a new investigation of the fully published inscriptions from a remote military outpost known as Kuntillet ʿAjrud.[30] This is one of the earliest corpora of Hebrew inscriptions dating to about 800 BCE. When this corpus of inscriptions is viewed as a whole, we see that they represent fragments of the entire range of an educational curriculum for an ancient Israelite scribe. They will also help us contextualize earlier Hebrew inscriptions such as the Gezer Calendar and the Qeiyafa Ostracon. And the outlines of this early scribal curriculum will correspond strikingly with the framework of the Mesopotamian scribal curriculum. Using these observations, we can reconstruct the framework for an elementary school curriculum for the scribes of the Bible. This discovery has profound implications for our study of the writing of the Bible itself. For the first time we have examples of the rudimentary scribal curriculum of ancient Israelite scribes and can show how their education shaped the composition of biblical literature.

Searching for a "Vector of Transmission": Mesopotamian Influence on the Alphabetic Curriculum

Scholars have questioned the timing and avenue of the influence of cuneiform literature on biblical writers. Many scholars have seen the Late Bronze Age as a time of transmission; others have pointed to the late Iron Age during Neo-Assyrian domination; and still others have suggested the exilic or postexilic periods.[31] An older view also saw the Solomonic period (i.e., tenth century) as the vector of transmission. James Crenshaw, for example, writes, "It makes a great deal of difference, therefore, whether an interpreter thinks Israel's schools evolved in the tenth century, when knowledge of Akkadian and Egyptian was essential for international relations, or in the eighth century, when familiarity with Aramaic would normally have sufficed."[32] Crenshaw's perspective reflects some older scholarly perspectives that envisioned a Solomonic enlightenment period.[33] Egyptian influence has been a focus for the study of education in ancient Israel, but in actuality Akkadian is a more viable vector of transmission. Indeed, Akkadian, not Egyptian, was the lingua franca in the Late Bronze Age. The Egyptian language was never essential for international relations, even in the heyday of the New Kingdom and certainly not in the tenth century or in the later Iron Age (eighth and seventh centuries). The Egyptians always used foreign languages and writing systems for international relations, whether Akkadian, Aramaic, or later Greek. To be sure, the foreign entanglements are complex, and the evidence is not as robust as we might hope. There is ample evidence for Egyptian administration in the Levant in the late second millennium, some of which lingered on after the collapse of the New Kingdom.[34] And there likely were influences of various types in all these periods, but this book is particularly concerned with the genesis of the educational rubrics of early Israel, which I will argue should be placed in the LB/Iron I transition.

William Morrow's concept of the "vector of transmission" is particularly useful in our discussion of the development of a scribal curriculum.[35] By vector of transmission, we refer specifically to the physical mechanisms by which literature or an educational curriculum could have been known and transferred from one culture to another. We refer to the basic questions: How, where, and when? Many books and studies discuss the relationship between ancient Near Eastern texts and biblical literature in general ways. This study is looking for the tangible points of contact—that is, for physical evidence of a vector of transmission between scribal cultures in the ancient world.

The starting point in this study is the concrete points of contact between the epigraphic record and scribal education. We may suspect, for example, that some biblical texts served in some way and in some period as a scribal curriculum, but we lack actual evidence in the inscriptional record to bolster this suspicion. So, for example, sometimes it is posited that the Book of Proverbs served as a scribal curriculum in ancient Israel, but the only seemingly direct point of contact is Prov 22:17–24:10 and its parallels with the Egyptian school text, *The Instruction of Amenemope*.[36] Yet even this example is problematic. We have no copy of *The Instruction of Amenemope* that was found in a Levantine context. As a result, there is a great deal of debate as to when and to what extent *The Instruction of Amenemope* was borrowed by the author or editor of the Book of Proverbs.[37] Up to this point, there is no physical evidence that proverbial sayings such as *The Instruction of Amenemope* were part of a scribal curriculum in the Levant during the Late Bronze Age or the Iron Age. Still, we do know that proverbial sayings were an important component of a Near Eastern scribal curriculum.[38] Thus scholars must infer on the basis of parallels that there must be some vector of transmission, even though the actual time and manner of contact is uncertain. This book will focus, as much as possible, on the tangible evidence of a scribal curriculum in the Levant from inscriptions—beginning with Hebrew inscriptions but also looking at other Levantine inscriptions in cuneiform. The physical evidence is fragmentary, but it is the place to begin. The completely published Kuntillet ʿAjrud inscriptions are now a major step forward in this search.

Mesopotamia has the earliest and best-documented example of an educational system that we have in the ancient Near East. Moreover, Mesopotamian texts like the Code of Hammurabi, the Enuma Elish, and the Vassal Treaty of Esarhaddon have often been cited as parallels to biblical literature. At the same time, some scholars have questioned the basis for the comparison. What was the vector of transmission, for example, by which the Code of Hammurabi came to be used by the author of the Covenant Code? David Wright offers a detailed comparison between the Code of Hammurabi and the Covenant Code in his book, *Inventing God's Law*, but he addresses the tangible vector of transmission only briefly.[39] In this case, it is difficult not to be brief since the only evidence for borrowing is the literary relationship itself. But what exactly is the possible vector of transmission? The general answer is that the Neo-Assyrian Empire exerted political and social control over the Levant and that the Laws of Hammurabi were part of the "Great Books" of the Neo-Assyrian libraries. A vector of transmission is inferred from these two observations. But there is no actual physical evidence that the Code of Hammurabi was being taught to foreign scribes. Are we to imagine that scribes from cities across the far-flung Neo-Assyrian Empire were brought to Nineveh, shown the Great Library of Sennacherib, Esarhaddon, and Assurbanipal, and then methodically taught the canonical works of the Akkadian scribal curriculum? That seems unlikely. It took many years of training for Mesopotamian scribes to learn cuneiform. Are we to imagine that foreign scribes would have been taught cuneiform when Akkadian was no longer being used as a lingua franca? No. This strains credulity.

One alternative is that Aramaic was the vector of transmission. Aramaic was a lingua franca in the West beginning in Neo-Assyrian times. Of course, it would be helpful if the traces of a translation from the Code of Hammurabi or the Enuma Elish were found in any Aramaic text. There are traces of Vassal Treaty traditions in Aramaic inscriptions (e.g., Sefire), which make it straightforward to posit a vector of transmission to Deuteronomy.[40] In general, however, the Akkadian scribal curriculum was restricted to the homeland during the Neo-Assyrian period. The empire very practically adopted Aramaic as the writing system for its administration. However, there is no evidence that the training of Aramaic administrative scribes included the teaching or translation of canonical Akkadian and Sumerian in the educational curriculum.

The spread of the cuneiform scribal curriculum throughout the Near East is actually located more narrowly in the Late Bronze Age. As Niek Veldhuis points out, "The late second millennium saw an unprecedented spread of cuneiform writing and Babylonian written culture over the entire Near East."[41] In this respect, the second millennium differs substantially from the Neo-Assyrian period. In the second millennium BCE, traditional cuneiform school texts appeared throughout the Levant at major centers like Ugarit, Emar, Nuzi, and Amarna in Egypt as well as at small local southern Levantine polities like Hazor, Ashkelon, Megiddo, and Aphek. I will demonstrate that this cuneiform school tradition directly influenced the development of the early Israelite alphabetic curriculum.[42] The scribes and bureaucrats that worked in the administration of the Egyptian Empire were trained in the Akkadian school curriculum (as we see most directly in the Amarna Scholarly Tablets). These bureaucrats were "left behind" when the New Kingdom's colonial empire collapsed at the end of Ramses VI's reign at the end of the twelfth century BCE.[43] Their scribal training and education was a technology that was taken over and adapted in the southern Levant.

Some recent scholarship dismisses the Late Bronze period as a context for the influence of cuneiform literature on the Bible. For example, Morrow contests the idea that knowledge of Akkadian literary texts could have been mediated to biblical writers through the Late Bronze Age (LBA) scribal culture. He suggests a resistance to borrowing cuneiform literature. He introduces the concept of "hybridity" from postcolonial theory, namely, how the relationship between the dominated and the subjugated often leads to new forms of cultural expression. Morrow gives Ugarit as a particular example. He points out that Ugaritic literature does not heavily borrow from Mesopotamian literature. However, his analysis breaks down for both Ugarit and the biblical writers in at least three ways. First, Akkadian was not emblematic of a dominant culture in the southern Levant during the LBA as it was at Ugarit. As Morrow himself points out, "While culturally influential, Mesopotamia was not politically coercive in LB Canaan."[44] This undermines the colonial model. The political situation was much different at Ugarit, which was dominated by North Syria. But even there, cuneiform was more of a lingua franca used by a variety of powers. In the southern Levant, Egypt was the dominant political force in the southern Levant. There Akkadian was actually viewed romantically as a heritage culture. This is illustrated archaeologically, as evidenced by the Amorite *koiné*,[45] as well as in biblical literature, which traces its ancestors to Mesopotamia (e.g., Abraham from Ur of the Chaldees). Second, the local scribes at Ugarit were bilingual and had access to Akkadian literature in the original languages. Scribes likely began their education by learning Akkadian.[46] But Akkadian was still not the native language of their overlords, the Hurrians. Furthermore, Ugarit was a multilingual and cosmopolitan port city. This contrasts sharply with the southern Levantine cities, where Akkadian was a completely foreign language. Third, while Ugaritic literature does not borrow from Akkadian, the elementary educational rubrics at Ugarit do directly mimic the Akkadian curriculum. This is easiest to see in the student letter exercises, which clearly imitate Akkadian texts. And an Ugaritic column is added to the traditional cuneiform *Ura* lexical lists. Elementary bilingual (Akkadian-Ugaritic) student exercises underscore Ugaritic borrowing and adapting of scribal rubrics.[47] Ugaritic adapted aspects of elementary education as it developed its own scribal curriculum. Morrow accounts for some of this under the term "hybridity," but it could be better described as adaptation.

In short, Ugaritic does show direct influence of Akkadian scribal rubrics even though Ugaritic literature (e.g., the Baal Epic) was not influenced significantly by Akkadian literature.

Vectors of scribal transmission have both magnitude and direction. The scribes themselves are most critical to understanding the transmission of an educational system. As soon as there were alphabetic scribes, they needed to develop a curriculum. In other words, the formation of an Israelite scribal curriculum had to be *at the very beginning of alphabetic writing* in the early Iron Age. The scribal curriculum would have already been formed by later periods, such as the Neo-Assyrian, Neo-Babylonian, or Persian periods. It could have been adapted and supplemented in these later periods, but it was not invented. In later periods, a new scribal curriculum would have had to compete with the old canons of education. In this respect, curriculum tends to be very conservative. The scope of scribal exercises at Kuntillet ʿAjrud illustrates what we previously could only assume—namely, that a scribal curriculum had already developed in early Israel. As this book will show, the Late Bronze Age cuneiform curriculum influenced the early alphabetic curriculum. The Late Bronze Age scribes were vectors for that transmission.

Even with new insights about the Hebrew scribal curriculum from the Kuntillet ʿAjrud inscriptions, we may still wonder how a cuneiform curriculum would have influenced the development of a Hebrew curriculum. Morrow's study of vectors of transmission suggests borrowing should be assessed in three categories: vocabulary, common intellectual culture and genres, and appropriation of literature. Morrow himself dismisses the first two and concentrates on the last area of borrowing. It is natural for scholars to concentrate on the potentially most interesting type of borrowing, namely, texts that reflect advanced scribal culture.[48] This is somewhat unfortunate since the appropriation of literature that implies quite advanced levels of scribal education. Few scribes would have achieved this in Late Bronze Age Canaan. Reflecting on the large influence of Akkadian administrative vocabulary, Morrow himself observes, "The scribal literature of LB Canaan is clearly connected to administrative functions. It is not a necessary conclusion that the same scribes also adapted Mesopotamian literature to their native traditions."[49] Where did this influence start? Undoubtedly it begins with the scribal education. For example, trilingual lexical lists that include a West Semitic column (like the one excavated at Ashkelon) would have actually facilitated lexical borrowing among scribes. In this example it becomes clear that the appropriation of literary texts is not the only way of discussing a vector of transmission. The vectors of transmission are much more broadly the scribes and administration. The paths of transmission include all aspects of the scribal curriculum as well as the technologies of writing and administration. These can be illustrated with both texts and archaeological remains.

Morrow essentially concedes the influence of cuneiform scribal c on early alphabetic scribes, while at the same time challenging the ext which Mesopotamian literature would have been appropriated by early alphabetic scribes. What is clear is that actual Mesopotamian literature—e.g., the Gilgamesh Epic, the Myth of Adapa—was known to Levantine scribes.[50] We have physical fragments of these texts in Levantine related contexts. So there is no problem with a vector of transmission from that perspective. The actual appropriation of Mesopotamian literature is a different question. Very little, if any, seems to have been directly borrowed and incorporated into biblical literature. Rather, it is better to speak of awareness of the themes, genres, and culture of this literature and how this general knowledge might have shaped biblical literature. For example, a story like the Tower of Babel (Gen 11) certainly shows an awareness of Mesopotamian religion and culture, but it does not borrow.[51] Likewise it is hard not to see an allusion to the Babylonian Creation myth, the Enuma Elish, where the goddess Ti'amat is a central character, in the reference in Genesis to "when God created the heavens and the earth . . . and darkness covered the *t*^{e}*hôm* [deep]."[52] There are many such parallels that show an awareness of Mesopotamian stories, themes, and genres, but they do not give evidence of direct appropriation. As such, they really offer little concrete temporal or logistical evidence for the vector of transmission.

Scholarly study about the influence of Near Eastern education has definitely focused on the advanced educational curriculum. For example, Carr writes, "If a given early Canaanite or Israelite scribe was trained in another culture's literature, he would not necessarily just learn what we would term 'wisdom' literature. Rather he (or occasionally she) would learn additional narrative, hymnic, and other materials as well."[53] But exactly when and how could a Canaanite or Israelite scribe be trained in another's culture? Did this really happen? It's certainly plausible if the other's culture were a scribal lingua franca. For example, Akkadian was a scribal lingua franca in the second millennium, and Aramaic became a lingua franca from the Neo-Assyrian period through the Persian period. Greek became a lingua franca in the Hellenistic period. It is difficult to imagine an advanced scribal curriculum being taught without the scribal language functioning as a lingua franca.

An elementary curriculum would have been the foundation for the spread of a scribal curriculum across cultures. An elementary curriculum is also the part of the ancient Near Eastern curriculum that is most rigid and invariable. For example, the inscriptional evidence shows that the elementary cuneiform curriculum was essentially the same in the entire Fertile Crescent during the Late Bronze Age, and it was largely unchanged over the course of the entire second millennium and into the first millennium BCE. In contrast, the advanced literary curriculum and even wisdom literature included an immense and varied repertoire. Moreover, much of this curriculum was purely "academic" for the professional scribes who would spend most of their days writing receipts, lists, and letters along with an occasional legal contract. Veldhuis points out that "a scribe learned far too much. A scribe had to be able to write contracts and business documents. . . . But a considerable part of the words he had learned in the lexical lists was obscure, obsolete, or for other reasons of no practical use. If we take into account the literary exercises the burden of 'useless' knowledge a scribal pupil had to digest is all the more impressive."[54] It is unclear how much scribes on the margins of Mesopotamian culture would have practiced or internalized such an impractical literary curriculum. For example, the bilingual Egyptian-Akkadian lexical list from Amarna (discussed in chapter 4) borrows from the cuneiform tradition, but also clearly simplies this tradition. Thus Mesopotamian curriculum provides the template, but the template is adapted for a more utilitarian purpose.

Judging from the fragments of the Gilgamesh Epic that have been recovered in the periphery (including Megiddo), some classic literary-type texts definitely reached Canaan. In other words, Mesopotamian literature could have been generally known. At the same time, it seems unlikely that they were central to the training of Levantine scribes or that much of this cuneiform literature would have directly influenced early alphabetic scribes. It is not surprising that scholars have been primarily interested in the influence on biblical literature of texts like the Gilgamesh Epic, the Enuma Elish, or the Code of Hammurabi. But on a practical level, their direct influence seems limited. To use Morrow's expression, there was no easy vector of transmission for such written texts. For this reason, some scholars appeal to *orality* as another vector in which such texts could have been transmitted. Indeed, such oral transmission may account for the parallels between Siduri speech in Gilgamesh and the Ecclesiastes 9 (discussed in chapter 7) or *The Instruction of Amenemope* and Proverbs 22:17–24:10 (discussed in chapter 6). To be sure, orality played a role, particularly for advanced literature. But I will illustrate a concrete vector for the *written* texts of elementary education.

Mesopotamian Influence on Alphabetic Writing at Ugarit

The influence of Mesopotamian education on an alphabetic culture can be usefully illustrated in a contemporary Late Bronze Age culture, the kingdom of Ugarit. This example is illustrative because it underscores that ancient cultures borrowed and adapted technology and tradition rather than reinventing it. Indeed, there was no need to reinvent the proverbial wheel. The connection between the cuneiform scribal curriculum and an emergent alphabetic curriculum is direct at ancient Ugarit. First of all, scribes at Ugarit learned both their own native Ugaritic language using a cuneiform alphabetic script as well as the Akkadian curriculum. In fact the situation at Ugarit is similar to that in early Israel, inasmuch as neither had their own scribal curriculum for their new alphabetic scribes. At Ugarit there are extensive examples of an Akkadian cuneiform curriculum but relatively few examples of an alphabetic curriculum. Nevertheless, there is evidence that the two writings systems were being learned together. For example, we have school exercise tablets with both Akkadian and Ugaritic writing, as is in Figure 1.2 (RS 94.2617 = *KTU* 5.34).[55]

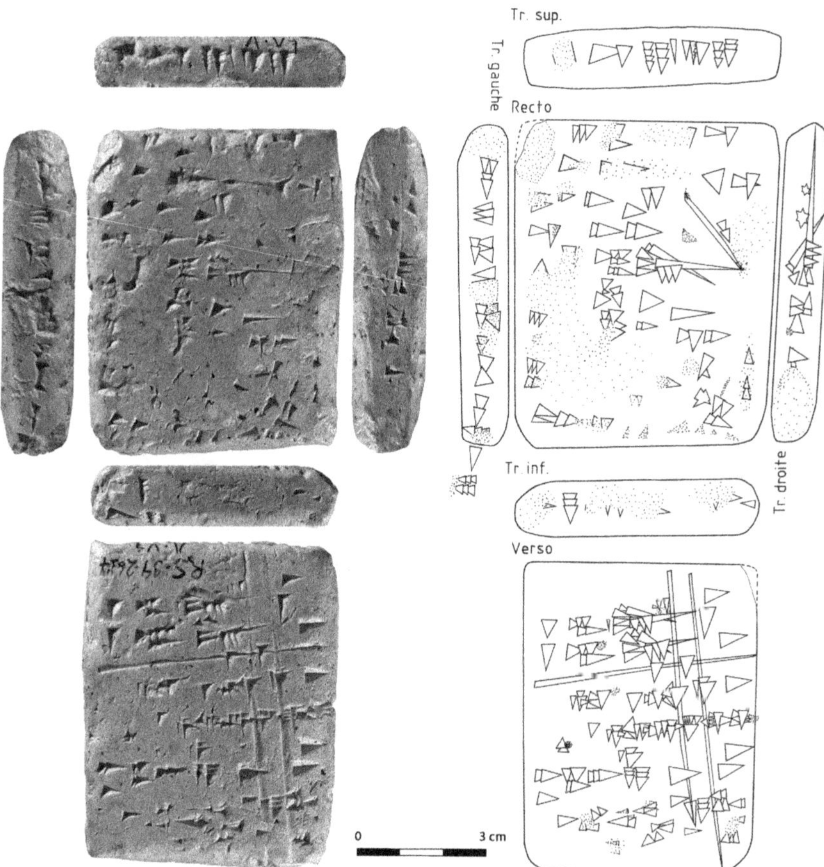

Figure 1.2 Bilingual Akkadian-Ugarit scribal exercise from Ugarit. Photograph courtesy of Projet PhoTEO, Mission de Ras Shamra. Copy courtesy of D. Pardee.

For the purpose of illustrating the mixture of Akkadian and Ugaritic, I transcribe as follows, with Ugaritic in lowercase and Akkadian in uppercase letters:

Top	
ʿmy.ly	my mother, to me
Left Side	
[]wlb⸢xx⸣q aḫty	[]and to ⸢PN?⸣, my sister
Obverse	
[]l⸢b⸣[xx]m	*practice letter shapes?*
[]ʿa ʿm	*practice letter shapes?*
paaʿṣ	*practice letter shapes?*
m aa	*practice letter shapes?*
^{M}EN.LUGAL	the lord-king
[]ʿ ʿ t	*practice letter shapes?*
d[]ḏ	*practice letter shapes?*
a[]⸢t⸣ ṯ	*practice letter shapes?*
pa[]b	*practice letter shapes?*
Right Side	
[]^{M}EN.LUGAL ṯṯ	[]the lord-king *ṯ ṯ*
Bottom	
aḫty r[g]m	my sister, speak!
Reverse	
^{M}EN.LUGAL t	the lord-king *t*
^{M}EN.LUGAL t	the lord-king *t*

A-NA ^{MD}UTU.A t	to Shamash *t*
A-NA ^{MD}A-ŠUR.KI.NA	to Assur (?)
abny t t t	*practice letter shapes*
t t t g ḫ	*practice letter shapes*
a b k a (upside down)	*practice letter shapes*
l q a (upside down)	*practice letter shapes*

This is clearly a practice tablet. Essentially it is little more than scribal doodling in Akkadian and Ugaritic. There is also varying depth to the cuneiform wedges, which indicates that the tablet was scraped and reused. In other words, it is a *palimpsest*, which is actually a technical term from Greek meaning "rubbed again," used to refer to manuscripts that have been used, erased (incompletely), and reused.[56] It is also difficult to accurately transcribe because the lines sometimes overlap and some signs are written upside down (i.e., written with the tablet flipped 180 degrees). Above all, this practice tablet illustrates a scribe writing both Akkadian cuneiform and Ugaritic alphabetic cuneiform. There are many other examples of tablets with both Akkadian and Ugaritic written on the same tablet, and they simply serve to illustrate that the rubrics of the Akkadian school curriculum were being used to learn Ugaritic.[57] This can also be seen in Ugaritic letters and other formal documents, where Ugaritic texts utilized the conventions of their Akkadian counterparts.

Another useful example of the mixture of Akkadian and Ugaritic on a student exercise tablet is RS 94.2273 (= *KTU* 5.33). On one side of the tablet are student exercises in Akkadian, and the other side has a practice letter in Ugaritic. This tablet is also a palimpsest. This is evident both by the shallow residual letters from a previous exercise and by the random placement of these letters around the outside and between the lines. This again illustrates the strong nexus between scribes learning Akkadian and also the new alphabetic Ugaritic cuneiform writing system. But the Akkadian school texts and training predominate. There are about twenty times more Akkadian school texts than Ugaritic school texts excavated at Ras Shamra![58]

The Akkadian school curriculum excavated at Ugarit reflects the robust diversity of the Mesopotamian tradition at the time, whereas the Ugaritic school texts are quite rudimentary (as one might expect from a neophyte writing system). The excavations yielded the full array of the traditional Akkadian cuneiform school curriculum. These include the basic exercises for learning cuneiform signs (e.g., TU-TI-TA exercises), trilingual and quadrilingual lexical lists (the *ḫubullu* [ur$_5$-ra]), as well as more advanced literary texts (including a fragment of the Gilgamesh Epic).[59] In contrast, the Ugaritic alphabetic school texts were limited in their scope; essentially they included only a few abecedaries and some practice letters.[60] There was no evidence for a well-developed school curriculum paralleling the Akkadian school texts preserved at Ugarit and known throughout the ancient Near East. This itself is a bit of a mystery. As a result, it is difficult to know exactly how advanced education in alphabetic literature was done at Ugarit, but it appears that all alphabetic scribes at Ugarit also had an education in Akkadian cuneiform.[61] While there are literary texts from Ugarit such as the Baal Cycle,[62] they do not seem to be purely school texts. They could have also been used as an advanced curriculum. For example, the Baal Cycle has internal evidence for oral recitation and scribal correction,[63] which can be indications that they were also used as school texts. By comparison, we may want to assume that some of the stories in Genesis, the poetry of the Psalter, or the wisdom of the Book of Proverbs served as a scribal curriculum in ancient Israel. But again, there is little internal indication, epigraphic evidence, or archaeological discovery that would substantiate this assumption. The concrete evidence points to a robust Mesopotamian cuneiform school curriculum at Ugarit, but only a rudimentary curriculum in the new alphabetic script. And this rudimentary curriculum borrowed from the principles and rubrics of the Mesopotamian curriculum.

When we turn southward to the early Israelite school curriculum, the influence of the Mesopotamian cuneiform curriculum on an early linear (including Hebrew) alphabet relationship is more indirect than at Ugarit. However, a compelling case for its influence can still be made. First of all, it is clear that the Akkadian school curriculum was being used throughout the southern Levant until the very end of the Late Bronze Age—that is, at the time of the transition to the early Canaanite alphabetic writing system. Fragments of Akkadian school texts have been found locally in Canaan at sites including Hazor, Taanach, Megiddo, Aphek, Jerusalem, and Ashkelon.[64] Second, the Amarna Scholarly Tablets evince aspects of adaption of the cuneiform school curriculum for local scribes (e.g., the bilingual Egyptian-Akkadian lexical list, EA 368, discussed in chapter 4). Thus, the Mesopotamian school curriculum was really the only foundation upon which to adapt and build an alphabetic school curriculum in the emergent southern Levantine polities, namely, Phoenicia, Israel, and Judah.

The Influence of the Mesopotamian School Curriculum

This book makes a bold claim: namely, that the rubrics of early Israelite scribal education were adapted from the Mesopotamian school tradition at the end of the Late Bronze Age. The two foundations for this claim are epigraphic and archaeological. The epigraphic evidence is manifold and robust: we have evidence of cuneiform school texts all around the periphery, including places such as Emar, Ugarit, Amarna, and Canaan. This, of course, is in stark contrast to the Iron Age, where there are relatively few cuneiform texts outside of Mesopotamia and no school texts. The archaeological considerations are also strong. Until recently scholars have assumed that there was an archaeological gap between the end of the Late Bronze Age and the emergence of the early alphabetic cultures of the southern Levant (i.e., Phoenicia, Israel, Judah). This is no longer the case. The archaeological evidence now allows for a stronger vector of transmission at the end of the second millennium BCE.

At this point we need to examine some of the specific details of the cuneiform school curriculum. A helpful visualization of the curriculum was done by Niek Veldhuis, which I have adapted as Table 1.1. In this book we will use this adaptation of his chart as a guide for assessing aspects of the early Israelite scribal curriculum (with my comments in brackets).[65]

This table will serve as a reference point moving forward to compare the scribal exercises from Kuntillet ʿAjrud. It will help identify and fill out the school

Table 1.1 Summary of Cuneiform School Curriculum (from Veldhuis, with Comments in Brackets)

Sign exercises	[compare abecedaries; chapter 3]
Sign elements	Tablets filled with horizontal, vertical, and oblique wedges
Syllable Alphabet B	Standardized sign exercise, introducing the most important cuneiform signs with lots of repetition
Tu-Ta-Ti	Sign list; triads of signs with alternating vowels (u-a-i)
Thematic lists	[i.e., classified vocabulary lists; see chapter 4]
Lists of names	Various lists of Sumerian and Akkadian names [personal names and geographic names]
Sumerian nouns and nominal phrases	Trees and wooden objects, reeds and reed objects, ceramics, hides and leather objects, metals and metal objects, animals, meat cuts, stones, plants, etc. (in six chapters)
Advanced lists	[see chapter 4]
Acrographic lists	Lists of Sumerian words ordered by first sign (compare alphabetic listing)
Advanced sign lists	Lists of signs with all possible readings (even very rare ones); list of special sign combinations (compound signs)
Numerical exercises	[see "Numerical Exercises" in chapter 2]
Metrological lists and tables	Weights, lengths, volume, etc., in standardized format
Mathematical tables	Multiplication tables and reciprocal tables
Phrases and sentences	[compare chapter 5 on "model letters" and 6 on "sayings"]
Sumerian proverbs	Multiple collections, using rare words and sign values acquired in earlier exercises
Model contracts	Realistic contracts, without witnesses or date [compare letters, treaties, monuments, etc.]

curriculum that we have in our Hebrew sources. To be sure, there are substantive differences in the cuneiform and (linear) alphabetic writing systems that make the comparison inexact. Moreover, the cuneiform school tradition has a history over the course of three millennia, whereas the Hebrew school tradition developed over the course of just a few centuries. In other words, the cuneiform school tradition was much more robust. At the same time, it is clear that school traditions are quite conservative and long-lived. *Moreover, these cuneiform school traditions were operating in Canaan until the end of the second millennium* BCE—that is, while the incipient alphabetic school traditions were first developing in early Israel. It would hardly be surprising that early Israel borrowed from this well-established cuneiform school tradition.

What are the features of this tradition, and how do they help us understand the alphabetic school curriculum? The elementary curriculum began with sign exercises in using a stylus, and the first real sign list (i.e., the Syllable Alphabet B) that a student practiced was organized by the shape of the cuneiform signs. This was followed by the TU-TA-TI tablets, that is, lists of signs organized by sounds (e.g., TU-TA-TI, NU-NA-NI, TUR-TAR-TIR, etc.). Indeed a considerable number of student exercises involved learning how to properly execute the signs. Alphabetic writing, of course, was much simpler to learn than the cuneiform writing system, so it did not need the same extensive number of student exercises. Yet the practice of writing the ABCs—that is, abecedaries—was a major component of early Israelite scribal training. In fact, abecedaries are the one category of scribal exercises that we have discovered in a variety of archaeological contexts from ancient Israel as well as Ugarit. Christopher Rollston, for example, has paid special attention to this one aspect of the scribal curriculum in his book *Writing and Literacy in the World of Ancient Israel*, arguing that the development of a consistent paleography—that is, the study of the forms of letters—in ancient Israel points to curricular activities. He argues that inscriptions reflect "a sophisticated and consistent production of letter morphology and stance considered standard during specific horizons. Moreover, the Old Hebrew script also reflects the fact that Old Hebrew scribes adhered to certain strict curricular conventions about the relative positions of certain sequential letters (e.g., *samek-pe*)."[66] The abecedaries are the beginning of physical evidence for the curricular exercises that resulted in the conventions that Rollston posits. This category will be discussed below in the context of Kuntillet ʿAjrud and elaborated upon in chapter 3.

The next exercises were thematic lists. These began with practicing writing personal names, and there were also lists with geographical names (including city names, water names, etc.). Such mundane names were critical to the fledgling scribe since most of the basic work involved administrative and economic texts of various types that required writing names. As Veldhuis points out, "The ability to write names is of the highest importance for the would-be bureaucrat. Most of the texts a scribe will write in his future life will be business documents, consisting of ever the same formulas. The names of persons involved, however, are not predictable."[67] This certainly bears itself out in ancient Hebrew inscriptions, many of which are administrative texts—e.g., letters, military personnel lists, receipts of various types, etc. It was essential to learn to accurately transcribe names.

After this, there were classified spelling lists—that is, lists organized by themes (e.g., trees/wood objects, animals, clay, leather, metal, clothing, food, etc.). Such vocabulary lists continue to be a staple of the educational system as well as student testing. The lexical tradition in cuneiform began in the fourth millennium BCE and became fixed and rigid during the Old Babylonian period (i.e., early second millennium BCE).[68] Excellent examples of the traditional Old Babylonian lexical lists are known in the periphery during the late second millennium BCE, including Emar and Ugarit, although the Emar examples have been more fully published.[69] In the periphery, these lexical lists often added columns for other languages, including Hittite, Ugaritic, West Semitic, and even Egyptian. In this respect, the lexical lists began to function as dictionaries in the periphery. The thematic lists continued into the Neo-Assyrian and Neo-Babylonian periods with continuing innovations, most notably the development of lexical commentaries.[70] Other categories of lists, such as grammatical lists and god lists, also developed. Grammatical lists included verbal paradigms and grammatical vocabulary, as well as lists of different categories of grammar (e.g., adverbs, conjugations, pronouns) in a variety of nonstandardized exercises.[71] A fragmentary example of such lists was excavated at Ashkelon dating to the end of the Late Bronze Age. This highlights the fact that such lexical lists were known and used as a new alphabetic scribal tradition emerged. The various types of lists will be discussed below in the context of Kuntillet ʿAjrud and elaborated upon in chapter 4.

Scribal education then advanced to numerical exercises. These included metrological lists and tables as well as mathematical tables. This category of curriculum also appears in the southern Levant; a small fragment of a combined multiplication table dating to the Late Bronze Age was actually excavated at Hazor.[72] Although the tablet was prepared at Hazor, it fits into the much larger cuneiform numerical tradition of scribal exercises. A well-developed and even advanced study of mathematics is well known in Mesopotamia,[73] but this study in ancient Israel was apparently limited to practical applications useful to accounting, administration, and economic activities. We have examples of basic numerical exercises in six ostraca from Kadesh Barnea,[74] and there are many examples of various weights and measures that utilize numbers and weights.[75]

This category also appears in the Kuntillet ʿAjrud inscriptions (and is discussed in chapter 2 under "Numerical Exercises").

The last part of the curriculum is described by Veldhuis as "phrases and sentences." This refers to proverbs and sayings as well as literary models of various genres. Some of the most prominent models for the purpose of studying ancient Hebrew inscriptions and biblical literature include treaties, letters, and monumental inscriptions. We have a few examples of a model letter from Kuntillet ʿAjrud, and I will deal with some of the implications of this genre in chapter 5. Unfortunately, we have no other examples of model contracts or treaties in the epigraphic record,[76] although the similarities between the Book of Deuteronomy and some Mesopotamian literature make it likely that such literature was part of the school curriculum. "Phrases and sentences" will be dealt with in chapter 6 under the heading "Proverbial Sayings."

Advanced scribal education falls outside of Veldhuis chart, which reflects the early and more rigid parts of the scribal curriculum. The more advanced stages of the scribal curriculum are also the least uniform. In the Mesopotamian context, well-known literature like the Gilgamesh Epic and the Enuma Elish could be used as advanced school texts. They were used even in the periphery; so, for example, a fragment of the Gilgamesh Epic was found at Megiddo. Indeed chemical analysis of the clay indicates that the tablet was actually written there, so it must have been part of the local school tradition.[77] However, the main types of advanced curriculum in the cuneiform tradition were liturgical texts.[78] It is important to recognize that the advanced curriculum included texts that were not strictly school texts. For example, an American student can study and memorize the Gettysburg Address or the Star-Spangled Banner, but these are not strictly school texts. There actually are general comparisons that can be made to this type of advanced literary texts that were used as scribal curriculum in the plaster wall texts represented at Kuntillet ʿAjrud. In chapter 7, I will explore how the plaster wall texts may reflect an advanced Hebrew scribal curriculum.

2

Scribal Curriculum at Kuntillet ʿAjrud

The inscriptions from Kuntillet ʿAjrud are the key to unlocking the Hebrew alphabetic curriculum. They provide the most varied set of school exercises within the ancient Hebrew epigraphic record, and they fill out the otherwise meager examples of school texts from other ancient Israel sites. The largely negative assessments of school texts known in ancient Israel predate the full publication of the Kuntillet ʿAjrud inscriptions. Indeed the piecemeal publication of these inscriptions prevented scholars from fully appreciating their significance.[1] Now the Kuntillet ʿAjrud inscriptions have been published in a complete edition with accompanying studies of the archaeological aspects of the site. And yet the new edition still does not treat the inscriptions as an interrelated corpus.[2] This chapter will give a holistic interpretation of the corpus that illustrates how the inscriptions reflect a variety of the curriculum for young scribes.

To appreciate the significance of the Kuntillet ʿAjrud material, it is useful to review other early alphabetic school texts from ancient Israel.[3] The examples are largely limited to abecedaries and disputed texts. For example, there are complete abecedaries at Izbet Ṣarta and Tel Zayit, as well as fragmentary examples from Lachish, Arad, Deir ʿAlla, Kadesh Barnea, and elsewhere.[4] In addition, there are lists of hieratic numerals and accounting abbreviations from Kadesh Barnea. The hieratic scribal exercises are especially important as they illustrate the necessary training for accounting, administrative, and economic texts that form the majority of scribal activities. Other examples include an ostracon from Arad, where a student apparently practiced writing the name of the site repeatedly—"Arad, Arad, Arad"—with rudimentary penmanship.[5] The Gezer Calendar has also often been understood as a school text, although there has been no consensus on this interpretation.[6] This brief survey underscores the dearth of actual epigraphic evidence for training of ancient Hebrew scribes. In fact James Crenshaw, in his book *Education in Ancient Israel*, took the most skeptical possible interpretation of the epigraphic evidence, summarizing it as follows: "The only site that has a strong claim to represent writing exercises, Kadesh Barnea, has yielded five ostraca."[7] To be sure, Crenshaw represents the most skeptical point of view, but it nevertheless highlights the significance of the

Kuntillet ʿAjrud inscriptions once they are properly understood as representing a variety of exercises for the training of Hebrew scribes.

The site is most well-known for its famous—or infamous—inscription that calls for a blessing from "Yahweh and his *ʾasherah*"—that is, from the God of Israel and apparently his divine consort. Often Yahweh was understood to be a confirmed bachelor. In this respect, this inscription (along with Khirbet el-Qom cave inscription) revolutionized our understanding of Israelite religion. But this reading of "Yahweh and his *ʾasherah*" has consumed scholarship, and the many other inscriptions from the corpus have received relatively little attention. As it happens, even this reading has now garnered significant skepticism in favor of "Yahweh and his shrine/sanctuary/temple," which may fit some of the inscriptional evidence (although it does not fit the Hebrew Bible well).[8] This debate is important for the history of Israelite religion, but it falls outside the scope of the present study. For the purposes of this study, "Yahweh and his *ʾasherah*" is simply part of a blessing formula used in scribal exercises.

Location and Function of Kuntillet ʿAjrud

In order to contextualize the corpus of inscriptions, it is first necessary to understand the location and function of the site. Kuntillet ʿAjrud sits in the barren wilderness of the central Sinai. The site itself was first discovered in 1869 by Edward Palmer, a British explorer who traveled the region. He published his observations in a book, *The Desert of the Exodus*.[9] Palmer recognized that the site must be interpreted as related to ancient trade and thought that he had found Gypsaria, a site on the old Roman road between Elath and Gaza. However, archaeological investigations detailed especially in Meshel's publication of the site proved him wrong about his dating and identification. Nevertheless, Palmer correctly intuited the strategic location of the site along an ancient trade route from the Red Sea to the Mediterranean Sea.

That ancient trade route is known today as the Darb el-Ghazza in Arabic, that is, "the Gaza Road." This route would have begun at the Red Sea near the site of ancient Eilat and/or Ezion-geber (Tell el-Kheleifeh),[10] gone up to Kuntillet ʿAjrud, then past Kadesh Barnea (Tel-Qudeirat),[11] up to Gaza, where it reached the Mediterranean Sea. This road connected the Red Sea with the Mediterranean coast long before the modern Suez Canal. The site of Kuntillet ʿAjrud lies along this route, though just to the west (about ten kilometers) of the most direct route through the Wadi Quraiya. It has been pointed out that neither Kuntillet ʿAjrud nor Kadesh Barnea lies on the most direct Darb el-Ghazza route, but they both provided convenient water sources near this trade route. Of course, desert trade routes do not always take the most direct path and must be sensitive to both topography and water sources.

The site of Kuntillet ʿAjrud itself lies perched on a solitary elongated hill overlooking Wadi Quraiya (M.R. 094954), approximately fifty kilometers south of Kadesh Barnea (see Figure 2.1). The excavators of Kuntillet ʿAjrud found several shallow wells nearby that would have provided a perennial water source suitable for a small fortress.[12] Indeed, the Arabic name means "hill of the water-well," which underscores its abiding importance as a way station in an arid region. The central Sinai receives less than three inches of rain per year, and water was particularly important for travelers and traders in the region. These wells provided one of the few water sources along the Darb el-Ghazza.

The function of the site has been debated in the scholarly literature. Meshel's official publication of the site subtitled it "an Iron Age II religious site," but his description is largely based on the religious content of some of the inscriptions and drawings. Yet, the evidence for a religious function offered by Meshel's site report is fragile. While the site has inscriptions and drawings with religious themes,[13] this does not necessitate an overall religious interpretation for the site. For example, with regard to the drawings, Tallay Ornan has pointed out that all the Kuntillet ʿAjrud drawings have direct parallels in neo-Assyrian *palace* reliefs.[14] In other words, they cannot be narrowly associated with a religious site. Meshel also argues that the unusual amount of linen found at the site supports a religious interpretation since linen was the typical material used for priests' garments. However, this argument is undercut by an appendix to the excavation report itself that admits that linen was also found in excavations at nearby Kadesh Barnea, which has not been interpreted as a religious site. A religious function for the site has also been questioned because the site has no temple, no shrine, and no significant cultic objects.[15] In sum, there is no evidence for a narrowly or specifically religious interpretation of the site. Rather, the site was simply a fortress built along a trade route because it had access to water in an arid region. Now that the entire corpus of inscriptions has been published, the contextual examination offered here further establishes that Kuntillet ʿAjrud was just a state-sponsored fortress along a desert trade route.[16]

The Inscriptions from Kuntillet ʿAjrud

A variety of inscriptions were excavated at Kuntillet ʿAjrud, but the examples of elementary scribal practice were found on two large storage jars, or *pithoi*. The two pithoi provide the primary data for reconstructing ancient scribal exercises,

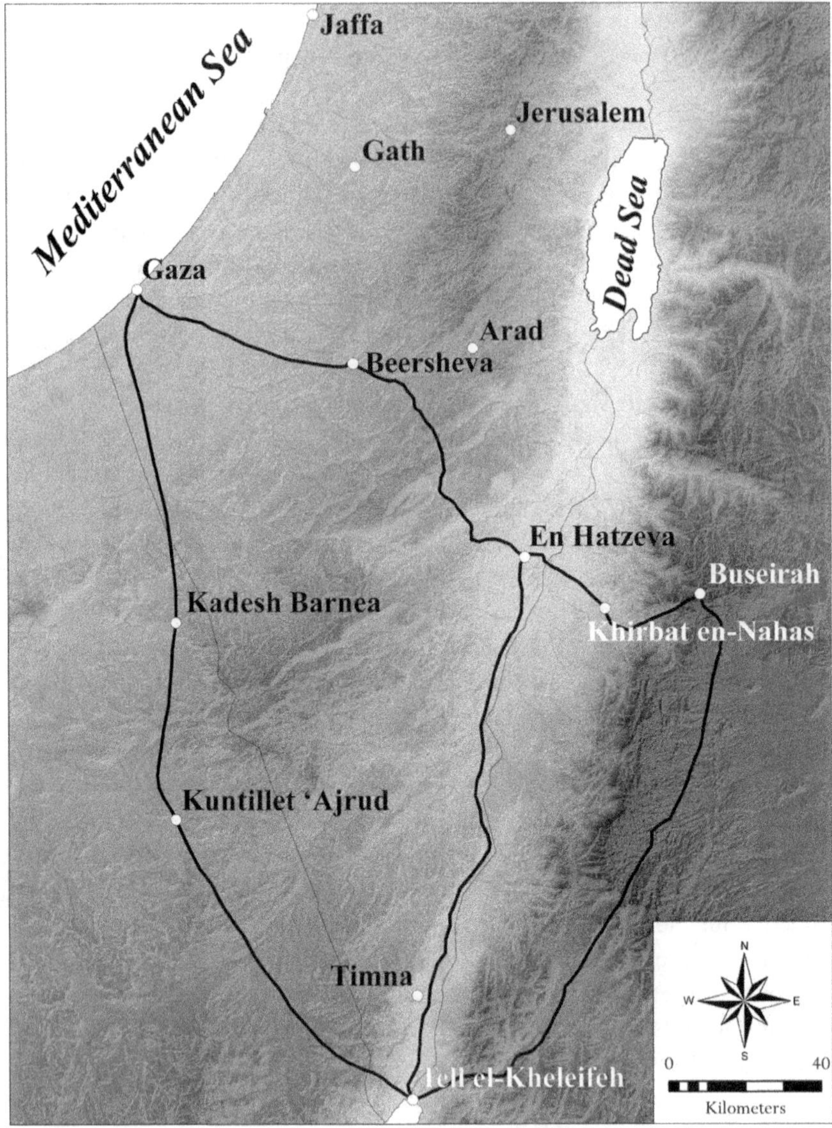

Figure 2.1 The location of Kuntillet ʿAjrud and related routes. Map courtesy of Amy Karoll.

but there were also fragmentary plaster inscriptions that originally decorated the walls of the fortress. Unfortunately they are in a poor state of preservation. They likely were texts that served as advanced scribal curricula; however, they are quite fragmentary and subject to different interpretations. I will discuss the

Figure 2.2 Pithos B inscriptions. Original drawing by N. Schechter and H. Kak; adapted by the author.

various possibilities of plaster wall inscriptions in chapter 7, but my main attention here will be on the pithoi inscriptions.

The first set of inscriptions are on Pithos B, which were published in the Kuntillet ʿAjrud volume with an excellent illustration by N. Schechter and H. Kak (see Figure 2.2).[17] The nature of these inscriptions as writing practice is first of all evident on the top left of the drawing, where we see the letter *yod* written over and over again at least ten times (labeled KA 3.15). On the far right side, to the immediate right of a long vertical scribal line, are parts of four separate abecedaries (labeled KA 3.11–14).

I have added labels to the Pithos B drawing to illustrate how the official publication treats each inscription separately rather than as a whole. This is most evident with the four abecedaries as if they were in order—3.11, 3.12, 3.13, and 3.14—when they are actually broken up by 3.7 and 3.8 (see more closely in Figure 2.3).

In KA 3.11, we can see most of the sequence, beginning with *ʾaleph* and ending with *tav*, in the two lines—or, perhaps more accurately, we should observe two parts in the alphabet pedagogy. Based on the remaining letters, I have reconstructed the first abecedary on the two lines—*ʾaleph* through *kaf* and *lamed* through *tav*. Michael Coogan has pointed out that these two parts were the way the alphabet was organized and learned based on evidence from later Hebrew abecedaries (e.g., Wadi Murabbaʿât, Qumran) and Greek evidence.[18] Even the word *ʾaleph* itself—spelled with an *ʾaleph*, then a *lamed*—seems to reflect the two parts to alphabet learning. In KA 3.11, then, we would have the first example of the two-part pedagogy of the alphabet learning in the Iron Age inscriptional corpus. And biblical acrostic poetry seems to confirm the two-part pedagogy of alphabet learning (see chapter 3).

The abecedaries illustrate the nature of this scribal practice with a master and apprentice(s). Although they preserve only partial sequences, they are clearly practice texts. Other aspects of the four separate abecedaries suggest a student practicing the elementary level of the scribal profession. Inscriptions 3.12 and 3.14 are written in red ink in a flowing, elegant hand, whereas Inscriptions 3.11 and 3.13 are written in black ink reflecting a more basic hand. The paleography of the red and black abecedaries at Kuntillet ʿAjrud certainly show at least two distinct hands, perhaps more.[19] This interplay of hands may point to a master and an apprentice. The black ink abecedaries are in a somewhat competent hand, even if they do not show the accomplishment of the red ink writing. Note especially the letter *shin* in KA 3.13, which is awkwardly written as two separate "v" shapes that are barely joined, instead of the more *correct* flowing "w" shape. And the letter *resh* is written as a triangle (Δ) and then a leg is attached to the right side, instead of a long vertical line (|) topped by a sometimes rounded "less than" shape (<). The awkward execution and stroke order of these letters proves that we are dealing with a novice scribe. In this respect, it cannot be argued that the different abecedaries merely represent different styles, cursive and lapidary. No, they reflect more and less accomplished scribes. To that extent, they are not dissimilar to the repetition in writing the letter *yod* on the top left of this same pithos (i.e., Figure 2.3).

KA 3.11, 3.7, 3.12, 3.13, 3.8, 3.14

<table>
<tr><td>3.11</td><td>1a)</td><td>ʾ b g [d] h [w z] ḥ [ṭ y k]</td><td>abecedary</td></tr>
<tr><td></td><td>1b)</td><td>[l m n s p ʿ ṣ] q r š t</td><td>abecedary</td></tr>
<tr><td>3.7</td><td>2)</td><td>]ʾb/m̊n̊ẙ[] |</td><td>]ʾB/M N Y (?) [</td></tr>
<tr><td>3.12</td><td>3)</td><td>]ṭ y k l m n s p |</td><td>abecedary</td></tr>
<tr><td>3.13</td><td>4)</td><td>]p ʿ ṣ q r š t |</td><td>abecedary</td></tr>
<tr><td>3.8</td><td>5)</td><td>]h. šmrn šʿrm. |</td><td>]H, Samaria, šʿrm (Shaʿaraim; gates; barley)</td></tr>
<tr><td>3.14</td><td>6)</td><td>]k l m n s p ʿ ṣ q r š | t</td><td>abecedary</td></tr>
</table>

The mixture of red and black ink is common in Egyptian texts but is unusual in ancient Israel.[20] An Egyptian scribe's palette normally had spaces for both red and black ink. Parkinson and Quirke note, "While black was the main ink, red ink was a practical means of highlighting phrases ('rubrics') and marking

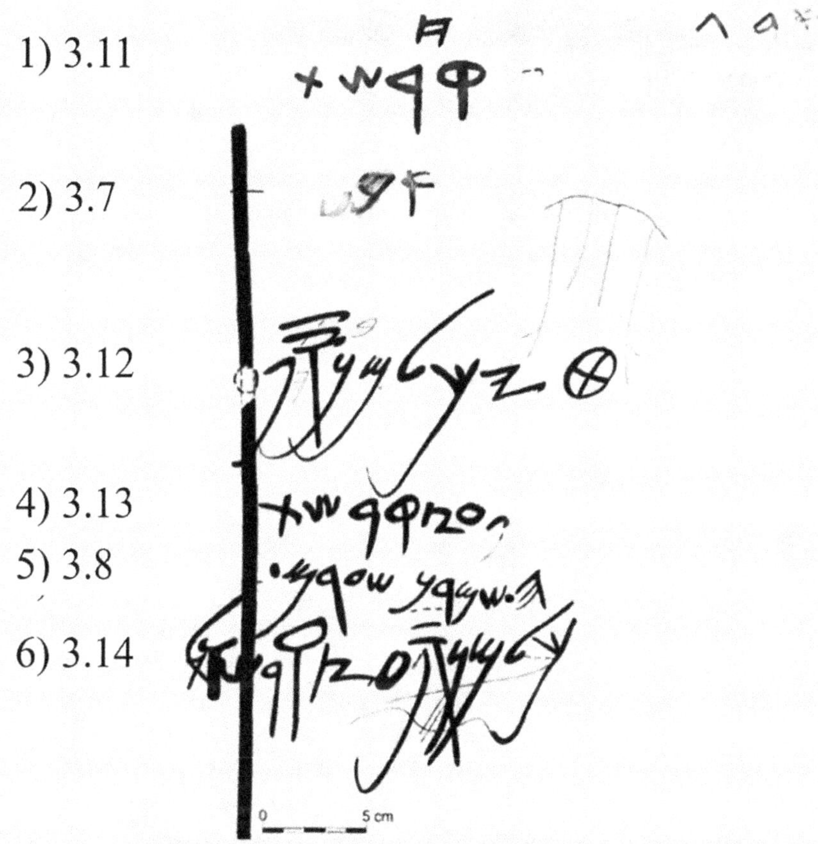

Figure 2.3 Pithos B, detail of abecedaries. Original drawing by N. Schechter and H. Kak; adapted by the author.

distinctions."[21] In official Egyptian texts, red ink was often used for headings and other paratextual notations, and it was also regularly used for instructions. In certain texts, red ink was used for corrections—that is, a master scribe correcting the work of an apprentice. Red ink was also used for drafting hieroglyphic texts on walls; the final text would then be written in black ink over the signs in red ink (probably done by the master scribe).[22] The fact that this is scribal practice is underscored by the faint traces of letters—an earlier exercise by a student that had been erased, cleaned up for a new set of practice exercises (see especially line 3 in Figure 2.3).

Abecedaries were certainly a foundation for early scribal education. In Rollston's article "Scribal Curriculum," he identifies two aspects of elementary education: script and spelling (i.e., paleography and orthography). Rollston infers these categories of education from synchronic consistency and diachronic development. Here we can ask what sort of scribal exercises were used to develop such consistency in script and spelling. The beginning of scribal curriculum was, of course, the practice of writing abecedaries. As for orthography, Rollston supports his assessment of a relatively standardized system of spelling from the corpus of inscriptions. But how was this standardized spelling learned? Presumably, such orthographic consistency would have been honed through copying lexical lists, including the types discussed below.

Lexical Lists

Lines 2 and 5 (KA 3.7 and 3.8) of Figure 2.3 seem to be related to lexical lists. The interpretation of these lines as lexical lists is based on two considerations. First, they are situated in the context of abecedaries as well as a model letter—that is, in a clear context of scribal practice. Second, one of the most typical scribal exercises is vocabulary lists. In other words, they must be understood as scribal exercises. The question then becomes, What kind of scribal exercises are they? Such lists would have been requisite for learning to spell properly—that is, creating the kind of orthographic consistency that Rollston identifies. As we saw in chapter 1, such vocabulary lists are well known in antiquity, particularly as cuneiform scribal exercises. Such texts could be organized in a variety of ways, but we mostly have cuneiform examples upon which to base our reconstruction. In cuneiform, one of the first practice lists was simply learning how to write names correctly.

Let's begin with the better preserved line, that is, line 5, which is designated as Inscription 3.8 in the official publication (see Figure 2.3). While it is sandwiched between a series of abecedaries (lines 1, 3, 4, and 6), it is clearly not an abecedary. What little is preserved in line 5,]*h. šmrn šʿrm.* | "]*H*, Samaria, *šʿrm* (Shaʿaraim; gates; barley; hair)," is in close alphabetical order—*shin-mem*, then *shin/śin-ʿayin*—that is to say, the alphabetical order is underscored by the abecedaries themselves. In this respect, the alphabetic order of the lexical items and the abecedaries are complementary. It is important to emphasize that this interpretation of a line as lexical practice is supported by its larger context, which is lost in the official publication that presents the abecedaries separately from line 5 as well as the model letter to the left of the scribal line (discussed below). In sum, Inscriptions 3.11, 3.7, 3.12, 3.13, 3.8, and 3.14 should be understood as six lines of the same practice text. At the same time, there is evidence of the hand of a master and at least one (maybe more) students in these lines.

The two words in line 5—]*h. šmrn šʿrm.* |—have been read in several ways.[23] This is the nature of the text itself. As a decontextualized list, it is polysemic.[24] Of course, in cuneiform writing and education, polysemy was a complex problem that a curriculum had to address. In Hebrew, the problem is less complex but still critical to education. It could mean many things, depending on how it is vocalized. And this is exactly the point in an educational context. A master scribe could use this to teach a student about the different ways to read both a single grapheme (ש as both *šin* and *śin*) and a lexeme (שערם).

The meanings of שערם could include "Shaʿaraim," "gates" (*šeʿārim*), and "barley" (*śeʿorim*), as well as other, more obscure meanings, depending on the context. The editors of the Kuntillet ʿAjrud material have proposed reading this word as "barley," although they admit, "This short and fragmentary text does not allow for an understanding of the relationship between the toponym Shomron and the plural form of the word 'barley.' "[25] But there is a context. It is on a jar with scribal doodling related to curriculum and education, and it is in the immediate context of abecedaries. Interestingly, the editors point out that the list would be organized by the *shape* of the letter rather than its sound; that is, the exercise would not distinguish between *šin* and *śin*. Material from the Hebrew Bible evidences this concern for graphemes that do not distinguish between *šin* and *śin* such as acrostic poetry, as in Prov 31:10–31. This is certainly valid, but actually the word serves to illustrate the dual phonemes of this single grapheme in an educational context. It was important to teach a fledgling scribe about the polysemy of the grapheme ש. And these two lexemes—the first referring to the capital of the Israelite kingdom and the second referring to either a place name, a typical commodity of exchange, or a part of a fortress and city architecture—were important for any would-be Hebrew scribe.[26] But the most important lesson might have been the lesson about polysemy in lexemes.

The second line also seems to be a fragment of a lexical list. Line 2 has only one certain letter (*ʾaleph*), but it does not appear to be an abecedary. However, it is too short and effaced for us to translate or to be certain about its purpose.[27] It should be some sort of student exercise. But what kind? In the overall context, I would tentatively suggest that one plausible interpretation is to understand this as a second fragment of a vocabulary list. I think we should imagine words that might teach young scribes about Hebrew phonetics, perhaps about the complicated nature of the pronunciation of the letter *ʾaleph* itself.

Taken together, lines 1 through 6 recall the cuneiform scribal exercises charted in the introduction. For the ancient Mesopotamian scribe, the "Syllable Alphabet B" taught shapes, and TU-TA-TI tablets taught sounds. Here, lines 1, 3, 4, and 6 are the exercises of a student practicing the shapes of the letters, and line 5 practices a list of words organized alphabetically. The alphabetic order also recalls the cuneiform practice of organizing words according to the shape of the first sign. In sum, this interpretation as a lexical list now gives some coherence to a whole text. It also begins to show how the cuneiform school tradition can give insight into aspects of the early Israelite scribal curriculum.

Pithos B gives another example of lexical lists—in this case, a list of personal names. On the left side of the pithos (Figure 2.2), there is a list of five or six personal names. Scribes had to learn to transcribe names accurately, and they practiced writing various names in lists as part of their elementary curriculum. As Niek Veldhuis points out "The ability to write names is of the highest importance for the would be bureaucrat. Most of the texts a scribe will write in his future life will be business documents, consisting of ever the same formulas. The names of persons involved, however, are not predictable."[28] In the cuneiform curriculum, these lists included exercises for personal names and titles of officials.[29] Although the thematic lexical lists have attracted more scholarly attention, the ability to accurately transcribe names was an important foundation to a scribal education.

Once we recognize lists of personal names as a critical scribal exercise, it opens up a new way to interpret Hebrew inscriptions. This has already been recognized, for example, by Aaron Demsky, who suggests the importance of practicing writing lists of names for the alphabetic scribal curriculum; he points to examples of name lists in the alphabetical school texts from Ugarit and notes the prominence of lists of names in the epigraphic record in Israel. Most recently, he has suggested that the Khirbet Qeiyafa inscription is merely a list of names (see discussion in chapter 4).[30] It is in this context that a list of names on Pithos B, published as Inscription 3.10, should be read, as follows:

1) *šknyw*	Shekanyaw
2) *ʾmṣ*	ʾAmotz
3) *šmryw*	Shemaryaw
4) *ʾlyw*	ʾEliyaw
5) *ʿzyw*	ʿUzziyaw
6) *mṣry*	an Egyptian

The last "name" is most likely a gentilic that should be translated as "an Egyptian," although it could be a personal name.[31] If this were just a list of names, then the last word—"an Egyptian"—might be a description of the previous name, ʿUzziyaw; however, this is an unlikely interpretation, as ʿUzziyaw is a typical Hebrew name that includes the Israelite theophoric suffix *-yaw* as an abbreviation for Yahweh. The very fact that ʿUzziyaw and "an Egyptian" (ll. 5–6) seem to be unrelated in the list further suggests that the list was used for scribal practice. Indeed the use of the gentilic "an Egyptian" may remind us of some of the Egyptian antecedents (e.g., ink, hieratic numerals, loanwords) for the scribal profession in ancient Israel. It also reminds us that the location of Kuntillet ʿAjrud is in the Negev Highlands, an area ruled by Egypt during the Late Bronze Age and reclaimed by Pharaoh Shishak (i.e., Shoshenq I, r. 943–922 BCE) via a military campaign in the tenth century BCE. "Egyptian" thus is a relevant lexical item for local students.

The spelling of the personal names with the *-yaw* theophoric is closely associated with the northern kingdom of Israel,[32] and this has attracted the most attention in the list of names. It corresponds to other elements of the site that have caused scholars to associate the site with the northern kingdom.[33] Of course, it would not be surprising if this particular list were the names of the Israelite soldiers who happened to be stationed at Kuntillet ʿAjrud at this particular time. Veldhuis actually suggests that cuneiform lexical lists of personal names "may well go back to an actual inventory of real people."[34] Perhaps the students at Kuntillet ʿAjrud used their own names for scribal practice, although this is mere speculation.

The paleography of this list of names does not nicely match either the abecedaries or the list of geographical names discussed above. The inscription here is written in red ink, but it does not exhibit the same quality of elegant and flowing characteristics of the abecedaries in red ink described previously. For example, the *yod* in line 5 is quite irregularly executed. The letter *shin* in lines 1 and 3 is not clearly articulated in the way it is in the abecedaries. What is the best way to account for these inconsistencies? Do we really have yet another student hand writing this list of names? It seems possible. Already there must be at least two, perhaps three or four scribal hands in the abecedaries and lexical list discussed above.

The list of names has sometimes been associated with five figures illustrated to the right of the list, although the relationship between the figures and the inscriptions is disputed. Some scholars believe that these images, as well as the other drawings on the pithoi, are not related to the inscriptions.[35] Some have thought the figures are a procession of religious worshippers,[36] but Ornan has compared this procession to royal supplicants in the palace reliefs of Assurnasirpal II.[37] That is, they are not necessarily worshippers but rather stylized figures in a typical processional pose of allegiance to the king. As mentioned above, Ornan has shown that all the drawings at Kuntillet ʿAjrud have parallels in neo-Assyrian royal iconography and consequently interprets them in the context of a royal trading fortress (as opposed to a temple or cultic context). There is no necessary relationship between the list of names and the procession of figures. Certainly the drawing does not undermine the interpretation of the list of names as a scribal exercise.

Numerical Exercises

The knowledge of accounting was critical to the bureaucracy of the ancient Near Eastern world. As such, scribal exercises using numerical exercises, accounting terminology, and mathematics played a critical role in preparing the would-be scribe for work in administration. Scribes were critical to state bureaucracy and the economy. As Veldhuis emphasizes, "Bureaucracy depended on loyal scribes."[38] As long as the bureaucracy was essentially generated by the palace and the state, the loyalty of the scribes would be to their main employer: the palace. The centrality of accounting in the duties of the scribe is reflected in the Hebrew terminology itself: the terms *sēp̱er*, "document, scroll," and *sōp̱ēr*, "scribe," come from the root *spr*, whose primary meaning was "to count" and only secondarily came to mean "to record, write."[39] Numerical exercises are known most prominently from several ostraca from Kadesh Barnea that write out hieratic numerals, including one that writes out the hieratic numerals in order from one to ten thousand.[40] Another probable example of a heiratic school text is found among the Arad ostraca (no. 34). These hieratic numbers are part of the technology of administration that was a legacy of the Egyptian hegemony in the Levant during the late second millennium BCE. Although the Kadesh Barnea scribal exercises are better preserved, Kuntillet ʿAjrud also has evidence of such scribal practice.

The inscriptions from Kuntillet ʿAjrud preserve this aspect of training in several examples. The hieratic numbers 1, 2, 3, and 4—which use simple strokes—are quite clearly written in sequence on Pithos A (see Figure 2.4). The numbers 5 and 6 seemingly appear inside the larger and smaller bull, although the hieratic numbers 5 and 6 are not usually written out simply with strokes. These numbers were also written inside the bull after the pictures were drawn, but there seems to be no particular reason other than the scribe's whim. Unfortunately the editors of the Kuntillet ʿAjrud inscriptions did not recognize the use of hieratic numbers on Pithos A; as a result, they could not be included in the otherwise very fine volume by Stefan Wimmer, *Palästinisches Hieratisch*, which catalogues all the use of Egyptian hieratic numerals in Hebrew inscriptions.[41] In Figure 2.4, it is clear that these numbers, as well as the practicing of the letter *yod*, were written after the iconography, since they are orientated 180 degrees to the pictures.[42]

One of the most interesting exercises is the so-called scribbles on Pithos A. This practice writing, described as "scribbles" in the official publication,[43] should be understood as practice in writing hieratic numerals. As with the repetition of *yod* on the far right side of the drawing, the student repeatedly practices writing various numerals. The number 10, which looks like a sans serif capital <T>, is written at least two times. Many of the rest of the "scribbles" look like attempts to write the hieratic number 70 as well as the numbers 50 and 30.[44] The shapes are too consistent to be dismissed as just scribbles. The number 70, which

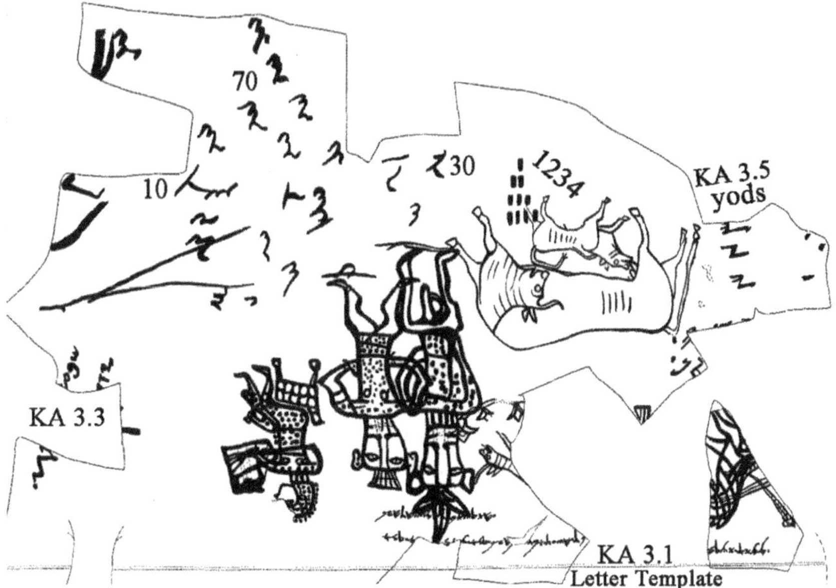

Figure 2.4 Pithos A (rotated 180 degrees). Original drawing by N. Schechter and H. Kak; adapted by the author.

looks like the number <3> with a tail on the bottom, is written at least eight times. In this respect, they are much like the example of the letter *yod*, which was practiced several times on both pithoi. Moreover, given the clear writing of the number sequence of 1 through 4 as well as the number 10, these scribbles should be understood as scribal practice in writing hieratic numerals. Here we should be reminded that six ostraca excavated at Kadesh Barnea (although dated a century later than the Kuntillet ʿAjrud examples) include well-preserved student lists of various hieratic numerals and accounting terms.[45] They remind us that accounting would have been quite useful in a remote trading post like Kuntillet ʿAjrud.

Models for Letter Writing

Letter formulary was another critical part of scribal training, and Kuntillet ʿAjrud provides three examples of the epistolary exercise: Inscriptions 3.1 (on Pithos A) and 3.6 and 3.9 (on Pithos B).[46] The best-preserved example, 3.6, will illustrate the formulary. All three examples are reconstructed in chapter 5 along with detailed discussions of the letter models, their ancient Near Eastern parallels, and their significance for biblical literature.

Inscription 3.6 is penned in an elegant hand in red ink to the left of a vertical scribal line. On the other side of the line are the abecedaries and lexical list discussed in connection with Figure 2.2. The model letter has been transcribed as follows:

1) *ʾmr*	“Message
2) *ʾmryhwʾ*	of Amaryaw: ‘Say
3) *mr l.ʾdnẙ*	to my lord,
4) *hš̈lm. ʾ*t .	are you well?
5) *brktk. ly*	I have blessed you to
6) *hwh tmn*	YHWH of Teman
7) *wlʾšrth. yb*	and his *asherah*. May He
8) *rk wyšmrk*	bless you and may He keep you,
9) *wyhy ʿm. ʾdn*	and may He be with my
10) *y* []	lord [forever].”

The nature of these inscriptions as scribal exercises is underscored by four observations. First, the examples include only the beginning of a typical letter—that is, a *praescriptio* that includes the address (i.e., “Message of PN, say to PN”) and the greeting (“how is your welfare? May the DN bless you”).[47] This is the only part of a formal letter that is always repeated in a letter that needs to be practiced by a student. A full template for letter writing typically refers to a blessing by God. Arad 16, for example, begins, “Your brother, Hanniah, send for the welfare of Elishib and the welfare of your house. I bless you to Yahweh.” In Ugaritic letters one typically finds formulas like “may the gods guard you and keep you well” (KTU 2:11:7–9). Practicing the *praescriptio* is also typical of other examples of scribal epistolary exercises, such as we find at Ugarit (e.g., *KTU* 5.9). Second, the present example is situated along the long vertical divider. Such dividers are known from Mesopotamian school texts, and the texts on the right side of the vertical divider (e.g., abecedaries, list) are also school texts. In other words, seen in its larger context on the pithos, this inscription is part of other student practice, including the physical rubrics of scribal exercises.[48] Third, once one recognizes this particular letter as an epistolary exercise, one can also see that it utilizes a grammatical pun on the root *ʾmr*, “to speak,” in lines 1–3. They begin, *ʾmr ʾmryw ʾmr l.ʾdny*, which might literally be rendered “An *ʾōmer* [i.e., ‘speech’] of *ʾAmaryaw* [i.e., ‘The-Speaker-of-Yahweh’]: *ʾemōr* [i.e., ‘Speak’] to my lord.” Although ʾAmaryaw is a personal name known in Hebrew inscriptions, as the editors point out, the name is also a play on the use of root *ʾmr* in the formula. In other words, ʾAmaryaw is probably not a real person but rather a scribal invention. Indeed we are reminded that cuneiform school texts included grammatical exercises,[49] and this type of punning is an effective teaching tool about the role of etymological roots in the Hebrew alphabetic writing system. Finally, the photographs of Inscription 3.6 indicate it is actually "a (partial) palimpsest";[50] that is, there is evidence that texts were being written, erased, and reused. The soldier-scribes were essentially using the large pithoi as a blackboard. Its recognition as a palimpsest further suggests it is a scribal exercise. In sum, there is little doubt that these texts are scribal exercises.

Proverbial Sayings and Liturgy

Finally, proverbial sayings and advanced literary texts were certainly an important part of the scribal curriculum. Proverbial sayings might seem to be a bit impractical, but they could be adapted and used in a variety of contexts. Mesopotamian scribes learned many proverbial sayings, often writing them singly on small round lentil tablets. Liturgy and advanced literature were another matter. These were often written out by more advanced scribes and memorized by students. Admittedly, there does seem to be little practical purpose in teaching a soldier-scribe advanced lessons in literature. Indeed this impracticality has been one of the justifications for understanding Kuntillet ʿAjrud as a religious site. At the same time, education often involves learning things that are not particularly practical. As Veldhuis said of Mesopotamian scribal training, "A scribe learned far too much. A scribe had to be able to write contracts and business documents. . . . But a considerable part of the words he had learned in the lexical lists was obscure, obsolete, or for other reasons of no practical use. If we take into account the literary exercises the burden of 'useless' knowledge a scribal pupil had to digest is all the more impressive."[51] Although we need not imagine that Israelite scribes had the same burden of useless knowledge as Mesopotamian scribes, it seems clear that Israelite education had a degree of impracticality that would have included literary texts.

There is a proverbial saying included in fragmentary text on Pithos B (Inscription 3.9). It is located at the top of the pithos between the letter template and abecedaries on the right side and the practice of the letter *yod* on the top left, and the list of names on the far left side (see Figure 2.2). This physical context is essential for understanding the purpose of the text. While we cannot make too much of this inscription because it is fragmentary, what remains is straightforward enough to translate. The first line looks to be a truncated blessing formula that may be reconstructed, "[I have blessed you] to YHWH of Teman and his *ʾasherah*." The blessing formula should likely be reconstructed as the beginning of a letter formula, as I argue in chapter 5. Such blessing formulas were especially used in letters, but they were also part of a more general scribal repertoire. For example, a blessing formula appears on a stone inscription at Kuntillet ʿAjrud (Inscription 1.2),[52] and it is, of course, part of the well-known Priestly Blessing (Numb 6:24–26) that is found in the Ketef Hinnom inscriptions.[53] Inscription 3.9, lines 2–3, look like some sort of wisdom saying or proverb. Learning such sayings and proverbs was a regular part of cuneiform education, and I will discuss this at length in chapter 6. The editors translate the saying as follows: "Whatever he asks from a man, that man will give him generously. And if he would urge—YHW will have him/according to his wishes." These lines point to general biblical parallels with texts like Pss 20:5; 37:21, 26; and 112:5 as well as a striking parallel with a line in the Aramaic Inscription from Panamuwa (KAI 214:4).[54] All these parallels point to a traditional wisdom saying that was used as a scribal exercise, which is the reason we find it on this pithos next to abecedaries, lists, and model letters.

A corpus of literary texts was also have been found at Kuntillet ʿAjrud. These are the plaster texts that were originally on the walls of the fortress; unfortunately, they are quite fragmentary. The fragmentary nature and debated reconstructions of the plaster wall texts somewhat limit their usefulness to this study. Were they school curricula? Did they serve a decorative purpose? Was there a cultic purpose? The exact answer is uncertain, and the inscriptions may have served several purposes. It is important to remember that advanced school curriculum often derives from repurposed texts. For example, a significant part of cuneiform advanced curriculum was liturgical texts that were repurposed in a school context. We can imagine something similar with the plaster texts at Kuntillet ʿAjrud. We can infer something of their purpose from the general archaeological context of the site and the other inscriptions, and we can utilize comparative evidence to suggest some of the uses of these plaster wall inscriptions. The physical context of these literary texts is definitely unique: the fact that literary texts such as these adorn the walls of a remote fortress on a caravan route from Eilat to Gaza. This is not where one might expect to find such literary compositions or wall decorations. This certainly should open the possibility that these literary texts were, in fact, repurposed as school texts. The contemporary plaster wall texts from Deir ʿAlla are also relevant here and bear some similarities to those at Kuntillet ʿAjrud. Taken together, they may offer a small glimpse into an advanced curriculum for alphabetic scribes within the epigraphic record of the early Iron Age (see further discussion in chapter 7).

The Kuntillet ʿAjrud plaster texts, even in their fragmentary condition, highlight repeated themes that are relevant to the location of the site. In Inscription 4.1, "Yahweh of Têman [*yhwh tymn*]" is mentioned twice. This description is comparable to the locative description, "Yahweh of Samaria [*yhwh šmrn*]," which we have in the practice letters. Têman is understood here as a specific location, perhaps in the southern part of Edom, but it can also be a general term meaning "south." In this respect, it is more contextually appropriate to the site than "Yahweh of Samaria." Inscription 4.2 seems to have a divine theophany where "El shines forth [*wbzrḥ ʾl*]"; as a result, "the mountains melt [*wymsn hrm*]" and "the peaks are crushed [*wydkn gbnm*]"—themes that seem to pick up on the frequent seismic activity along the Great Rift Valley (or the East African Rift).[55] Theophany is accompanied by the repeated concept of theomachy— "on the day of war [*bym mlḥmh*]"—which underscores the military aspects of a state-sponsored fortress garrisoned with soldiers. The theme of divine conflict is quite typical of Near Eastern mythology, and theomachy figures in central texts like the Song of the Sea, the Ugaritic Baʿal Epic, and the Babylonian Creation Epic. In fact, all these literary texts would also serve adequately as school texts.

There are also religious themes in the Kuntillet ʿAjrud plaster texts. El, Yahweh, and Baal all seem to be mentioned in the fragmentary texts. To be sure, these are religious themes, but that would not preclude them from being part of an advanced scribal curriculum. Indeed it would be difficult to think of Near Eastern literary texts that did not have religious themes. The themes of the texts, though fragmentary, certainly are appropriate to the location of Kuntillet ʿAjrud. Kuntillet ʿAjrud should serve as a cautionary example regarding the association of the scribal profession with religion, the temple, and priests. Although several scholars have suggested that Kuntillet ʿAjrud might have been occupied by a group of priests or perhaps was a prophetic "school,"[56] it was a remote fortress on a desert trade route that was more likely populated by soldiers stationed there by the palace. The concept of a soldier-scribe that needed to train apprentices to take over the post is a much more straightforward interpretation of the data. The fact that the nearby site of Kadesh Barnea has scribal exercises in writing hieratic numerals underscores the economic and administrative functions of these sites, as opposed to a religious interpretation. Literary themes like the "day of war" and the theophany of "Yahweh of Têman" were simply relevant literary texts to soldier-scribes stationed at Kuntillet ʿAjrud.

The Context and Implications of Kuntillet ʿAjrud

In sum, a holistic understanding of Kuntillet ʿAjrud yields tangible and substantial inscriptional evidence of early Israelite education. This begins with the natural function of a fortress on a trade route from the Red Sea to the Mediterranean. The site was chosen because it provided access to water for travelers in the desert. The fortress was part of state-run caravansaries—apparently, operated by the kings in Samaria, judging from the personal names and the reference to "Yahweh of Samaria." The inscriptions on two pithoi reflect a variety of elementary and practical scribal practice. While the purpose of the literary texts written on the walls must be approached tentatively, it makes sense to see them as the advanced lessons of soldier-scribes rather than pointing to a special religious or cultic site. These literary texts were outside the purview of the daily work of scribes, but then (like now) students often learned much more than they needed to. The pithoi inscriptions, however, reflect the education necessary for the day-to-day work of ancient Israelite scribes. This curriculum will provide the outline for this book and will illustrate how ancient Israelite scribes learned to write the Bible.

The example of Kuntillet ʿAjrud also has implications for the spread of writing in early Israelite society. It is hard to imagine that the site would have been occupied by more than a half-dozen people. And yet it had a scribe and students. There are multiple hands writing these inscriptions, some accomplished, some not. Perhaps, as Aḥituv and Eshel have suggested, there was an individual soldier who was also trained as a scribe and was training other soldiers. The role of literacy within the military is implied by the "Letter of the Literate Soldier" from Lachish. A scribe at Kuntillet ʿAjrud had the opportunity to train one or more apprentices. This training included a gamut of educational curricula: the alphabet, numbers, epistolary formulas, onomastic and lexical lists, and literary texts. In other words, already by the end of the ninth century BCE, even remote desert fortresses would have scribes who were trained in basic skills relating to trade and state bureaucracy.

Soldier-Scribes

The scribal role of soldiers might also be indicated by these inscriptions. It seems unlikely that someone who was purely a scribe and an administrator could have functioned effectively at such remote sites as Kuntillet ʿAjrud or Kadesh Barnea. These were small forts with contingents of soldiers. Furthermore, soldiers who served as scribes appear in the well-known Egyptian text Papyrus Anastasi I, which is the best exemplar of the school text "The Craft of the Scribe."[57] Anson Rainey notes that the Egyptian expression *sš mhr* in this "Satirical Letter" should be understood as "soldier-scribe"; he draws parallels with the use of the term *mhr* in administrative texts from Ugarit and suggests it is a Semitic equivalent to the well-known *maryannu*, "chariot-warrior."[58] James Allen states that this Semitic term in Papyrus Anastasi I denotes "an officer concerned with logistics and reconnaissance."[59] Demsky likewise suggests that "military logistics" was likely part of the advanced curriculum of scribes.[60] There is a biblical echo of the military scribe in the term *šōp̄ēr māhîr*, "skilled scribe" (see Ps 45:2; Ezr 7:6). Although Rainey dismissed the association with that biblical expression, with its Ugaritic and Egyptian antecedents, it is difficult to completely dismiss the strong etymological connection. Rather it seems likely that *šōp̄ēr māhîr* represents a later semantic development of the "soldier-scribe," perhaps in the postexilic period, when it lost its original connection with the military (e.g., note the use in Aramaic, *Aḥiqar* 1).

Although the biblical text does not explicitly develop the military association of scribes, we may infer it on the basis of ostraca found in a fortress like Arad (which span the tenth through the seventh century BCE) or the gate of Lachish (dated to the Babylonian destruction). It is quite explicit in one ostracon excavated at Lachish, the "Letter of the Literate Soldier."[61] This letter was apparently written by a junior military officer who had been told by a senior officer to hire a scribe. On the one hand, the letter suggests that the services of a professional scribe might be necessary for a soldier; on the other hand, it indicates that military officers often had some rudimentary scribal training. As Rollston has noted, "A fairly high percentage of the Old Hebrew epigraphic corpus hails from sites that were military in nature"; he proposes the title "scribe of the army" to reflect this aspect of ancient Israelite scribal profession.[62] Basic scribal training would have been useful for administrators and soldiers stationed at smaller forts or caravansaries.

A complicated relationship between scribes and soldiers is also expressed in Papyrus Anastasi I. At various times, we read different assessments of the scribe;[63] for example, it states unequivocally, "Look, you are the army's command-scribe" (6.8). However, later it backtracks, "You have said to me: You are not a scribe nor are you a soldier" (11.8). And then later the scribe retorts, "You will find my name on the list as a soldier of the great stable of Ramesses II, LPH, and you will learn of the command of the stable, with a bread-ration in writing in my name. Then I will be (seen to be) a soldier, then I will be (seen to be) a scribe" (11.8). This back and forth over the title of soldier-scribe and a theme of the text more generally has to do with the level of logistical competence required for a soldier-scribe. In this respect, the text shares a common theme with the Hebrew "Letter of the Literate Soldier," which also questions the competence of a soldier-scribe.

Scribal Apprentices at Kuntillet ʿAjrud?

Kuntillet ʿAjrud may actually have a reference to these scribal apprentices among its inscriptions. In the Hebrew edition of the Kuntillet ʿAjrud inscriptions, Ahituv, Eshel, and Meshel publish the reconstruction of Erhard Blum that combines fragments 4.1.4, 4.1.3, and 4.1.12 (and renumbers them as 4.2.2), which I would transcribe and translate as [*l*]*nʿry.* ⌜*ś*⌝*rʿr*, "[For] the Apprentices of the Commander of the Fortress."[64] The placement of these fragments, as pictured in Figure 2.5, is particularly important to its interpretation.[65]

The "Apprentices of the Commander of the Fortress" must be the title or header for the inscription.[66] The reconstructed text, fragments 4.1.4 + 4.1.3 + 4.1.12 (see Figure 2.6), belongs to the larger poetic inscription 4.1. Based on the location of their excavation and paleography, these fragments are part of the two-line inscription originally published as 4.1. This inscription clearly has a blank space above the first line and below the second line. This precludes a full third line that includes "Apprentices of the Commander of the Fortress." As such, it must be a title or header at the beginning of the first line, or just above the first line of Inscription 4.1. In some respects, this inscription bears similarities to the Deir ʿAlla Plaster Text, which also begins with a title header followed by a poetic literary text: [. . .] *spr*[. *blʿm. br . bʿ*]*r. ʾš . ḥzh . ʾlhn*, ". . . the Account of [Balaam, son of Be]or, a man who was the seer of the gods."[67] In the Deir ʿAlla text, the titular nature of this is also indicated by the use of red ink for the title. If [*l*]*nʿry.* ⌜*ś*⌝*rʿr* is the header in the Kuntillet ʿAjrud text, then it would be especially instructive since it suggests an addressee and thereby purpose of the text. Moreover it is difficult to imagine that "The Apprentices of the Commander of the Fortress" is actually part of the literary poem itself. Not at all. So it is likely the header. Actually, one might imagine it like the headings in the biblical Psalms. The headers are not part of the liturgical poems. In the present case, this is a text written for "the apprentices of the Commander of the Fortress."

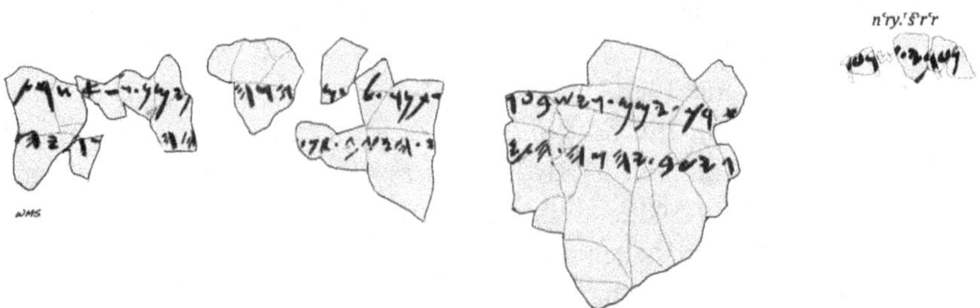

Figure 2.5 The placement of *NʿRY.ŠRʿR* as title for Inscription 4.1. Drawing by the author.

Figure 2.6 *NʿRY.ŚRʿR*, reconstructed from fragments 4.1.4 + 4.1.3 + 4.1.12. Reconstruction by Erhard Blum. Drawing by the author.

The heading begs the question: Who is this "Commander of the Fortress"? This is a figure that is repeatedly mentioned in the inscriptions at Kuntillet ʿAjrud, occurring three other times in the pottery inscriptions (Inscriptions 2.4, 2.5, 2.6).[68] In the English edition, *śrʿr* is translated by Ahituv, Eshel, and Meshel as "the governor of the city"—but this is an unfortunate English translation.[69] The term *śrʿr* must be understood as a title composed of two elements: *śr*, "commander, official, leader," and *ʿr*, "fortress." Thus the title *śrʿr* can be understood with reference to the site of Kuntillet ʿAjrud and its local official. In addition to the reconstructed expression from the plaster wall inscription, three examples of the title appear on storage jars, including one completely restored jar with its full inscription, *lśrʿr*, "belonging to the Commander of the Fortress" (see Figure 2.7). According to the official publication, "Inscriptions 2.4–2.6 are identical, and were incised by the same person on storage jars, after firing."[70] The complete jars provide a good context for understanding the title. These were provisions specifically for the commander in charge of this remote fortress. In many biblical contexts as well as in the epigraphic evidence, *śr* can be understood as a military commander. For example, the term *śr* is used twice in the Yavneh Yam ostracon in reference to the official in charge of the small fortress there.[71] In Lachish Letter 3, we find a more explicit military context with the expression, *śr hṣbʾ*, "commander of the army." Lachish Letter 6 mentions military communiqués, *spry hśr*, "letters of the commander." At the same time, there are many uses of the term *śr* in biblical literature that suggest a wider semantic range, including "prince" or "an official" or "the leader of a group."[72] The term *śr* certainly designates a "leader" or "official" in its more general sense, but its nuance must be interpreted according to the context—in this case the meaning of *ʿr* as well as its use as an official in charge of the fortress.

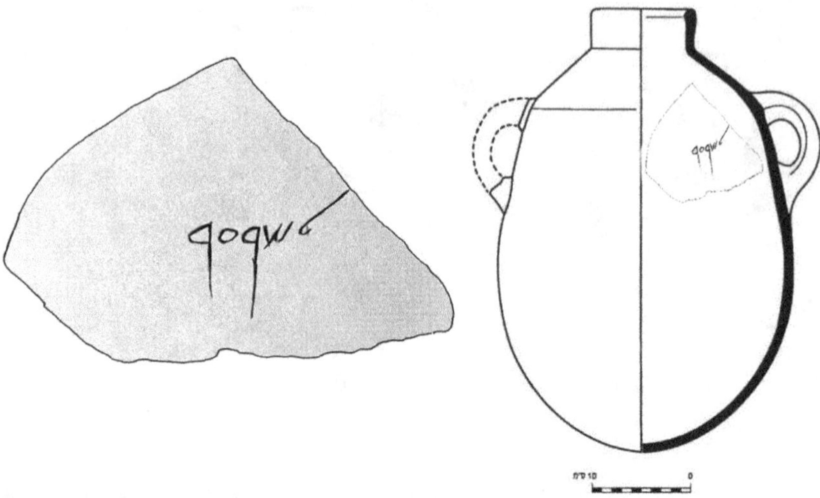

Figure 2.7 "Belonging to the Commander of (the) Fortress." Inscription on a storage jar from Kuntillet ʿAjrud. Drawing of the ostracon by the author.

The term *ʿr* obviously refers to the fortress at Kuntillet ʿAjrud. This is striking because the biblical word /ʿîr/ (always spelled with the *yod* [עִיר] as a vowel letter) usually refers to a "city." Kuntillet ʿAjrud is not a "city." A seal impression reading *lśrʿr* from Jerusalem dating to the late eighth century (see Figure 2.8) should not mislead us into translating *ʿr* in these inscriptions as "city" instead of "fortress."[73] The Jerusalem bulla was published in a Hebrew article, but it was also presented to the mayor of the city of Jerusalem and appears in press reports using the traditional translation "Belonging governor of the city." This excavated seal impression adds to the two unprovenanced examples published in *West Semitic Seals*, one reading *lśr hʿr* and the second reading simply *lśr*.[74] The semantic range of biblical *ʿîr* certainly included "fortress" or "walled settlement."[75] The meaning "fortress" is even attested etymologically in Old South Arabic, where *ʿr* means "mountain, fortress." An illustration of this meaning in Hebrew may also help explain its semantic development as "city." In 2Sam 5:7, a scribe adds an editorial comment using the term *ʿîr*: וַיִּלְכֹּד דָּוִד אֵת מְצֻדַת צִיּוֹן הִיא עִיר דָּוִד, "And David captured the fortress of Zion—that is, the *ʿîr* of David." The comment offers an explanatory gloss clarifying that the *fortress* (*m*^{e}*ṣūdāh*) of Zion is now known as the *ʿîr* of David. This explains why standard lexicons include "walled settlement" as one of the translations for *ʿîr*.[76] It also explains why a fortress like Kuntillet ʿAjrud could have been referred to as an *ʿr*. It is possible that the urbanization of the Levant in the late monarchy resulted in a semantic shift in the word,[77] which

Figure 2.8 "Commander of the Fortress Bulla" from Jerusalem. Drawing by the author.

would not be linguistically unusual. The Iron IIC period (beginning already in the late Iron IIB) witnessed a striking urbanization of Judean settlements (as well as much of the Neo-Assyrian Empire), so the semantic range of *ʿîr* may have shifted. In other words, the biblical term *ʿîr* came to refer more generically to a "city" instead of its narrower and older sense of a "fortress" or "walled settlement." Kuntillet ʿAjrud, of course, was no city. It was a simple small fortress in the remote reaches of the Sinai.

Another noteworthy aspect of the *śrʿr* inscriptions is the lack of a personal name. This is unusual for Hebrew seals and inscriptions, where figures are almost always named. It is particularly striking in the storage jar inscriptions from Kuntillet ʿAjrud. These jars do not belong to a person but a position. Likewise the seal impressions with this title (from outside of Kuntillet ʿAjrud) lack personal names. Very few known seals lack a personal name. Seals from the late Iron Age usually place primary emphasis on the personal name.[78] The most notable exception to this is the *lmlk* seal impressions, which simply read "Belonging to the King" in the first register and give the name of an administrative center (Ziph, Hebron, Socoh, and the mysterious *mmšt*) in a second register.[79] But these are administrative seals belonging to the bureaucracy, not necessarily to a particular king. We may surmise that the lack of a personal name also highlights the administrative nature of the title "Commander of the Fortress."

Now that we have established that the four examples of *śrʿr* at Kuntillet ʿAjrud can be understood as referring to "the Commander of the Fortress," we may turn to his *apprentices* (*nʿr*). The term *nʿr* occurs 244 times in the Hebrew Bible and can be translated by a variety of terms.[80] Most frequently, the term is understood to refer to a young boy or adolescent, but there are many examples where it must refer to a servant or an apprentice. One of the more prominent examples is its use for the young boy Samuel. After he was weaned, his mother called him a *naʿar* because he would become a "servant" or "apprentice" to Eli (see 1Sam 1:22–27).

One of the more significant and often cited biblical examples for our purposes is the incident in Judges where Gideon captures a *naʿar* after a local conflict and enlists him to write down the names of his foes: "When Gideon son of Joash returned from the battle by the ascent of Heres, he captured a *naʿar* from the men of Succoth and questioned him; and he [the *naʿar*] wrote down for him the officials and elders of Succoth, seventy-seven people" (Judg 8:13–14). Some scholars have used this example to argue for widespread literacy, even among young boys (as reflected in the *naʿar*); however, the term *naʿar* is at best ambiguous in this context.[81] But it does seem to refer to a young person, as we see later in the story: "But the *naʿar* did not draw his sword, for he was afraid, because he was still a *naʿar*" (8:20). In this context, *naʿar* seems to be someone in training with the military, not yet a seasoned soldier. The use of the expression *nʿry.śrʿr*, "apprentices of the Commander of the Fortress," may shed some further light on its use in Judges. If we accept that *naʿar* can be a young person receiving military training, an apprentice, then this might account for the relationship to the "Commander of the Fortress" as well as the general scribal exercises that are evident on Pithos A and B. One of the responsibilities of the "Commander of the Fortress" may have been to pass along a rudimentary scribal education to those under his command at the fortress.

A military nuance for *nʿr* is further supported by other Near Eastern parallels. For example, Egyptian texts use *naʿar* as a generic term for "soldiers; special detachment"; for example, in Papyrus Anastasi I, we read, "O distinguished scribe, *mahir* of ready hand, leader of the *nʿrn*, head of the troops."[82] The term *mahir* here in the context of *nʿrn* has a sense of an official in charge of logistics, in this case military logistics.[83] The *nʿrn* also play a role in Ramesside descriptions of the battle of Qadesh, where they seem to play a subordinate role.[84] The term *nʿr* also appears in Ugaritic; in his study of Ugaritic military personnel, Rainey argues that *nʿr* refers to "first class experienced fighting men."[85] This may overstate their prowess; in any case, it is only one aspect of *nʿr* in Ugaritic. The use of *nʿr* is complex at Ugarit, just as it is in the Hebrew Bible.[86] John MacDonald points out that the term in Ugaritic and Hebrew could refer to a variety of "distinctive classes or guilds."[87] It is, for example, included among lists of professions (e.g., RSOu 14 34; *KTU* 9:436:2'). There are military aspects of its use in Egyptian and Ugaritic texts of the New Kingdom period, but the precise meaning of *naʿar* is dependent on its context. In the present example, the *nʿry* must be interpreted by their relation to *śrʿr*, the Commander of the Fortress.

The *nʿry.śrʿr* as "apprentices of the Commander of the Fortress" can be further contextualized by a more extended reflection upon the Egyptian text "The Craft of the Scribe" (Papyrus Anatasi I) mentioned above.[88] There, a master scribe for the military and administration of the Levant chides and teases a young apprentice about all the knowledge that he must acquire. The master tells the apprentice, "Look, you are the army's command-scribe" (6.8). The master points out that he himself writes "without calling a scribe for dictation" (7.9). The very fact that he does not need a scribe indicates that scribal skills were only one part of his duties. In fact, it suggests that such skills were not always well acquired but that they were always highly valued in his position. He was a special type of scribe with military and administrative responsibilities. This reminds us that learning to write could be part of many different professions, in this case a "command-scribe." Military scribes undoubtedly received the same basic education of anyone learning to write, and then would have had special scribal training relating to their profession.

In the "Craft of the Scribe," much of the specialized scribal knowledge relates to geography; for example, the master asks, "Oh *mahir*, where is Raphia? What is its wall like? How many river-miles is it in going to Gaza? Answer quickly, give me a report, that I may call you *mahir*" (27.2). In summation, the master says, "You are a scribe of the great double gate, who reports the needs of the lands . . . you relate them and become with us an esteemed official of the treasury" (28.6). This is a scribe with administrative duties, but he is expected to have a vast amount of practical knowledge attained through both education and experience. Furthermore, the system of learning was expressly related to apprenticeship, as the master relates: "My father has taught me what he knew" (28.1). This serves as a good model for the role of the *nʿry.śrʿr*, "apprentices of the commander of the fortress" at Kuntillet ʿAjrud (for a more extensive discussion of *mahir*, see chapter 6 "Egyptian *mhr* and Biblical Hebrew *mahir*: Military Scribes").

Finally, it needs to be stated that the fact that we have soldiers doing scribal exercises does not mean that Kuntillet ʿAjrud was a "school." Some scholars have even suggested certain types of schools. Kuntillet ʿAjrud was not a "military school"; it was not a "school for priests"; it was not a "prophetic school." Kuntillet ʿAjrud was not a "school" at all. It was a military fortress along a trade route.[89] The training of scribes was not done in an institutional school-type system but rather in an apprentice-type system. This is especially clear from the example of

Late Bronze Age Emar but is also suggested by the use of the term "son(s) of" in the descriptions of scribes that point to guilds, families, and apprentices.

In sum, Kuntillet ʿAjrud was a special type of environment for scribal learning. The training there was undoubtedly specialized for the type of work done by the "Commander of the Fortress" as well as those assigned to serve there. Therefore, their education would focus on trade and requisite knowledge of the geography of the region. It might have also required general military training to protect the fortress and travelers along the route from brigands and marauders. For our purposes, we are fortunate that the elementary scribal education reflected in the pithoi inscriptions is generic and universal. These inscriptions are the foundations of learning to read and write and function with basic scribal literacy.

3
Alphabets and Acrostics

Modern literate cultures that use an alphabet tend to assume that the alphabet is a logical extension and expression of speech and learning to write. It is not. Actually, the alphabet is problematic. As a writing system, the alphabet is unusual because we do not speak in letters, but with words and syllables.[1] If writing systems are symbolic expressions of language—or, more precisely, spoken language—then the alphabet is a poor expression. Most writing systems that have been invented—e.g., hieroglyphics, cuneiform, Chinese, Mayan, Minoan, Indus Valley, etc.—are based on words, syllables, or a combination of words and syllables. These are natural expressions of speech. In contrast, while letters are an economical invention, they are not a natural transcription of spoken language. For this reason, the very invention of the alphabet is exceptional. While there are many writing systems in the world, all alphabetic writing systems are derived from a singular invention of alphabetic writing in the second millennium BCE. All other alphabets are borrowed and adapted from this one original invention.[2]

The modern European writing systems evolved from the early Canaanite (or "Phoenician")[3] alphabet, which the Greeks modified to include vowels. Peter Daniels has divided the "alphabet" into different systems: the early Canaanite *abgad* (also called an *abjad* or *abugida*) that denotes only consonants and the later Greek *alphabet* that encodes both consonants and vowels.[4] He also rejected a historical understanding that sees the *abugida* as a subtype of the full *alphabet*. However, the Greek alphabet directly borrowed and adapted the early Canaanite linear alphabet, so it is difficult to understand his rejection of the historical approach. Moreover, as Florian Coulmas points out, "all phonographic writing systems, however refined and concerned with phonetic detail, omit great numbers of phonetic distinctions."[5] In other words, the fact that the early Canaanite alphabet omitted vowels does not make it less of an alphabet or even that unique. All alphabetic writing systems omit details. None is a faithful transcription system. In any case, a variety of different alphabets—e.g., Arabic, Aramaic, Syriac, Dhivehi, Ethiopic, Coptic, Latin, Cyrillic, Runic, Armenian—can be traced back to the singular invention of an alphabet that can be traced back to the early second millennium BCE. The linear alphabet, however, was not widely used or significantly developed until the very end of the second millennium.

The most abundant record of alphabetic writing in the Late Bronze Age comes from Ugarit, where more than 1,500 tablets in alphabetic cuneiform have been excavated. By the fourteenth century BCE, Ugaritic scribes had adapted the alphabet into a thirty-letter cuneiform alphabet that used the *abgad* order in its school texts (this is the basic sequence adopted later in Phoenician, Hebrew, Greek, and later), and this cuneiform alphabet was widely used for writing local Ugaritic literature. A dozen examples of a thirty-letter alphabet in the *abgad* order (e.g., *ʾa b g d*) are known from Ugarit.

Two other variations of alphabetic order were known at ancient Ugarit.[6] For example, there is one exemplar of an abecedary in the *halaḥam* order (RS 88.2215).[7] This *halaḥam* order is also attested in an abecedary from Beth-Shemesh as well as a bilingual Egyptian–West Semitic ostracon from a Theban tomb (discussed later). The *halaḥam* order is different from the traditional *abgad*, which was widely known from Phoenician and Hebrew and was borrowed and adapted in Greek and Latin. The *halaḥam* order, however, is known from later South Semitic alphabets (e.g., Old South Arabic, Ethiopic). Now there is clear evidence that this *halaḥam* order was known at an early date, perhaps even before the *abgad*. In addition, alphabetic cuneiform texts provide evidence for a shorter alphabet following the same *abgad* order; this shorter alphabet would be developed into the linear alphabet known from early Canaanite inscriptions (e.g., Izbet Ṣarta). The shorter cuneiform alphabet is known from other locations such as Sarepta (i.e., early coastal Canaanite city-states) and attests to the emergence of the shorter Canaanite/"Phoenician" alphabet by the end of the thirteenth century BCE. The short, twenty-two-consonant early Canaanite alphabet spread throughout the eastern Mediterranean in the early Iron Age (1200–900 BCE). Particularly important for the spread of the alphabet is the Tel Fekheriyeh inscription. It uses archaic letter forms dating as early as the eleventh century BCE even though the inscription itself dates to the ninth century BCE.[8] The archaic letter forms point to an early date for the spread of the twenty-two-letter linear alphabet. This twenty-two-letter alphabet spread in spite of the problems that its limited graphemic inventory posed for the phonetics of other eastern Mediterranean dialects, like Hebrew, Moabite, and Aramaic. But the reduced twenty-two-letter graphemic inventory seems to have mapped better onto the phonemes of the coastal Canaanite dialects in cities such as Tyre, Sidon, and Sarepta (i.e., the "Phoenicians"), which was likely its origin.

Comparative and historical linguistic evidence for spoken Hebrew demonstrates that it had at least twenty-five consonantal phonemes, and yet its scribes adopted an alphabetic writing system with only twenty-two letters. This is not that surprising. As writing systems spread, they are often used by new languages to which they are not particularly well-suited. A striking example of this may be seen in the way that Akkadian adopted the Sumerian cuneiform writing system in spite of its shortcomings for writing a Semitic language. Hebrew and Aramaean scribes similarly adopted a writing system with some shortcomings. The consonants *shin* and *śin*, for example, would have to be written with a single grapheme, ש, until the Masoretes came along more than a millennium later and added a dot to distinguish them. The phonemes /ḥ/ and /ḫ/ were both written with ח, and the /ʿ/ and /ǵ/ were both written with the grapheme ע. For example, later Septuagint transcriptions of proper nouns like Gaza (Greek Γάζα; Hebrew עזה) testify to the preservation of the pronunciation of phonemes in Hebrew (e.g., /ǵ/) that could not be represented precisely in an alphabet with only twenty-two letters. Thus, it was a restricted twenty-two-letter alphabet that was taught and passed along by early Israelite scribes in the early Iron Age. It functioned, but it was not a precise transcription system.

When we recognize the singular and unique nature of the alphabet as well as its idiosyncrasies, the process of teaching and learning the alphabet becomes more profound. Linguists have shown, for example, that "alphabetic segment analysis"—that is, the ability to distinguish different letters—is not spontaneously acquired but rather requires special training.[9] This is because alphabetic segmentation is not a natural part of speech; speech is segmented syllabically or by words. Interestingly, some reading problems, such as dyslexia, are specifically related to alphabetic scripts and do not relate to syllabic or logographic writing systems.[10] That is to say, there is something cognitively unique and difficult about learning to read and write in an alphabetic script. In this respect, the famous quip by W. F. Albright, that "the 22 letter alphabet could be learned in a day or two by a bright student and in a week or two by the dullest,"[11] as an expression of the superiority of the alphabet is a bit misguided. Logographic and syllabic writing systems are much more straightforwardly related to speech than is alphabetic writing. The alphabet requires a level of abstract phonological segmentation that must be learned and taught. Given the unique and special nature of alphabetic writing, its origins and adoption by the early Israelites were part of a revolutionary change in ancient writing and literacy.

The Egyptian Origins of the Alphabet

The evidence for alphabetic writing was discovered in Egypt and dates back to the early second millennium BCE.[12] The earliest alphabetic writing system was discovered at a remote Egyptian mining settlement in the middle of the Sinai Desert known as Serābiṭ el-Khâdem.[13] These alphabetic inscriptions are usually dated to around 1700 BCE. A second example of early alphabetic writing was later discovered along a remote Egyptian trade route in the desert of Middle Egypt known as Wadi el-Ḥol. Scholars date the two alphabetic graffiti there to around 1800 BCE.[14] The most exciting new evidence for the early West Semitic alphabet was more recently published. A bilingual Egyptian hieroglyphic–West Semitic alphabetic abecedary was excavated in a Theban tomb and dates to the fifteenth century BCE.[15] Taken together, the locations of these discoveries in diverse places that were under Egyptian hegemony suggest an Egyptian connection for the invention and spread of the alphabet.

Scholars have long noted that the early alphabetic letters bear striking resemblances to Egyptian hieroglyphs.[16] For this reason, Alan Gardiner, who deciphered the first proto-Sinaitic inscription, argued that the alphabet was an Egyptian invention.[17] This identification has been challenged,[18] but it remains the best hypothesis. An alphabetic concept was already present in Egyptian "group writing," that is the monoconsonantal hieroglyphs used especially for writing foreign words. For example, when Gardiner analyzes the writing of the geographical name Djeba in the *Ancient Egyptian Onomastica*, he observes that "this seems to imply a consciousness of the alphabet as such which some have recently been rather unreasonably inclined to doubt."[19] But the use of monoconsonantal hieroglyphs to write foreign words was a functional, if limited, type of alphabetic writing. It certainly was a solid basis to adapt and invent a West Semitic alphabet. For example, an Egyptian school text, "The Craft of the Scribe" (Papyrus Anastasi I), is littered with West Semitic words written using "group writing." The Semitic words—that is, foreign words—have their own writing system within the Egyptian system that was a convenient basis for inventing a foreign writing system: the alphabet.[20] The alphabetic writing system thus was a clever adaptation of Egyptian concepts of writing, especially those used for writing foreign words.[21]

The dissemination of the alphabet also points to its Egyptian connection. The early alphabet appears in Egypt proper (Thebes, Wadi el-Ḥol) as well as the Sinai. From there, it moved up the coast of the eastern Mediterranean to the coastal Mediterranean port of Ugarit; not coincidentally, it spread during the heyday of Egyptian internationalism. Ugarit itself was an Egyptian vassal in the fourteenth century—that is, about the time the alphabetic idea was adapted in Ugarit. By the Late Bronze Age, this original iconic alphabet was simplified into the linear form that I would call "Early Canaanite."

The most important inscription for the invention of the alphabet may be the bilingual hieratic-alphabetic ostracon excavated from a tomb in Thebes and dated to the fifteenth century BCE (see Figure 3.1).[22] The ostracon has already been the subject of a few studies, all of which agree upon the identification of the *halaḥam* order of a West Semitic alphabet on the obverse.[23] Thomas Schneider

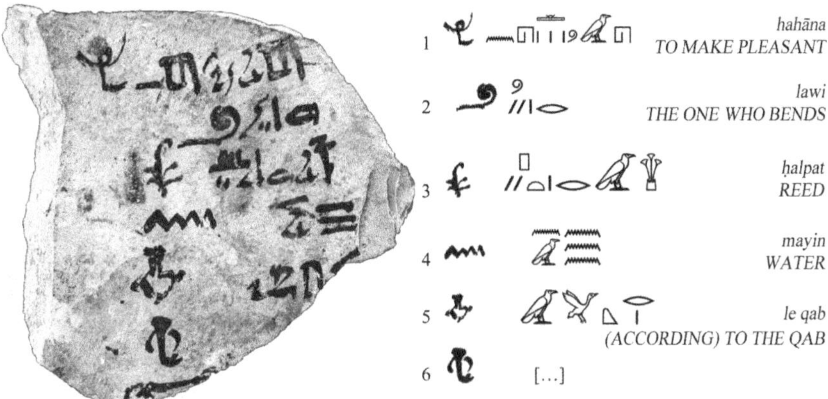

Figure 3.1 Ostracon TT99 obverse from Thebes. Reconstruction and drawing by Thomas Schneider. Photograph by Nigel Strudwick. Courtesy of Nigel Strudwick, Thomas Schneider, and ASOR.

has now offered a striking decipherment that understands the Egyptian column as using Egyptian words and group writing to create a mnemonic verse that playfully records the *halaḥam* abecedary (see Figure 3.1).[24] The use of group writing to create mnemonic verse is both unusual and important. It highlights the scribal and educational nature of this text, but it also associates this abecedary to the origins of the alphabetic idea in Egyptian monoconsonantal writing. The use of a mnemonic device to learn or teach the alphabet would hardly be surprising.[25] Indeed, such devices are used this very day to teach schoolchildren their ABCs. In the case of the Theban tomb bilingual ostracon (TT99), it seems clear that some sort of mnemonic device was playfully teaching the West Semitic linear alphabet.

The *halaḥam* order was one of the unexpected aspects of the bilingual TT99 ostracon. To be sure, the *halaḥam* order was already known before this discovery. It was most familiar from its use as the standard sequence in Classical Ethiopic as well as from the ancient South Semitic scripts.[26] The *halaḥam* order was also known from two alphabetic cuneiform inscriptions, one from Ugarit and a second from Beth-Shemesh (discussed earlier).[27] The *halaḥam* order now seems like a specifically Egyptian order.[28] Taken together with the TT99 ostracon, the evidence of the later South Semitic *halaḥam* alphabet as well as the Classical Ethiopic *halaḥam* order seems decisive. The South Semitic and Ethiopic alphabets have long pointed to a southern origin for the *halaḥam* order, but this order was often understood as secondary to the *abgad*. The new TT99 bilingual abecedary now firmly puts the *halaḥam* order in Egypt in the middle of the second millennium BCE, before the first known *abgad* alphabets appear in Ugarit and Canaan. Indeed we may now suggest that the creation and adoption of the *abgad* order in the Levant in the late second millennium had a typical linguistic anthropological explanation: it was created as a local Levantine order for the alphabet to distinguish it from its Egyptian counterpart. By creating a new arrangement for the alphabet, the *abgad* becomes a specifically Canaanite alphabet in distinction from the *halaḥam* alphabet.

The eventual spread of alphabet also owes something to ancient Egypt—or, more specifically, the New Kingdom. During the New Kingdom, an Egyptian colonial administration controlled the Levant, and this colonial administration set up a "vector of transmission" for writing systems—first, Canaano-Akkadian cuneiform, and then the alphabet. The Egyptians used the Akkadian cuneiform writing system in their international relations. The most extensive evidence for this use of the Akkadian cuneiform writing system comes from Tell el-Amarna. The Canaanite Amarna letters include more than three hundred letters sent from the various Canaanite city-states under Egyptian hegemony in the fourteenth century BCE. The corpus of texts from el-Amarna also includes non-Canaanite texts, such as letters from north Syrian polities like the Hittites and other city-states outside of Egyptian administrative oversight as well as cuneiform school texts.[29] However, the Canaanite Amarna letters were written in a peculiar dialect of Akkadian, which has been called "Canaano-Akkadian," as opposed to the other Akkadian texts from el-Amarna that reflect expected aspects of peripheral Akkadian of the Late Bronze Age. These Canaanite Amarna letters were written in a relatively standardized dialect and paleography—in spite of the fact that they came from widely dispersed and often competing city-states within the Egyptian hegemony.[30] This standardization of Canaano-Akkadian among the various city-states under Egyptian rule in the New Kingdom period sets an important backdrop for the spread of the linear alphabet in the beginning of the Iron Age. The early Canaanite alphabet demonstrated a similar standardization as it spread in the early Iron Age (i.e., 1200–900 BCE). Furthermore, the early Canaanite alphabet did not splinter into local manifestations with their own graphemic inventories and local paleographic tendencies. Rather, the early Canaanite alphabet maintained its short, twenty-two-letter graphemic inventory and a relatively standard script.[31] By this time, however, the twenty-two-letter alphabet was already well-entrenched, in spite of its shortcomings for expressing the phonetic inventory of early Hebrew. If we think of the early scribes as members of a transnational guild that learned and disseminated writing systems,[32] then the horizons of early alphabetic are much like Canaano-Akkadian.

At the same time, the early alphabet was not completely uniform. There were different orders to abecedaries, varying numbers of graphemes, and different representations in script. The standard Ugaritic alphabet known in more than a dozen exemplars had thirty graphemes in the *abgad* order. The so-called Ugaritic cuneiform alphabet was probably already created by the fourteenth century BCE, although most of the texts date to the late thirteenth or early twelfth century BCE.[33] This was the order that was adopted and adapted for the early Canaanite linear alphabet in the twelfth century BCE. This Canaanite alphabet—a close forebearer to the Hebrew alphabet—spread rapidly in the eastern Mediterranean after the demise of the Egyptian Empire in the twelfth century BCE. Examples of Canaanite alphabetic inscriptions dating to the early Iron Age (ca. 1200–980 BCE) have now been found at a variety of places, including Jerusalem, Lachish, Beth-Shemesh, Jaffa, Izbet Ṣarṭa, and Gath.[34]

Principles of the Abecedary

The first student exercise that a fledgling alphabetic scribe learned is an *abecedary*—a word derived from the order of the letters, or the ABCs. In contrast to cuneiform, where a student began by learning shapes of signs and groups of syllables—e.g., TU-TA-TI, NU-NA-NI, etc.—the Israelite scribe began by learning letters in an alphabetical order: *ʾaleph, beth, gimel, dalet,* etc. The earliest example of an abecedary in the Hebrew alphabet was excavated at the Israelite settlement of Izbet Ṣarṭa (probably biblical Eben-ezer) and dates to about 1100 BCE. The original publication reads the inscription as five lines:

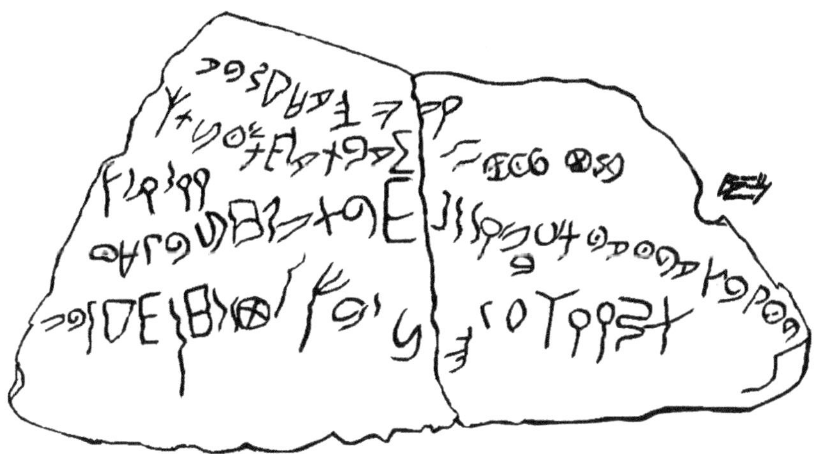

Figure 3.2 Early Iron Age abecedary from Izbet Ṣarta. Drawing courtesy of Brian Donnelly-Lewis.

1) ʾ b/l š d ḥ ʾ t ? ʾ ʿ
2) k t n ʿ q ḥ ʾ t l/b ʾ d ? ṭ ʿ b/l ṭ ṭ
3) ṣ ? q š q q
4) ʿ q p b/l n ḥ g ʾ t b/l h d z q b/l ʿ ? ʿ ʾ ʿ b/l ʾ ḥ b/l r ʿ b š
5) ʾ b g d h w ḥ z ṭ y k l m n s p ʿ ṣ q r š t

The first four lines remain undeciphered, and the fifth line is an abecedary in what appears to be rudimentary student handwriting.[35] Other examples of abecedaries have been discovered at Tel Zayit, Kuntillet ʿAjrud, Kadesh Barnea, Lachish, and Deir ʿAllā.[36] This scribal learning tradition predates the emergence of early Israelite scribes. There is evidence for abecedaries in the cuneiform alphabets from Ugarit, a *halaḥam* from Beth-Shemesh, and now in the bilingual Hieroglyphic-Semitic inscription from a Theban tomb (TT99).

Abecedaries were primarily a beginning student exercise. Most scholars understand them in this context, although it is sometimes suggested that they had some sort of mantic function. Stuart Weeks notably argued for this aspect in his discussion of "schools in Israel"; for example, he dismisses the plausibility that the Kuntillet ʿAjrud inscriptions could have been school exercises.[37] Now that the Kuntillet ʿAjrud corpus has been fully published, however, his position is no longer tenable. As shown in chapter 2, Kuntillet ʿAjrud had a variety of student scribal exercises. The Kuntillet ʿAjrud abecedaries are just one part of a larger corpus of student exercises. Perhaps abecedaries could have had a mantic function in some contexts, but this is not a convincing approach to abecedaries in general. Students needed first to learn their ABCs. As Aaron Demsky put it, "There can be no doubt that learning the linear alphabet, by writing the letters in a standard sequence and repeating their names, is the key to alphabetic literacy."[38] The abecedaries represent the beginning of scribal literacy, and most examples of abecedaries in the inscriptional corpus must be interpreted in this manner.

The abecedaries have clear educational parallels in cuneiform exercises like the TU-TA-TI tablets. While the alphabet was a much more circumscribed corpus to learn (as compared to cuneiform signs), it was no less critical. One of the more interesting examples for the present study is a fragmentary bilingual Ugaritic-Akkadian abecedary discovered at Ugarit (*RS* 19.159/*KTU* 5.14). It was inscribed on two sides and used the standard *abgad* order that we find in Ugaritic, but it was lined as a table using a typical Akkadian scribal convention and arranged in two columns, the Ugaritic cuneiform on the left and a parallel Akkadian column on the right. As shown in Table 3.1, the Akkadian column may give the first syllable of the name of the Ugaritic letter.

A much later similar example occurs in a Neo-Babylonian context with an Aramaic alphabetic abecedary written in cuneiform.[39] These inscriptions

Table 3.1 Bilingual Ugaritic-Akkadian Cuneiform Abecedary (*KTU* 5.14)

	Ugaritic Cuneiform	**Akkadian Cuneiform**
obv. 1	ʾa	a
2	b	be
3	g	ga
4	ḫ	ḫa
5	d	di
6	h	ú
7	w	wa
8	z	zi
9	ḥ	ku
10	ṭ	ṭí
11	. . .	
rev. 20	. . .	
21	[p]	⸢pu⸣
22	ṣ	ṣa
23	q	qu
24	r	ra
25	ṯ	ša
26	ǵ	ḫa
27	t	tu
28	[ʾi]	i
29	ʾu	u
30	s_2	sú

suggest a conceptual adaptation of the cuneiform elementary sign exercises to an alphabetic context. Another parallel reflecting conceptual adaptation is the trilingual lexical tablets (discussed in chapter 4), which add a West Semitic column to traditional cuneiform lexical lists (as in the lexical fragment from Ashkelon as well as examples from Emar and Ugarit).[40] These examples adapted the traditional cuneiform lexical list to include a West Semitic language.

A few things become clear in the Ugaritic-Akkadian abecedary. First of all, the sounds of the two languages did not map exactly. So, for example, in lines 4 and 26 we see that the Ugaritic *ḫ* and *ǵ* are both represented by the Akkadian syllabic sign *ḫa*. Simply put, Akkadian did not have an equivalent for the Ugaritic guttural phoneme ǵ. A similar issue appears in line 9, where the Ugaritic guttural ḥ is rendered in Akkadian as *ku*. These linguistic issues underscore the difficulty that different writing systems have for accurately encoding the phonemes of a language for which they were not designed. This also occurred when Hebrew scribes adopted the early twenty-two-letter proto-Canaanite alphabet. A similar problem arose when Egyptian loanwords were written with Hebrew script. For example, Egyptian writing did not have separate graphemes for /l/ and /r/. Thus in the TT99 ostracon discussed above, the *halaḥam* might be transcribed as *h-r-ḥ-m*! While the Ugaritic-Akkadian bilingual abecedary (*KTU* 5.14) is an attempt to transcribe Ugaritic letter names with the Akkadian writing system, TT99 seems to have had much grander aims using mnemonic devices (as both Haring and Schneider have recognized). In Thomas Schneider's clever attempt at a translation, he suggests that the Egyptian column is not merely an attempt at writing the name of a West Semitic letter; rather there is a poetic element to this bilingual inscription. *KTU* 5.14 has much less grand purposes. It merely seems to provide a transcription of the Ugaritic letter with the first syllable of its name written in Akkadian syllabic. Still, we should remind ourselves of Florian Coulmas's observation that "all phonographic writing systems . . . omit great numbers of phonetic distinctions."[41] That is to say, there is nothing unusual here.

At Kuntillet ʿAjrud, the abecedaries are part of a variety of student exercises. Other examples, like the abecedary carved in stone from Tel Zayit or even abecedaries carved into pottery shards like the Izbet Sarta ostracon, are a bit less certain. In the Zayit abecedary, for example, we have the carving of the alphabet on a large stone, which does not immediately evoke the idea of a school exercise. However, Menachem Haran's suggestion that such examples could be practice by apprentice craftsmen seems plausible.[42] Craftsmen did have to practice their craft, but it is difficult to be certain about an inscription like Zayit without further context. Likewise, the Izbet Sarta ostracon has little other context to suggest its purpose. It has four undeciphered lines followed by the abecedary in the fifth line. There are no other associated texts or scribal exercises excavated at the site. The rudimentary writing seems like it should be understood as a student exercise, but we cannot be certain. This lack of larger contextual evidence with many other inscriptions is what makes the Kuntillet ʿAjrud inscriptions so valuable.

Learning the Alphabet

The alphabet was the beginning of the educational curriculum, and it was a staple of some of the most basic poetry in the Bible: acrostics. The acrostic poetry encodes what some scholars have called "alphabetic thinking."[43] I would frame it differently. It reflects the centrality and even mystery of writing as well as the beginning of education. The notion of "alphabetic thinking" makes acrostic poetry far too abstract. It seems that this terminology was likely influenced by Marshall McLuhan, who in his seminal work, *The Gutenberg Galaxy*, introduced the notion of an "alphabetic effect."[44] However, the "alphabetic thinking" of the acrostics is quite different. There is really no abstract thinking in acrostics; rather it is fundamentally mechanical and scribal. This order is visual, not aural. Acrostic poetry is visually arranged by the first letter of the word, and it does not work if it is not visually arranged.

The alphabetic acrostic poem depends on the order of the alphabet, but this is a bit sketchier than is generally known. As discussed above, in the earliest period, there were two different orders for the alphabet: the *abgad* and the *halaḥam*. The *abgad* order became the standard Canaanite version, which is known from examples at the early Israelite sites of Izbet Ṣarṭa (eleventh century) and Tel Zayit (tenth century BCE).[45] The *abgad* order was apparently a coastal Levantine localization of the Egyptian alphabetic tradition (the *halaḥam* order). In this manner, the alphabetic tradition was adopted and given its own curricular tradition in the Levant. Through the curricular development of the *abgad* order, the alphabet lost its Egyptian connection and became localized at sites like Ugarit, the eastern Mediterranean coastal cities, and early Israel.

The Israelite *abgad* alphabetic tradition has its own story and idiosyncrasies.[46] One of the more well-known idiosyncrasies of the Hebrew tradition is the varying order of *ʿayin* and *peh*, which finds differing expressions in various inscriptions and in acrostic poetry. The Tel Zayit abecedary, however, adds three previously unknown interchanges to the well-known *peh-ʿayin*, with an inverted order for *heh-waw* (*waw-heh*), *zayin-ḥet* (*ḥet-zayin*), and *kaf-lamed* (*lamed-kaf*). Thus, Tel Zayit reads *a b g d <u>w h</u> <u>ḥ z</u> ṭ y <u>l k</u> m n s <u>p ʿ</u> q r š t*. A conclusive explanation for these variations has not emerged. Seth Sanders plausibly suggests the influence of the *halaḥam* order,[47] and there were likely also regional (i.e., Israelite vs. Judean) or perhaps diachronic influences to the variation. In the end, the *abgad* order becomes the standard school tradition for the Levantine polities and writing systems (e.g., Hebrew, Phoenician, Aramaic).

Biblical Acrostic Poetry

There are a limited number of acrostic poems in the Hebrew Bible. These include Nahum 1:2–8*, Psalms 9–10, 25, 34, 37, 111, 112, 119, 145; Proverbs 31:10–31; Lamentations 1–4. To these may be added the acrostic poem in Sirach

51:13–20 and Psalm 155. There are also a number of partial acrostic poems, which are significant for understanding their use and transmission. Some acrostics are partial (e.g., Nah 1:2–8, Pss 9–10), and others are missing lines (e.g. Pss 25, 34, 145). Some of the variant acrostics likely arose from problems in transmission. So, for example, Psalm 145 is missing the *nun* line, but the *nun* verse appears in the Septuagint, in the DSS 11QPs[a] manuscript, in some later Hebrew manuscripts as well as the Syriac. In other words, the missing *nun* is evidently a scribal transmission error rather than a deliberate omission. However, the omission is quite remarkable given that it ruins the acrostic in the psalm. It is almost as if the acrostic was not evident to the scribe, or it was no longer important. Other examples, like the incomplete acrostic in Nahum 1:2–8 or the jumbled acrostic in Psalms 9–10 do not show evidence of textual corruption based on the Septuagint and later text critical evidence. This may be explained in two ways. First, they could have been corrupted at a much earlier period in the scribal transmission (e.g., before the Babylonian exile or earlier). As a result, the complete original acrostics would not show up in the various textual versions. More likely, the jumbled or incomplete acrostics might have been intentional adaptations of earlier texts. It is important to recognize that such omissions and errors undermine the very acrostic structure, and they likely reflect a lack of scribal interest during transmission in the acrostic as a structuring principle. In other words, the acrostic structure no longer served the scribe's purpose or, for that matter, a reader's interest.

Let's be candid, the acrostic structure is—in a word—pedantic. Already the early twentieth-century German scholar P. A. Munch suggested, "von diesen Gelehrten geradezu für den Unterricht gedichtet" and that they had "starken pädagogischen Zweck" (that is, they were composed by scholars primarily for teaching and with strong pedagogical purpose).[48] At the same time, Munch recognized the possibility that the alphabetic acrostic form became detached from its original *Sitz im Leben* in education and became a form unto itself.[49] Early commentators on the acrostic poems in the Bible were quite critical of the "poetic" aesthetic of the alphabet. Herman Gunkel, for example, regarded acrostic poetry as typical of the latest phase of biblical psalmody and wrote, "The outward decoration of the alphabetic form appears particularly pleasing to this period, a decorative form which can only be appreciated by the eyes while offering nothing for the ear or the spirit."[50] Gunkel here reflects the rather biased and jaded view that Israelite literature underwent a devolutionary process, and acrostic psalms reflect the degeneration of Hebrew literature. In this, he misses the pedagogical point of acrostic structure. For example, *The Cat in the Hat* is not a degenerate poem but rather brilliant literature of elementary education. The same may be said for Hebrew acrostic poetry. As an advanced form of elementary education, they are striking. However, they are not a high literary accomplishment. With the canonical context, an elementary educational *Sitz im Leben* disappears. As a result, the acrostic order of the original poem could even be corrupted.

The pedagogical value of acrostic poetry was certainly not as an aid to memory. Although this explanation of acrostic poetry is frequently cited,[51] it is unclear how these poems really would have had mnemonic value. Aids to memory are based on aural devices, whereas acrostic poetry is purely graphic. Acrostic organization presumes the knowledge of the alphabet; it does not enable its memorization. The acrostic may be a student exercise that enshrines and elevates the elementary knowledge of the alphabet, but the acrostic poems that we have do not aid the memorization of the alphabet. Theoretically, scribes may have designed acrostic poems to aid memorization of the alphabetical order. We do not have an example of such design in the Hebrew Bible, but the Egyptian–West Semitic abecedary (TT99) may suggest the existence of such design in acrostic poems.

Acrostic poetry may have been sung and, in this manner, memorized. The singing of curricular exercises is attested in Egypt. For example, in a classic Old Kingdom school text we read, "Do not kill a man whose efficiency you know, with whom you once sang the writings."[52] Al Wolters sees Prov 31:10–31 as a song, arguing that it formally follows the characteristics of a "hymn" or "song of praise" known from Gunkel's form-critical categories.[53] To be sure, in this manner acrostic poetry could be memorized, but the graphic aspects of the song would certainly be obscured. In other words, the alphabetical arrangement does not help itself in the memorization of an acrostic hymn even when it is sung.

The graphemic (rather than phonetic) nature of the acrostic poems is underscored by the fact that there are only twenty-two letters—not twenty-three, twenty-four, or twenty-five letters—in acrostic poems. Most textbooks will speak about the twenty-two-letter Hebrew alphabet, but this minimally reflects the conflation of the letters *šin* (שׁ) and *śin* (שׂ) because the superlinear dot that distinguishes them is a much later Masoretic invention. While ancient inscriptions have only one letter (ש), it is also clear there were two sounds even in antiquity, /š/ and /ś/. Acrostic poems in the Bible conflate the two phonemes under the single grapheme, and this also underscores the fact that the acrostic poems were primarily a visual scribal technique. They do not work as an aural device. In his guide to Hebrew poetry, Wilfred Watson sums up the two characteristics of the acrostic poems as reflecting "the highly *artificial* nature of such a scheme and its *non-oral* character, these poems being intended to appeal to the eye rather than the ear."[54] It is artificial only in as much as it reflects writing practice, not spoken rhetorical devices.

An additional example of graphic alphabetic exercises is the *ATBaSh*. This was an advanced manipulation of the letter order as a code. Demsky explains,

"Since learning the alphabet was a function of a formal curriculum, we can assume that there were different exercises for memorizing the order of the letters already at an early period. An exercise that is already documented in the sixth century BCE is the *ATBaSh* exercise which is based on the equal division of the twenty-two letters of the alphabet, correlating the first and last letter, the second and 21st letter and so on."[55] Thus we find three separate examples in the Book of Jeremiah (25:25, 26; 51:1, 41): *ššk* (i.e., ששך) for *bbl* (i.e., בבל "Babylon"), *lbkmy* for *kśdym* (Chaldeans), and *zmry* for *ʿylm* (Elam). In sum, the *ATBaSh* indicates that a variety of alphabetic exercises was likely part of ancient alphabetic learning. Understood together with the abecedaries in the inscriptional corpus, it provides a glimpse into the first scribal exercises. The biblical acrostic poetry underscores the importance of this alphabetically ordered scribal education to early scribal education.

The acrostic poem as a form is essentially restricted to alphabetic cultures, and biblical poems are the first examples of the form. Alphabetic poems, for example, are not found in the extant Ugaritic literature. Still, the play with the symbols of language certainly did not begin with biblical acrostic poetry. One of the most famous cuneiform comparisons is to *The Babylonian Theodicy* (or *Ludlul bēl nēmeqi*, "The Poem of the Righteous Sufferer"), which was a classic of Babylonian literature. It was used as a school text and found in many copies in cuneiform libraries, and it is a "constrained poem" that is sometimes also described as an acrostic.[56] The Akkadian cuneiform poem comprises twenty-seven stanzas of eleven lines each, and all eleven lines of each stanza begin with the same (multivalent) cuneiform sign. Stanza 13 can illustrate:[57]

> I will abandon my home [. . .]
> I will desire no property [. . .]
> I will ignore (my) god's regulations, and trample on his rites.
> I will slaughter a calf, and [. . .] the food,
> I will go on the road and learn my way around distant places.
> I will open a well and will let loose a fl[ood?],
> I will roam like a bandit about the vast outdoors.
> I will stave off hunger by forcing entry into one house after another,
> I will prowl the streets, casting about, ravenous.
> I will [. . .] like a beggar inwards [. . .],
> [. . .] good fortune is distant.

Each line begins with the KAŠ logogram, which is rendered syllabically in the poem as *bi*, *bé*, and *pí*. That is, the similarity is purely graphic, not aural. I have rendered the beginning of each line with the translation "I will" to highlight the graphic uniformity, but the cuneiform does not mirror the aural uniformity of my translation. The cuneiform writing system allows for the graphic nature of the poem because it relies on one repeated logogram that has many possible syllabic realizations in each line of the stanza. The aesthetic is primarily graphic.

More important for our purpose is that *The Babylonian Theodicy* adapts an elementary school text for its graphic aesthetic. In this graphic aesthetic, it seems to borrow from Akkadian lexical lists. The earliest lexical texts were thematically arranged, giving lists of objects. These early school texts—essentially, vocabulary lists—usually began with the same determinative logogram. Thus a lexical list concerning trees and wood had every line beginning with the determinative GIŠ, which means "wood, tree."[58] This gives the list a visual uniformity. These thematic lexical lists are the most elementary level of scribal learning. *The Babylonian Theodicy* develops this elementary school form into a more developed advanced literary text used for advanced scribal education.[59] A similar development may be envisioned for biblical acrostic poetry, which takes the elementary exercise of writing the alphabet and creates a graphic poem.

A characteristic of school exercises should be an appropriately limited vocabulary. This actually fits quite well with acrostic poetry. As Wilfred Watson observed in his book *Classical Hebrew Poetry*, "The repertoire of words and phrases found in these acrostics is very limited."[60] The acrostic poems also tend to use keywords over and over again. The most extended acrostic is Psalm 119, with its 176 verses, but it is a psalm themed on the "law" with a repetition of eight terms for the *torah*,[61] with overall a relatively limited vocabulary. The psalm divides into eight lines for each of the twenty-two letters of the alphabet, beginning the with statement "Happy are those whose way is blameless, who walk in the *torah* of the LORD." Soll points out that one of the eight *torah* words—תורה "*torah*," עדות "stipulations," פקודים "precepts," חקים "statutes," מצות "commandments," אמרה "word," דרך "word," and משפטים "judgments"—is used in each line through the structure of the 176 verses.[62]

Nahum's Partial Acrostic (Nah 1:2–8): The Didactic Theophany

As was mentioned, there are several are partial or defective acrostics (Nah 1:2–8; Pss 9–10, 25, 34, 145). The case of the partial acrostic in Nah 1:2–8 is particularly useful to illustrate. Since the nineteenth century, scholars have generally understood that Nah 1:2–8 derives from an acrostic poem.[63] However, it is certainly deficient as an acrostic. Not only does the acrostic cover only half the alphabet, from *aleph* to *kaf*, but it is also missing letters in the formal acrostic structure so that the poem needs to be emended to create even the half acrostic.[64] These deficiencies derive from its transmission as a purely didactic poem to its literary adaptation and integration as a theophany within the prophetic book.

Let us begin by pointing out all deficiencies in this "half" acrostic hymn. To begin with, the rigid line-for-line form is not followed in the poem; extra poetic lines appear in verses 2b–3a. Clearly, the poem has undergone significant reworking and adaptation. In addition, some emendation must be done to recognize the acrostic order of the hymn. In verse 4b, various scholars have proposed emendations to create the requisite *dalet* for the poem; in verse 6a, the word *lipnê*, "before," needs to be eliminated to get the requisite *zayin*; and, in verse 7b, the letter *waw* must be erased so that we get the requisite *yod* for the poem. Finally, the Masoretic versification further underscores the fact that the acrostic underpinnings of Nah 1:2–8 have been lost, especially when compared with pristine examples of acrostic psalms like Psalm 119. In spite of this, there is strong consensus that recognizes the underlying acrostic structure to the poem. The emended poem in Nah 1:2–8 with its acrostic structure might look like this:[65]

2 אל קנוא ונקם יהוה נקם יהוה
נקם יהוה לצריו ונוטר הוא לאיביו 3 יהוה ארך אפים וגדול כח ונקה לא
ינקה יהוה
בסופה ובשערה דרכו וענן אבק רגליו
4 גוער בים ויבשהו וכל הנהרות החריב
<דלל?>/{אמלל} בשן וכרמל ופרח לבנון אמלל
5 הרים רעשו ממנו והגבעות התמגגו
ותשא הארץ מפניו ותבל וכל ישבי בה
6 {לפני} זעמו מי יעמוד ומי יקום בחרון אפו
חמתו נתכה כאש והצרים נתצו ממנו
7 טוב יהוה למעוז ביום צרה
{ו}ידע חסי בו 8 ובשטף עבר
כלה יעשה מקומה ואיביו ירדף חשך

[*Aleph*] 2 The LORD is a jealous and avenging God,
the LORD is avenging and fierce in wrath;
the LORD takes vengeance on his adversaries
and rages against his enemies.
3 The LORD is slow to anger but great in power,
and the LORD will by no means clear the guilty.
[*Beth*] His way is in whirlwind and storm, and the clouds are the dust of his feet.
[*Gimel*] 4 He rebukes the sea and makes it dry, and he dries up all the rivers;
[*Dalet*] Bashan and Carmel <shrink,> and the bloom of Lebanon fades.
[*He*] 5 The mountains quake before him, and the hills melt;
[*Waw*] And the earth heaves before him, the world and all who live in it.

[*Zayin*] **6** Who can stand {before} his indignation? Who can endure the heat of his anger?
[*Ḥet*] His wrath is poured out like fire, and by him the rocks are broken in pieces.
[*Ṭet*] 7 The LORD is good, a stronghold in a day of trouble;
[*Yod*] {and}he protects those who take refuge in him, **8** even in a rushing flood.
[*Kaf*] He makes an end of his adversaries, and his enemies he will pursue into darkness.

The acrostic underlying Nah 1:2–8 cobbled together several themes that emerged in the scribal curriculum and exercises. The acrostic was then rewritten, losing much of its original didactic form, as a hymn reflecting a divine theophany. At the same time, the "half" acrostic makes a certain sense from a pedagogical point of view. The alphabet was learned as two halves: *aleph* through *kaf* and *lamed* through *tav*.[66] In this respect, one might expect acrostic poetry to be written in two parts. Although we have preserved only the first part of a two-part acrostic, the very nature of the division underscores one aspect of the pedagogy of the alphabet itself.

The themes of the acrostic are known from biblical literature as well as extra-biblical literature. The acrostic begins in verse 2 with the well-known divine attribute formula "The LORD is a jealous God," which features prominently in the Decalogue (cp. Exod 20:5; 34:14; Deut 5:9; 6:15). Verse 3a uses three well-known expressions that describe divine attributes: *ʾp ʾpym*, which is often translated as "slow to anger," *gdwl kḥ*, "great in power," and *nqh lʾ ynqh*, "He will by no means clear the guilty."[67] These expressions can be found in assorted lists of Yahweh's divine attributes (e.g., Exod 20:7, 34:6–7; Num 14:18; Joel 2:13; Pss 85:15, 103:8, 145:8; Neh 9:17). Verse 4a is an allusion to the Red Sea story, particularly as it was known in the historical psalms (cp. Ps 106:9), and verse 4b uses the poetic pairing of Bashan and Carmel, and the second stitch adds Lebanon; the three are often associated in biblical poetry (cp. Isa 2:13, 29:17, 33:9; Jer 22:20, 50:10; Mic 7:14). Verse 5 has the central theme of the hymn: the earthquake metaphors of a divine theophany known elsewhere (cp. Ps 18:8; Amos 9:5; 1Kgs 19:11). It is worth noting here that this theophany theme and language also appears in the plaster texts from Kuntillet ʿAjrud (KA 4.2, lines 2–4). Not surprisingly, divine wrath then accompanies the theophany in verse 6. The hymn ends with the familiar liturgical exclamation, "The LORD is good" (cp. Pss 34:9, 100:5, 145:9; Lam 3:25; Jer 33:11), and then enumerates those who find this divine favor.

In sum, there is something very familiar and nothing unexpected in this little hymn. It utilizes well-known themes in a way that suggests an original didactic purpose, but it repurposes them. The acrostic background of Nah 1:2–8 was obscured as it was reworked, and the repurposed hymn now introduces the prophetic book as a whole. In this respect, as some have argued, it is not an acrostic poem. Or, more precisely, it is *no longer* an acrostic poem. But it illustrates something important about the educational curriculum: that it can be repurposed. Nahum 1:2–8 could begin as a student exercise (as I would suggest it was originally), then be adapted and repurposed. Alternatively, it can conceivably go in the other direction: literature or liturgy can be incorporated into a school curriculum (as I shall argue in chapter 7). This latter process is easy enough to understand; for example, the Declaration of Independence or the Magna Carta can become part of a school curriculum. Both processes are important. On the one hand, the elementary scribal curriculum could be reworked and adapted for new literary or liturgical purposes. On the other hand, literary or liturgical texts could be incorporated into the scribal curriculum. Just because a text was or became a school text does not mean it could be only a school text.

Psalm 34 as a Scribal Exercise

Perhaps the best exemplar of an acrostic poem in the Bible is Psalm 34. Several scholars have suggested that it reflects "alphabetic thinking" because its use of the alphabet goes well beyond merely beginning each line consecutively with letters of the alphabet.[68] The so-called alphabetic thinking, however, is a purely scribal exercise. But it is an important scribal exercise. Below, I offer a somewhat liberal translation of Psalm 34 in order to highlight some of the alphabetic organization of the poetry:

Ps 34:1 לדוד בשׁנותו את־טעמו לפני אבימלך ויגרשׁהו וילך:
2 אברכה את־יהוה בכל־עת תמיד תהלתו בפי:
3 ביהוה תתהלל נפשׁי ישׁמעו ענוים וישׂמחו:
4 גדלו ליהוה אתי ונרוממה שׁמו יחדו:
5 דרשׁתי את־יהוה ועני ומכל־מגורותי הצילני:
6 הביטו אליו ונהרו ופניהם אל־יחפרו:
7 זה עני קרא ויהוה שׁמע ומכל־צרותיו הושׁיעו:
8 חנה מלאך־יהוה סביב ליראיו ויחלצם:
9 טעמו וראו כי־טוב יהוה אשׁרי הגבר יחסה־בו:
01 יראו את־יהוה קדשׁיו כי־אין מחסור ליראיו:
11 כפירים רשׁו ורעבו ודרשׁי יהוה לא־יחסרו כל־טוב:
21 לכו־בנים שׁמעו־לי יראת יהוה אלמדכם:
31 מי־האישׁ החפץ חיים אהב ימים לראות טוב:
41 נצר לשׁונך מרע ושׂפתיך מדבר מרמה:
51 סור מרע ועשׂה־טוב בקשׁ שׁלום ורדפהו:
61 עיני יהוה אל־צדיקים ואזניו אל־שׁועתם:
71 פני יהוה בעשׂי רע להכרית מארץ זכרם:

81 צעקו ויהוה שמע ומכל־צרותם הצילם:
91 קרוב יהוה לנשברי־לב ואת־דכאי־רוח יושיע:
02 רבות רעות צדיק ומכלם יצילנו יהוה:
12 שמר כל־עצמותיו אחת מהנה לא נשברה:
22 תמותת רשע רעה ושנאי צדיק יאשמו:
32 פודה יהוה נפש עבדיו ולא יאשמו כל־החסים בו:

0 (Superscription: *Of David. When he feigned madness before Abimelech, so that he drove him out, and he went.*)

1 A At all times, I will bless the LORD; Be in my mouth, his praise shall Continually.

2 B By the LORD, my soul boasts; let the humble hear and be glad.

3 G Come, magnify the LORD with me, and let us exalt his name together.

4 D Delivering me from all my fears, when I sought the LORD and he answered me.

5 H Ever look to him, and be radiant; so your faces shall never be ashamed.

6 Z For This poor soul cried, and was heard by the LORD, and was saved from every trouble.

7 Ḥ Great is the messenger of the LORD who encamps around those who fear him, and delivers them.

8 Ṭ Taste and see that the LORD is good; happy are those who take refuge in him.

9 I Indeed, fear the LORD, you his holy ones, for those who fear him have no want.

10 K Kitten-like lions suffer want and hunger, but those who seek the LORD lack no good thing.

11 L Let us come, O children, listen to me; I will teach you the ABCs of the fear of the LORD.

12 M May you desire life, and covet many days to enjoy good?

13 N No, keep your tongue from evil, and your lips from speaking deceit.

14 S See, depart from evil, and do good; seek peace, and pursue it.

15 ʿ Oh, the eyes of the LORD are on the righteous, and his ears are open to their cry.

16 P Please, the face of the LORD is against evildoers, to cut off the remembrance of them from the earth.

17 Ṣ Since the righteous cry for help, the LORD hears, and rescues them from all their troubles.

18 Q Quite near is the LORD to the brokenhearted, and saves the crushed in spirit.

19 R Righteous ones have many afflictions, but the LORD rescues them from them all.
20 Š **She** guards all their bones; not one of them will be broken.
21 T Treachery brings death to the wicked, and those who hate the righteous will be condemned.
22 P **At the end**, the LORD redeems the life of his servants; none of those who take refuge in him will be condemned.

The major English translations do not reflect the acrostics of the poem, although many make a note of the alphabetical order in one way or another. However, the alphabetic aspects of the psalm go beyond the simple ABC order of the verses.[69] For example, the consonants of the first line spell out the Hebrew word *ʾaleph*—the name of the first letter—using the first (א), middle (ל), and last (פ) consonants (represented in bold). The word itself underscores something of the pedagogy of the alphabet, with its letters representing the two parts as well as its completion. Michael Coogan even suggests that the Hebrew root *ʾlp* is denominalized as a verb meaning essentially "to learn the *ʾaleph*."[70] The word *ʾaleph* is, of course, the basis for the English word *alphabet*, which comprises the first two letters of the Hebrew (and Greek) alphabet. The middle letter of the Hebrew alphabet is *lamed*, which as a verb means "to study, learn"; the psalm incorporates its verbal root, √*lmd*, "to learn," in the verse for the letter *lamed*. Finally, the psalm ends by appending a verse beginning with the letter *peh*, which is the last letter of the word *ʾaleph*. The last letter of the alphabet, *tav*, also seems to play on the alphabet by beginning with a word using the last letter of the alphabet and ending with a word that uses the first letter of the alphabet.

Moreover, the syntax of the Hebrew is sometimes awkward or unusual because of the rigid formula of the acrostic structure. Thus, for example, in the final line (v. 23 [22, English]), the Divine name, Yahweh/LORD, is normally the first word of any verbal sentence, but not in this case.[71] However, the final sentence begins with the verb (which uses the *peh*) rather than the more normal syntax that would begin with "Yahweh." In verse 3 (2, English), there is the unusual syntax that begins a sentence with a prepositional phrase. I highlight some of these aspects of the psalm in my Hebrew transcription, which uses larger letters to make these devices more apparent. In its translation, I created a hybrid form of the English and Hebrew alphabets as a heuristic way of signaling the unique role of the Hebrew alphabet in framing the psalm.

The structure of this psalm must be understood with the alphabetic structure as central to its purpose. It encapsulates the logic of the psalm. Commentators have often struggled to find a thematic thread in the psalm. Mitchell Dahood, for example, writes, "Being acrostic in form, the psalm offers a sequence of sentiments whose logical connections are not always immediately evident. The reader and the exegete must accordingly take into account the formal element and its logical consequences."[72] Indeed the form frustrates the coherence of the psalm, but this presupposes that the psalm has some thematic thread. It has sometimes been called a "wisdom psalm," which is a way of making an excuse for its lack of coherence. But it has coherence when we understand that the alphabet is its theme. As we shall see in the next chapter, the alphabet would also be used as an organizing principle for vocabulary lists.

4

From Lists to Literature

Elementary education continued with lists. Lists (and various types of administrative documents) compose as much as 80 percent of the ancient epigraphic record. And, not surprisingly, a variety of lists found their way into the Hebrew Bible.[1] Most prominently, genealogies throughout the biblical corpus catalogue peoples and names. There are also lists of military and temple personnel. But scribal lists go far beyond personal names. There are, for example, lists of commodities, such as wine, oil, garments, and foodstuffs. There are tribute lists and land grant lists. There are lists for journeys—like the Israelites' wilderness wanderings (e.g., Numbers 33)—as well as military campaigns. Even the Ten Commandments are a type of list. Lists also appear pervasively in other ancient Near Eastern polities and writing systems, ranging from the cuneiform of Mesopotamia and Ugarit to the hieroglyphs of Egypt. They provide an enormous trove of comparative data. They were essential to the work of a scribe. They were the heart of scribal education. And the fingerprints of this part of scribal education can be recovered throughout the Bible.

What do all these lists mean? Earlier scholars constructed a rather grandiose purpose for these lists, complete with a good German neologism: *Listenwissenschaft*.[2] The term was popularized in a seminal study by the Assyriologist Wolfram von Soden and later used for biblical literature by scholars such as Albrecht Alt and Martin Noth.[3] These earlier scholars conceived lexical lists as a kind of ancient science for categorizing reality (*Ordungswille*). To be sure, there is some truth to the philosophical ruminations about the nature of lists and what their creation implies for human society. Thematic lists especially require an abstraction of reality. Jack Goody, for example, in his seminal book, *The Domestication of the Savage Mind*, suggests that lists create "boundaries" that attempt to understand the world by classifying it.[4]

At the same time, lists can just be mundane scribal exercises. They are elementary education, and they do not pretend to teach fledgling scribes about the nature of reality. They were practical tools. Indeed the first lists in the cuneiform scribal curriculum were arranged simply by the forms of the signs. They had no grand meaning. They simply taught the scribe how to form signs and categorize them according to their shapes. After teaching the shapes and sounds of the graphemes, cuneiform lists started teaching the student vocabulary. That was their primary purpose. They were not some grand *Ordungswille*, but rather just a way to learn how to write words. Thematic lists had a mundane purpose in elementary education, even if their design highlights aspects of abstract thinking. Their design reflects the advanced education of master scribes. Thematic lists do classify the universe, even if at their most basic level they are just spelling lists. They trained scribes for basic administrative and economic activities. This purpose is especially clear in peripheral Akkadian texts where scribes added extra columns to the lexical lists to give glosses for Akkadian and Sumerian words in Hittite, Ugaritic, West Semitic, and even Egyptian. In this respect, lists were designed and organized as reflections of early science, but they also served as merely mundane tools for teaching spelling and vocabulary.

In his book on biblical lists, Benjamin Scolnic emphasizes that even though lists are central to Hebrew literature, there is not a single Hebrew word for "list."[5] However, I do not think this is a complete representation of the situation. There are several words and expressions relating to lists in the Hebrew Bible. As noted earlier, the Hebrew word for "scribe," *sōp̄ēr*, comes from the root *spr*, which means "to count, write." The verbal form often refers to things related to accounting, that is, "to enumerate, count out," for example, when Joseph measures and records amounts of grain as the viceroy of Egypt (Gen 41:49). It is used explicitly to refer to making a written record (e.g., Jer 36:23; Ezek 9:2; Ps 45:2, 87:6), and the root is nominalized as *sēp̄er*, "a written document." The word *sēp̄er* "scroll, written document," was used in construct with a variety of terms to distinguish different types of written lists. And, the word *sēp̄er* often pairs with another word to indicate a type of document; for example, *sēp̄er dib̄rê hayyāmîm* is a "list of daily events" or "annals" (cf. 1Kgs 14:19, 29; 15:7, 23). The Book of Esther mentions a similar concept, noting that the Persian king kept a *sēp̄er hazzik̄rōnôt dib̄rê hayyamîm*, "list of the records of daily events" (Esth 6:1). The root *yḥś* relates to being enrolled in a genealogical list, and the expression *sēp̄er hayyaḥaś* is the "document of registration" or a genealogical list (Neh 7:5). There are also a variety of types of name lists, including *sēp̄er tôlĕdôt*, "a list of descendants" (Gen 5:1); *sēp̄er zikkrôn*, "book of remembrance" (Mal 3:16); and the famed *sēp̄er ḥayyim*, "book of life" (Ps 69:29). Thus a variety of words complement the term *sēp̄er*, "written document," to create technical terms for different types of lists in Hebrew.

We can assume that word lists were part of the basics of Hebrew scribal education just as they were in Mesopotamia and Egypt.[6] Indeed spelling lists continue to be an essential part of elementary education even in the modern world. Unfortunately, we have precious little by way of examples of spelling lists from ancient Israel. However, Kuntillet ʿAjrud does give us fragments of a couple lists.

And, fortunately, there is an enormous amount of comparative evidence from the cuneiform tradition to help inform our study.

Ancient Near Eastern School Tradition of Vocabulary Lists

Both Mesopotamia and Egypt had lively school traditions of vocabulary—or lexical—lists.[7] In Mesopotamia, these lexical lists were quite extensive and formalized. Many scholars, however, question—as James Crenshaw does—how much this influenced ancient Israelite education: "To what degree Israel's intelligentsia participated in this lively culture is debatable."[8] Yet there is direct evidence of contact with these Near Eastern lexical traditions throughout the eastern Mediterranean world. "The late second millennium," as Niek Veldhuis points out, "saw an unprecedented spread of cuneiform writing and Babylonian written culture over the entire Near East."[9] Traditional Mesopotamian lexical lists from that time have been found throughout the eastern Mediterranean world, including Ugarit, Nuzi, Egypt, and Hazor. While the overall number of cuneiform texts discovered in Israel is rather modest, a number of them are lexical lists.[10] These include two lexical tablets from Aphek as well as one each from Ashkelon, Hazor, and Megiddo. This evidence illustrates the spread of cuneiform school tradition—and particularly the lexical tradition—throughout the West. Even though the actual cuneiform lexical tablets from Israel are all quite fragmentary, the evidence can be reconstructed by the larger cuneiform tradition. Word lists are admittedly not one of the more exciting aspects of cuneiform scribal tradition. Lists are not sensational, but they were ubiquitous and their influence far-reaching.

The cuneiform list curriculum followed a straightforward developmental order.[11] Veldhuis offers the following progression that was outlined in chapter 2: (1) sign exercises (e.g., Syllable B, TU-TA-TI); (2) thematic lists (lists of names, nouns, and phrases); and (3) advanced lists (acrographic lists organized by first sign, advanced sign lists with all possible meanings). Thematic word lists began with names—for example, personal names or geographical names. This was followed by lists organized thematically by semantics—for example, trees and wood, lists of animals, professions, metals, etc. The earliest thematic word lists date back to the fourth millennium BCE and document aspects of the emergent ancient administrative systems.[12]

Beginning in the Old Babylonian period, thematic lists always start with lists of "trees and wooden objects" (marked with the Sumerian determinative GIŠ). The lexical lists were essentially unchanging. This conservative nature of the lexical school tradition is illustrated in the compilation by Benno Landsberger in the *Materialien zum sumerischen Lexikon* series.[13] The Ura (also referred to as Ur_5-ra or *ḫubullu*) cuneiform lexical series was standardized into six sections in the following order: (1) trees and wood objects, (2) crafts, (3) animals, (4) natural entities, (5) geographical names, and (6) food.[14] These thematic lists continued into the Neo-Assyrian and Neo-Babylonian periods, albeit with innovations so that the "trees and objects" series was no longer necessarily first or the most prominent.[15] In the later standardized version of the *ḫubullu*, "trees and wood objects" became Ura tablets 3 and 4. Excellent examples of the traditional Old Babylonian series in the West during the second millennium BCE are preserved at both Emar and Ugarit, although the Emar examples have been more fully published.[16]

The standard Old Babylonian lists were monolingual, using only Sumerian. During the second millennium, an Akkadian column translating the Sumerian was added to these lists. Students committed the Akkadian translations of the Sumerian vocabulary lists to memory. As the use of the cuneiform writing system spread to the periphery in the Late Bronze Age, further columns with other languages, including West Semitic, Ugaritic, and Hittite, could be added. There are many references in cuneiform texts to the importance of memorization, particularly of lexical texts. For example, David Carr cites the following Akkadian text to illustrate the importance of memorization in education: "If you have learned the scribal art, you have recited all of it, the different lines, chosen from the scribal art, (the names of) the animals living in the steppe to (the names of) artisans you have written (but) after that you hate (writing)." The scribe can then say that he can recite "the whole vocabulary of the scribal art."[17] Carr thus highlights the importance of memorization in general, although this example refers specifically to the memorization of lexical lists. In the above citation, the thematic lists of animals and professions (i.e., artisans) are recalled. While memorization was important in general, lexical lists were a particular foundation to elementary cuneiform education.

More complicated lists developed the lexical tradition in the late second and first millennium BCE in Mesopotamia. For example, later scribes began to write commentaries (known as Murgud, or HAR-gud) on lexical lists.[18] These lexical commentaries appear in many Neo-Assyrian libraries, including the famous library of Assurbanipal. In other places, new columns were added to the original lexical lists. The practicalities of the curricula setting resulted in more flexibility in lexical lists as well as a multidimensionality reflecting the complex linguistic situation of the second millennium, especially in the periphery.[19] At Ugarit, for example, there are polyglot lexical lists with four languages: Sumerian, Akkadian, Hurrian, and Ugaritic.[20] The spread of cuneiform writing into other cultures resulted in the adaption of lexical lists into advanced multilingual dictionaries. Lists were excerpted, enhanced, and elaborated.

The excavations at Tell el-Amarna (a site dating to the Late Bronze Age) unearthed a particularly interesting adaptation of traditional cuneiform school texts.[21] The pragmatic adaption of word lists is illustrated by a bilingual dictionary (EA 368) that begins with an Egyptian word in the first column written in syllabic cuneiform, followed by its Akkadian translation in a parallel column (Figure 4.1):[22]

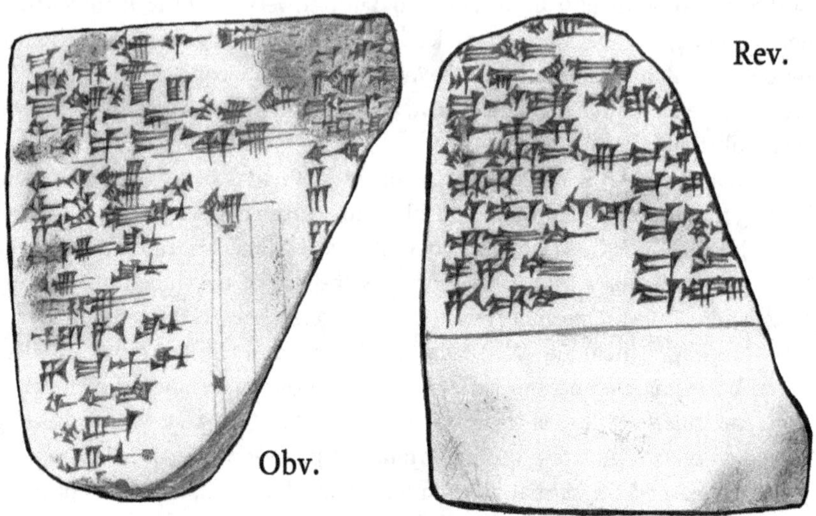

Figure 4.1 Lexical list of Egyptian words using cuneiform script. EA Tablet 368. Drawing by the author based on collation by Jeremy Black.

EA 368

	Egyptian	**Akkadian**	**Translation**
1.	*ma{}aḫ pi*	LUGAL xx[ru] bi nu	"king . . ."
2.	*nam*-DU-*ú*	*mal-la-mu*	"the words . . ."
3.	*ma aḫ tu lu*	*a-ḫi-a-tu*$_4$	"foreign"
4.	*pi-da-aš ni mu ú uḫ*	*da* GIŠ *qa x x (x) di*	"case"
5.	*x mu ḫat-ma-*⸢*DU*⸣*-ú*	*šaq-la-*[*a*]	"they are paid"
6.	*ši-na-aḫ*	*ši-qí-*[*il* KÙ.BABBAR]	"weight/shek[el of silver]"
7.	*ši-na-aḫ-wu*$_4$	*2*	"two [e.g., dual]"
8.	*ḫa-am-tu*$_4$ *šu-nu-uḫ*	*3*	"3"

9.	*⌜pi-du⌝-ú šu-nu*	*4*	"4"
10.	*ṭí-ú šu-nu*	⌜5⌝	"5"
11.	*⌜ša⌝-ú*	[6]	"6"
12.	*šap-ḫa šu-nu*	[7]	"7"
13.	*ḫa-ma-an šu-nu*	[8]	"8"
14.	*pi-ši-iṭ*	[9]	"9"
15.	*mu-ṭu*	[10]	"10"
16.	*⌜tí⌝-ib-nu*	[]	

Reverse

1'-4'. *broken*

5.	*⌜pi⌝-pa-ru*	[GIŠ]⌜É⌝[]	"house"
6.	*pu-us-bi-ú*	GIŠ.I[G]	"door"
7.	*DU-ḫu-lu*	GIŠ.SI[.GAR]	"bolt"
8.	*na-ab-na-su*	GIŠ.N[A]	"door post/socket"
9.	*DU-as-bu*	GIŠ.G[U.ZA]	"chair"
10.	*pa-ḫa-tu*$_4$	GIŠ.NA[]	"bed"
11.	*ḫa-DU-pu*	GIŠ.BANŠUR	"(offering) table"

The tablet is broken but still clearly a lexical list with two columns. The obverse has a series of words related to trade and economic administration, presumably categorized under the relationship to the "king" (in line 1). A scribe divided the obverse of the tablet with physical line that divide lines 1–5 from lines 6–11. Lines 1–5 may be some sort of title for the lexical list, and the list itself begins in line 6 with numbers. The reverse preserves a local adaption of the standard cuneiform lexical list that begins with the determinative GIŠ, that is, words relating to "wood." This is the first of the thematic lists (Ura 3). It categorizes the "wood" under the general rubric of the "house." (A blank space is left where the GIŠ sign would be in line 5, indicating that this entry is the general topic for the following entries.) While this list is not an exact copy of the formal Mesopotamian lexical lists, it clearly depends on that tradition.

Local adaptation is important for understanding how Mesopotamian school traditions could be altered for different types of educational settings. In this case, an Egyptian-Akkadian bilingual scribal school based their exercise on a Mesopotamian forerunner. Presumably, the scribe knew Akkadian and was learning how to write Egyptian words with the Akkadian writing system.[23] If the text were meant for a scribe whose first language was Egyptian, then it would make the most sense to use hieratic for the Egyptian words. But the writing of Egyptian words is in syllabic cuneiform, which would be useful for learning how to transcribe Egyptian words into Akkadian but irrelevant for learning how to write in the hieroglyphic script. This is not an equivalency of writing systems but rather an adaptation of a traditional cuneiform school text for teaching the writing of Egyptian words using cuneiform syllabic script. Apparently the scribe was learning to write Egyptian words for diplomatic purposes but was not being taught to write using hieroglyphs. This also underscores that Egyptian scribes used hieroglyphic writing only for local Egyptian purposes. Their script and writing system was not taught to foreigners. Akkadian (and its cuneiform writing system), on the other hand, acted as a lingua franca that could serve as a diplomatic tool in the Egyptian Empire.

The Egyptian Onomastic Tradition

Lists (or "onomastica," as Egyptologists refer to them) were also critical in the hieroglyphic scribal curriculum in Egypt.[24] Like scribes in Mesopotamia, Egyptians compiled classified lexical lists of plants, animals, geographical terms, professions and titles, etc. In other words, the use of lists in school curricula was not unique to cuneiform culture within the ancient world. The copying of lists formed part of general school practice in the ancient Near East.

Furthermore, the Egyptian onomastic tradition did not develop as a continuation of cuneiform tradition. The educational purpose of Egyptian lists is described in the introduction to the *Onomasticon of Amenope* (dating to the Late New Kingdom):

> Here begins the teaching, in order to expand the mind, to teach the ignorant, to know everything that is: What Ptah created, what Thoth brought in being, the sky and its objects, the earth and what is in it, what the mountains spew forth, what Nūn covers, all things on which Rēʿ shines, everything that grows on the back of the earth, conceived by Amenope, scribe of the holy books in the House of Life.[25]

Lexical lists were a beginning and foundation of education in ancient Egypt. Indeed, in an influential essay Gerhard von Rad argued that Yahweh's speech in Job 38 was dependent upon Egyptian *onomastica*, particularly the *Onomasticon of Amenope*, which was thought to represent a kind of scientific encyclopedia.[26] However, the comparison is not particularly convincing. There is no concrete evidence of direct knowledge of Egyptian onomastic lists among Canaanite scribes. This is in direct contrast to the situation with cuneiform lexical texts, which have been found throughout the Levant. No Egyptian school texts are known outside of Egypt. Moreover, relatively few hieroglyphic or hieratic texts have been found in Israel. While there are clear indications of Egyptian influence in scribal *technology* (e.g., ink, papyrus, technical loanwords), the Egyptian writing system itself was used only by the Egyptians. As the *Onomasticon of Amenope* states, Egyptian lexical lists were given to a "scribe of the holy books." In other words, there is little evidence to suggest that outsiders would have been taught using Egyptian onomastica or other scribal curricula. Michael Fox suggests that a primary purpose of these Egyptian lists was to teach a scribe how to write; therefore, he argues, "it is doubtful that they would have been known in Israel, where the alphabet created quite different pedagogical needs."[27] It was not simply the practical issue of teaching different writing systems. No, it is also imbedded in Egyptian linguistic ideology. In this respect, it is hard not be struck by the contrast with the Akkadian language and the cuneiform writing system. Cuneiform spread from Sumerian to Akkadian as a borrowed writing system, and then cuneiform spread throughout the Near Eastern world. Hieroglyphs, in contrast, were always a local Egyptian writing system that was closely tied to Egyptian religion and cultural identity.

Lists in Hebrew Inscriptions from Israel

Like Mesopotamian and Egyptian scribal traditions, lists were certainly part of the elementary scribal curriculum in ancient Israel. As stated previously, the scribal exercises from Kuntillet ʿAjrud provide two examples of such lists: a catalogue of personal names and a list of geographical names. Ostraca from the nearby site of Kadesh Barnea contain school exercises with lists of hieratic numerals. Outside of these examples, the Hebrew corpus of inscriptions does not provide much evidence. On the other hand, the majority of inscriptions are administrative and economic texts composed of lists of names and commodities.[28] For example, the excavations at Arad yielded more than one hundred inscriptions; although many of Arad inscriptions are quite fragmentary, at least twenty-seven of them are lists of some kind.[29] Other sites, such as Ḥorvat ʿUzza, Tel Masos, and Tel ʿIra, offer examples of the use of lists of personal names for military purposes, economic receipts, or ration lists.[30] Thus the epigraphic record demonstrates the importance of teaching scribes how to record lists of people, places, and things.

The lists at Kuntillet ʿAjrud were already discussed in chapter 2, but it is worth summarizing some of the argument here. At least one, and probably two, fragmentary lists are part of a text with a number of abecedaries and a practice letter. For the reader's convenience, I provide again the inscription along with the KA numbers reflecting the way they were originally published. According to my interpretation (introduced in chapter 2), line 5 is a fragmentary list of geographical names, and line 2 was probably also a list but too fragmentary to be certain:

KA 3.11, 3.7, 3.12, 3.13, 3.8, 3.14

1a)	*ʾ b g [d] h̊ [w z] ḥ [*	abecedary
1b)	*]q r š t*	abecedary
2)	*]ʾm̊n̊ẙ[ ] |*	]ʾ*M/BNY* (?) [
3)	*]ṭ y k l m n s p |*	abecedary
4)	*]p ʿ ṣ q r š t |*	abecedary
5)	*]h. šmrn šʿrm. |*	]*H*, Samaria, *šʿrm* (Shaʿaraim; gates; barley)
6)	*]k l m n s p ʿ ṣ q r š | t*	abecedary

My assessment of line 5 was based on two considerations. First, it is situated in the context of abecedaries; second, lists are among the most typical scribal exercises. As discussed in chapter 2, the two words in line 5—*]h. šmrn šʿrm.* |—have been read in several ways. While it seems preferable to understand them as a geographical list in alphabetical order, "Samaria, Shaʿaraim," alternative readings (e.g., "gates" or "barley") are also possible. Indeed in this decontextualized list, a master scribe could have used this obscure place name from a geographical list to actually teach polysemic aspects of the writing system. More than this, given the educational context of Pithos B, this may have been precisely the purpose for including this lexeme.

Another example of a lexical list at Kuntillet ʿAjrud appears on Pithos B on the opposite side of KA 3.8. It is a list of personal names. Scribes had to transcribe names accurately, and cuneiform scribes practiced writing personal names and titles as part of their training. For the reader's convenience, I provide the list of names again here:

KA 3.10

1)	*šknyw*	Shekanyaw
2)	*ʾmṣ*	Amotz
3)	*šmryw*	Shemaryaw
4)	*ʾlyw*	Eliyaw
5)	*ʿzyw*	Uzziyaw
6)	*mṣry*	an Egyptian

The interpretation of this list of names as a scribal exercise is supported by its physical context on a large pithos as well as the fact that the list is accompanied by other scribal exercises on the jar. To be sure, this evidence is frustratingly fragmentary, but it opens up a new avenue for thinking about other inscriptions.

Gezer Calendar as a List

The interpretation of the Gezer Calendar has been a scholarly crux. It seems to be a list of months according to agricultural activities.[31] The transcription and translation of the text have found general consensus, even though its interpretation has garnered considerable debate. W. F. Albright first described the Gezer Calendar as a school exercise.[32] Many scholars have followed Albright's assessment, but there remains considerable debate.[33] The tablet pictured in Figure 4.2 may be transcribed and translated as follows:

Figure 4.2 The Gezer Calendar. Drawing by the author.

ירחו 1. two? months of ingathering (olives) / months
אספ·ירחו ז 2. of sowing (cereals) / months of late sowing
רע·ירחו לקש 3. a month of hoeing weeds (for hay)
ירח עצד פשת 4. a month of harvesting barley
ירח קצר שערמ 5. a month of harvesting and measuring
ירח קצר וכל 6. months of grape harvesting
ירחו זמר 7. a month of ingathering summer fruit
ירח קצ 8. Abi[yaw?]
אבי Edge

The crude form of the letters already makes a good case that the inscription should be understood as a school text. The scribe writes with the poor hand and execution indicative of a beginner. A more telling observation relates to the soft limestone material on which the text is written; there are traces of erased letters on both sides of the tablet that suggest it was reused, perhaps by as student; that is, the tablet is a palimpsest. Most drawings of the Gezer Calendar do not capture this aspect of the inscription, with the notable exception of the drawing by Johannes Renz (see Figure 4.2).[34] For these reasons, it seems likely that the Gezer inscription functioned as a school exercise. But what kind of school exercise?

The inscription presents several problems that have elicited an enormous secondary literature and a wide variety of solutions.[35] First, it is unlikely that it was a simple calendar.[36] The relation between the agricultural cycle and the months of the year is, at best, loose. For example, Oded Borowski offers a general alignment of the Gezer Calendar with the cycle of the agricultural year in his book *Agriculture in Iron Age Israel*, and it generally can be forced to work. At the same time, he observes that the agricultural cycles are much more complicated than this simple "manual," as he calls it.[37] In fact, it is not a manual or even a calendar. No farmer would find any use in it. It is a lexical list with different "months" as they relate to agricultural activities. The description as a "calendar" depends largely on understanding the *waw* four times appended to *yrḥ* as a dual, thus translating "two months" and totaling twelve months. But this would be twelve lunar months—not particularly useful as a perennial calendar. The *waw* has also been a crux for the interpretation because *waw* is not the usual Hebrew plural morpheme (we expect *-mem*), thus it is usually explained as a proleptic suffix where the plural or dual would be unmarked.[38] An alternative explanation has been to see the *waw* as the remnant of a case ending for plural nouns, which is known in the Zenjirli inscriptions (e.g., *KAI* 214:2, 215:17). Thus the portrayal of the inscription as a calendar is hardly tight or entirely straightforward.

The scholarly problems with interpreting the Gezer Calendar can be solved by comparing it with aspects of the cuneiform lexical tradition. Helpful parallels can be found in the cuneiform lexical tradition in both form and language. The first thing to note is the formal style of the text, with each syntactic unit beginning by repeating the word *yrḥ*, "moon; month." In fact, apart from the second line, every physical line begins with the same word, which is a feature common to lexical texts. The first section (from Ura 3) of a Neo-Assyrian lexical text from Nippur will illustrate (see Figure 4.3):[39]

This particular example comes from the canonical cuneiform school text with the series on "trees and wood items," but there are many other examples from a variety of periods with a variety of initial signs. The first sign in each line is the determinative GIŠ used to mark "trees and wood items." This repetition of the initial GIŠ sign gives the text a kind of visual aesthetic.

Figure 4.3 An Ura 1 lexical text concerning "Wood Objects" with each line beginning with the determinative GIŠ. Image courtesy of the UCLA Collection.

The Gezer Calendar also has the visual aesthetic of a lexical list. It begins with *yrḥ* on lines 1, 3, 4, 5, 6, and 7; the exception in line 2 is actually a result of a student error, corrected in the following lines. In line 1 the student had available space and mistakenly wrote *yrḥ* in a continuation of the line. This practice, however, was not continued in later lines—even where there was space to continue. There was ample space in lines 2, 3, and 6 for a scribe to continue and write *yrḥ*, but the scribe did not. On the other hand, in line 4 there was not enough room to complete the final word on the line (שערמ); rather than simply continue on the next line, the scribe completes the line by writing the final letter *mem* just below the line after the *resh*. This allows the next line to begin with *yrḥ*. The visual aesthetic of lists goes beyond ancient texts. For example, the arrangement of Ecclesiastes 3:2–8, the famous passage "A Time for Everything" is laid out in some Hebrew manuscripts (e.g., Leningrad Codex, Figure 4.4) to emphasize the repetition of the Hebrew word for "time."

Another interesting aspect of the Gezer Calendar is the repeated use of the lexeme *yrḥ*, which is usually translated as "moon" in Hebrew (vocalized as *yārēaḥ*). This is itself a bit unexpected. As scholars have pointed out, *ḥdš* is the expected Hebrew lexeme for "month" and is also known in Ugaritic and other West Semitic dialects. To be sure, the lexeme *yrḥ* is also used for "month" in biblical texts (vocalized as *yeraḥ*). However, the term *yrḥ* is the common term in West Semitic for "month," and its Akkadian cognate, *arḫu*, is in fact used in the Ura lexical tablets. The term is found both in the Akkadian and Ugaritic texts discovered at Ras Shamra. The traditional cuneiform lexical text Ura, Tablet 1, contains a section relating to linguistic construction relating to the various months.[40] This lexical text relating to months was known throughout the Near East, and versions have been published from both Emar and Ugarit.

The Gezer inscription should be understood as a local alphabetic adaption of the Mesopotamian lexical tradition. It picks up themes well known in the canon of cuneiform lexical texts, but it is not a simple translation into Canaanite. It is an adaptation. For example, in the Mesopotamian lexical list, Ura 1, there are phrases related to reaping and harvesting (lines 148–56):[41]

še-kin-kud	*e-ṣe-du*	"reaping (of the barley)"
še-kin-kud-šè	*a-na e-ṣe-di*	"until the reaping (of the barley)"
u_4-še-kin-kud	UD-*me e-ṣe-di*	"the time of the reaping (of the barley)"
egir-še-kin-kud	*ar-kàt e-ṣe-di*	"the time after reaping (the barley)"
EBUR	*e-bu-ru*	"harvest"

EBUR-šè	*a-na e-bu-ri*	"until harvest"
u_4-EBUR-šè	*a-na* UD-*me e-bu-ri*	"until the harvest season"
egir-EBUR-šè	*a-na ar-kàt e-bu-ri*	"until the season after the harvest"
mu-un-du-EBUR-šè	*a-na šu-ru-ub-ti e-bu-ri*	"until the bringing in of the harvest"

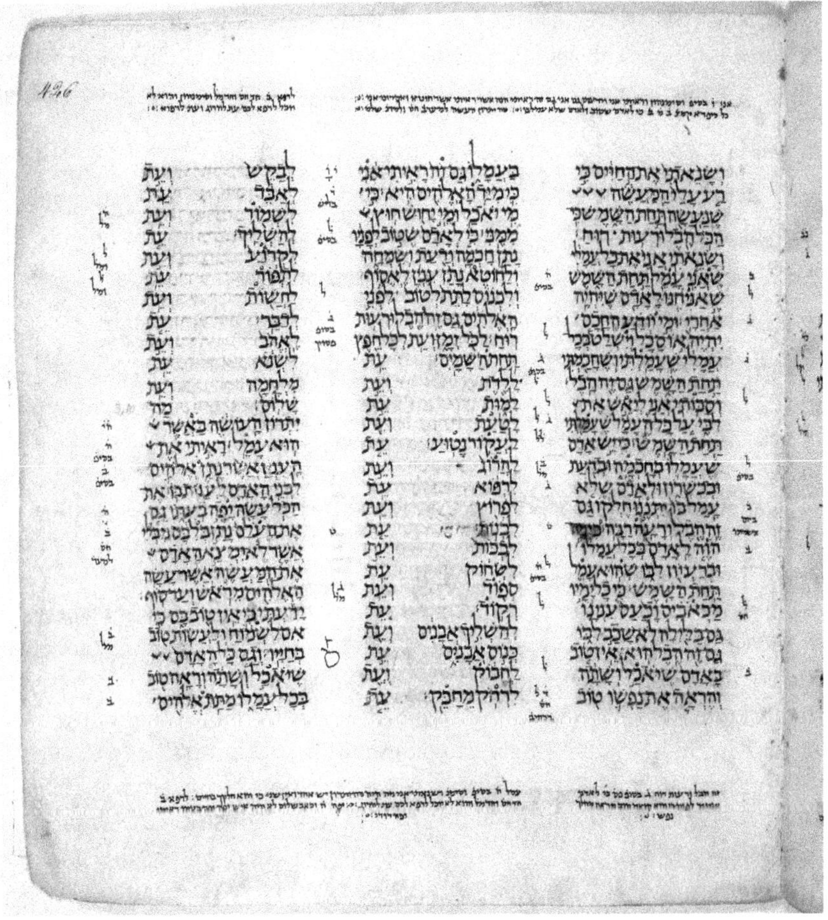

Figure 4.4 Visual aesthetic of Ecclesiastes 3, "A Time for Everything," in Leningrad Codex. Photograph by Bruce and Kenneth Zuckerman, West Semitic Research, in collaboration with the Ancient Biblical Manuscript Center. Courtesy of Russian National Library (Saltykov-Shchedrin).

While these are certainly not a close parallel to the Gezer inscription, the flavor of the lexical list and repetitions begins to be evident already in this short selection. Some of the terminology is even cognate with the Gezer inscription, such as the use of *eṣedu*, "reaping," which is cognate with *ʿṣd* (עצד) in line 3 of the Calendar.[42] It is also worth pointing out that the verbal constructions in this section of Ura use the infinitive,[43] just as we have in the Gezer Calendar. This section of Ura continues in a similar fashion with various agricultural themes and terminology (lines 157–75).

The next section of the canonical Ura lexical list (1, 176–234) is also related to a theme of the Gezer Calendar, namely, a list of words and expressions related to time. It begins with a section related to the "day" (UD-*mu*), moves to the canonical section on *arḫu*, "months," and concludes with the year (*šanat*). Lines 211–16 relate to the "month":

itu	*ar-ḫu*	"month"
itu-šè	*a-na ar-ḫi*	"within a month"
ud-itu-šè	*a-na* UD *ar-ḫi*	"within the period of a month"
sag-itu-šè	*a-na ri-eš ar-ḫi*	"until the beginning of the month"
egir-itu-šè	*a-na ar-kàt ar-ḫi*	"until the end of the month"
u_4 $kaš_4$-a	UD-*mu li-is-mu*	"day of the running" (announcing month)
u_4-sar	*ar-ḫu*	"new moon"

There can be no doubt that this particular lexical list was familiar to Canaanite scribes because this section of Ura was actually found in the fragmentary lexical text excavated at Ashkelon! The fragment dates to the very end of the Late Bronze Age, probably the twelfth century. As John Huehnergard and Wilfred van Soldt reconstruct it, there were three columns: Sumerian (ITU), Akkadian (*arḫu*), and West Semitic (*ia-ar-ḫu* = *yarḫu*).[44] It is especially important to emphasize that this fragment varies from the canonical version of Ura by adding a West Semitic column. This was not part of the normal Mesopotamian lexical tradition, but it is a tradition known from peripheral sites like Emar and Ugarit. That is to say, the text already shows the willingness to adapt scribal curricula in the West Semitic tradition. In fact, the influence from the traditional term *arḫu*, "month"—or, *yarḫu* in West Semitic column—in the cuneiform lexical series may explain the preference for the term *yrḥ* (as opposed to *ḥdš*) in the Gezer inscription. This fragment provides tangible evidence of a "vector of transmission" of the cuneiform lexical tradition for early Canaanite and Hebrew scribes. The Ashkelon tablet demonstrates that this lexical series was known and being adapted in the southern Levant on the eve of the Iron Age.

Khirbet Qeiyafa as a List

Another possible example of a lexical list among early Hebrew epigraphic texts may be the enigmatic inscription from Khirbet Qeiyafa. Although this inscription has already yielded an array of differing scholarly transcriptions and interpretations,[45] both Alan Millard and Aaron Demsky have independently suggested reading the ostracon as a list of names. Demsky points to parallels at Ugarit with scribal exercises in writing names (e.g., *KTU* 5.1, 5.7, 5.18, 5.22). Matthieu Richelle agrees with the approach of Millard and Demsky, although he limits his efforts to the first two lines.[46] In this respect, Richelle takes a more prudent approach given the great variety of transcriptions that may be found for this inscription, especially for lines 3–5. To be sure, any interpretation must be tentative, but I agree with the interpretation of the ostracon as a list of names. It is not an exciting interpretation, but this would make the Qeiyafa Ostracon a very typical ancient document.

The inscription is written in ink on the concave part of a pottery sherd. The writing in ink is, of course, an Egyptian technology that was utilized in early alphabetic writing. This is one of the earliest examples of an alphabetic inscription written with ink. In my opinion, the ostracon should be dated to the late eleventh century BCE based on its archaeological context, C14 dating, and paleography.[47] The ostracon is lined with four lines separating the five lines of text (see Figure 4.5). This itself is unusual, although it has received scant attention in many publications.[48] Demsky has suggested a school function to the lines: "This pedagogic choice would facilitate the exercise in recognizing and writing letters in different directions, guided by lines drawn in order to focus the attention of the learner."[49] It is worth noting that cuneiform school exercises are often lined, and administrative lists quite frequently are individually lined.[50] More generally, the use of lines in cuneiform literary texts and letters tends to separate discrete sections of a text. But in school texts and lists every textual line is often scribed with a dividing line, as we have in the Qeiyafa Ostracon. So the lines themselves should be understood as part of the text and suggest its interpretation as a list.

For the reader's convenience, I will offer a tentative transcription and translation. I make no attempt to be particularly original in this reading, but rather follow my assessment of the best readings offered in the many readings of the text. The problem of the interpretation lies in the relatively poor state of preservation, which has resulted in different reconstructions of the inscription (which

Figure 4.5 An early alphabetic list from Khirbet Qeiyafa. Drawing courtesy of Brian Donnelly-Lewis.

are heavily dependent on the overall interpretation of the inscription). Apart from technology that renders the inscription easier to read, every interpretation will be necessarily tentative. The most generous way I could describe some of the attempts to make a readable narrative or poem from these lines is imaginative. There is little consensus in the more ambitious interpretations, but there is an emerging group of scholars who have understood this inscription as some sort of list of names. Along those lines, I offer the following transcription and translation:

	Transcription	**Translation**
1)	*ʾltʿš⌜tr⌝ʿbdʾ*[*l*]	"Ellat-ʿAshtar ʿEbed-El
2)	*špṭ*|*bwʾlm*[]*špṭyt*	"Shaphaṭ BWʾ LM[] Shaphaṭyat

3)	*lr|bʿll/ʿ[]m[]*	"[]LR x Baʿal-[]
4)	*ʾ[]m⸢wn⸣qmybdm⸢l⸣kg[t]*	"[] and Naqmay [] Bodmilk Ga[th]
5)	*ḥ/srm/nʿ[]grt[]*	"???"

In addition to the lines, the crude execution of the letters, which many scholars have noted, also points to interpreting this ostracon as a writing exercise. Indeed one of the more curious aspects of this inscription is the different orientations of the same letter. For example, the four *ʾalephs* in lines 1, 2, and 4 are oriented in three different directions! Is there some meaning to these orientations? Or do they have something to do with its function as a school exercise? We simply do not have enough data to offer a definitive conclusion. And the difficulty in arriving at a consensus on the transcription of the ostracon further prevents a definitive interpretation. However, once we have arrived at the conclusion that this is a writing exercise, the most likely interpretation is that it is a lexical list of some type.

The Use of Lists in Biblical Literature

The list is ubiquitous in biblical literature. The classified lexical lists may be implicit in the very first "school" setting—namely, the Garden of Eden where "the man gave names" to all the animals (Gen 2:20). There are a variety of types of lists in biblical literature. The most common type of list is the genealogy, but there are also geographical lists, king lists, personnel lists, tribe and clan lists, ritual lists, object lists (i.e., booty, temple objects, merchandise), and achievement lists. In his book on biblical lists, Benjamin Scolnic gathers and classifies examples:[51] David's Mighty Men (2Sam 23:9–11), Royal Officials (e.g., 1Kgs 4:1–6); Edomite King List (Gen 36:31–40; cp. 1Chr 1:43–51); Administrative Districts and Personnel (e.g., 1Kgs 4:7–19); Palace Provisions (1Kgs 4:22–23); Levitical City List (Josh 21; cp. 1Chr 6:39–66), List of Returnees (Neh 7:5-73; [ET, 7:6–72]; Ezra 2), List of Nations (e.g., Ex 3:8, 17; 13:5; 23:23; 33:2; 34:11; Deut 7:1; 20:17; Josh 3:10; 9:1; 11:3; 12:8; 24:11; Judg 3:5), List of Unconquered Nations (Judg 1:1–36), Lists of Foreign Officials (e.g., Jer 39:3), Genealogies (e.g., Gen 5, 10; 1Chr 1–9, etc.), and more.

These are some of the most obvious examples of lists, but the influence of lists goes far beyond these examples. Lists were used as an organizing tool in the composition of biblical literature. As a way of understanding the role of lists in biblical literature, I will illustrate the use of lists in two different ways: autonomous lists embedded into the narrative and the use of lists to create a literary text.

Naturally, lists exist outside of a narrative context. These can be lists of names, lists of commodities, or even lists of months like the Gezer Calendar. They do not necessarily require a narrative context. They can have a social context outside of literature. This would include school texts, whether they be lists of personal names, geographic names, deity lists, or thematic lists, such as a list of "trees and wood items" or other items. Some biblical lists are really autonomous and not well integrated into their context. Others could be autonomous but are well integrated into the fabric of the narrative.

The centrality of lists seems to illustrate Solomonic wisdom and knowledge. In one passage, the context of Solomonic knowledge suggests the learning of lists: "He discoursed about all the trees—from the cedar in Lebanon to the hyssop that grows out of the wall; and he discoursed about the animals—of birds, of reptiles, and of fish" (1Kgs 5:13; [ET] 4:33).[52] Scholars have sometimes suggested that Solomonic knowledge here might be a general allusion to an onomastic school tradition. Some have appealed to Mesopotamian and Egyptian lexical lists, which focus quite a bit on things like trees and animals, but James Crenshaw and others have dismissed the appeal to the comparative material as unnecessary historicizing of King Solomon.[53] John Gray, for example, wrote, "The precise significance of the tradition of Solomon's sayings or discourse about natural phenomena is uncertain."[54] John Day also objected: "It is clearly not the case that Solomon's wisdom was actually onomastic in character, for against this it may be noted that Solomon is said to have *spoken* of the trees and beasts, which does not seem appropriate for a mere catalogue of names such as we find in the Egyptian and Mesopotamian onomastica."[55] C. F. Burney regarded the use of the "trees" as "late" or "poetical."[56] Albrecht Alt suggested that Solomon had appropriated the lexical lists by transforming them into proverbs and songs, but Day dismisses this, suggesting that this type of transformation "is nowhere else attested."[57] All of these suggestions are rather general, and the adaptation of the Gezer Calendar suggests a more direct and tangible knowledge of the cuneiform lexical tradition.

One expression of Solomon's knowledge and wisdom is his ability to discourse about trees and animals. Why would the illustration of Solomon's great wisdom begin with his being able to discourse about trees? The answer can be found in the traditional cuneiform lexical curriculum. Cuneiform school curricula included the learning of thematic lexical lists; these lexical lists always began with lists of "trees and wooden objects." This order for thematic word lists continued in the cuneiform tradition throughout the second millennium and is even found in peripheral Akkadian. In this respect, the reference to Solomon's wisdom seems to be an intentional allusion to the systematization of lists in the traditional cuneiform school curriculum—that is, the order that begins with lists of "trees and wooden objects," followed by a comprehensive knowledge of "animals," which is one of the next elements of the traditional thematic cuneiform lexical list. These two taken together are more than coincidental. In this respect, the passage seems to draw on traditional cuneiform lexical curricula to represent Solomon's encyclopedic knowledge.

The adaptation of lexical lists is illustrated already by the addition of West Semitic columns to the lists in the West, including the one from the site of Ashkelon (discussed above). This is important for establishing a "vector of transmission" for the influence of the cuneiform lexical tradition. Moreover the recent publication of Niek Veldhuis's monumental *A History of the Cuneiform Lexical Tradition* now makes it clear that these scholars understate the ways in which lexical lists were developed and transformed in antiquity. Beginning in the Old Babylonian period, there emerged a great number of new variations on the traditional lexical list. New compositions of a variety of types emerged. For example, Amarna scholarly tablets illustrate how a traditional lexical list was adapted into a kind of bilingual Egyptian-Akkadian dictionary. Veldhuis concludes, "Something more fundamental is going on, a new understanding of what knowledge is and how it may be employed."[58] In other words, the lexical tradition became an educational foundation for "a broad trend in textualization knowledge and freeing textual genres from some of their traditional constraints."[59]

Veldhuis points out that lexical lists were used in the education of the crown prince.[60] Of course, the Assyrian king Assurbanipal famously boasted of his literacy, and the veracity of this claim has been discussed by many scholars.[61] The boasting of Assurbanipal begins as follows: "I learnt the lore of the wise saga Adapa, the hidden secret of the scribal art. I can recognize celestial and terrestrial omens and discuss them in the assembly of scholars."[62] The list of Assurbanipal's knowledge also includes divination, mathematics and accounting, Sumerian, and an ability to interpret archaic texts. Striking evidence for the crown prince's study of lexical lists comes from a text in Assurbanipal's own library (K 2016a+); the colophon reads:

> Fourth tablet of the series Ura = *hubullum* [i.e., wooden furniture and boats]. For the consultation of the crown prince of the succession house of Esarhaddon, king of the world, king of the land of Assur, governor of Babylon, king of the land of Sumer and Akkad, Aplāya, the junior apprentice scribe, son of Kēni, the scribe of the crown prince, wrote it and provided it for the crown prince, his lord, as a prayer.[63]

This lexical series is a continuation of the "trees and wood objects" (GIŠ) series that began the traditional thematic cuneiform lexicon.

In this context, it is worth comparing an oft-mistranslated text in the Book of Deuteronomy. The "Law of the King" concludes with the injunction that "after the king takes his throne, he shall write for himself a copy of this *torah* upon a scroll" (Deut 17:18). Many English translations mistranslate this as a passive (e.g., "he shall have a copy of this Teaching written for him," NJPS), but the Hebrew is clearly an active verb and recalls the scholar-king portrait of Assurbanipal.[64] According to the Book of Proverbs, the men of Hezekiah copied down a collection of Solomonic proverbs (25:1). This evidence suggests that Solomon (and other kings) were being represented in a Neo-Assyrian scholastic tradition as being able to write.

A scholastic background can be posited for many examples of lists in biblical literature that can be cleanly extracted from their narrative contexts. Genealogies are the most frequent example of this, but there are a variety of types of examples. One example of an autonomous list is the "Table of Nations" in Genesis 10. The list is introduced by the statement "Now these are the generations of Noah's sons" (verse 1a), and the list is closed with a framing repetition, "These are the families of Noah's sons according to their generations" (verse 32). Within the chapter, the genealogical list is punctuated by the phrase "and the sons of PN" (PN-ובני, see verses 3, 4, 6, 7, 20, 22, 23). There are elaborations within the list such as the description of Nimrod, who was both "the first man of might on the earth" and "a mighty hunter by the grace of the LORD" (verses 8–9). Some parts of the list itself seem to be autonomous, like the description of Shem's descendants, which is framed itself by a bracketing inclusio (verses 21 and 31). But the list as a whole could exist as an autonomous catalogue. On the other hand, the list is framed at the beginning and end to integrate it into the larger narrative. In verse 1, the list is tied to the previous flood narrative: "sons were born to them after the Flood." In verse 32, the closure of the list foreshadows the Tower of Babel narrative that follows: "from these the nations were spread out in the earth after the Flood."[65] In this way, independent sources like lists, which reflect the foundations of scribal education, could be integrated into larger narratives.

Another example of an integrated list is the priestly narrative of the building of the Tabernacle (Ex 25–29, 35–40; Lev 8–10; Numb 7). For example, an editor embeds an independent archival list preserved in Numb 7:12–88 into a larger narrative development.[66] The first indication of an archival list is a typical pattern of citing qualities in a list—that is, item/quantity; for example, verse 17 may be rendered as follows:

> *for his sacrifice of well-being*:
> bulls, 2
> rams, 5
> he-goats, 5
> yearling, 5.

This is the pattern found throughout Numb 7:12–88. Baruch Levine illustrates the independent archival character of this list by translating verses 12–88 as a chart.[67] Another indication of the archival list origin of these verses is the absence of *waws*, separating the items in the list; for example, in verse 15:

פר אחד	"bull, 1 (from the herd)
בן־בקר איל אחד	ram, 1
כבש־אחד	lamb, 1
בן־שנתו לעלה	(yearling for a burnt offering).

The fact that these verses go on, item after item, each followed by a number but not separated by *waws*, suggests that they were originally formatted by line breaks in a list, as we find in many inscriptions. The list is embedded with a narrative introduction in verses 10–12: "The chieftains also brought the dedication offering for the altar on the day its being anointed." The narrative presentation of the archival list is then tied up in the end (verse 88) with a total:

וכל בקר זבח השלמים
עשׂרים וארבעה פרים
אילם ששים
עתדים ששים
כבשים בני־שנה ששים
זאת חנכת המזבח אחרי המשח אתו

"*Total of the herd animals for sacrifices*:
24 bulls;
rams, 60;
male goats, 60;
yearling lambs, 60.
This was the dedication offering for the altar after its anointing."

An inclusio embeds the entire list into the narrative beginning in verse 10 and ending in verse 88, from "on the day of its anointing [ביום המשח אתו]" to "after its anointing [אחרי המשח אתו]," using the distinctive *niphal* infinitive verbal form of the root *mšḥ*, "anointing," which highlights the editorial bracketing repetition.

The order and repetition of lists can serve as a starting point and structuring device in literary texts. This can be illustrated with a couple of features of lists in the "Oracles against the Nations" in Amos 1:3–2:16. To begin with, the judgments are framed as complaints against a geographical list: Damascus (verse 3), Gaza (6), Tyre (9), Edom (11), Ammon (13), Moab (2:1), Judah (2:4), and Israel (2:6). Each oracle is introduced by the messenger formula "thus says the

LORD" (כה אמר יהוה), and most are concluded by a clipped repetition of this formula, "says the LORD" (אמר יהוה). These oracles famously also begin with the repeated formula "for three transgressions of GN, and for four, I will not revoke punishment." In this way, the repetitive aspects of lists help frame biblical literature.

Another type of repetitive list is a travelogue. For example, Benjamin Scolnic has an extensive discussion of Numbers 33, "the journey through the wilderness," in his book *Biblical Lists* as an example of an independent list.[68] The list begins with a framing introduction that points to a list: "These were the daily marches of the Israelites" (verse 1). It then intentionally points out that "Moses recorded the starting points for their daily marches [ויכתב משה את־מוצאיהם למסעיהם]" (verse 2). Verses 5–37 are all structured the same:[69] "and they set out from GN, and they camped at GN [ויסעו מ-GN ויחנו ב -GN]," so that the text looks unmistakably like an itinerary list. In fact, this itinerary list follows a pattern well-known in Neo-Assyrian texts. A variety of comparisons may be found in Akkadian military annals, which have as their basic framework an itinerary formula: *ištu* URUGN *at-tu-muš ina* URUGN *a-sa-ka-an be-dàk*, "From city GN, I departed. In city of GN, I spent the night."[70] This formula is then elaborated upon in a variety of ways. For example, in an annal of Assurnasirpal II:[71]

> *From the city of* Magarisi, *I departed,* and I marched to the district of the river Habur. *In the city of* Shadikanni, *I spent the night.* The tribute of Shadikanni—silver, gold, lead, vessels of copper, cattle, and flocks—I received.
>
> *From the city of* Shadikanni, *I departed. In the city of* Qatnu, *I spent the night,* and I received the tribute of the Qatnites.
>
> From the city of Qatnu, I departed. In the city of Dūr-katlimmu, I spent the night.
>
> From the city of Dūr-katlimmu, I departed. In the city of Bīt-Ḫalupê, I spent the night.

The itinerary formula is marked by italics, and the scribe was able to insert additional details—e.g., records of tribute—into the list relevant to the purpose of the military list. Likewise, we may compare elements in the composition of Numbers 33. A few verses from the chapter will illustrate the rigid structural backbone of the list as well as the ability to add notes that are not unlike the Assyrian military itineraries. In verses 7–15, we read:

> *They set out from* Etham and turned about toward Pi-hahiroth, which faces Baal-zephon, *and they encamped before* Migdol.

> *They set out from Pene-hahiroth* and passed through the sea into the wilderness; and they made a three-days' journey in the wilderness of Etham, *and they encamped at* Marah.
>
> *They set out from* Marah and came to Elim. There were twelve springs in Elim and seventy palm trees, *and they encamped* there.
>
> They set out from Elim, and they encamped by the Sea of Reeds.
>
> *They set out from* the Sea of Reeds, *and they encamped in* the wilderness of Sin.
>
> They set out from the wilderness of Sin, and they encamped at Dophkah.
>
> They set out from Dophkah, and they encamped at Alush.
>
> *They set out from* Alush, *and they encamped at* Rephidim—it was there that the people had no water to drink.
>
> *They set out from* Rephidim, *and they encamped in* the wilderness of Sinai.

The structure is quite repetitive, as befits an itinerary list. As in the Assyrian annal, however, additional relevant information could be worked into the list.

In the preface to the itinerary (verses 1–5a), an editor integrated the list into its larger Pentateuchal context with two *Wiederaufnahme* that mention the larger Exodus narrative.[72] The introductory framework emphasizes the textual nature of the list: "Moses recorded the embarking locations of the journey" (verse 2a). At the conclusion of the list, an editor uses the repetition of the last location to connect the list with the location of the previous narrative. Specifically, an editor repeats the location of the last encampment of the list, "in the plains of Moab by the Jordan at Jericho" (verses 48b and 50a). This repetition of the location frames an elaboration of the location—"they camped as far as Abel-Shittim" and there "the LORD spoke to Moses"; this takes the reader back to the previous narrative in Numb 25:1, where "Israel was staying at Shittim." The result is that an editor has taken an independent itinerary list and knitted it into the larger narrative. The traces of editing are clear enough, but the result is a coherent narrative.

The poetic structure of the poem in Ecclesiastes 3, "A Time for Everything," also functions as a list (see Figure 4.4). The visual aesthetic of this list of "time" (עת) is enhanced if the word "time" is lined up in a column, as you would have in many lexical lists. Indeed this is the way that many Hebrew manuscripts (such as the Leningrad Codex) presented the text. I present the following arrangement of the translation:

> For everything there is a season, and a time for every matter under heaven:
> a time to be born, and a time to die;
> a time to plant, and a time to pluck up what is planted;
> a time to kill, and a time to heal;
> a time to tear down, and a time to build up;

a time to weep, and a time to laugh;
a time to mourn, and a time to dance;
a time to cast stones, and a time to gather stones;
a time to embrace, and a time to refrain from embracing;
a time to seek, and a time to lose;
a time to keep, and a time to discard;
a time to tear, and a time to sew;
a time to be silent, and a time to speak;
a time to love, and a time to hate;
a time for war, and a time for peace.

The aesthetic of the poem is highlighted both by the repetition of the word "time" (עת) and by the use of the Hebrew infinitive for the verbal constructions. In fact, without reflecting on the nature of Eccl 3:2–8 or the Gezer inscription as lists, Jacqueline Vayntrub has observed some striking formal parallels.[73] She points out that both comprise the elements of "time" and "activity." Indeed this juxtaposition is also a feature of the Ura lexical list. And just as in the Gezer Calendar (and the section of Ura), the verbal constructions in Eccl 3:2–8 use the infinitive (except in the culminating verse, "a time for war and peace"). For these reasons, I would describe Eccl 3:2–8 as a "lexical poem."

At the beginning of this section, I listed some of the many examples of lists in the Hebrew Bible. Understanding the importance and breadth of this part of scribal education begins with the comparative evidence adduced from the cuneiform tradition. The cuneiform tradition helps us correctly identify the fragmentary evidence from Kuntillet ʿAjrud, as well as properly interpret texts like the Gezer Calendar and the Qeiyafa Ostracon. It is with this context that we can identify the fingerprints of scribal lists and lexical traditions in biblical literature. I have illustrated just a few examples of the many lists in the Hebrew Bible. The purpose of this has been threefold. First, I wanted to show that lists were part of the curriculum of early Israelite scribes and that this curriculum could be found in a variety of places in the Bible. Second, I wanted to illustrate the ubiquity of lists in the Hebrew Bible. They are found throughout the corpus. Sometimes they are largely independent and are incorporated with minimum editing; sometimes lists were adapted in a variety of ways in composing biblical literature. While there is good reason to downplay the grandiose idea of a *Listenwissenschaft*, lists were nevertheless an essential part of scribal education and exerted far-reaching influence in the composition and editing of the Hebrew Bible. They were a primary means to teach writing, and the impact of these educational exercises are widely felt throughout biblical literature.

5

Letters, Paragraphs, and Prophets

Elementary education continued with the copying of literary models of various genres. The most important and well-known of these literary models was the letter. There are other well-known models of genres, such as treaties and legal contracts, but writing letters was part of the daily activity of a scribe. Not surprisingly, we find dozens of letters in the Hebrew epigraphic record, and it is clear that practicing letter writing was basic and essential to the elementary scribal curriculum. From the various types of model texts that scribes may have had to learn to write, the only scribal exercise preserved in Hebrew are model letters. As a result, it should hardly be surprising that the genre of letter writing influenced biblical literature in a variety of ways both small and great. In this chapter, we will explore various forms and technical terms of learning to write letters, and the way these forms and terms were used and adapted in biblical literature.

Letters have a long history as part of Near Eastern scribal curriculum. They were already used as part of the Mesopotamian school curriculum dating back centuries before the earliest Hebrew writing. Moreover such letter exercises in the Akkadian curriculum were adapted and used in the alphabetic cuneiform of the ancient city-state of Ugarit. There, letters served as one of the primary school exercises. It is hardly surprising, then, that we have three actual examples of this scribal exercise in the inscriptions from Kuntillet ʿAjrud.

The Prominence of Letter Writing throughout the Ancient Near East

Ugaritic, Egyptian, and Mesopotamian corpuses include many literary texts with narrated scenes of letters being sent and received. Interestingly enough, one Mesopotamian account even explains the invention of writing as resulting from the need to write letters accurately. In *Enmerkar and the Lord of Aratta*,[1] Enmerkar ruled in Uruk as "priest-king" and forced the ancient city of Aratta to submit to his rule. The lord of Aratta challenged Enmerkar by sending him messengers who each posed a series of seemingly insurmountable problems. Enmerkar in response dispatched messengers with the solutions. Finally, in one particular instance, Enmerkar's message became too long for his messenger's memory. To solve the problem, the priest-king invented writing so that his messenger could take a written response—a letter—with him to Aratta. This story nicely illustrates that the need to transmit ideas between polities was foundational to the invention of writing itself, which explains why learning to write letters was fundamental to scribal education.

The importance of letter writing was also part of the literary canon in Egypt. For example, the well-known story "The Report of Wenamun" (dated to ca. 1100 BCE) recounts the story of an unfortunate Egyptian emissary traveling up the eastern Mediterranean coast in order to acquire Lebanese timber for the bark of Amun-Re.[2] Wenamun arrived in the Nile delta at Tanis bringing "*dispatches* of Amun-Re, King of the Gods. They had them read out before them and they said: 'I will do, I will do as Amun-Re, King of the Gods, our lord has said.'" With this literary dispatch couched in the traditional messenger *Sitz im Leben*, he begins his perilous mission. After making port in Dor, where he was robbed, Wenamun traveled to Byblos, where he is unwelcome. According to the story, he sent and the prince of Byblos daily messages back and forth for twenty-nine days: "Then the prince of Byblos sent to me: 'Leave my harbor!' I sent to him, saying: 'Where shall I go? If you have a ship to carry me, let me be taken back to Egypt!'" Letters were simultaneously being sent back and forth to Egypt: "(The prince of Byblos) placed my letter[s] in the hand of his messenger . . . and sent them to Egypt." The entire narrative thread of the story is carried by these types of messenger scenes and the traditional formulations of letters.

Ugaritic literature also utilizes letters as a means of carrying its literary narratives. For example, messenger scenes carry the narrative in the Ugaritic epic poem known as *The Baal Cycle* (see *KTU* 1.1–6).[3] The use of letter formulae are illustrated nicely in the account where Yamm's messengers arrive at the Great Assembly and frame the message as follows: "Speak to the Bull, his Father, El: the message of Yamm" (line 33). This is a standard formula of Ugaritic letters. And messengers, messages, and messenger formulae are critical to the narrative. Although the beginning of this particular epic is missing, when it picks up, El is sending messengers to the goddess Anat. The narrative then recounts their journey to deliver El's message. El later sends messengers to the craftsman god, Koṯar-wa-Ḫasis. Then the god Yamm returns messengers to El. The latter scene is clearly depicted and can illustrate the way the story uses messengers to move the narrative thread (*KTU* 1.2:i:11–17):

> Yamm *sends messengers*, Ruler Naharu sends an embassy.
> They rejoice . . .

Go, young servants, don't delay,
head for the Great Assembly, to Mount Lalu.
Do not bow down at El's feet,
Do not prostrate yourself before the Great Assembly.
Standing, make your speech, repeat your information.
Speak (*rgm*) to the Bull, my father, El, repeat to the Great Assembly.
Message (*tḥm*) of Yammu, your master, of your lord River [Naharu].

The narrative is framed by performative speech acts derived from the reading of letters, even in other places where messengers and letters are not specifically mentioned. The scene type of the messenger carrying a letter to be read out loud before the recipient is deeply embedded into the narrative poetry. Most revealing is the usage of technical terminology known from the letter genre—namely, "message (*tḥm*) of Sender" and "speak (*rgm*) to Recipient." These are the exact terms from the many letters in the Ugaritic corpus, and their repeated usage directly points to the role of the letter genre in carrying the narrative thread. In sum, the social context of letters, letter writing, and messengers has shaped Ugaritic narrative poetry.

Likewise, the formula from the letter genre can be seen in biblical narratives.[4] For example, in the story of Jacob's confrontation with Esau on his return to the land, we read as follows in Gen 32:4–14:

> *Jacob sent messengers* ahead to his brother Esau in the land of Seir, the country of Edom, *and instructed them as follows*, "Thus shall you say, 'To my lord Esau, *thus says your servant Jacob*: I stayed with Laban and remained until now; I have acquired cattle, asses, sheep, and male and female slaves; and I send this message to my lord in the hope of gaining your favor.'" *The messengers returned to Jacob, saying*, "We came to your brother Esau; he himself is coming to meet you, and there are four hundred men with him." . . . Then after spending the night there, Jacob took from what was at hand and sent presents for his brother Esau.

In this narrative, we witness the oral *Sitz im Leben* from which the written genre of letters arises. Messengers are sent and received. Originally, these were oral performances (without the aid of letters), as suggested by the Mesopotamian etiology of *Enmerkar and the Lord of Aratta*. The oral conventions of messengers and messenger performances actually become encoded in the letter genre itself. For example, "thus says your servant Jacob" is an oral convention that was textualized in the letter genre. It is often difficult to know whether physical letters were actually sent, as in the above narrative. The oral conventions, however, become fixed in the letter genre.

The story of David and Bathsheba in 2 Samuel 11 also illustrates the role of messengers and letters. It begins with David sending "messengers" to fetch Bathsheba (verse 4). When she becomes pregnant, she "sends word" to David (verse 5). We may assume (though it is not explicit) that this part of the story utilized oral messengers although the private nature of the interaction might suggest written letters. But the story quickly moves explicitly to messengers carrying letters. David sends messengers to Joab to recall Uriah from the battle. When Uriah refuses to sleep with his wife, David conceives of his plot using a letter: "David wrote a letter to Joab, which he sent with Uriah" (verse 14). Joab receives the letter, and he fulfills David's plot, resulting in the death of Uriah. Joab then sends messengers back to David with the news. The story ends with David sending the messengers back to Joab, implicitly signaling his approval of Joab's role in the plot (verse 25). An actual written letter in this story is mentioned only in verse 14, that is, when the message needs to be concealed from Uriah (who is also the messenger). Many other biblical stories utilize messengers and letters,[5] and it is clear that the setting and literary genre were widely known in ancient Israelite culture.

Model Letters in School Exercises from Ugarit

Before the rise of Hebrew scribal education, we already have examples of model letters in the alphabetic curriculum from ancient Ugarit. Given the limited evidence for school exercise letters in ancient Israel, it will be helpful to look at a couple parallels of these epistolary exercises from Ugarit. Ugaritic letters draw upon the formal elements of the Near Eastern letter genre that have been isolated in a variety of studies.[6] These elements draw from the genre in Akkadian letters, albeit with local modifications. A full Near Eastern introductory formula might include an address formula, a prostration formula (when appropriate), a greeting formula, and a request for divine blessing. All these elements are not present in actual letters where an economy of expression was often preferred.

There are as many as four examples of model letters from the archives at Ugarit (*KTU* 5.9, 5.10, 5.11, 5.33), but two examples in particular can shed some light on aspects of the training of alphabetic scribes. The first example of a model letter was published as *KTU* 5.9 (= *RS* 16.265).[7] This tablet was written on both the front and back as well as all four sides. The recto has a complete model letter (see Figure 5.1).

While the front is a complete model letter, this tablet actually consists of four different types of scribal exercises: a practice letter (recto), abecedaries (sides),

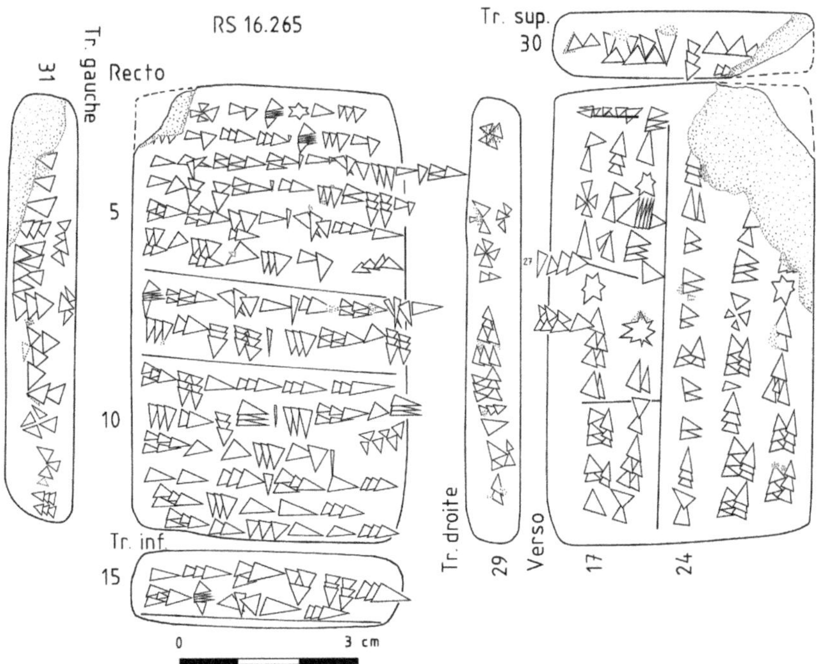

Figure 5.1 Practice letter, abecedaries, and lexical items. Copy courtesy of Dennis Pardee.

lexical items (verso), and practice signs (verso).[8] On the front (recto), down to the lower edge, we find a practice letter that may be transcribed as follows:

<u>*KTU* 5.9: Recto to Lower Edge</u>

(1) *[t]ḥm iṯtl*	Message of ʾIṯtēlu
(2) *l mnn.ʾlm*	to whomever. May the gods
(3) *tǵrk.tšlmk*	guard you, keep you well,
(4) *tʿzzk.ʾalp ym*	strengthen you, for a thousand days
(5) *w rbt šnt*	and ten thousand years
(6) *bʿd ʿlm*	through eternity.

————————————

(7) *iršt.aršt*	A request, I request,
(8) *l aḫy.l rʿy*	to my brother, to my friend.

————————————

(9) *w ytnnn*	And may he grant it [impf/energ]
(10) *l aḫh.l rʿh*	to his brother, to his friend,
(11) *rʿ ʿlm.*	an eternal friend.
(12) *ttn.w tn*	May you give [juss], and give [impv]!
(13) *w l ttn*	and may you indeed give [asseverative l],
(14) *w al ttn*	and would you not give [rhetorical]?
(15) *tn ks yn*	Give a cup of wine [impv],
(16) *w ištn*	and I shall drink it [impf/energic].

Several aspects indicate that this is no ordinary letter but rather an embellished scribal exercise. To begin with, in line 2 the letter is addressed to *mnn*, which should be understood as the Ugaritic indefinite particle *mn*, "whomever," with a suffixed enclitic *n*. This addressee is unusual. We do not have this lexeme as a personal name in Ugaritic. Indeed it would be strange to have a personal name based on the indefinite meaning "whomever"! The scribe must have intentionally used the indefinite "whomever" even though the second part of the letter will wax eloquent as a request to "his brother, his friend, his eternal friend." These lines seem like rather cheeky embellishments since there is no particular addressee. Of course, as it is scribal practice, there is no need to have a specific addressee.

The letter also heaps up parallelism. In lines 3–4, we find three possible blessing words—*nǵr, šlm*, and *ʿzz* ("to guard," "to be well," and "to strengthen")—that all have cognates in Hebrew (נער, שלם, and עזז). This full blessing triad can be found in a just one Ugaritic letter (*KTU* 2.4); typically, Ugaritic letters would use just one or two of these terms, whereas practice exercises used the entire array. Students learned the full variety of formulae and terminology in practice exercises, but actual letters reflected an economy of expression.

Most practice letters ended with the introductory section of a message as only the formal introduction of a letter could be practiced and repeated. The body of a letter obviously varied. Therefore, in the Ugaritic example cited above, the exercise continued with grammatical, lexical, and semantic practice. In lines 8 and 10, we have the alternative terms *aḫ*, "brother," and *rʿ*, "friend," which are never used together in an actual Ugaritic letter; they are not a logical parallel, though they are part of the larger semantic field of relationships that are typically found in letters. Using a relational term like "mother," "brother," "son," or "servant" is quite typical in letters, but "my brother, my friend" is purely a scribal flourish in this student exercise. Line 11 embellishes further by adding "an *eternal* friend." Such flourishes reflect the freedom of the scribe to adapt and be creative even within the confines of the exercise. Such creativity would become even more important as scribes used and adapted their learning in a variety of real-world situations.

The body of the letter also embeds grammatical exercises. In line 7 there is an unusual cognate accusative structure, "a request I request," with a nominal and verbal formulation of the root *ʾrš*, "to request." In lines 9–15, five different verbal formulations of the Ugaritic verbal root *ytn*, "to give," appear. The last of these instances creates the jocular request "give me a cup of wine so that I may drink!" One might suppose that granting this request is what makes "his brother" an "eternal friend"! In the end, this letter is not really a letter at all because it is missing one of the most standard features of a letter, namely the word *rgm*, "speak!," which is a critical part of the performative aspect of the ancient missive.[9] But this is not a letter to be performed; rather it is a scribal exercise framed by traditional message conventions.

As an aside, we should also observe that scribal exercises continue on the edges of the tablet with partial abecedaries. On the right edge (line 29), there is preserved the first eleven letters of the Ugaritic alphabet: *abgḫdhwzḥṭy*. And again, on the left edge (line 31), there was originally the first eleven letters of the Ugaritic alphabet: [*a*]*bgḫdhwzḥṭy*. Finally, on the upper edge (line 30), there is a partial abecedary with just five letters preserved that looks to have been written by a different, less accomplished student: *ad<b>gḫd*[xx]. The letters are poorly formed and spaced, and the student actually confuses the *d* with the *b*. The student "handwriting" is so different that the tablet must be a palimpsest; that is, the tablet was likely inscribed by an apprentice scribe who made typical mistakes (e.g., confusing *b* with *d*), then a more advanced student (incompletely) scraped the tablet and reused it, leaving the upper edge (line 30) from the earlier scribe untouched. Such reuse for practice tablets is quite typical and can be seen quite clearly in *KTU* 5.33 (see Figure 5.2) as well as the jars from Kuntillet ʿAjrud (see Pithos B, *KA* 3.6).

The reverse of the tablet has different exercises. They include lexical items, practice writing different graphemes, and a conclusion reversing the letter introduction from lines 1–2 (Figure 5.1).[10] I offer the following transcription:

Verso

(17) *ʿbd*	"servant"
(18) *qrq*	QRQ "sounds"?
(*Column II*)	
(24) *qnṣṣ.bṣṣṣpn*[ ]	random letter shapes?
(25) *ddn.dḥld*[ ]	random letter shapes?

(26) *ddwaṯd*[ ]	random letter shapes?
(*Column III*)	
(19) *prṯ*	PRṮ (PN?)
(20) *pṯ*	PṮ (PN?)
(*Column IV*)	
(21) *tḥm* +palimpsest	"Message
(22) *ḏ mn* +palimpsest	of whomever
(23) *l iṯtl*	to ʾIṯtēlu"

No actual Ugaritic tablet has such a confusing arrangement of lines and columns. I would suggest that it was not meant to actually to be a coherent whole but was merely a variety of exercises. Still, it is possible to offer a reading that makes some sense out of the scribal practice. Line 18 begins with the well-known term *ʿbd*, "servant," which is frequently found in letters and is one of the more common Ugaritic words. Line 19 might be related to the root *qr*, meaning "sounds" or "to hiss"; I speculate that this may be an allusion to the random letters to follow. The student separated the exercise with a long horizontal line across the entire tablet. Such dividing lines are often used in letters to separate the introduction from the body. Here, the body of the message (lines 24–26) seems to be merely practicing Ugaritic penmanship. One can compare the graffiti on the two Kuntillet ʿAjrud pithoi where a scribe practices writing *yod* over and over again. Perhaps lines 24–26 here are referred to by the "servants of sound" (*ʿbd qrq*, lines 17–18)—that is, the practice of the alphabetic cuneiform letters. Column III (lines 19–20) is just as unclear as the preceding sections. Perhaps it is more sign practice or perhaps these are personal names. Column IV (lines 21–23) is a bit clearer. It unmistakably echoes the beginning of the practice letter starting with *tḥm*, "message of," and the same lexemes of sender and receiver; now, however, the sender and the recipient are reversed. I suggest reading lines 21–23 as the conclusion of the tablet because it intentionally reverses the beginning of the practice letter; that is, the "Message of ʾIṯtēlu to whomever" (lines 1–2) becomes "the message of whomever to Iṯtēlu" (lines 21–23). The scribal exercise of letter writing here was not some rote form; rather the form became the basis for creative practice by the student.

One of the best examples of a practice letter exercise and a palimpsest is *KTU* 5.33 (*RS* 94.2273), which was mentioned in chapter 2 because it is written in Akkadian on one side and Ugaritic on the other. Here, we will take a closer look at the Ugaritic practice, as seen in Figure 5.2.[11]

Figure 5.2 A practice letter with palimpsest. Photograph courtesy of Projet PhoTEO, Mission de Ras Shamra. Copy courtesy of Dennis Pardee.

1)	*[tḥ]m.abny ql[t]*	Message of Abniya: I fall
2)	*[l.]ur{b}ṯṯb.l pʿn*	before Urteṯuba, before
3)	⌜*a*⌝*ḫy.hllm.* + *signs*	my brother, indeed,
4)	*mrḥqtm* + *signs*	from afar
5)	*qlt.šbʿd* + *signs*	I fall, seven times
6)	*ṯmnid qlt* + *signs*	even eight times, I fall.
7)	*ilm.tǵrk.tš[lmk]*	may the gods guard you, may they keep you[well.]
8)		*palimpsest* letters

This is only the beginning of a letter, the formal introduction. It includes the formal elements of Near Eastern letters: an address formula ("Message of Abniya"), a prostration formula ("I fall down before Urteṯuba"), and the divine blessing ("May the gods guard you"), and omits the greeting formula. One of the more notable aspects of the tablet is the remnants of an earlier exercise that may be seen clearly at the end of lines 3–6, on the bottom (i.e., line 8), and even in between letters (especially between lines 6 and 7). There is also an example of a student error in line 2, where the student incorrectly wrote *b*, then overstruck it with the correct letter, *t*. Sometimes Ugaritic letters included a greeting formula asking, "Are you well?," which also occasionally appear in ancient Hebrew letters.[12] In sum, this is another typical practice letter.

Variations were also illustrated in practice letters in Ugaritic, as we see in *KTU* 5.33 (= *RS* 94.2273). This letter illustrates a lack of rigid uniformity: "[Mess]age of Abniya. [I] fall before Urteṯub, before the feet of my brother. Here from afar I fall. Seven times, even eight times I fall. May the gods guard and keep you well." The scribe actually seems to have made an error by skipping the addressee part—instead of saying "Message of Abniya to Urteṯub," the student skips into a series of deference statements with the repetition of "I fall."[13] Such deference statements are used especially in letters to rulers and royalty by those whose status is decidedly lower. Such deference statements are particularly well known from the El-Amarna correspondence, which illustrates the borrowing of the cuneiform tradition into Ugaritic. This practice introduction to a letter seems focused on that aspect of the model letter, but it also illustrates the necessary flexibility in the student exercises. Taken together with the first example, these two letters illustrate different possible pieces to the introduction of a letter.[14] Just as we shall see in the exemplars from Kuntillet ʿAjrud, there was flexibility because the exact introduction of a letter depended on the context. Letters could be formal or informal, written from an inferior to a superior or vice versa, or written between two peers.

Model Letters in School Exercises from Israel

Several aspects of the Ugaritic practice letters find striking parallels in the scribal exercises from Kuntillet ʿAjrud. Perhaps the first and most important observation is that these texts show evidence of being palimpsests. Usually palimpsests are identified and discussed as part of more expensive writing materials, like parchment or papyrus. Often the earlier text can be of particular interest because it is a completely different text (sometimes even written in a different language or writing system). Furthermore these earlier texts may have been written decades or even centuries before the later text. Here, however, the previous text is more like a poorly erased blackboard or whiteboard. It is difficult to make sense of the earlier text, but it seems it was all part of the day's work of a student doing excises.

The three practice letters (3.1, 3.6, and 3.9) from Kuntillet ʿAjrud illustrate aspects of the three formulaic parts of the letter genre in Hebrew: the address, the greeting, and the blessing. Two letters have versions of an introductory formula, but they represent two different types of letters, reflecting the different relationships between sender and addressee. A third practice letter is fragmentary with only the blessing from the letter remaining. The introductory formulas on the first two read as follows:[15]

Inscription 3.1: Superior to Inferior
1) *ʾmr.ʾ[šyw.]hm[l]k.ʾmr.lyhl⌜y⌝.wlywʿśh.wl[. . .]brkt.ʾtkm.*
2) *lyhwh.šmrn.wʾšrth*

"Message of A[šyaw,] the k[in]g: "Say to Yaheli and to Yoʿasah and to [PN]. I have blessed you by Yahweh of Samaria and to his *asherah*."

Inscription 3.6: Inferior to Superior

1) *ʾmr*
2) *ʾmrywʾ*
3) *mr l.ʾdn⸢y⸣*
4) *hšlm.ʾt*
5) *brktk.ly*
6) *hwh tmn*
7) *wlʾšrth.yb*
8) *rk wyšmrk*
9) *wyhy ʿm.ʾdn*
10) *y*

"Message of Amaryaw, say to my lord: 'Are you well? I have blessed you by Yahweh of Teman and his *ʾasherah*. May he bless you and may he keep you, and may he be with my lord.' "

Inscription 3.1 reflects a shorter practice exercise that is more typical of actual letters. Letters from those of superior or equal status did not require all the embellishments of a letter sent from an inferior to a superior. To be sure, the most important part of a practice letter was the introductory formula since this is the only part of the formula that was invariably utilized, but there was still quite a bit of flexibility in the formulas that were used. For example, "Yahweh of Samaria" (in 3.1) might have been more appropriate in a letter from an Israelite king, whereas "Yahweh of Teman" (in 3.6) would be appropriate for a letter emanating from the military outpost at Kuntillet ʿAjrud. In general, however, the introductions show an economy of expression. They are usually quite abbreviated, especially in everyday correspondence, and most actual letters known from the epigraphic corpus are quite mundane, with abbreviated introductions.

Inscription 3.6 is a fuller presentation of a possible introductory formula because it was addressed to a superior, as indicated by "my lord." In contrast, 3.1 is a more concise formula that was apparently from a superior to an inferior. The personal name in this letter is probably modeled after Joash, who was likely the contemporary Israelite king, hence "Ashyaw, the king"; the orthographic difference between *ʾšyw*, "ʾAshyaw," and biblical *ywʾš*, "Joash," simply reflects the difference of the divine theophoric Yahweh (in this case, "-yaw" or "Jo-") as either a prefix or a suffix that we see with other names (e.g., Ahaziah [2 Kgs 8:24] or Jehoahaz [2 Chr 21:17]; Jehoiachin [2 Kgs 24:6] or Jeconiah [Jer 24:1]).

The reconstruction of a fictive king as an addressee in a practice letter is further confirmed by an example from the Amarna scholarly tablets—that is, the cuneiform student exercises from the New Kingdom–era school. There are three fragmentary practice letters among the Amarna scholarly tablets (EA 342–44).[16] EA 333–44 have the expression *ana* LUGAL "to the king." Although they are quite fragmentary, they seem to be practicing writing letters to and from a king. The significance of these particular examples goes further. They are geographically and temporally proximate to the Late Bronze–Iron Age transition of the scribal curriculum. In this respect, these Amarna school tablets illustrate how cuneiform scribal culture may have been adapted for later alphabetic traditions. It is not hard to imagine that the multilingual scribal school at Amarna adapted the cuneiform curriculum in ways not much different from the scribes during the Late Bronze–Iron I transition in the southern Levant.

The formal language of the Kuntillet ʿAjrud letters finds close parallels in biblical literature. For example, the use of the root *ʾmr*, "to say, speak," found in 2Kgs 22:15, the words of the prophetess Huldah, are couched in letter format: "And (Huldah) said to them: 'Thus says [*ʾmr*] Yahweh, the God of Israel: Say to [*ʾmr l-*] the man who sent you to me . . .'" Here we see both the sender and the addressee identified as we have in the practice letters. And the identification is made with the repeated *ʾmr* to reference both the speaker and the addressee—which we may generalize as "Thus *says* Sender" and "*Say* to Addressee."

The prominence of the root *ʾmr*, "to speak," in practice letters should alert us to the well-known prophetic introductory phrase "Thus says/said the LORD (*kh ʾmr YHWH*)." The phrase has its specific origins in the letter genre that begins, *ʾmr* PN, which is often translated as "Message of the Sender." The formula "Thus says YHWH" is thus directly related to the *Sitz im Leben* of Near Eastern messengers. Moreover, the textualization of the writing prophets should likewise be associated with the textualization of the Near Eastern messenger scene.[17]

There is a third example of a practice letter, KA 3.9, but the opening address is missing in this fragmentary text. This letter is at the top of Pithos B (see Figure 2.2). With the formal opening missing, scholars have not generally recognized that this is also a practice letter and usually interpret it as a dedicatory inscription. But the dedication is typical of that used in letters, and, given the overall context of inscriptions on the pithos, the introductory formulae of a letter is a straightforward and contextually supported reconstruction. The inscription consists of three lines written on the very top of Pithos B.[18]

Transcription and Translation

1) [*ʾmr* PN^1 *ʾmr l*PN^2 *brktk*]*lyhwh.ht*⌜*m*⌝*n wlʾšrth.*

2) [———]*kl ʾšr yšʾl mʾš ḥnn hʾ wʾm pth wntn lh yhw~*

3) *klbbh*

1) [Message of PN^1, say to PN^2: I bless you]by Yahweh of the Teman and by his *Asherah*.[19]
2) [And now,] whatever he asks from a man, he will give generously. And if he petitions, then Yahwe(h) will give to him
3) according to his heart.

The blessing formula is well known as part of the formal introductions to letters, but they were adapted for other contexts as well. This explains why scholars have not heretofore recognized this as a practice letter.[20] But this must be understood as some sort of scribal exercise. Given this context, the missing beginning would most likely be part of a practice letter. The obscured space is about seventeen to twenty letters, which gives room for the reconstruction for a letter introduction according to the pattern that we have in 3.1 and 3.6. The second part (lines 2–3) utilizes a proverbial saying (discussed in chapter 6) as the body of the letter.

Admittedly, the fragmentary nature of KA 3.9 has fostered some scholarly debate about its interpretation and reconstruction. Many scholars, for example, see the first line as part of a dedicatory inscription. However, this fails to account for the larger context on the pithos that is entirely school exercises. The two most telling physically related inscriptions are to the top left, where a student was practicing writing the letter *yod*, and to the right side, where there is a complete letter template separated by a school line from a series of abecedaries (see Figure 2.2). The overall picture cannot be any clearer. Ergo, one should expect KA 3.9 to also be some sort of student exercise.

Another sort of general comparative context will also support the student exercise interpretation. The combination of the letter genre with another student exercise is paralleled in one Ugaritic school text, *KTU* 5.9. This parallel text was discussed above (see Figure 5.1), but it is worth recalling it here since it also incorporates a different type of student exercise into a practice letter. Indeed the verso of *KTU* 5.9 continues with lexical and writing exercises, so it actually mixes a variety of types of student practice into one tablet. The main point to this parallel is simply that the body of a practice letter can provide the opportunity for a student to practice other traditional parts of student exercises. Many exercises in writing letters may just include the first part, that is, the formal introductory elements. These are rigid and repeatable. The content of a letter, however, must be completely flexible. This opens up the possibility for playful student exercise in *KTU* 5.9 as well as the pious proverbial saying in the Kuntillet ʿAjrud example. (The saying will be discussed further in chapter 6.) In the playful and practical adaptations of student exercises, we begin to witness scribal creativity that would be a foundation for authoring literature.

The introductions to such model letters tend to be more complete than in actual letters. In our Hebrew exemplars, the most complete practice letter is exemplified by KA 3.6 on Pithos B.[21] Two aspects of the Ugaritic practice letter are especially notablein comparison. First, the triple invocation of the gods' protection is unusual; in actual Ugaritic letters, there is never more than one or two of these phrases, typically "may the gods of Ugarit keep you well" (Ugaritic, *šlm*; cp. Hebrew, שלם). But students probably learned all the possible permutations of such formulas. Likewise, the time period expressed in the Ugaritic example is pure scribal hyperbole, with three different and expanding time periods. Again, actual letters evince more economy, whereas practice exercises can reflect nice scribal flourishes as well as the combination of different types of school texts.

Many of the Arad letters skip most of the elements of the introduction except an abbreviated address formula (e.g., *ʾl ʾlšb*, "To Eliashib"; see Arad letters 1–11; or, *ʾl ʾdny ʾlšb*, "To my lord, Eliashib"; Arad 18:1–2).[22] A more complete address formula with a greeting is found in Arad 16: *ʾḥk ḥnnyhw šlḥ lšlm ʾlšb wlšlm bytk*, "Your brother, Hananiah, sends greetings to Eliashib and greetings to your house." The divine blessing is one of the standard parts of a form letter that is preserved in several letters (e.g., *brktk lyhwh*, "I bless you to Yahweh"; Arad 16:2–3, 21:2, 40:3). An alternative type of divine blessing is found in most of the Lachish letters but not in the Arad correspondence: "May Yahweh cause you to hear a report of peace (or a good report)" (see Lachish 2:1–2, 3:2–3; 4:1–2; 5:1–2; 8:1–2; 9:1–2).[23]

In general, the letters found at the major Judean city of Lachish have more complete, formal introductions than the abbreviated introductions found in the remote fortress of Arad. However, even the most complete introductions in Hebrew letters do not include the prostration formula; they are not included in any Hebrew letters preserved in the epigraphic record, not even in the fuller practice letters from Kuntillet ʿAjrud. To be sure, the idea of self-deprecation is evident in the content of some letters. For example, a couple Lachish letters ask, "Who is your servant, (but) a dog?" (see Lachish 2:3–4, 5:3–4). Such self-deprecation is known, for example, in the Amarna letters (e.g., EA 71:16; EA 201:15; 379:18). In general, however, the type of prostration formulae known in the Amarna letters or in Ugaritic letters is not preserved any Hebrew letters. The formal parts of the introductions in Hebrew letters were restricted to the address formula, a greeting formula, and the divine blessing.

Student exercises indicate that there was no rigid form to actual letters, even though there are a number of typical elements. Students needed to learn the various permutations of the introduction as well as the transition. In Hebrew letters, typical elements begin an introduction (*praescriptio*) that includes an address formula. The introduction sometimes includes a greeting formula or a divine benediction.[24] The introduction is then followed by a formal transition to the body of the letter, "and now (*wʿt*)." The body of the letter, of course, was entirely variable. There was apparently no rigid form to the model letter that students practiced. In this respect, we should not be surprised by the differences between the two practice letters from Kuntillet ʿAjrud.

Letter Writing Exercises and Biblical Literature

The content within ancient Hebrew letters also illustrates the central role of letters and messengers in ancient Israel. Several mention letters and messengers as a subject matter discussed within the letter (see Arad 16, 24, 40; Lachish 3, 5, 6, 7, 16, 18). Lachish Ostracon 3 nicely illustrates an interaction with multiple letters:

> [Introduction] Your servant Hoshaiah sends (*šlḥ*) to report (*ngd*) to my lord Yaush: May Yahweh cause my lord to hear a good report.
>
> [Body] And now (*wʿt*), please explain to your servant the meaning of the letter (*spr*) that you sent (*šlḥ*) to your servant yesterday. For your servant has been sick at heart ever since you sent (*šlḥ*) it to your servant. And, because my lord said, "Don't you know how to read a letter (*spr*)?" As Yahweh lives, no one has ever tried to read me a letter (*spr*)! And also, any letter (*spr*) comes to me, I can read it. And moreover, I can recount everything in it.
>
> And, as for your servant, it has been reported (*ngd*), saying (*lʾmr*), "The Commander of the Army Koniah son of Elnatan has moved south in order to enter Egypt." He has sent (*šlḥ*) (messengers) to fetch Hodaviah son of Ahiah and his men from here.
>
> And, as for the letter (*spr*) of Tobiah, servant of the king, which came to Shallum son of Yadaʿ, from the prophet saying (*lʾmr*), "Beware," your servant has sent (*šlḥ*) it to my lord.

The body of the letter begins with a direct response by a junior officer to a superior officer questioning whether he was able to read or needed a scribe to help with the letter. The scribe's claim to be able to recite the content of the letter also recalls the etiological origins of letter writing—that is, as an aid to memory in the oral delivery of messages. In the next paragraph, the junior officer relates a communiqué about the commander of the army traveling to Egypt. He apparently is sending letters (*šlḥ*) to fetch some other personnel to his location. Finally, in the last paragraph, he relays a message from an unnamed prophet written in a letter from a royal servant named Tobiah to Shallum. Thus, in addition to his own correspondence, he is relaying the contents of two other, separate correspondences. This is not unusual. Another letter, Lachish 6, mentions other letters passed along to him from the king and military officers that apparently contained some disconcerting news, although the exact content is not relayed. Judging from Lachish 4, we may assume that it was bad news concerning the (impending?) Babylonian invasion of Judah. These examples serve to underscore how significant the writing of letters had become in Judean bureaucracy at all levels.

The terminology utilized in ancient Hebrew letters would also be used in biblical narratives. These terms include *l'mr*, "saying"; *spr*, "letter"; *ngd*, "to report";[25] *šlḥ*, "to send"; and *šlm*, "welfare" (as illustrated in Lachish 3 above). These are some of the most common terms and expressions in the Hebrew Bible. One of the more intriguing expressions in the Hebrew Bible, which is difficult to translate, is the infinitive verbal form *l'mr*, which is sometimes rigidly translated as "saying," but is really the introduction of a direct quote. The phrase occurs about nine hundred times in the Hebrew Bible. Two of the more interesting examples of this expression in biblical literature underscore its close association with the letter genre. In 2Kgs 5:6, a messenger from the king of Aram "brought the letter from the king of Israel, saying (*l'mr*): 'And now (*w'th*) . . .'" And according to 2Kgs 10:1–2, "Jehu wrote letters and sent them to Samaria, to the rulers of Jezreel, to the elders, and to the guardians of the sons of Ahab, saying (*l'mr*): 'And now (*w'th*) . . .'" Both of these examples are striking because they incorporate—without adaptation—the standard transitional expression that is found in the Hebrew epigraphic corpus, "and now" (*w't*); this directly connects the use of *l'mr*, "saying," with the letter genre (see further discussion later).[26] In other words, although *l'mr* often seems to just repeat the idea of the speech act already expressed in the narrative framing, it is actually the formal introduction to direct speech drawn out of the *Sitz im Leben* of messenger formulas and the letter genre.

In the translations of the Hebrew Bible, *l'mr* often seems untranslatable. It seems like a throwaway word. Very "literal" Bible translations (that is, translations using "formal equivalence") such as the old King James Version or the New American Standard Bible would simply translate *l'mr* as "saying." Many more recent Bible translations, such as the New Revised Standard Version, moved toward a "dynamic equivalence" (or "functional equivalence") translation theory, which has led them to leave *l'mr* untranslated, marking it only by the use of quotation marks. In either approach, the close association between *l'mr* and the textualized messenger scene should be emphasized.

The background of *l'mr*, "saying," in the letter genre is further underscored by the two practice letters from Kuntillet ʿAjrud. These letters use the same verbal root in the prefatory introduction, "Speech (*'mr*) of PN." The introduction to the letter is not direct speech; rather it introduces the direct "speech," /*'ōmer*/ by the sender of the letter. The connection is further developed in the use of the expression "thus *says* PN" (*kh 'mr* PN) in the messenger formula. This is well known in the expression "thus says Yahweh," but it can be used more generally as in "thus says Pharaoh" (Exod 5:10), "thus says Balak" (Num 22:16), or "thus says Ben-Hadad" (1Kgs 20:5). These latter examples are the origin of what becomes the more frequently used expression in the Bible, "Thus says YHWH." Other epigraphic Hebrew letters actually use the term *l'mr* within the letter to introduce direct quotes (e.g., Lachish 3, 6).

The messenger formula also reveals how deeply rooted the letter genre was in oral culture. The sending of messages with messengers did not require actual written letters. But with the advent and spread of writing, the letter became a physical witness in the oral performance by a messenger. The letter genre finds a variety of expressions in biblical literature. The most well-known of these is prophetic speech—"Thus says YHWH"—which borrows directly from the genre and *Sitz im Leben* of letter writing. The role of the messenger and written letters is also a trope in biblical storytelling. But the influence of practicing to write letters can also be quite prosaic.

The expression, *wʿt(h),*[27] "and now," was an important device that functioned as a new paragraph marker and was learned by ancient scribes when practicing the writing of model letters.[28] The use of *wʿt(h)* is especially important in ancient Hebrew because the writing system did not have many auxiliary markers to mark semantic functions in the way we have in modern languages (e.g., commas, periods, spaces, line breaks, tabs, paragraphs, etc.). The only regularly used auxiliary marker in epigraphic Hebrew was a dot "•" that was often used as a word divider. By the time of the Dead Sea Scrolls, the "•" was replaced by the space.[29] In addition, paragraphing and larger breaks using empty space were beginning to be seen in the Scroll manuscripts. However, there is little evidence that such conventions were used in epigraphic Hebrew. For this reason, the use of *wʿt(h)* as a paragraph marker is especially critical in the early development of Hebrew writing.

Paragraph dividers in letter writing serve a universal semantic function. In the Amarna letters and Ugarit, auxiliary scribal markers served as a functional equivalent to the lexical *wʿt(h),* "and now." Both the Amarna letters and Ugaritic regularly employed a horizontal line in a variety of ways to distinguish logical semantic units in texts, and this included marking off sections (or "paragraphs") within letters.[30] Alphabetic Ugaritic letters often utilized a single horizontal line to separate the *praescriptio* (that is, the address and the greeting) from the body of a letter. Frequently, Ugaritic letters separated both elements of the *praescriptio* with a line. Occasionally, they omitted the line, so it is not entirely consistent. A couple examples can illustrate the practice:

KTU 2:10 (RS 4.475)
(1) *tḥm . ỉwrḏr* (2) *l . plsy* (3) *rgm*

---

(4) *yšlm . lk*

---

(5) *l . trǵds* (6) *w . l . klby* (7) *šmʿt . ḫ̮tî* (8) *nḫ̮tů. ht . . .*

(1–3) Message of Iwriḏarri: To Pilsiya, say:

(4) "May it be well with you.

(5–8) Regarding Tarǵudassi and Kalbiya, I have heard that they have suffered defeat"

KTU 2:16 (RS 15.008)

(1) *tḥm .* ⌜*t*⌝*lm[y]*⌜*n*⌝ (2) *l ṯryl . ůmy* (3) *rgm*

---

(4) *yšlm . lk . îly* (5) *ůgrt . tǵrk* (6) *tšlmk . ůmy* (7) *tdʿ . ky . ʿrbt* (8) *l pn . špš* (9) *w pn . špš . nr* (10) *by . mîd . . .*

(1–3) Message of Talmiyāni: To Ṯarriyelli, my mother, say:

(4–10) "May it be well with you. May the gods of Ugarit guard you, may they keep you well. My mother, you must know that I have entered before the Sun and (that) the face of the Sun has shone upon me."

While the horizontal line works as an auxiliary scribal device marking sections, Ugaritic did not have a lexical equivalent to *wʿt(h)* that was employed regularly.

The use of *wʿt* (always with the shorter spelling) as a sectional divider in Epigraphic Hebrew letters is quite consistent and impressive. It either occurs or can be restored from context in seventeen of the Arad letters (1:2, 2:1, 3:1, 5:1–2, 6:1, 7:1–2, 8:1, 9:1, 10:1, 11:2, 14:1, 16:3, 17:1, 18:3, 21:3, 40:4); it appears five times in the Lachish letters (2:3, 3:4, 4:1–2, 5:2–3, 9:3); and it also appears once in a Wadi Murabbaʿat papyrus.[31] Other Iron Age Canaanite letters use *wʿt* as well; for example, it is found in an Edomite letter from Horvat ʿUza and an Ammonite letter from Tell El-Mazār.[32] In all of these cases, *wʿt* served as a transitional particle denoting the shift from the *praescriptio* (that is, the formal address and greeting) to the body of the letter. From a formal point of view, *wʿt* marks the progression from the scribe announcing the sender (and sometimes a formal stereotyped greeting) to the actual content of the message. This makes explicit the shift in speaker from the scribe himself to the scribe as mouthpiece of the sender. The paragraph marker *wʿt* realigns the focus from the metapragmatic structure of the letter to the actual letter itself.[33] A few examples will illustrate both the variety and the consistency of its usage in inscriptions:

1) Arad 1:1 *ʾl.ʾlyšb.w*
   1:2 *ʿt.ntn. lktym*
   "To Elyashib: And now, give to the Kittim"
2) Arad 16:1 *ʾḥk.ḥnnyhw.šlḥ lšl*
   16:2 *m.ʾlyšb.wlšlm bytk br*

16:3 *ktk lyhwh.wʿt kṣʾty*
"Your brother, Hananiah, sends for the welfare of Elyashib and for the welfare of your house. I bless you by Yahweh. And now, when I left"

3) Mura. 1:1 *ʾmr.*[——]*yhw.lk*
1:2 *wʿt.ʾl.tšmʿ lk*[l] *dbr. ʾšr ydbr.ʾlyk*
"Message of [XXX]yahu to you: And now, do not listen to every word that he says to you"

4) Lachish 3:1 *ʿbdk.hwšʿyhw šlḥ.l*
3:2 *hgd lʾdny yʾwš.yšmʿ*
3:3 *yhwh ʾt ʾdny šmʿt šlm*
3:4 *wšmʿt ṭb*[.]*wʿt.hpqḥ*
"Your servant, Hoshayahu, sends to tell my lord Yaush: May Yahweh cause my lord to hear a report of peace and a good report. And now, please open . . ."

5) H. ʿUza 1:1 *ʾmr.lmlk.ʾmr.lblbl*
1:2 *hšlm.ʾt.whbrktk*
1:3 *lqws.wʿt.tn.ʾt.hʾkl*
"(Thus) says Lumalak, say to Balbal: Are you well? I bless you by Qaus. And now, give the food"

The use of *wʿt* is as a transition marker so consistent in Iron Age inscriptions that one must assume it was a device scribes learned to use in writing letters.

The paragraph marker was also used in a variety of Aramaic dialects as well. Beginning with biblical Aramaic, the Book of Ezra uses *wkʿnt, wkʿt,* and *wkʿn*—which may all be translated "and now"—as opening transitional particles in its letters (4:11, 17; 5:17; 7:12). The Aramaic Hermopolis Papyri frequently employ *wkʿt* (e.g., 1:3, 2:4, 4:4, 5:2, 6:3, 10:2), and we also find *wkʿn, kʿn, kʿnt,* and *wkʿt* in the Elephantine papyri.[34] These are close functional parallels to the use of *wʿt* in Epigraphic Hebrew. For example, in Ezra 4:11–12 we read: "This is a copy of the letter that they sent: 'To King Artaxerxes: Your servants, the people of the province Beyond the River, send greeting': 'And now (*wkʿnt*), may it be known.'" There is some orthographic variation in the transitional particle here as well as in other Aramaic inscriptions (*wkʿt, wkʿn, kʿnt,* and *kʿn*), and the length of the *praescriptio* can vary from elaborate to minimalist. Yet functionally it follows the pattern that we know from Iron Age inscriptions. However, this usage disappears in later Hebrew and Aramaic.[35] We may surmise then that the use of *wʿt* and semantic cognates continued to be taught in the scribal curriculum only until the demise of the Persian Empire. Moreover, it shows that the use of *wʿth* in biblical literature was closely tied to scribal learning. When the scribal curriculum changed, the expression *wʿth* disappeared with it.

So how did this rudimentary element of letters impact biblical literature? The expression *wʿth* (always with the full spelling) is remarkably common in biblical Hebrew, appearing 273 times. In other words, more than half of the 435 occurrences in biblical literature of the word *ʿth* (עתה, "now") are with the conjunctive particle *waw*, thereby underscoring its predominant usage as a transitional expression.[36] This is unusual. The word *ʿth*, "now," should be a common enough word, but the even more frequent use of *wʿth* is noteworthy. This frequent construction reflects the basic scribal education where the expression *wʿth* was taught to all young scribes as part of the rubrics of letter writing. The usefulness of *wʿth* as a transition particle in letters was then adapted in a variety of contexts in biblical literature.

The use of *wʿth* diminishes and finally disappears in postbiblical Hebrew. The expression *wʿth* continued to be used in Qumran Hebrew, although some of its uses are curious. For example, *wʿth* is the first word of the Damascus Document from the medieval manuscript from Cairo Geniza (CD), which certainly would not fit into its use as a transitional particle. H. A. Bongers observed that it never appears as an introduction to direct speech.[37] For this reason, Bongers was suspicious of this opening of CD, pointing out that it never appears as an introduction to direct speech. And it turns out that his suspicions were well founded. When the fragments of this manuscript from Qumran caves were published, 4Q266 indicated that the text originally had a prologue. Thus *wʿth* actually did serve as a transitional particle from the prologue into the body of the Damascus Document. In general, Qumran usage of *wʿth* is biblicizing. In the Mishnah, it essentially disappears, appearing only once when it is quoting Gen 20:7 (mBabaQ 8:7). Given that Rabbinic Hebrew is generally considered a textualization of a vernacular dialect, this is a noteworthy development.

The use of the expression *wʿth* within oral discourse is complicated by its role in the scribal rubric. The oral aspects of the expression are evident in biblical literature. For example, *wʿth* is sometimes followed by an imperative of *šmʿ*, "hear, listen" (e.g., Gen 27:8, 43; Deut 4:1; 1Sam 8:9, 15:1, 26:19, 28:22), and the Dead Sea Scrolls also feature this construction (e.g., CD 1:1, 2:2, 2:14, 4Q185, 4Q525). This use of *wʿth* with an imperative of *šmʿ*, "hear, listen," can be taken as evidence of its use as a marker in oral discourse. For example, Dennis Pardee suggests, "Such a usage arose from standard speech wherein *wʿt* marks the point of transition between a preamble of any kind (historical, circumstantial, causal) and the point of a given statement."[38] This suggestion is substantiated by a survey of its use in biblical literature. Indeed all twenty-six occurrences of *wʿth* in the Book of Genesis appear within direct speech. For example, in Gen 3:22 we read (using the NRSV translation for illustrative purposes), "Then the LORD God said, 'See, the man has become like one of us, knowing good and evil; *and now* (*wʿth*), he might reach out his hand and take also from the tree of life.' "

In one respect, these examples precisely represent the use of *wʿth* in the context of a letter. It transitions the introduction to the body of the model letter as follows: "Message/Speech of the Sender to the Recipient: May you be blessed by YHWH. How is your well-being? *And now*, [Body of the Message]." Thus, *wʿt(h)* was formally embedded in direct speech, and it was also learned as a textual formula. If the origin of the expression was as a regular feature of oral discourse, then we would expect it to continue in vernacular Hebrew, especially Rabbinic Hebrew. But it did not. It disappears in Rabbinic Hebrew. On the other hand, if a primary role of *wʿt(h)* was as a scribal marker for a semantic transition, that is, as a formal scribal device taught to scribes as a marker of a new section within a messenger's speech, then the disappearance in later Hebrew can be explained with a change in scribal education. In this respect, the disuse of *wʿth* and its Aramaic cognates in letter writing parallels the decline of the Aramaic chancellery of the Achaemenid Empire. In other words, the regular use of *wʿt(h)* was closely tied with scribal education in ancient Israel.

The relationship between the use of *wʿt(h)* in Epigraphic Hebrew and in Standard Biblical Hebrew warrants some reflection. To wit, how is its regular usage as a transitional particle, essentially a paragraph divider, reflected in biblical literature? It is quite regularly used in biblical speeches as a transitional marker in the speech. In addition to marking transitions in oral discourse, there are instances that recall its more formal use in letter writing. For example, we read in 1Sam 15:1, "Samuel said to Saul, 'YHWH sent me to anoint you king over his people Israel; and now (*wʿth*), listen to the words of YHWH.'" Here the function of *wʿth* is both transitional and metapragmatic, as in Epigraphic Hebrew. Likewise, the use of *wʿth* followed by the imperative *šmʿ*, "hear," seems to harken back to the messenger formula utilized in letters.[39] For example, the narrator subtly employs features of a formal messenger scene in 1Sam 28:21–22, "The woman came to Saul, and when she saw that he was terrified, she said to him, 'Your maidservant has listened to you; I have taken my life in my hand, and have listened to what you have said to me. And now, you also listen (*wʿth šmʿ-nʾ*) to your maidservant: let me set a morsel of bread before you.'" The role of *wʿth* in letters is most explicit in 2Kgs 5:6, "He brought the letter (*hspr*) to the king of Israel, which read (*lʾmr*): 'And now (*wʿth*), when this letter reaches you, know that I have sent to you my servant Naʿaman that you may cure him of his leprosy.'" Similarly, we read in 2Kgs 10:1–2, "So Jehu wrote letters and sent them to Samaria, to the rulers of Jezreel, to the elders, and to the guardians of the sons of Ahab, which read (*lʾmr*): 'And now (*wʿth*), your master's sons are with you.'" In these last two examples, the use of *wʿth* most closely reminds us of Epigraphic Hebrew with regard to their context of written letters; it is worth noting that *wʿth* actually follows *lʾmr*, which is traditionally translated "saying" but is functionally a metapragmatic marker of a direct quotation translated in these contexts as "which read." These examples indicate an awareness and probably the influence of the metapragmatic use of *wʿt* known from Epigraphic Hebrew letters. Since writing lacks many of the semiotic cues of speech, developing semiotic markers like the dot (•) as a word divider (i.e., a "space"), *lʾmr* as a quotation mark, and *wʿth* as a paragraph marker gave biblical authors the pragmatic tools needed to help readers understand the written word.

While the origin of *wʿt(h)* was probably as a marker in oral discourse, it was borrowed for formal use in the practice of writing letters—one of the main tasks of the scribal enterprise and one of the foundations of early scribal education. It was this formal use that in turn explains why *wʿt(h)* came to be used so commonly in biblical texts. It certainly was a textual device of great familiarity to the scribes of biblical literature, just as it was a regular feature in letters written in Epigraphic Hebrew.

From Letters and Messengers to Prophetic Speech

The most striking adaption of the letter genre in biblical literature is prophetic speech, although most scholars emphasize its roots in the *Sitz im Leben* of the messenger and messenger speech (e.g., Gen 32:4–14).[40] The messenger scene involved a sender, a messenger, a message, and an audience. These elements were all part of prophetic speech.

God sent (*šlḥ*) the prophet, his messenger, with the "word of God" (the message), to an audience—usually, the Judean people as a group. One of the titles that became associated with prophet is *malʾāḵ*, "messenger." In postexilic biblical literature, the term developed into a synonym for a prophet. The last book of the Hebrew canon is, in fact, the prophetic book of Malachi, literally "my messenger." The prophet Haggai was given the title "the messenger of God" (1:13); the Book of Chronicles concludes by referring to the prophets as divine messengers (2Chr 36:15); and Deutero-Isaiah refers to the prophets as "my messengers" (Isa 44:26). This adoption of the term *malʾāḵ*, "messenger," for the prophets reflected the fact that they were sent (*šlḥ*) by God; for example, in 2Sam 12:25, "YHWH sent (a message) by the hand of the prophet Nathan" (also see Judg 6:8; 2Kgs 17:13; Jer 14:14–15, 23:21, 25:4; etc.).

The prophetic message was the "word of YHWH"—a technical term in the Hebrew Bible that refers to a divine speech.[41] Thus we find the formal expression "the word of YHWH came to the prophet" repeated frequently (more than forty times) within the Hebrew Bible.[42] The meaning and form of the "word of YHWH" was transformed in the postexilic period.[43] Specifically, prophetic speech—"the word of YHWH"—was textualized and broadened. For example, it came to be equated with *Torah* as a written text (e.g., 2Chr 34:21; 35:6). The genre of the letter itself facilitated this shift from the oral message ("word of YHWH") to a physical manuscript ("scroll of the Torah").[44] But the shift from oral to written was easily facilitated by the shift in the messenger *Sitz im Leben* from an oral message to a messenger carrying written texts. In this respect, the transition from the early (oral) prophets like Nathan and Samuel to the so-called writing prophets of the Hebrew Bible was shaped by the development of the scribal curriculum itself—particularly in the development of letter writing. That is, the development of the letter genre and its linguistic formalities paved the path for the writing prophets.

Royal bureaucracy may have also played a role in the adaptation of the messenger formula. As the writing prophets became royal counselors in a bureaucracy that increasingly utilized writing, so also the prophets adapted the tools of that bureaucracy—in this case, letter writing. Some of the most famous prophets of the Hebrew Bible were, in fact, members of the royal administration. These include, for example, Nathan and Isaiah. Of course, it was not necessary to be a part of the royal administration for prophets to be acquainted with the protocols of sending messengers or writing letters. Prophets like Jeremiah were clearly outside of the official bureaucracy, yet the Book of Jeremiah shows evidence of adapting the protocols of letter writing in its presentation of the "word of YHWH" (e.g., Jer 29). This observation accords well with John Holladay's classic essay "Statecraft and the Prophets of Israel," where he argues that royal letters were one of the categories of Assyrian statecraft that had a particular influence on the rise of the writing prophets. Holladay asserts that the royal messenger was a figure and a form that transcended boundaries, and he describes "the spectacular rise to prominence of the royal herald as an essential instrument of imperial government."[45] As we recall from *Enmerkar and the Lord of Aratta*, writing was actually invented in order for a messenger to transmit the precise words of the sender.

The introductory language of the message is reflected in prophetic speech. The expression "Thus says YHWH (*kh ʾmr yhwh*)," is adapted from "the typical letter form."[46] Almost a century ago, Jack Lundblom pointed out that this formula had strong parallels in Near Eastern letter writing, and new discoveries have only further confirmed his observation.[47] "Thus says YHWH" is the most pervasive form of the formula, occurring 293 times in the Hebrew Bible. Sometimes a specific audience is addressed, as in the following examples:

2Kgs 19:32, "Thus says YHWH to the King of Assyria" (cp. Isa 37:33)
Isa 29:22, "Thus says YHWH to the House of Jacob"
Isa 18:4 "Thus says YHWH to me" (also Isa 31:4; Jer 17:19; 27:2)
Isa 45:1 "Thus says YHWH to his anointed, to Cyrus"
Jer 4:3 "Thus says YHWH to the people of Judah and the inhabitants of Jerusalem"
Jer 22:11 "Thus says YHWH to Shallum"

Jer 29:16 "Thus says YHWH to the king who sits on the throne of David"
Jer 29:31 "Thus says YHWH to Shemaiah of Nehelam"

These cases emphasize a different or special audience, which is then specified. A variety of comparisons can be drawn from the ancient Near East. For example, Neo-Assyrian letters begin typically with the introduction *abat* LUGAL *ana* ^{MD}PA.BÀD.PAB, "The word of the king to PN."[48] Usually, however, the biblical audience remains unnamed, and we assume that the prophetic speech was addressed corporately to the people of Israel/Judah. There are many examples of letters in the inscriptional corpus where the sender or the addressee is unmentioned; presumably, these are contexts where this information is known.

The letter genre lent authority to the prophetic word. As pointed out above, there are two formal forms to a letter: one from a superior to an inferior and one from an inferior/equal to a superior/equal. The prophetic messenger formula naturally followed the form of a letter from a superior to an inferior. The most common ancient Near Eastern example for this was letters written from a king. In Marc Brettler's study *God Is King: Understanding an Israelite Metaphor*, he discusses the many parallels wherein divine kingship draws directly upon human kingship.[49] His study mentions the use of messengers and the adaptation of the letter genre for prophetic speech, although it could be fruitfully extended by some of the observations discussed here. In the Hebrew Bible, God is like a human king in his use of messengers, and prophetic speech is essentially an adaptation of the royal letter genre.

One of the more striking examples of prophecy by letter is in Jeremiah 29. The chapter begins, "These are the words of a letter that the prophet Jeremiah sent." It also mentions the scribe who served as the messenger (verse 3): "The letter was sent through Elasah, son of Shaphan and Gemariah, son of Hilkiah." A second letter is then mentioned in Jer 29:24–32:[50]

> To Shemaiah the Nehelamite you shall say: Thus says YHWH of Hosts, the God of Israel: Because you sent letters in your own name to all the people in Jerusalem, to Zephaniah son of Maaseiah, the priest, and to the rest of the priests, saying, "YHWH appointed you priest instead of Jehoiada, the priest, to exercise authority in the House of YHWH over every madman who plays a prophet, to put him into the stocks and into the pillory. Now why have you not rebuked Jeremiah of Anathoth, who plays a prophet among you? For he has actually sent a message [in a letter] to us in Babylon, saying: 'It will be a long time. Build houses and live in them, plant gardens and enjoy their fruit.'" The priest Zephaniah read this letter in the hearing of Jeremiah, the prophet. And the word of YHWH came to Jeremiah: Send a message [in the form of a

> letter] to all the exiles, saying: "Thus says YHWH concerning Shemaiah the Nehelamite: Because Shemaiah prophesied to you, though I did not send him, and has led you to trust a lie, assuredly, thus says YHWH: 'I am going to punish Shemaiah the Nehelamite and his offspring. There shall be no man of his line dwelling among this people or seeing the good things I am going to do for My people'—declares YHWH —for he has urged disloyalty toward YHWH."

In these letters, the textualization of the prophetic word is actualized in the form of letters. Of course, the letter genre more generally became the genre of prophetic speech, but these examples give this textualization an explicit narrative framing. One might even suggest that the word of YHWH was commissioned as a text in the form of letters. In a sense, these examples offer justification for the textualization of the divine word, that is, for the genre of the writing prophets.

In sum, the student exercise of learning to write letters flexed its muscles in a number of ways in biblical literature. The sending of messages forms one of the backbones for biblical narratives. And the technical terminology of letter writing also influenced the shape of biblical literature. To begin with, the very structuring of texts using the expression "and now" as a paragraphing device depended on the school lessons of letter writing. Other devices, such as the use of "saying" (*lēmôr*) as a marker of direct speech was dependent on the sending and delivering of letters through messengers. Finally, the form of biblical prophecy was directly adapted from the *Sitz im Leben* of the sending and receiving of letters. The impact was wide-ranging and impressive.

6

Proverbial Sayings

Ancient elementary education advanced in its last stage to proverbs or sayings. These sayings were copied, memorized, and recited. This type of curriculum is well known in cuneiform as well as hieroglyphic writing. In cuneiform, we find both collections of proverbial sayings and individual sayings written on small, round tablets called "lentils". The small "lentil" tablets would only contain one proverb or saying, which highlights an important aspect of their role in curriculum; namely, the singular sayings were individually memorized. Their singularity, as opposed to collections, was a significant aspect of the genre. At the same time, while young scribes did memorize individual sayings, master scribes also edited proverbs into collections. Both types of proverbial sayings are evident in biblical literature, yet until now we have had almost no epigraphic evidence of any sayings among alphabetic inscriptions. Now, however, Kuntillet ʿAjrud gives us a single example of a wisdom saying. This little bit of evidence serves to confirm a genre of educational curriculum abundantly known from elsewhere in the ancient Near East. In these sayings and proverbs, scribal learning added an oral component that would be vital for education. Here, scribal education advanced past the mechanical aspects of learning forms and formulas to add content that would be used and adapted in a variety of contexts.

The best comparative evidence for proverbs and sayings comes from cuneiform curriculum. In Mesopotamia, students copied Sumerian proverbs and then learned the Akkadian translations and instruction orally. We do not find the same sort of multilingual texts for proverbs that we have with the lexical lists. Niek Veldhuis summarizes the situation as follows: "The last subject in the first phase of scribal education was proverbs. Most proverbs are short sayings, commonly arranged in thematically organized collections. Some of the animal proverbs are expanded into short stories, not unlike Aesop's fables."[1] He continues, "With the proverb collections the first phase of the education ended and evolved into the second phase: literary texts."[2] One of the best-known proverbs concerns the industrious ant (cp. Prov 6:6, 30:25), and long ago W. F. Albright pointed out striking parallels in the Amarna letters (e.g., EA 252:15–19), where this proverbial saying is incorporated into diplomatic correspondence.[3] Short wisdom stories are also incorporated into biblical narratives in several places, for example, in Jotham's fable of the trees (see Judg 9:7-20;). Jotham's fable actually derives from a list of trees—that is, the first themed cuneiform lexical list—which gets remade into a proverbial story. Scribes learned such proverbial sayings and stories in their curriculum, then adapted and incorporated them in their daily work.

Wisdom Sayings as Part of the Israelite Curriculum

The Kuntillet ʿAjrud inscriptions now have the first actual example of a wisdom saying used in a Hebrew scribal exercise. KA 3.9 includes a fragment from the sayings genre (lines 2–3) as part of a student exercise that begins with a practice letter. The whole inscription consists of three lines written on the very top of Pithos B. For the reader's convenience, I recall the text and translation here:

Transcription and Translation
1) [*ʾmr* PN^1 *ʾmr l*PN^2 *brktk*]*lyhwh.ht*⸢*m*⸣*n wlʾšrth.*
2) [——]*kl ʾšr yšʾl mʾš ḥnn hʾ wʾm pth wntn lh yhw~*
3) *klbbh*
1) [Message of PN^1, say to PN^2: I bless you]by Yahweh of the Teman and by his *ʾasherah.*
2) [——]whatever he asks from a man, he will give generously. And if he petitions, then Yahwe(h) will give to him
3) according to his desire.

The first line is the fragmentary introduction to a practice letter, and lines 2–3 are a pious proverbial saying. These formulas are well known as part of the formal introductions to letters, but they were adapted for other contexts as well. As reconstructed and discussed in the previous chapter, the beginning is probably part of a letter formula. The second part then utilizes a traditional proverbial saying as the body of the student exercise. It is a two-line saying, which actually touches on an issue that has been discussed in the study of the Book of Proverbs. Namely, scholars argue about the development of the form of individual proverbs, whether they were originally one line or two lines.[4] The saying in KA 3.9 is two lines, which is similar in form to the second major section of Proverbs (10:1–22:16). However, it seems unwise to make too much of this one example in this respect.

Indirect parallels to KA 3.9:2–3 can be found in a variety of places. For example, in an Aramaic inscription from eastern Turkey, the Samʾalian king Panamu wrote, *wmz ʾšʾl mn ʾlhy ytn ly*, "And whatever I shall ask from my god, may he give to me" (*KAI* 214:4), and also in the same inscription, *wmh ʾšʾl mn ʾlhy mt ytnw ly*, "and whatever I shall ask from my god, surely he shall give me" (lines 12–13). There are close linguistic parallels here with the terms *šʾl*, "to ask," and *ntn*, "to give" as well as with the syntactic structure. Scholars have also suggested a number of biblical correlates for Kuntillet ʿAjrud inscription, including:

Ps 20:5 *ytn lk klbbk*, "He shall give to you according to your desire"
Ps 37:21 *ṣdyq ḥwnn wnwtn*, "the righteous is generous and gives"
Ps 37:26 *kl hywm ḥwnn wmlwh*, "he is always generous and lends"
Ps 112:5 *ṭwb ʾyš ḥwnn wmlwh*, "all goes well with the man who lends generously"

We may imagine that such language would have been learned and memorized from school exercises, then applied in a variety of literary contexts. The example from Ps 112, which is an acrostic psalm, might itself have its origins as an adapted school exercise (see chapter 3).

Arguably, the most striking parallel to the Kuntillet ʿAjrud wisdom saying is Psalm 20:5. First, as a whole, Psalm 20 may have originally been a northern psalm as it appeals to the "God of Jacob." This, of course, is notable given the northern traits of the site of Kuntillet ʿAjrud and its inscriptions, although the psalm was edited and revised for the Judean psalter. It also has some salient motifs that point to its use in royal liturgy.[5] For example, the psalm ends with the enjoinder, "O Yahweh, give victory to the king!" (verse 10a [English, 9a]). This is also significant given the royal motifs in the iconography of the Kuntillet ʿAjrud drawings, as well as the apparent mention of a king in one of the letter templates (KA 3.1).

The combination of the letter genre with a different scribal exercise is paralleled in one school tablet from Ugarit, *KTU* 5.9. This example was already discussed in chapter 5 in the context of letters, particularly with regard to the introductory formulae. In this context, the body of Ugaritic practice letter becomes our focus. After the introduction, the letter (lines 7–16) presents a reciprocal saying ("a request, I request") followed by a humorous grammatical exercise (e.g., using the verbal forms of the word *ytn*, "to give"): "And may he give it to his brother, to his friend, an eternal friend. May you give, and give! And may you indeed give, and would you not give? Give a cup of wine, and I shall drink it." The content of an actual letter, unlike its introduction, must be completely flexible, depending as it does on the situation and circumstances. This opens up the possibility of attaching the playful student exercise that we find in *KTU* 5.9, or adding a pious proverbial saying as we find in the Kuntillet ʿAjrud example. What is relevant here is the way the genre of a letter allows the student to adapt the body of the letter to various types of practice.

The proverbial saying in KA 3.9 is more significant than first meets the eye. In this particular case, such sayings were learned by scribes and employed especially in diplomatic correspondence (although they could be adapted and used for various purposes). Once we recognize the pattern, we can adduce further parallels. For example, scholars have long noted certain correlations between the liturgical contexts in the biblical Psalms and the Amarna diplomatic corpus.[6] One example is Ps 21:3 (Eng. verse 2), [תַּאֲוַת לִבּוֹ נָתַתָּה לּוֹ

[וַאֲרֶשֶׁת שְׂפָתָיו בַּל־מָנַעְתָּ], "You give him the desire of his heart, and you do not withhold any request." This also has a certain general resonance with KA 3.9 but has an even more impressive parallel with a Babylonian letter to Pharaoh (EA 9:7–10):

> *ul-tu ab-bu-ú-a-a ù ab-bu-ka it-ti a-ḫa-mi[-iš] ṭa-bu-ta id-bu-bu šu-ul-ma-na ba-na-a a-na a-ḫa-mi-iš ul-te-bi-i-lu ù me-re-el-ta ba-ni-ta a-na a-ḫa-mi-iš ul ik-⌈lu-⌉ù*, "From the time my fathers and your fathers mutually spoke in friendship, they sent good gifts to one another, and they did not withhold any request."[7]

As Avi Shveka points out, this Babylonian letter uses diplomatic language typical of requests. It was stock terminology evoking a mutual relationship or "brotherhood." This particular parallel is notable because of the unusual word אֲרֶשֶׁת in Ps 21:3. The lexeme is a clear cognate to the Amarna term *mēreltu*, "request" (< Akkadian, *mēreštu*) from the root *erēšu*, "to desire, request."[8] However, while Ps 21:3 employs this Akkadian term, it is a *hapax legomenon* in Biblical Hebrew, and it never appears in later Hebrew.[9] The word appears to be an older loanword from Akkadian. Shveka also latches on to the last part of the expression, "they did not withhold any request," as a "common idiom" deriving from diplomatic correspondence. The reciprocity results in requests and desires being mutually fulfilled by the diplomatic "brothers." This is not the only example. Shveka notes a variety of other occurrences, such as a letter from Ebla: "You are a brother, and I am a brother. Brother, whatever desire from your mouth I will fulfill, and you, my desires fulfill" (TM.75.G.2342).[10] Moshe Weinfeld explains this fulfilling of desires as a part of diplomatic exchange intended to create good relationships. Within the biblical narrative, this dynamic is especially clear in the messages between Israel and Phoenicia.[11] The example of Solomon and Hiram illustrates this well. In fact, Hiram's letter to Solomon encodes the general paradigm in 1Kgs 5:22: "Hiram sent word to Solomon: 'I have heard that you have sent to me, and I will do all that which you desired [אֲנִי אֶעֱשֶׂה אֶת־כָּל־חֶפְצְךָ].'" Or, to paraphrase in the language from the Amarna letters or Ps 21:3, Hiram received Solomon's request, and he will not withhold any request.

Diplomatic terminology also creates the backdrop to the playful phrasing in *KTU* 5.9:7–8, the Ugaritic school text referenced above, *iršt.aršt/l aḫy.l rʿy*, "A request, I request, to my brother, to my friend." Indeed, this Ugaritic phrase employs the exact same root (*ʾrš*) as Psalm 21:3 and the Amarna correspondence. In the case of *KTU* 5.9, the reciprocal formula is also a grammatical exercise—namely, nominal and verbal forms from the same root—that plays with the diplomatic terminology. The Ugaritic school text also goes on to utilize comically diplomatic reciprocity in its extended grammatical exercise on the forms of the verb "to give" (cited above): "And may he give it to his brother, to his friend, an eternal friend. . . . and I shall drink it." It looks like just a playful little grammatical exercise using verbal forms, and it is. But this playful scribal exercise has its roots in the diplomatic terminology and relationships. In this Ugaritic school text, we make the straightforward connection between diplomatic language and their practice in school curriculum.

What these examples seemingly lack is the invocation of a deity, which Ps 21:3 implies and KA 3.9 makes explicit. There are, however, ancient Near Eastern monumental inscriptions that supply such parallels. In two separate places in the Aramaic inscription of Panamuwa, we read as follows: *wmz ʾs[ʾl m]n ʾlhy ytn ly*, "And whatever I shall ask from my god, he shall grant me" (*KAI* 214:4) and *wmh ʾšʾl mn ʾlh[y] mt ytnw ly*, "And whatever I shall ask from my gods, surely they will grant me" (*KAI* 214:12–13). These phrases echo quite strikingly the example from KA 3.9. Here, the diplomatic language of request and receipt was adapted for a monumental Aramaic inscription. As in 3.9, the inscription writes of reciprocity between deities and their subjects, but the roots still must be traced back to common school sayings of Near Eastern scribes.

A much later parallel in Papyrus Amherst 63 (or PapAm 63) reflects the long and conservative reach of scribal curriculum. PapAm 63 is a long text with twenty-three columns that was known already at the end of the nineteenth century. However, it was not deciphered because it was an Aramaic text written in Demotic script. Richard Steiner and Karel van der Toorn have recently begun to unlock this difficult text.[12] Psalm 20 seems to have been translated, adapted, and incorporated into PapAm 63 column XII. As Raik Heckl has suggested, it seems likely that "the text served for instruction in the Aramaic language."[13] This is one way to account for the use of Demotic script to write Aramaic, namely, it could have been used by Egyptian scribes learning Aramaic. This recalls the bilingual Egyptian-Akkadian lexical text (EA 368, discussed in chapter 4), which uses cuneiform script to write Egyptian words in a school text. An educational scribal context helps explain the transmission of the psalm (as well as some of the other parallels discussed by Steiner, van der Toorn, and others). Steiner understands the papyrus as related to the military camp of Jews at Elephantine; van der Toorn connects the liturgical composition with refugees from the northern kingdom of Israel.[14] The specific parallel relevant for KA 3.9 is found in lines 14–16, but a more general context will be instructive:[15]

PapAm 63, Column XII, 11–16	Psalm 20:2–5
[11] May Yaho answer us in our troubles, [12] May Adonai answer us in our troubles.	[2] May YHWH answer you in the day of trouble, may the name of the God of Jacob protect you.
O bow in heaven [13] crescent moon, shine forth.	
(and) send your emissary from the temple of Arash, and from Zaphon [14] may Yaho help us.	[3] May he send you help from the sanctuary and may he support you from Zion.
	[4] May he remember all your offerings and may he favor your burnt offerings.
May Yaho give us the desire of our hearts. May [15] *Mar* [i.e., the Lord] give us according to our hearts. All plans, Yaho should fulfill. May Yaho fulfill—may Adonai not be deficient [16] in satisfying—every request of our hearts.	[5] May he give you the desire of your heart, and may he fulfill all your plans.

The parallels between PapAm 63 and Psalm 20 are convincing, but they are blurred by layers of transmission and translation. As is evident in the parallel columns, PapAm 63 is not a simple translation of Psalm 20, but a reworking of it.

We now can add KA 3.9 to the scholarly discussion of Psalm 20 and PapAm 63. Given the parallel between KA 3.9 and Ps 20:5, it seems more than coincidental that Psalm 20 is also echoed in PapAm 63. The saying in KA 3.9 seems to have been copied and transmitted among scribal circles and then adapted in a variety of ways in different contexts. It was not scripture, but rather a school saying that could be used and adapted to serve a variety of different functions. We see a glimpse of its origins as a school text in Kuntillet ʿAjrud. The text was then adapted into the psalter, as we see in Psalm 20, where it retains some of its vestiges as a northern text of the "God of Jacob" but has been thoroughly tailored as Judean liturgy in the psalter.[16] We finally see another guise of this school text as it is repurposed in PapAm 63, where it becomes part of a liturgy composed in Aramaic and dressed up in the Egyptian garment of the Demotic script. Line 16 of PapAm, which refers to the "request" which should be satisfied, actually brings us back to the Amarna letters and the Ugaritic letter that were discussed earlier. To be sure, PapAm 63 is quite distant from KA 3.9, *KTU* 5.9, and the Amarna letters, but its triangulation through Psalm 20 confirms an original curricular setting. The persistence of these themes and language in various guises underscores the conservative nature of the educational curriculum.

To be sure, scholars have debated the origin of these parallels. Early on, the shared phrasing between Psalms and the Amarna correspondence led to the suggestion that the language reflected lament terminology along the lines of form criticism. Others have proposed that they reveal a common origin in Canaanite religious psalms. More recently, scholars have pointed to the diplomatic nature of these expressions and understood their original environment to be political correspondence.[17] Form criticism is actually a useful approach to understanding these sayings, although form criticism does not typically include the setting of the scribal education. But, it should. In this case, Richard Hess was on the right track when he suggested, "It would seem that the reasonable conclusion from the evidence available would be to find a common source in Canaanite scribal tradition for these expressions."[18] He gives the generic suggestion that "such correspondences reflect the common purposes and concerns of the authors."[19] But we can now suggest something much more concrete. The preceding analysis provides the so-called smoking gun—that is, the common origin in the scribal curriculum. In the Ugaritic school text, we see that the terminology and expressions were part of school exercises. KA 3.9 continues this tradition of school exercises. It actually parallels the Ugaritic letter *KTU* 5.9 quite nicely. The first half of both exercises are the introduction template of a letter, then the second part reflects sayings useful in diplomatic and political contexts. As we see in the example of the Aramaic Panamuwa inscription, these school lessons could be adapted for a variety of contexts. The origin in the school curriculum gave wide latitude for these formulas and terminology to be adapted and used, including for political correspondence, monumental inscriptions, and even the writing of psalms.

The Amenemope Collection

One of the most substantial examples of borrowed Near Eastern school curriculum in the Hebrew Bible is the *Instruction of Amenemope* in the Book of Proverbs. But scholars have yet to come to a consensus on its vector of transmission. The *Instruction of Amenemope* comes from the Egyptian school tradition. As many scholars have noticed, Prov 22:17–24:10 has striking parallels with *Amenemope*.[20] But how and when did these Egyptian proverbs come to influence the Book of Proverbs? As J. D. Ray observes, "The discussion of this sometimes has a circular quality about it, in the absence of precise knowledge about the date of the text and the mechanism of the transmission into Hebrew."[21] The *Sitz im Leben* is a more advanced Egyptian scribal curriculum, which was memorized and recited. Thus it is unlikely that the *Instruction of Amenemope* was known textually by alphabetic scribes. It was known orally as part of a memorized curriculum. It was then adapted and incorporated into the early Israelite curriculum and eventually made its way into the Book of Proverbs.

Our understanding of Proverbs and *Amenemope* has been furthered by the recent edition of the *Instruction of Amenemope* by Vincent Laisney.[22] Laisney follows earlier scholars in suggesting that there was no direct connection between Proverbs and *Amenemope*, but proposes rather that it was mediated by an older Hebrew text that was edited during the Saitic period (i.e., seventh century BCE).[23] This seems unlikely, however, as there is no straightforward vector for transmission. Although the most complete copy of this text does date to the seventh century BCE, Laisney concedes that the language of the text dates the *Instruction of Amenemope* to the New Kingdom period. Moreover, our earliest fragments of the text—the Stockholm Papyrus and the Cairo Ostracon—also date to this Ramesside context. Laisney was struggling with the mechanism of transmission, but the Saite period is not a solution since there is little evidence of direct Egyptian presence in the Levant at that time. Michael V. Fox suggests an Aramaic translation as the vector, but this is mere speculation with no concrete textual or linguistic evidence. Indeed, there is simply no evidence for a direct written translation of *Amenemope* into Hebrew or Aramaic in any period.[24] So the text most likely was transmitted to alphabetic scribes orally. We know that this type of scribal curriculum was memorized and recited. And the twelfth century BCE works better than the seventh century or even the Persian period for oral transmission. As pointed out earlier in this book, new archaeological discoveries point to a continuation of an Egyptian presence in the Levant to the end of the twelfth century BCE, that is, at the same time of emerging alphabetic writing traditions. Thus, the late Ramesside period (i.e., twelfth century BCE) is the best context to understand the mechanisms of transmission for the *Instruction of Amenemope*.

The relationship between the *Instruction of Amenemope* and Proverbs 22:17–24:10 is still not extremely close, but rather general. This can be illustrated by a few commonly suggested parallels. Fox, for example, presents one of the most convincing sections of correspondence:[25]

Proverbs	*Instruction of Amenemope*
(22:17bc) Words of the wise. Incline your ear and hear my words, and direct your hear to my knowledge.	(3.9–10) Give your ears, that you may hear the things that are said. Give your heart to understand them.
(22:18a) for it will be pleasant if you keep them in your belly.	(3.13) Let (my words) rest in the casket of your belly.
(22:18b) (that) they may all be secure on your lips.	(3.16) They will be a mooring ring on your tongue.

Proverbs	*Instruction of Amenemope*
(22:20–21a) Have I not written to you Thirty sayings in counsel and knowledge, to teach you the truest of words,	(27:7–9, 30) Look to these Thirty chapters: they divert, they instruct. They are the foremost of all books. They make the ignorant wise.

On the one hand, these parallels are somewhat remarkable. It is hard to believe that such analogous language in the Book of Proverbs can be accounted for without some knowledge of the *Instruction of Amenemope*. For example, Fox points out that Proverbs adopts distinctly Egyptian ideas, such as that thought resides "in your belly." On the other hand, the wording of the parallels is not precise, and the translation process can only partially account for this. The relationship between Prov 22:17–24:10 and *Amenemope* is best described as quite loose. For example, in creating this parallel structure, Fox liberally omits lines from the *Instruction of Amenemope*.[26] While the parallels themselves are compelling, they do not reflect a direct translation of the Egyptian school text. In other words, the scribe of Prov 22:17–24:10 did not model his work on an Egyptian manuscript. And it seems unlikely that a physical copy of such an Egyptian school text would ever have made its way to the Levant at any time. Rather, the Hebrew parallel seems to be based on a scribe's *memory* of a school tradition. Orality offers the best solution to the transmission problem. Egyptian scribal administrators working in the Levant knew the *Instruction of Amenemope*.[27] While there are striking parallels between Proverbs and *Amenemope*, it in no way requires a direct translation of a physical copy of the Egyptian text. Moreover, it underscores that the Book of Proverbs is an edited collection that is no longer simply a scribal curriculum even if it may have some heritage in school texts like the *Instruction of Amenemope*.

To be sure, it is impossible to know with certainly how the editor(s) of Proverbs came to know the *Instruction of Amenemope*.[28] Yet it is clear that the *Instruction of Amenemope* was a New Kingdom composition, and the only time there was an extensive presence of Egyptian administrators who could have known and transmitted these sayings in the southern Levant was during the New Kingdom period. Moreover, we know that some (if not most) Egyptian administrators were left behind in the Levant and found employment in the emergent polities of the Iron Age. In short, we have connected most of the dots about when and how the *Instruction of Amenemope* could have come to be known by early alphabetic scribes during the Late Bronze Age to Iron Age transition. Once the Egyptian sayings were adapted and incorporated into the scribal curriculum, the sayings could have persisted for centuries and eventually were further adapted and integrated into the literary framework of the Book of Proverbs.

A few hints indicate that an awareness of this Egyptian school tradition was lost over time. First of all, it is widely acknowledged that the beginning of the collection makes an oblique reference to the *Instruction of Amenemope*. Verse 20 is often translated something like this: "Indeed, I have written for you *Thirty Sayings* of counsel and knowledge." This has a striking parallel with the "Thirty Chapters" in *Instruction of Amenemope* cited above. And, as it happens, the Hebrew section in Prov 22:17–24:10 has about thirty sayings. However, the Hebrew term for "thirty sayings" was confused by ancient scribes, as reflected by the *Qere-Ketiv*, which has the (nonsensical) *šālîšîm/šilšôm* (שִׁלְשׁוֹם [שָׁלִישִׁים])—neither the *Qere* nor the *Ketiv* actually say "thirty," although almost all commentators assume the Hebrew *šelōšîm*, "thirty," is the correct reading. While the exact number of sayings in Proverbs has been debated, John Emerton shows that it is either precisely thirty or about thirty.[29] The collection has undoubtedly undergone editing over time, so the fact that it still seems to be about thirty sayings is quite compelling. At the same time, the scribes that transmitted this collection no longer realized there were "thirty sayings" nor that it had a connection with the "Thirty" of the *Instruction of Amenemope*.

A second hint comes from another challenging phrase in the introduction to Proverbs' "Amenemopet Collection." The Masoretic Text of Prov 22:19b reads as follows: *hôdaʿtîkā hayyôm ʾap ʾattâ* [הוֹדַעְתִּיךָ הַיּוֹם אַף־אָתָּה], which might literally be translated something like "I made [them] known to you, today, surely to you."[30] But the Hebrew is ambiguous. The difficulty begins with the *Hiph'il* form of the verb *ydʿ*, "to make known," which in Hebrew grammatically requires an object, but the Masoretic Text does not supply one.[31] What was being made known? I provided the ambiguous "[them]" in my translation above, which is also found in many modern translations. A Hellenistic Greek translator in the Septuagint felt this lacuna and supplied a subject—καὶ γνωρίσῃ σοι τὴν ὁδὸν αὐτοῦ, "and he made *his way* known to you"; at the same time, the Greek translator completely omitted the final Masoretic expression, "today, surely to you [הַיּוֹם אַף־אָתָּה]," in his translation. One must assume that this translator read the final phrase as some sort of textual corruption in Hebrew. Perhaps he surmised that the text should have read *ʾrḥtyw*, "his ways," in Hebrew and translated this into Greek. Given the struggles in the Septuagint with this verse, it is easiest to suppose the text has been corrupted in some way requiring some form of solution.

The textual corruption of verse 19b and its solution begins with understanding the direct object for the verb *ydʿ*, "to make known." How would such a radical textual corruption occur? The reconstruction of the Septuagint makes perfect sense, but it is not a strict translation. And it is hard to understand how a perfectly sensible

Hebrew text (as reconstructed by the Greek) became so completely mangled in the Masoretic Text. The Greek version is a clue, but not a solution. We must assume that the original text was so radically corrupted that it no longer made sense to later copyists and then translators. This leads us to a clever solution proposed by Gary Rendsburg, namely that the Hebrew text originally read, *ymnmʾpt*—that is, "Amen-em-opet."[32] This solution actually preserves and explains most of the letters preserved in the Masoretic Text. It also solves the grammatical problem of the passage since *Amen-em-opet* becomes the object of the verb "to make known." And it makes sense of the context since what follows is a collection of sayings with parallels in the *Instruction of Amenemope*. Finally, it renders a nice parallelism in verses 19–20 that is typical of Hebrew proverbs (using Rendsburg's translation):

> That your trust may be in the LORD,
> I make known to you *Amen-em-opet*,
> Behold, I have written for you the Thirty,
> in counsel and knowledge.

On the basis of this reconstruction, I have labeled Prov 22:17–24:19 the "Amenemope Collection." The corruption of Amenemope's name is easy to understand because it is a reference to a relatively minor Egyptian wisdom collection from the Ramesside period. Its origins would have become increasingly obscure to Judean scribes in the late monarchy, the Babylonian exile, and the Persian period. Once the original connection with the *Instruction of Amenemope* was forgotten, the reference was misunderstood and corrupted. Later scribes and translators then made sense of it as best they could.

Finally, a third hint suggesting a twelfth-century vector of transmission is the use of the term *māhîr* (מָהִיר) in the "Amenemope Collection". First of all, this usage is one of the conspicuous parallels between Proverbs and the *Instruction of Amenemope*:[33]

Prov 22:29a	***Amenemope* 30:16–17**
Have you seen a man, a *māhîr*, in his work? He will stand before kings.	As for the scribe (*sš*) skilled in his office. He is found worthy to be a courtier.[34]

The parallel is noticeable but not exact. This passage in *Amenemope* concludes the work, while in Prov 22:29 it is buried in the middle of the "Amenemope Collection." While *Amenemope* is explicitly speaking of a "scribe," Proverbs seems to take a step away from that particular connection by speaking generically of a "man" who is characterized with the Hebrew term *māhîr*, which is often translated as simply "skilled." The Masoretic version of Proverbs then would refer to any skilled person, not just scribes. Yet Egyptians used *mahir* to refer to a soldier-scribe-administrator stationed in the Levant, and we may posit an Egyptian background or influence for the Hebrew *māhîr*.

Egyptian *mhr* and Biblical Hebrew *māhîr*: Military Scribes

The Egyptian term *mhr*, usually vocalized as *mahir*, is rooted in the New Kingdom administration of the Levant. The word *mahir* appears prominently and repeatedly as a West Semitic loanword in the well-known Egyptian school text "The Craft of the Scribe" (Papyrus Anastasi I), which dates to the Ramesside period.[35] In this text, the term *mahir* is used fifteen times and is always written in "group writing"; that is, it is transcribed by the semisyllabic writing used by Egyptian scribes for foreign words. This use of *mahir* is crucial, yet it is almost completely neglected by scholars discussing the use of the term *māhîr* in the Hebrew Bible. This may be partially explained by the fact that its meaning was forgotten by or unknown to later Hebrew scribes.[36] But "The Craft of the Scribe" explains what the West Semitic *mahir* did. Papyrus Anastasi uses the framework of an extended model letter written by an accomplished scribe to a young scribe. The master patronizes the fledgling scribe and gives him a sense of the extensive scope of scribal training. The *mahir*'s education necessitated knowledge of colonial military logistics and the geography of the Levant in addition to basic scribal training. It begins by saying, "you are the army's command-scribe," and it states the purpose of the letter as follows: "I wrote to you like a friend teaching one greater than him to be an accomplished scribe." The author then introduces the varied scribal duties of logistics and reconnaissance by saying, "I am a scribe and *mahir*," and he continues, "I will explain to you the manner of a *mahir*, and let you see what he has done." He relates one story where the *mahir* was forced to carry a chariot and another where he was robbed in a foreign city, and then he says, "Now you know what it's like to be a *mahir*." Furthermore, the master scribe asks the young apprentice many questions about logistics and reconnaissance, for example: "Where does the *mahir* march to Hazor? What is its river like? . . . Don't withhold your teaching: let us know them." It admonishes the apprentice scribe, saying, "you select scribe, *mahir* who knows his hand, leader of the *na'aruna* [special forces], first of the *djabi'u* [troops]." Finally, only when the young scribe can answer all questions about logistics and reconnaissance quickly, then "I may call you *mahir*." The text concludes by stating, "You are a scribe of the great double gate, who reports the needs of the lands . . . See I have told you the manner of a *mahir*, gone around Retenu [i.e., Levant] for you, and assembled the foreign lands to you in one place, and the towns according to their systems." In Egyptian terms, the addressee was a scribe learning the logistics of the Egyptian military's occupation of the Levant. The use of *māhîr* in Proverbs should be understood in the context of "The Craft of the Scribe." Such an understanding would make the use of the term *māhîr* in the "Amenemope Collection" quite interesting—namely, Proverbs employs a West Semitic administrative term prominent in an Egyptian school text.

The term *mahir* is not present in the main corpus of Canaanite administrative letters from the New Kingdom period—that is, in the Amarna Letters. This omission is rather surprising, but there are general considerations that explain it. First, the Amarna Letters (ca. 1350 BCE) predate the Ramesside period of Egyptian domination by a century. Second, the Amarna Letters are written in Akkadian (albeit with some strong Canaanite features) and are not West Semitic. The Akkadian term *rābiṣu* is used in the Amarna Letters as the functional equivalent to *mahir*.[37] Some of the best demonstrations of this appear in the Amarna Letters from Tyre, which exhibit a number of striking Egyptianisms,[38] and the term *rābiṣu* has military connotations in these texts. For example, in Abimilki's letter to pharaoh, he states that pharaoh assigned him "to guard the city of Tyre" (EA 149:10). He repeatedly mentions that his position depends upon pharaoh, as in line 14: *a-na-ku* LÚ.MAŠKIM LUGAL *be-li-ia*, "I am a commissioner of the king, my lord."[39] Elsewhere, the *rābiṣu*, "commissioner," seems to be an Egyptian military liaison between pharaoh and various Canaanite rulers that is written using a logogram, MAŠKIM. Since it is not spelled syllabically, it serves equally well for the Akkadian term *rābiṣu* and the Egyptian title *mahir*. This is well illustrated in EA 148:46–47, where we find an appeal to the *rābiṣu*'s knowledge of military reconnaissance and logistics: *li-ei-al* LUGAL LÚ.MÁŠKIM-*šu ša i-de*$_4$ KUR *Ki-na-á*ʾ*-na*, "May the king ask his commissioner who knows the land of Canaan." Such examples suggest that the Akkadian *rābiṣu* corresponds with the West Semitic *mahir*. Other cases are also instructive. For instance, in EA 151:21–24, we read the following appeal: "May the k[ing], my lord, ask his commissioner whether I have turned my face to the presence of the king, my lord." In this case, the *rābiṣu* was the arbiter of loyalty to pharaoh. Furthermore, the *rābiṣu* was in charge of allocating Egyptian resources from pharaoh (EA 155:36–39): "the commissioner has not done [as] the kin[g commanded]; he has [not] given w[ood and water a]s the ki[ng] commanded." Jeffrey Zorn concludes that *rābiṣu* "represents an Egyptianized form of the West Semitic *mhr*," which is unknown in Akkadian.[40]

The Hebrew term *māhîr* finds a rather limited usage in the Bible, appearing only three times.[41] The term does not continue in later Hebrew; for example, it does not appear in Qumran Hebrew or the Mishnah. In all these cases, the original connection of this term with the West Semitic lexeme repeatedly used in the Egyptian "The Craft of the Scribe" seems forgotten. The term remains in the Bible as a vestige of a bygone era. In the Bible, the only place where the term stands alone, so to speak, is in Prov 22:29: "do you see a man, a *māhîr*, in his work? He shall stand before kings." In the other two cases, the term *māhîr* is expanded in the expression *sōpēr māhîr*. For example, it appears in Ps 45:2, "I speak my verses to a king, my tongue is the pen of a *sōpēr māhîr*." As with Prov 22:29, Ps 45:2 is contextualized with "kings," which should suggest a royal or even an administrative context. That is to say, it makes good sense when read in the context of "The Craft of the Scribe." The expression *sōpēr māhîr* also appears in the much later description of the scribe Ezra as an official in the Babylonian court (Ezra 7:6), but there it likely borrows directly from Ps 45:2. In Ps 45:2, *sōpēr*, "scribe," looks like an editorial gloss on *māhîr*. In other words, the meaning of the West Semitic term *māhîr* was becoming obscure, so an editor added *sōpēr* to clarify the meaning. Alternatively, *māhîr* may simply augment the meaning sōpēr, that is, indicating a specific type of scribe.

The expression *sōpēr māhîr* has a striking parallel in "The Craft of the Scribe": "I am a scribe and *mahir*."[42] Here in "The Craft of the Scribe," *mahir* does function as a sort of gloss—that is, it gives a West Semitic equivalence to the Egyptian word for "scribe." The Hebrew term *māhîr* is sometimes understood by appeals to Ethiopic, where the root *mhr* means "to teach, learn" and later in Arabic "to be skilled," but these seem like later developments in the meaning of the term.[43] Alternatively, *sōpēr māhîr* is often translated as "a skilled scribe" or "a ready scribe," and its meaning is explained by reference the Hebrew root *mhr*, "quick."[44] This interpretation, however, is strained; it only can explain the use in Ps 45:2 and cannot explain Prov 22:29 where *māhîr* stands alone without the term *sōpēr* "scribe." A West Semitic etymology makes more sense. In Ugaritic, for example, the term *mhr* was commonly associated with warriors or soldiers,[45] with a nuance that may be related to the soldier-scribe in "The Craft of the Scribe." The later Aramaic school text, *The Words of Ahiqar*, begins with a description of *spr ḥkym wmhyr*, "a wise and capable scribe"—that is, Ahiqar, who was an official in the court of King Esarhaddon. But we hardly need to appeal to later Aramaic texts for this idea of a "capable scribe." Very early texts like the Sumerian *School Days* also reflect on this theme. As pointed out, the Ramesside Egyptian school text "The Craft of the Scribe" is essentially dedicated to this idea in using the term *mahir* fifteen times to explain what it means to be "a scribe and a *mahir*." The term *mahir* forges a nice link between the Egyptian scribal and administrative culture at the end of the Late Bronze Age and the development of alphabetic scribal culture in the beginning of the Iron Age.

The Use of Proverbial Sayings in Biblical Literature

The epigraphic evidence for understanding the influence of proverbial sayings is quite limited. On the one hand, it is quite clear from comparative evidence, especially in the cuneiform world, that proverbial sayings were the critical last stage in the elementary scribal education. On the other hand, the Hebrew inscriptional evidence in ancient Israel is *almost* nonexistent. To be sure, the one example from Kuntillet ʿAjrud supports our appeal to the comparative evidence. The proverbial sayings were likely a part of the scribal curriculum in ancient Israel. And yet it is only one short saying. Moreover, KA 3.9 is only loosely related to biblical proverbs. Nevertheless, it does encourage further reflection about what kind of proverbial sayings may have been part of the scribal curriculum as well as how and where proverbial sayings may have influenced biblical literature.

Proverbial sayings are known both as individual sayings and collections in the ancient Near East. We have clear examples of collections of proverbs in the cuneiform corpus,[46] and for this reason the Book of Proverbs has often been considered a school text. But the Book of Proverbs was not a scribal curriculum. In its final form, it was a literary work, not a corpus of schoolboy exercises. Indeed, Proverbs is not really a book at all but rather a compilation of collections. This should remind us that the more widely used physical form of cuneiform sayings written and recited by students were the "lentil" texts with individual sayings. This fact in itself should suggest to us that the Book of Proverbs is a secondary genre made up of collections rather than a school text itself. This is most obvious in the final chapters of the book, which name a series of autonomous collections of proverbial sayings that are being gathered into the Book of Proverbs:

22:17 "The words of the Wise" (i.e., the "Amenemope Collection")
25:1 "These are the sayings of Solomon, which the men of Hezekiah collected"
30:1 "The sayings of Agur, son of Jakeh"
31:1 "The sayings of King Lemuel"

These statements all begin discrete collections of sayings. On the basis of these examples, we may conclude that the editors of the Book of Proverbs utilized the scribal curriculum, collecting individual sayings and compiling collections, but that the canonical book was not intended as a school text itself. Rather, individual proverbial sayings were more typical schoolboy exercises.

Numerical Sayings

An important form of proverbial sayings was numerical sayings.[47] These are an adaptation of lists, and they became a well-known form in wisdom literature. In Proverbs 30, for example, they serve to classify knowledge and wisdom. Sometimes they can be derived from a lexical theme like zoology, as in verses 24–28:

> Four things on earth are small,
> yet they are exceedingly wise:
> ants are a people without strength,
> yet they provide their food in the summer;
> badgers are a people without power,
> yet they make their homes in the rocks;
> locusts have no king,
> yet all of them march in rank;
> lizards can be grasped in the hand,
> yet it is found in kings' palaces.

We are reminded here of the passage expressing Solomon's encyclopedic knowledge, which involved his composition of proverbs, and culminates with the statement, "He would speak of the animals, of the birds, of the reptiles, and of the fish" (1Kgs 4:33 [Heb, 5:13]). As I pointed out in chapter 4, animals are, of course, one of the main categories of traditional Mesopotamian lexical lists. In Prov 30:24–28, the numerical saying may reflect a more advanced scribal exercise that involved adapting a thematic list of vocabulary.

There are a variety of different types of numerical sayings in biblical literature. One of the more well-known examples using an x/x + 1 pattern appears in Amos 1–2. There we have the repeated numerical expression "for three transgressions and for four, I will not revoke punishment." So, for example, it begins in verses 3–5:

> For three transgressions of Damascus, and for four,
> I will not revoke the punishment;
> because they have threshed Gilead with threshing sledges of iron.
> So I will send a fire on the house of Hazael,
> and it shall devour the strongholds of Ben-hadad.
> I will break the gate bars of Damascus,
> and cut off the inhabitants from the Valley of Aven,
> and the one who holds the scepter from Beth-eden;
> and the people of Aram shall go into exile to Kir, says the LORD.

The numerical sayings formula is applied to a geographical list that begins with Damascus (verse 3) and proceeds to Gaza (6), Tyre (9), Edom (11), Ammon (13), Moab (2:1), Judah (2:4), and finally Israel (2:6). In this way, three traditional educational rubrics were combined to create a powerful literary text; a sayings formula and a geographical (i.e., lexical) list are couched within the prophetic message formula (i.e., letter template).

Not surprisingly, numerical sayings are well known in the Book of Proverbs. For example, we read in Prov 6:16–19:[48]

> There are six things that the LORD hates,
> seven that are an abomination to him:
> haughty eyes, a lying tongue,
> and hands that shed innocent blood,
> a heart that devises wicked plans,
> feet that hurry to run to evil,
> a lying witness who testifies falsely,
> and one who sows discord in a family.

Such numerical styling can be understood as a general feature of educational literature. But these numerical sayings may be incorporated into literature in a variety of ways. For example, in the Baal Cycle we find the following (1.4 iii, 17–18):[49]

> For two feasts Baal hates, Three, the Cloud-Rider:
> A feast of shame, a feast of strife,
> And a feast of the whispering of servant-girls.

Some scholars have even suggested that the numerical proverb has its origins in Canaanite tradition.[50] They identify parallels with Ugaritic literature and understand them as a result of borrowing. Yet these kinds of parallels should be understood as a typical teaching rubric. For example, one may recall the use of numerical lists in the traditional Passover Seder; at the end of the meal, the children sing:

> Who knows one? I know one.
> One is our God in heaven and on earth.
> Who knows two? I know two.
> Two are the tablets of the covenant.
> . . .
> Who knows thirteen? I know thirteen.
> Thirteen are God's principles;
> Twelve are the tribes of Israel;
> Eleven are the stars of Joseph's dream;
> Ten are the Commandments;
> Nine are the months of childbirth;
> Eight are the days before circumcision;
> Seven are the days of the week;
> Six are the sections of the Mishnah;
> Five are the books of the Torah;

Four are the Matriarchs;
Three are the Patriarchs;
Two are the tablets of the covenant;
One is our God, in heaven and on earth.

As we can see, this type of numerical listing as a teaching rubric is universal. Examples could be cited from world literature more generally.[51] What is more particular and striking is the x/x + 1 formula, which finds a comparative Near Eastern parallel and can hardly be coincidental. It is assumed, although there are no actual Epigraphic Hebrew examples, that such rubrics were learned in student exercises.

The repeated use of proverbs in different contexts could also suggest memorized student exercises. An excellent example of this in biblical literature is the "sour grapes" proverb used in Jer 31:29 and Ezek 18:2:

> In those days they shall no longer say: "The parents eat sour grapes, and the children's teeth are set on edge." (Jer 31:29)

> What do you mean by quoting this proverb concerning the land of Israel, "The parents eat sour grapes, and the children's teeth are set on edge"? (Ezek 18:2)

Given that proverbs were a genre of student exercises, it is tempting to see this example as a proverb memorized and copied by scribes as part of their training. However, it is just as easy to imagine this as a part of common Israelite culture—that is, a proverb that all people knew apart from scribal education. It likely reflects a more complex relationship between writing, memory, and culture. For example, American proverbs such as "There are no gains without pains" (later, "No pain, no gain") and "A penny saved is two pence dear" (later, "A penny saved is a penny earned") were collected or written by Benjamin Franklin for his *Poor Richard's Almanack*.[52] These adages survived because they were written, but they became well known and adapted through popular culture rather than school exercises.

Another example of a proverbial saying embedded in a narrative is found in the story of David's conquest of Jerusalem. We read in 2Sam 5:6–9,

> The king and his men marched to Jerusalem against the Jebusites, the inhabitants of the land, who said to David, "You will not come in here, even the blind and the lame will turn you back"—thinking, "David cannot come in here." Nevertheless David took the stronghold of Zion, which is now the city of David. David had said on that day, "Whoever would strike down the Jebusites, let him get up the water shaft to attack the lame and the blind, those whom

David hates." Therefore it is said, "The blind and the lame shall not come into the house."

Daniel Pioske insightfully identifies the repeated and reworked saying about "the blind and the lame" as a proverbial saying rooted in the oral background of early Israelite scribalism. He understands this as "a confluence of the oral and written forms of discourse woven together by scribes unaccustomed to making a sharp distinction between them."[53] However, I think these type of oral sayings were practiced and memorized in scribal training precisely for the purpose of adapting them into various contexts—stories, letters, liturgy, etc. They were not unaccustomed to this integration, but rather they were trained precisely to make this type of integration of memorized sayings in various written contexts. In the above example, the reworking of the oral saying between its two citations evidences precisely the type of adaptation that scribes were trained to do. Indeed, the purpose of memorization of sayings in part was to give the scribe an arsenal of tools that could be employed in a variety of genres.

The Book of Proverbs as an Educational Curriculum

The influence (or lack thereof) of the Book of Proverbs in biblical literature has been something of a scholarly crux. If Proverbs were central to scribal education, why does it seem to exert only marginal influence in biblical literature? As Katherine Dell points out, the influence of Proverbs "tends to be less of ideology than the occasional proverb or expression that echoes the wisdom stance."[54] Moreover, why doesn't Proverbs deal with the themes of the Exodus or *Torah*? This omission is conspicuous and contrasts with later wisdom literature, including the Wisdom of Sirach and the Sapiential literature from the Dead Sea Scrolls. According to David Carr, this is because Proverbs lies at the outset of the formation of biblical literature rather than during its latest period.[55] His explanation is cogent. The Book of Proverbs itself is a connection to an ancient Near Eastern instructional curriculum. This begins with references to collections from non-Israelite sages (Prov 30:1, 31:1), and it is underscored by the extensive borrowing from the *Instruction of Amenemope*. Outside of Proverbs, these connections are further highlighted. Solomon dialogues with Hiram of Tyre (1Kgs 5:21 [Eng. 5:7]) as well as the Queen of Sheba (1Kgs 10:1–9). Two "wisdom" psalms (see Ps 88:1, 89:1) are attributed to Heman, the Ezrahite, who was apparently an Edomite (see Gen 36:22; 1Kgs 5:10–11 [Eng. 4:30–31]). In this respect, the Book of Proverbs hints at a vector of transmission from the

Near Eastern scribal curriculum to its adoption and adaptation among ancient Israelite scribes.

Scholars sometimes suggest that the Book of Proverbs is the product of a "wisdom school" or even that the prophet Isaiah was trained in a "wisdom school."[56] Examples like KA 3.9 should return us to the realia of scribal education. It is better not to envision "schools"—wisdom or otherwise. Rather, there was curriculum and scribal exercises. Scribes copied, memorized, and recited individual sayings as part of learning to read and write. In this respect, there was no canonical Book of Proverbs to influence scribes. Moreover, different specialties for scribes—for example, military scribes—might require specialized knowledge, like geography; however, it is difficult to imagine a particular scribal profession that would have required specialized knowledge in proverbs, sayings, and wisdom literature. These curricular exercises would have been useful to a variety of scribes, even military scribes. To be sure, wisdom literature may have been particularly important for elite scribes to master, but this hardly suggests a physical "wisdom school" where a scribe went to become one of the "wise." It is much better to think of wisdom as a genre of texts and literature studied by all scribes, to some extent at least, rather than a "school."[57] And it is best to think of proverbial sayings as being memorized individually by fledgling scribes to be adapted and used in a variety of ways.

The direct influence of the Book of Proverbs on the writing of biblical literature is limited. Proverbs as a late literary compilation creates for itself a fiction that is the backbone of ancient Israelite education (e.g., "these are the proverbs of Solomon," Prov 1:1, 10:1, 25:1). But it was not. The literary fiction is based in a certain realia, namely, the scroll was likely compiled from scribal curricula resources. But the Book of Proverbs itself was not a school text. In this respect, it is not surprising that Proverbs exerts little tangible influence on the writing of the Hebrew Bible. This begins with its very language. It is unusual and isolated linguistically.[58] Gary Rendsburg explains this by positing an Israelite origin for the Book of Proverbs, which was "transferred" to Judah in the wake of the Assyrian invasions.[59] This could indeed explain some of the lack of influence: Proverbs was not a central text for *Judean* scribes. But in any interpretation, the Book of Proverbs is an edited and collected work, not a simple text of a scribal curriculum.

The problem is not merely linguistic. Proverbs did not extensively influence other biblical literature through inner-biblical interpretation. For example, Michael Fishbane's landmark study on inner-biblical exegesis makes only passing mention of texts in Proverbs.[60] Still, scholars do cite a few examples for the scribal influence of the Book of Proverbs, especially in the Book of Deuteronomy.[61] For instance, the relationship between Prov 22:28 and Deut 19:14 is unmistakable: Deuteronomy echoes Proverbs word for word in enjoining Israel, "Do not move the boundary marker" (לא תסיג גבול). As Carr observes, Deuteronomy elaborates upon the saying from Proverbs, which makes the proverbial saying (in Prov 22:28) the likely source for Deut 19:14.[62] Unfortunately, such clear instances of the borrowing and reuse of the Book of Proverbs are not numerous. Carr summarizes a variety of examples that have been brought forth, but he points out that the direction of influence and the closeness of the parallels are not as convincing as Prov 22:28 and Deut 19:14.[63] We can explain this in part because the point of sayings was not necessarily to quote them, but rather to adapt them in a variety of contexts. Indeed, Carr correctly understands that educational as well as oral aspects can account for the looseness of the parallels. This was also the case in our one example from KA 3.9. This example had a variety of loose parallels, but no exact quotes. In other words, it is not a case of mechanical borrowing and precise reuse. Creative adaption is the modus operandi for the scribal curriculum. But in the end, it is not really an oral context that creates the loose reuse of proverbial sayings. Indeed, they are memorized in the context of training scribes to read and write. Proverbial sayings are part of scribal training.

In sum, proverbial sayings were an important part of scribal education. Scribes copied, memorized, recited, and adapted them as they learned to write. Fortunately, we now have one hint of this type of scribal curriculum in the inscriptions from Kuntillet ʿAjrud. This one particular example from Kuntillet ʿAjrud actually points to a textualization of an oral dimension of education. The would-be scribe copied and memorized a variety of sayings that could be used and adapted in a variety of written contexts, including stories, letters, and liturgy. Adaptations of the saying known from Kuntillet ʿAjrud are amply illustrated in parallels from all these genres in ancient Near Eastern and biblical literature.

7
Advanced Education

Moving toward my conclusion, this chapter will wade into more turbulent waters: advanced scribal education. This book has focused on the scribe's elementary curriculum, but some reflection on advanced learning seems warranted. The advanced curriculum was naturally more flexible than elementary education in ancient Israel. Different scribal positions required different types of education and varying levels of proficiency. Even though it is difficult to know for certain what constituted the advanced curriculum for ancient Israelite scribes, we can offer some conjectures based on comparative evidence, analysis of the Hebrew Bible, ancient inscriptions, and particularly the plaster texts from Kuntillet ʿAjrud and Deir ʿAlla. In this summary, I reflect upon some of the texts that may have been part of the advanced scribal training in ancient Israel. The focus of my exploration continues to be on the tangible evidence for an advanced curriculum. With regard to the comparative Near Eastern evidence, I continue to pay special attention to the "vector of transmission." The evidence here is fragmentary, and we must be quite tentative.

Advanced education extends beyond the narrow purposes of this book. What do I mean by this? Well, by its nature (and based on what we know of the cuneiform advanced curriculum) an advanced curriculum was much more variable. Ancient Hebrew scribes did not necessarily use the same advanced curriculum for all positions, all times, and all places. Elementary curriculum was standardized and generally quite conservative, which allows us to reconstruct curriculum from our rather fragmentary evidence. For advanced curriculum, this approach is much more problematic. Indeed, the scope of advanced curriculum and the role that it played in shaping ancient Hebrew scribes is much more nuanced as well as diverse.

Scholars have begun to recognize the critical role of the scribes themselves in Hebrew literature. In this book I have repeatedly argued for the importance of adaptation as part of scribal training. When we begin to tackle advanced curriculum, the role of the individual scribe as well as the different scribal roles—government, priests, military, economic—come to the fore. The critical role of the individual scribes comes to the fore in a groundbreaking book by Seth Sanders. Sanders points out, for example, that Adapa along with Enoch were icons for the ancient scribe, and this may be their most lasting legacy on Hebrew literature.[1] Adapa was an ancient Mesopotamian scribal figure who unwittingly refused the gift of immortality, and Enoch was a legendary biblical figure who "walked with God" (Gen 5:21–24) and in later tradition was understood as a scribe who recounted his heavenly journeys. For Sanders, these are the ideal typological figures of antiquity that serve as signposts for his exploration of elite scribal culture. Yet, as Sanders also acknowledges, "the connection between Mesopotamian and Judean learning was widespread and pedestrian."[2] Sanders makes this observation as a way of investigating "a shared set of assumptions about a shared high culture."[3] There are differences between the shared high culture and the rudimentary foundations of the scribal enterprise upon which this book has focused. Or, put another way, the early scribal curriculum had a more uniform and basic impact on the shaping of the Hebrew Bible, whereas Sanders has the more elevated aspiration of grasping "what these cultures meant to the scribes themselves."[4]

Advanced Curriculum: The Cuneiform Parallels

The advanced curriculum of scribes was not fixed. This is confirmed by the robust material that we have in Mesopotamian cuneiform. The popularity and distribution of the cuneiform curriculum should be a main consideration in assessing its influence. As Sanders points out, "The rule of popularity gives a simple guideline for judging plausibility: widely distributed material is more likely to be known."[5] This is certainly fair, although our specific assessment of "widely distributed" must include the geographical dispersion as well as numerical accumulation and chronological distribution. So, for example, on the basis of Near Eastern cuneiform evidence, it is clear that the Epic of Gilgamesh was a widely known and circulated school text. Perhaps even more important for our purposes is the fact that there are fragments from several places in the periphery of Mesopotamia, including Ugarit and Megiddo. In contrast, the myth *Adapa and the South Wind* was not as widely circulated, but it was found among the Amarna Scholarly Tablets. It may therefore have served as a local school text during the Late Bronze Age, perhaps only in Egypt.[6] As for the Code of Hammurabi, it was widely circulated and studied by elite scribes within Mesopotamia, but not necessarily as a school text.[7] And apparently it was not widely circulated outside of Mesopotamia. These observations should be accounted for when appealing to these laws as influencing biblical scribes. More generally, cuneiform texts that appear within the Levant provide the most direct, useful, and clear evidence of possible vectors of scribal transmission. More excavations may uncover more cuneiform literature in the southern Levant and change our reconstructions, but at present we must begin with our actual evidence.

The chronological spread of the cuneiform school curriculum also warrants our attention. For example, there are no copies of the cuneiform school curriculum from the southern Levant that date to the first millennium. More generally, the cuneiform curriculum is not found outside the Mesopotamian heartland in the first millennium. In contrast, it is found throughout the Levant in the second millennium BCE. Therefore the best evidence of a vector of transmission for cuneiform influence on the development of the Hebrew scribal curriculum was the late second millennium BCE. In addition, the Levantine copies of the cuneiform curriculum from the second millennium skew heavily toward an elementary curriculum. For this reason, we have focused on the fundamental curriculum up until now.

Orality and memorization were other important aspects of advanced education. The advanced curriculum was not only learned and practiced by scribes; it was recited and memorized as well. This component of ancient education was a particular focus of David Carr's book, *Writing on the Tablet of the Heart.* Up to now, it has not figured prominently in our discussion because the elementary curriculum was learned mostly by repetition in writing, not by recitation. The advanced curriculum, however, was different. Memorization and recitation were also critical. This began already with proverbs and sayings and continued to advanced curriculum. An excellent illustration may be seen in the colophon to the Babylonian creation epic, the Enuma Elish. The epic concludes as follows (VII:145–50, 157–58, emphasis added):

> The wise and the learned should ponder them together,
> *The teacher should repeat them and make the pupil learn by heart. . . .*
> This is the revelation that an Ancient, to whom it was told, wrote down and established *for posterity to hear.*

If we accept this literally, the student did not copy the text but merely repeated after the teacher. The student learned this literary classic "by heart." As Karel van der Toorn points out, "The verb here translated as 'established' (*šakānu*) is used for putting a text on the scribal curriculum, which is likely what is being referred to here."[8] Scribes also made "library copies," but this advanced scribal curriculum was primarily written down in copies to be recited and memorized "for posterity to hear." In this way, oral recitation alongside scribal copying could have had a lasting impact on biblical literature throughout the Iron Age.[9] From our textual evidence we must suppose that after the Late Bronze Age firsthand knowledge of cuneiform literature would have only become available again to Judean scribes during the Babylonian exile.[10] Thus memorization and oral recitation offer a vector of transmission that could transcend narrow and particular historical periods.

One of the most well-known and important literary school texts was the Gilgamesh Epic. Copies and versions of the tales of Gilgamesh are known for three millennia. In the Late Bronze Age in particular, as cuneiform scribal culture spread throughout the Fertile Crescent, the Gilgamesh Epic spread with it. Versions of the tale appear at sites ranging from ancient Iran to Ugarit and Emar and to the Southern Levant at Megiddo.[11] As the editor of the critical edition of *The Babylonian Gilgamesh Epic*, Andrew George, points out, "These finds demonstrate that copying the poem of Gilgameš was part of the curriculum of scribal learning in the West throughout the Late Bronze Age."[12] George describes not only the pervasiveness of Gilgamesh in cuneiform scribal curriculum but also its popularity in the broader culture.[13] As Steve Tinney has pointed out, the distribution of these compositions indicates that they were not critical only to bureaucratic education, but rather that they belonged to the realm of advanced scribal education.[14] The popularity of the tales was also reflected in their integration and adaptation into new forms of literature.

The Gilgamesh Epic was not circulated as a whole. Instead students copied certain individual tales from the Epic. For example, in the Tablet House at Nippur, dating to around 1740 BCE, twenty-one copies of "Gilgamesh and Huwawa" and fifteen copies of "Gilgamesh, Enkidu, and the Nether World" were excavated.[15] The fragment from Megiddo also belongs to the "Gilgamesh, Enkidu, and the Nether World" episode, which is Tablet VII in the Standard Babylonian edition.[16] This fragment likely dates to the fourteenth century based on paleographic parallels within the Amarna corpus, as well as the episode's correspondence to the House of Nippur texts. Thus the Megiddo Gilgamesh fragment fits generally into the cuneiform school tradition of the second millennium.

Four fragments of the Gilgamesh Epic dating to the twelfth century BCE were also excavated at Ugarit.[17] According to George, the somewhat garbled nature of the Ugaritic fragments indicates that they were school copies.[18] The Ugaritic fragments, however, are not simple school copies. Sara Milstein has shown that the peculiarities of the Ugaritic fragments are examples of "revision through introduction."[19] In other words, the addition of a new introduction essentially reframes an old piece of literature, in this case an episode from the Gilgamesh Epic. Although the Gilgamesh Epic was standardized in the first millennium, the second millennium fragments from Ugarit, Megiddo, Emar, Hattusa (the Hittite capital also known as Boğazköy), and other peripheral sites reflect different versions of the standardized set of stories.

The tales of Gilgamesh certainly were widely known, and this may account for their rather fragmentary legacy in biblical literature. Scholars have pointed out how Gilgamesh tales influenced biblical texts as diverse as the Jacob Cycle, the Flood Narrative, and the Book of Ecclesiastes,[20] but there is no evidence that ancient Judean scribes actually *read* the Gilgamesh Epic. The impact is either limited (as in Qohelet) or quite vague and thematic (as in the Book of Genesis). This minimal impact could be a legacy of oral tradition. Fragments or memories of the epic may have been retained and adapted into Israelite education, but the text itself was unknown. Sanders warns about the complexity of the transmission of Gilgamesh to Levantine scribes: "Part of the problem is that small, highly portable pieces of culture like catch-phrases, clichés, and forms of discourse are likely to have circulated in more than one channel of communication." He continues, "The Gilgamesh example also demonstrates the weaknesses of the literary approach in its tendency to focus our attention on loose verbal parallels *without plausible direct historical connections*, let alone rich or informative actual contexts" (emphasis added).[21] Of course, the existence of the Gilgamesh Epic fragment from Megiddo points to one plausible and direct historical connection. Copies from Ugarit and Emar further underscore how widespread its dissemination was during the Late Bronze Age.

Alternatively, some scholars suggest that the Gilgamesh Epic could reflect the influence of contact with Mesopotamian scribal culture during the Neo-Assyrian period or after the Babylonian exile.[22] For example, Gilgamesh (*glgmyš*) appears in the Qumran fragments of the Book of Giants (from 1 Enoch), and Humbaba (*ḥwbbš*) is one of the giants.[23] Stephanie Dalley observes that the Book of Watchers contains a story about Gilgamesh and points out that "another episode has been pieced together from Qumran which relates a dream of Gilgamesh about a divine court of judgement set up in a heavenly garden with trees. The interpreter of the dream is Enoch, who takes the part that Enkidu played in the Akkadian Epic of Gilgamesh."[24] All this to point out the deep roots that the Gilgamesh Epic had in Near Eastern culture. But these references certainly do not necessitate that a written version of the Gilgamesh Epic was known to the Qumran community, but rather that the oral versions of the Gilgamesh tales were broadly preserved, circulated, and adapted.

One notable parallel of Gilgamesh appears in the Book of Ecclesiastes. This parallel has been noticed by many scholars, although a vector of transmission is difficult to pin down. The parallel appears in a speech by the barmaid Siduri to Gilgamesh:[25]

Gilgamesh **OB version 3, 6–14)**

As for you, Gilgamesh, let your belly be full.
Day and night enjoy yourself in every way.
Every day arrange for pleasures,
Day and night, dance and play,
Wear fresh clothes.
Keep your head washed; bathe in water
Appreciate the child who holds your hand
Let your wife enjoy herself in your lap,
For this is the task of [mankind/woman].

Ecclesiastes **9:7–9**

Go, eat your bread with gladness,
and drink your wine with joy;
for long ago
God approved your actions.
Let your clothes always be fresh;
let not oil be lacking on your head.
Indeed, enjoy life with the wife whom you love, all the days of your fleeting life that are given you under the sun, because that is your portion in life and in your toil at which you toil under the sun.

The organization and themes are strikingly similar. The one thing missing from Ecclesiastes is the mention of "the child," which was enough for Robert Gordis to dismiss a literary connection and argue that this was merely a reflection on the universal human condition.[26] However, most find it difficult to dismiss the similarities entirely. Still, this is also not a straightforward translation. It seems much more likely that Qohelet represents a local adaptation of a well-known oral tradition. In such a case, there was no need to preserve precise wording. The speech from the Gilgamesh Epic had become material for a later scribe to adapt and re-create. There are also further apparent allusions to Gilgamesh enumerated by Shawna Dolansky.[27] She points, for example, to a central theme of Ecclesiastes—the futility of "chasing after the wind" (e.g., 1:6, 14, 17; 2:11, 17, 2:26, etc.), which recalls Gilgamesh's advice to the Enkidu: "Mankind can number his days. Whatever he may achieve, it is only wind" (Yale Tablet, Old Babylonian Version). There is some thematic similarity here, but again it might best be accounted for by oral tradition within scribal schooling. She offers another general parallel in the story where Gilgamesh persuades Enkidu that two are stronger than one, "A three-stranded cord is hardest to break" (Standard Babylonian Version, IV, iv). This certainly echoes the proverbial saying in Ecclesiastes, "Two are better than one, because they have a good return for their work. . . . Though one may be overpowered, two can defend themselves. A cord of three strands is not quickly broken" (4:9–12). Again, however, we do not need to think ancient Israelite scribes were actually reading cuneiform tablets to explain such striking thematic parallels. The scribal practice of memorization and recitation actually better explains these striking but limited parallels.

The longevity of the Gilgamesh tradition is striking, but in some ways it is no more striking then the proverbial saying from KA 3:9 (discussed in chapter 6), which had parallels from Amarna, Northwest Semitic, and Ugaritic as well as Psalm 20:5; and, it was also adapted in a version of Psalm 20 incorporated into the much later Papyrus Amherst 63. In sum, the legacy of scribal learning and curriculum could be at times remarkably diverse and long lasting.

The "Schoolhouse" at Deir ʿAlla

Another example of the long and broad legacy of scribal learning is the biblical tradition of the prophet Balaam, which has a remarkable parallel in the plaster texts from Tell Deir ʿAlla. The site of Deir ʿAlla, which probably should be identified with biblical Succoth, was located in the Jordan River Valley about five miles east of the Jordan River and a mile north of the Jabbok River. The excavations there uncovered what may be an Iron Age "schoolhouse" (roughly contemporary with Kuntillet ʿAjrud)—Room EE335 is reconstructed in Figure 7.1—where apprentice scribes learned their craft.[28] The site has achieved notoriety as the location of literary texts inked on a plastered wall with an account of the "teachings of Balaam, son of Beor." The text is reconstructed from plaster fragments from the rubble of a collapsed wall. The purpose of the texts has been debated. Perhaps they were associated with religious institutions or the state. Could there have been a school of prophets—like Balaam—who studied there? Or, based on the content of these "teachings of Balaam, son of Beor," perhaps the texts were related to dream incubation.[29] Or were these texts part of more general scribal education?

An educational context for the inscriptions makes sense on both textual and archaeological grounds. First of all, the inscriptions were found in an unusual archaeological context: a large room with benches. Not enough attention has been given to this *Sitz im Leben*. As Gareth Wearne points out, "The layout of the bench-room (room EE335) and its relative segregation suggest that the room had a highly specialized function, distinct from the more mundane aspects of life in the settlement."[30] Wearne's detailed analysis of the room follows along the lines of Andre Lemaire's seminal study of the plaster texts.[31] Lemaire also thought it was important to consider the inscription's physical context. When one looks carefully at the room, it becomes clear that the plaster texts played a central role in the use of the space. While the benches are positioned to read the text, advanced school texts were not simply copied and read; they were also memorized and recited. Wall inscriptions could have served such a performative function in a setting intended for training young scribes.

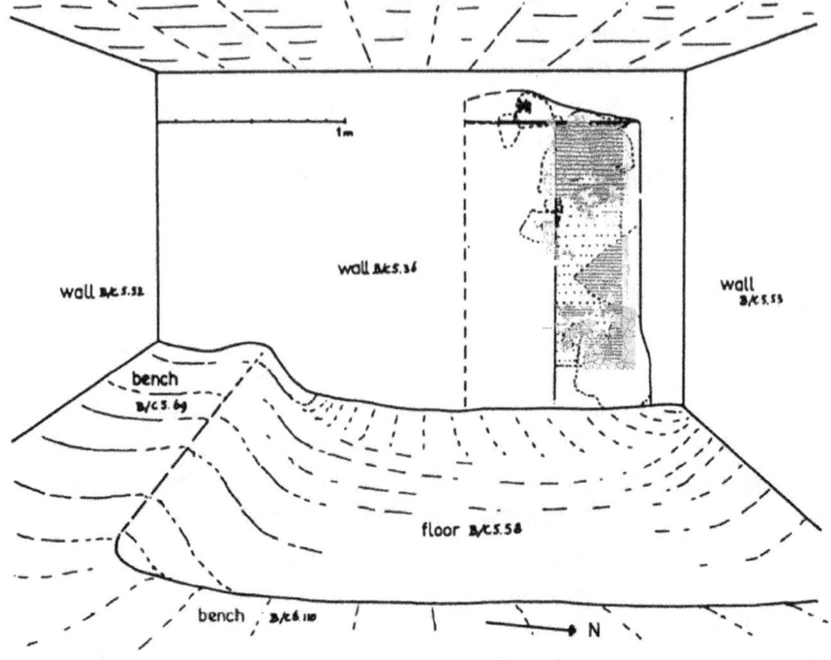

Figure 7.1 Reconstruction of Room EE335 with Deir ʿAlla plaster texts. Original drawing courtesy of Gerrit van der Kooij.

One additional inscription has been suggested to provide some evidence of an educational context. An ostracon with five clearly incised, though poorly drawn, letters was also found at Deir ʿAlla. In Figure 7.2, we can see that it begins with the first four letters of the alphabet, ʾ *b g d*, which might indicate an abecedary. However, the fifth letter is *zayin*, which would omit the *heh* and *waw* in the traditional Hebrew alphabetic sequence. The excavators suggested that this sequence could be a consonantal abecedary, which would be unique and for that reason must be considered speculative. And there are unusual aspects in the shape and execution of these letters that seem to reflect a student rather than a master scribe.[32] However, this interpretation is hardly conclusive. Alternatively, the *zayin* could be simply translated as a relative particle thus: "Abigad, who[. . .]" or even "the father of Gad, who[. . .]." The latter alternative seems particularly appealing given the association of this region with the Israelite tribe of Gad. We should also heed Jo Ann Hackett's warning in her edition of the Deir ʿAlla plaster texts, where she cautions against making sweeping conclusions on the basis of fragmentary texts.[33] Thus, it is difficult to put too much weight on the possible fragmentary abecedary.

Figure 7.2 A possible consonantal abecedary (ʾ *b g d z*[. . .]) from Deir ʿAlla. Drawing by the author

The plaster texts themselves offer further clues for an educational context. Figure 7.3 gives a general picture of the reconstruction. The precise reconstruction is not critical for our argument, and we will proceed based on the broadly agreed outlines of the text.[34] Most important for the present purpose is the observation that it is a literary text that clearly uses school rubrics. These rubrics include the use of red ink for an apparent title to the text and instructions within the text as well as a frame to the text.[35] In addition, the text uses red ink to frame itself almost as if it were copying the framing rubrics used in papyrus documents. Scholars should take more notice that the red ink framing the inscription on the top extends as if they were planning a second column to the left (see my reconstruction in Figure 7.3). However, no writing is clearly part of a two column to the left. The main column begins with a title that refers to the "Teachings in Book of Balaam, the son of Beʿor" (A, 1).[36] The lower half (Combination B [II]) includes a rubric that refers to memorization and performance: "Do not you understand the art of writing? Recite and memorize it! May you have skillful and elaborate speech!" (B, 17).[37] Erhard Blum offers a plausible reconstruction here. More than this, he notes that various repetitions and parallelisms make it probable that the text was designed as verse poetry, even though the fragmentary state of preservation does not allow for an arrangement of verses.[38] Poetic parallelism would further lend the text to fledgling scribes memorizing and reciting the text. Frank Polak observes that the Balaam tale—both in Numbers and Deir ʿAlla—have elements, including parallelism and the interchange of divine names, that reflect oral composition and recitation.[39]

Figure 7.3 The layout of the Deir ʿAlla plaster texts. Reconstruction by the author.

The two combinations of the text may be summarized as follows. It begins with Balaam being visited by gods who are delivering a message of doom from El. Balaam is distressed. He weeps and fasts and tells his associates about his vision. There is a council of various gods who seem to oppose the coming doom. However, the heavens are sewn up, producing darkness, which creates panic on earth. There is a long list of birds that apparently are part of the panic. Balaam interprets the vision about the impending doom. But then the text becomes even more fragmentary and unclear. It seems the impending doom does not come to fruition. The next combination seems to be with El engaging in lovemaking and then constructing the netherworld. The Hebrew word *Sheol* may even occur in the text here. There is an unnamed wise counselor in the text—perhaps also Balaam—who is apparently denied his gift to pronounce oracles and execrations. Most interestingly, the second combination includes a rubric that apparently enjoins the reader to memorize and recite the text. Unfortunately, the text is so fragmentary that it is unclear how this rubric fits within the reading or performance of the text.

As enigmatic as the Deir ʿAlla plaster texts may be, they share with the biblical narrative the story of a theophany to the seer Balaam. In this respect, Deir ʿAlla also shares something significant with the Kuntillet ʿAjrud plaster texts. In both texts, we have divine theophanies. Theophanies are type scenes, which are staples of biblical literature.[40] They are central to biblical narratives like Exodus 14 and 19, but also to Hebrew liturgy in texts like Exodus 15 and Psalm 18. So it would hardly be surprising to see stories or liturgies describing theophanies incorporated into an advanced school curriculum. And the school rubrics employed in the Deir ʿAlla plaster texts certainly indicate that they were used as advanced curriculum for training scribes.

Legal Traditions

Legal codes were not a regular part of the advanced scribal curriculum. For example, in the famous Tablet House from Nippur that included 1,425 fragments of mostly school texts, legal codes were noticeably absent.[41] Among all these advanced school texts (which included twenty or more copies of the "Song of the Hoe," "Gilgamesh and Huwawa," and many other texts) only one fragment of a legal code was excavated: the Law Code of Lipit-Eshtar. And, unlike the *Gilgamesh Epic*, the Code of Hammurabi has not been found outside of the heartland of Mesopotamia. Additionally, no law codes were preserved at Ugarit, even though the site possessed many legal documents.[42] In other words, law codes were not central to the scribal school curriculum itself. Rather, they were a specialized curriculum. In this respect, the following paragraphs might be viewed as a digression. Yet, scholars do agree that Mesopotamian legal codes influenced the Covenant Code in Exodus. How, where, and when did this happen? There continues to be debate over the nature of the vector of transmission for this influence.[43] One thing seems certain: the influence was not the result of a widely distributed school curriculum. Yet the biblical legal codes are so significant and so much a part of the formation of biblical literature that some discussion seems warranted.[44]

Mesopotamian law was known and applied widely outside of the heartland. As Dalley points out, Hammurabi's laws, such as the river ordeal, "were widely used beyond Mesopotamia, in Iran, Syria, and Anatolia."[45] But if we wish to argue that the Code of Hammurabi or other Mesopotamian law codes were studied textually by ancient Israelite scribes, we are pressed hard by the actual physical evidence. When it comes to law codes, as Martha Roth points out, "the rare and fortunate scribes might be called upon to help collect, organize, and publicize a larger formal collection of laws and cases, possibly with a royal sponsor and patron. One such collection is that promulgated under the name of King Hammurabi of Babylon in 1750 B.C.E., which was copied and recopied in the scribal centers for over a thousand years."[46] Law codes were a specialized curriculum, but there were legal exercises among school texts. For example, general student exercises included works such as the *ana ittišu* lists, which influenced daily legal matters. Lexical lists of legal terms and formulas were copied and memorized by all aspiring scribes. Roth notes, "Most students used the lessons learned from these to draft the daily contracts of local life."[47] Even the most well-known legal code—the famous Code of Hammurabi, which became more popular in the Neo-Assyrian period—was not part of the scribal curriculum.[48] In the tens of thousands of documents recording lawsuits, court cases, legal transactions, and the like, there is no explicit reference to the Code of Hammurabi or any other legal code.[49] Still, the Code of Hammurabi did become part of a scholastic "canon"; that is, it was among the works copied by "the rare and fortunate scribes." Within the world of such elite cuneiform scribes, the Code did exert considerable literary influence.[50]

Could legal codes have been a legacy of the Late Bronze Age in the southern Levant? Perhaps. But it is very difficult to prove such a thesis. Alternatively, could a few Judean scribes have learned some Akkadian and some legal traditions during the period of Neo-Assyrian hegemony? Perhaps, but this is pure conjecture. Could a few Judean scribes have been tutored in the courts of Babylon during the exilic period? Perhaps, although this too is difficult to prove. Did Judean scribes ever study Akkadian? Unlikely. Maybe they learned cuneiform law codes orally? Arguments have been made for all these positions, but it will difficult to be certain unless more evidence is uncovered.

Establishing a vector of transmission for legal codes is critical to understanding the formation of biblical law codes. Scholars have argued for a wide array of dates for the Covenant Code based on its relationship to other (later) laws in Deuteronomy. Usually scholars have seen the Covenant Code influencing Deuteronomy,[51] but arguments have gone in the other direction as well.[52] Nevertheless, there seems to be a general consensus that the Covenant Code preceded Deuteronomy. Depending on the dating of the legal core of Deuteronomy (chapters 12–26), this seems to require at least a Neo-Assyrian date for the Covenant Code, although an even earlier date must be considered. Here, in the dating question, we confront the tangible vector of transmission problem. The most important book in recent years relating to this problem is David Wright's *Inventing God's Law: How the Covenant Code of the Bible Used and Revised the Laws of Hammurabi*. Wright opts for a Neo-Assyrian context for the Covenant Code and the influence of Hammurabi. He sees the parallels between the Code of Hammurabi and the Covenant Code to be quite close, but I think he overstates his case. I agree instead with David Carr, who observes that "the particular character of the adaptation of the Code of Hammurabi in Exod 22:22–23:33 (especially 21:1–22:19), along with its relative lack of reflection of monarchy in its laws (cf. Deut 17:14–20), points more toward an adaptation of the Code of Hammurabi (or a pre-Israelite, local version of it) early in the development of the monarchy."[53] As Bruce Wells points out, Wright has shown the Covenant Code is influenced generally by Near Eastern legal traditions, but not specifically by the Code of Hammurabi. Still, how scribes—in any period—came to know Near Eastern legal traditions has remained a problem until recently.

The possibility of a "local version" of the Code of Hammurabi has received some confirmation by two fragmentary cuneiform legal tablets that were recently discovered at Hazor.[54] The tablets date to the second millennium BCE and are vaguely similar to the Code of Hammurabi. The larger fragment, pictured in Figure 7.4, has been compared with the Laws of Eshnunna, but the parallel is not exact. Wayne Horowitz, Takayoshi Oshima, and Filip Vukosavović have suggested that the fragments represent the publication of a local law code, the "Hazor Code," as it were. This is an important contribution. Even before the Hazor Code had been published, Gary Knoppers and Paul Harvey had already posited local law codes in order to explain biblical law, but they could only cites examples from Greek and Roman law.[55] The Hazor Code is a striking confirmation of their intuition here. The Hazor Code now provides a much more concrete vector of transmission for the Covenant Code than the Code of Hammurabi.

The Hazor Code is a local legal tradition, independent but related to other Mesopotamian legal codes including the Code of Hammurabi. The

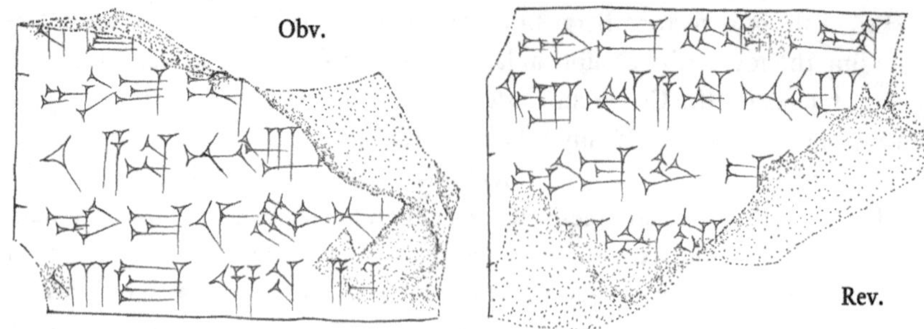

Figure 7.4 The "Hazor Code": Hazor 18, Fragment A. Drawing courtesy of Takayoshi Oshima.

Hazor Code preserves a section of laws delineating how an owner ought to be compensated for injuries to a slave. Such laws are known from the Code of Hammurabi, as in §199: *šumma īn warad awīlim utappid eṣemti warad awīlim ištebir misil šīmišu išaqqal*, "If he (an *awîlum* = man) should damage the eye of the slave of a man (or) break the bone of the slave of a man, he shall pay out one-half of his (the slave's) value." The Hazor Code, unfortunately, is much more fragmentary. The main fragment may be translated as follows:

Hazor 18 Fragment A

Obverse

[*šum-ma* . . .]	[If it is an eye . . .
12 ⸢GÍN⸣ [KÙ.BABBAR *a-na* . . .]	12 shekels of [silver to the . . .
šum-ma ⸢*ap*⸣-[*pu-um* . . .]	If (it is) the n[ose . . .
10 *a-na be-el* Ì[R . . .	10 (shekels of silver) to the owner of the sla[ve . . .
šum-ma ši-in-nu-[*um* . . .	If (it is) a tooth [. . .
3 GÍN KÙ.BABBAR ⸢*a*⸣-*n*[*a be-el* ÌR . . .	3 shekels of silver t[o the owner of the slave . . .

Reverse

šum-ma le-et [. . .	If the cheek of [the slave he has slapped
ù ÌR *a-na be-el* Ì[R . . .	[. . .] and the slave to the owner of the s[lave . . .]

šum-ma LÚ GIŠ.P[I.TUG . . .	If a man, the e[ar . . .]
⌜*ù*⌝ ÌR *i*[*m* . . .	and the slave [. . .]

The Laws of Eshnunna give us another parallel to the Hazor Code:

> *šumma awīlum appi awīlim iššukma ittakis 1 mana kašpam išaqqal īnum 1 mana šinnum 1/2 mana uznum 1/2 mana meheṣ lētim 10 šiqil kašpan išaqqal*, "If a man bit the nose of another man and thus has cut it off, he shall pay 1 mina (60 shekels) of silver; an eye, 1 mina; a tooth, ½ mina (30 shekels); an ear, 1/2 mina; a slap to the cheek, he shall pay out 10 shekels of silver."

The parallels from the Code of Hammurabi and the Laws of Eshnunna reflect a common topic, with slightly different enumerations in the respective texts. They emanate from a common legal tradition, but there is no straightforward textual relationship. The Hazor Code also includes independent legal traditions otherwise unknown in the Bible or other cuneiform law codes.[56] In other words, this is not a simple matter of textual copying. The Hazor Code is a similar, yet independent, tradition. Although the Code of Hammurabi is the best known of the legal traditions, there is no reason to assume biblical traditions depend directly or intimately on the Code of Hammurabi. The Hazor Code provides a corollary that now gives tangible evidence for suggesting a much more general relationship between Near Eastern legal traditions and the Covenant Code.

Can we posit some special relationship between the Hazor Code and the later development of the biblical Covenant Code (Exod 21–23)? This is a stretch. First of all, there is little known of the Hazor Code. It is just a couple fragments, although we may assume from the fragments that it belonged to a more extensive legal code like the Covenant Code, the Laws of Eshnunna, or the Code of Hammurabi. The Hazor Code also seems to date to the Middle Bronze Age, perhaps around 1700 BCE, and not the latest phase of the Bronze Age. The other examples cited in this book have quite consciously been taken from the last phase of the Late Bronze Age, when there would have been a more straightforward connection with an early alphabetic scribal curriculum. Still, it is not hard to imagine that this Hazor Code would have been passed on for generations in Canaan. By analogy, the remnants of the Old Babylonian cuneiform tradition continued into the Canaano-Akkadian texts from Amarna.

Many scholars have dismissed the possibility that Late Bronze Age cuneiform traditions influenced biblical law and scribes. Wright, for example, argues that cuneiform scribal schools "ceased to exist around 1200 BCE with the urban collapse at the end of the Late Bronze Age."[57] As a result, there could not be "maintenance" of the cuneiform legal tradition, unless it was completely oral. Wright believes the only plausible vector of transmission for the Covenant Code is the Neo-Assyrian period, that is, when Assyria exerted political and cultural influence over Judah.[58] However, Wright is wrong. He assumes the old model of an urban collapse and a two-century gap until the emergence of new polities (e.g., Israel, Phoenicia), which would require a purely oral transmission across centuries. But recent archaeological evidence suggests there was no such gap. Early Levantine polities emerged on the heels of the Late Bronze Age collapse at the end of the second millennium BCE. On the one hand, legal texts like the Hazor Code were part of the cuneiform scribal tradition in the Levant in the second millennium BCE; that is, there is a direct vector of transmission that may be posited. On the other hand, the Code of Hammurabi was not taught outside the borders of the Neo-Assyrian Empire in the eighth and seventh centuries BCE. The Assyrians used Aramaic as a lingua franca to administer their empire. There is no evidence that Code of Hammurabi was part of this administration. While Assyrian scribes still copied the Code of Hammurabi in Akkadian cuneiform, there is no evidence that they translated it into Aramaic. Nor do we have direct evidence that they taught any of their vassals the Code.

Another problem is that legal codes were not at all central to the cuneiform school curriculum.[59] There is no direct evidence to suggest that a cuneiform law code would have been needed for an early alphabetic scribal curriculum. Could a cuneiform law code have been translated and transmitted into early alphabetic? We now have some indication that there were cuneiform law codes like the Hazor Code that were known in the Levant in the second millennium. So this adds some plausibility for an early vector of transmission. Much of the answer depends on whether we see the late second millennium as a more plausible vector of transmission for a legal code than the Neo-Assyrian period or even the Neo-Babylonian period. There is little evidence to indicate that Judeans (or other peripheral vassals) needed to learn Akkadian in the Neo-Assyrian period or at any time. In fact, the Assyrians used Aramaic as a bureaucratic lingua franca so that foreigners did not need to be taught Akkadian cuneiform. The few cuneiform inscriptions in the West dating to the Neo-Assyrian period are monuments and bureaucratic texts—that is, they are evidence of Assyrian presence and a projection of Assyrian power, not evidence that Akkadian was actually taught in the periphery. In other words, if the Code of Hammurabi became known at all in the periphery, it was likely taught orally rather than learned scholastically in Akkadian.[60] From this point of view, the late second millennium might offer a more tangible *textual* vector of transmission, whereas the Neo-Assyrian period might suggest an *oral* vector of transmission. The evidence is thin for either alternative, although I prefer the late second millennium because at least there is some fragmentary evidence of a cuneiform legal tradition.

The implausibility of Judeans knowing Akkadian and the Code of Hammurabi during the Neo-Assyrian period led scholars like John van Seters and William Morrow to suggest a Neo-Babylonian context.[61] At least in the Neo-Babylonian period, Judeans were actually physically in the palaces of Babylon, although why they would have been studying Neo-Babylonian cuneiform is a bit puzzling. By the Neo-Babylonian period, cuneiform learning was increasingly a narrow scholastic topic. Aramaic was firmly entrenched as the lingua franca, and the purpose of borrowing from Akkadian law codes to create new law codes for a defunct state and exiled people also takes more than a little imagination. The physical presence of exiles in Babylon makes a vector of transmission seem more plausible, but it still seems quite unlikely that the Code of Hammurabi would have been known to Judean exiles *in Akkadian cuneiform*. Again, however, we need only be speaking of a single scribe, and it is difficult to account for what a single scribe may have learned at any moment in the historical process.

Finally, the Code of Hammurabi was a textual monument. It was important for scribes to create such monuments, and these monumental traditions were part of the larger scribal craft. This is indicated not only by an imposing physical example but also by a literary prologue dedicated to the ruler. It projected monumental symbolism both as a textual artifact and as a physical inscribed statue. In this respect, although the Code of Hammurabi is often compared to the Covenant Code, it actually has a striking similarity to the Ten Commandments in its status as a textual monument. The Ten Commandments stand as a victory commemoration in the Exodus narrative. They come after Yahweh's victory over the Egyptians at the Red Sea. As Timothy Hogue has pointed out,[62] the Israelites travel to a liminal boundary after their victory—Mount Sinai—and God gives the Ten Commandments, which begin in the traditional manner of Northwest Semitic monumental stelae: "I am the LORD, your God, who brought you out of the land of Egypt" (Ex 20:1). Compare the Mesha Inscription, "I am Mesha, son of Chemoshyat" (KAI 181:1), or the Kilamuwa Inscription, "I am Kilamuwa, son of Hayya" (KAI 24:1), or the Panamuwa Inscription, "I am Panamuwa, son of Qarli" (KAI 214:1). Indeed, Hogue points to numerous other examples of the similarities between Northwest Semitic monumental inscriptions and the Ten Commandments. In Exodus, the Ten Commandments are a textual monument, but in the Book of Deuteronomy they first become directly associated with a physical monument: the two tablets (Deut 4:13, 5:22, 9:9–17). These monuments, however, were not school texts. And biblical literature does not present them as such. Indeed in Deuteronomy Moses locked the tablets of the Ten Commandments within the inaccessible Ark of the Covenant. Thus, from a biblical perspective, they were not school texts. On the other hand, the creation of textual monuments was part of shared West Semitic scribal tradition as "I am PN" formula illustrates.

In sum, what type of texts would have made up an advanced curriculum in ancient Israel? Based on the Mesopotamian curriculum, we may surmise that an advanced curriculum consisted of liturgical and ritual texts as well as canonical literary texts such as the Gilgamesh Epic.[63] Liturgical texts—that is, hymns and poetry—made up the preponderance of the advanced school curriculum in ancient Mesopotamia. Such texts are perfect for memorization and oral recitation. At the same time, such an advanced scribal curriculum was not practical for a would-be scribe who spent most of his time with mundane bureaucratic texts—letters, lists, receipts, contracts. Perhaps this is why an advanced curriculum was mostly memorized and recited as opposed to written and copied. This observation should frame our analysis of the Kuntillet ʿAjrud plaster fragments, which were decidedly not elementary school texts. And they were originally not school texts either. Rather they are poetic texts, perhaps some sort of liturgy. But we also know that liturgical and poetic texts in the cuneiform tradition were exploited for use as school texts. We may posit the same for the Kuntillet ʿAjrud plaster texts.

Advanced Hebrew Curriculum and the Kuntillet ʿAjrud Plaster Fragments

The plaster texts at Kuntillet ʿAjrud include six inscriptions excavated in two areas, KA 4.1–3 in the front gate area and KA 4.4–6 near the rear storage area. The front area with the gate actually has benches (like the room with the Deir ʿAlla plaster texts), which might have been conducive to teaching. The two inscribed pithoi were found in the vicinity of the gate area. While the ink inscriptions on Pithoi A and B are quite straightforwardly school exercises, the plaster texts are the subject of more debate.[64] Were they religious texts? When Zeev Meshel subtitled his publication of the site of Kuntillet ʿAjrud as *An Iron Age Religious Site*, the inscriptions—including both the pithoi and the plaster wall texts—were a contributing factor in his interpretation. As we have seen, however, the pithoi inscriptions were scribal practice and school exercises. What about the plaster wall texts? Were they school texts like the pithoi? The plaster inscriptions are certainly religious texts, but this does not preclude them from also being school texts. Indeed most advanced cuneiform curricula were composed of religious texts, especially liturgy and ritual texts, because religion was part of the fabric of ancient society. It would be strange if an advanced curriculum had no religious content. For this reason, the larger context of the inscriptions is critical. With regard to its geographical context, Kuntillet ʿAjrud was a remote fortress along a desert trade route. And, as we have established, it had a large number and variety of scribal exercises. It would be unique and unusual to interpret such a site as a strictly religious enclave. It is natural to consider whether the plaster wall texts were more than strictly religious.

Advanced literary texts were an important part of the scribal curriculum. But why would they be located at a remote fortress? Surely soldier-scribes did not need to learn such religious texts to be effective. As discussed in chapter 2, Kuntillet ʿAjrud was a military outpost, not a priestly community. A desert fortress on a caravan route from Eilat to Gaza is not exactly where one might expect to find such literary compositions. There seems to be little practical purpose in teaching a soldier-scribe advanced lessons in literature. For these reasons, most scholars have generally avoided reading the Kuntillet ʿAjrud literary inscriptions as school texts. The significant exception among scholars has been André Lemaire, who has long argued that these inscriptions should be considered school texts.[65]

Impracticality is not an obstacle to interpreting the plaster texts as advanced school curricula. Education often involves learning things that are not particularly practical. This truism certainly also applies to ancient scribal education. We should recall again the observation by Niek Veldhuis cited at the beginning of the book regarding Mesopotamian scribal training: "A scribe learned far too much. A scribe had to be able to write contracts and business documents. . . . But a considerable part of the words he had learned in the lexical lists was obscure, obsolete, or for other reasons of no practical use. If we take into account the literary exercises the burden of 'useless' knowledge a scribal pupil had to digest is all the more impressive." Although we need not imagine Israelite scribes had the same burden of esoteric knowledge as the Mesopotamian scribes, it is not a problem to assume that Israelite education had a degree of impracticality that would have included literary texts like the Kuntillet ʿAjrud plaster inscriptions. Moreover liturgical texts similar to the Kuntillet ʿAjrud plaster inscriptions are typical of the advanced curriculum that we know from Mesopotamia.

An excellent illustration of the scope of the Mesopotamian curriculum was found in the excavations of the Tablet House in Nippur.[66] There was found a cache of nearly 1,500 tablets related to scribal training that have been analyzed and classified. Seven of the ten works of advanced cuneiform curriculum from the Tablet House—the so-called Decad of the advanced curriculum—are hymns or songs. These hymns and songs are found in large qualities in the Tablet House at Nippur even though it was not a temple or a temple school. This illustrates that the reappropriation of liturgical texts is typical for advanced scribal training. The fact that the hymns are found among the Decad shows how such religious texts could be reappropriated in a school context. For example, the Kesh Temple Hymn, which had twenty-four copies in the Nippur Tablet House, was certainly still used as a religious text. But in the Tablet House, it was part of a scribal school curriculum. Thus, the religious nature of the poetry at Kuntillet

ʿAjrud does not make the site a temple or a shrine, nor does it make the scribes a group of priests or prophets. Religious poetry was part of the scribal curriculum, and its context at a remote fortress like Kuntillet ʿAjrud suggests just such a function.[67]

Discerning the purpose of the plaster inscriptions is not helped by their fragmentary preservation. The excavators identified and published six separate inscriptions written with ink on the plastered walls of the fortress.[68] Three inscriptions were near the entrance and three near the backroom of the fortress. Only one of the poorly preserved inscriptions (KA 4.3) was found partially intact on a wall. Because of the laconic nature of these fragmentary texts, there is not much to be gained in the philological analysis of these texts that definitively answers the question of their purpose.

The plaster wall inscriptions were the work of several different scribes over a period of time. One of the more curious aspects of the plaster texts from Kuntillet ʿAjrud is that five of the six inscriptions are written in Phoenician script as opposed to the Hebrew script of the pithoi. The fact that there are several different scribal hands within the Phoenician inscriptions complicates matters further. As several scholars have pointed out, the scribal handwriting in the plaster inscriptions is quite distinct from the pithoi inscriptions. The language of the plaster inscriptions, however, is still distinctly Hebrew. And the orthography has been thought to be specifically Judean because of the preservation of diphthongs (e.g., *tymn* and *qyṣ* in KA 4.1 and 4.3), but the evidence for this as a distinguishing Judean linguistic feature is rather thin.[69] The comparative corpus for Israelian inscriptions is quite minimal, and this feature cannot bear the entire weight for labeling these inscriptions as reflecting aspects of Judean Hebrew. The limited comparative material certainly adds another layer of complexity to the interpretation of the wall inscriptions. Nevertheless, the paleographic analysis still points to multiple scribes and phases during the fortress's occupation.

The location of the inscriptions within the fortress is also important to their interpretation, particularly for the plaster inscriptions. For example, there is a large number of incised inscriptions (KA 2.1–2.28) at Kuntillet ʿAjrud that are essentially labels on pottery. Not surprisingly, incised inscriptions are concentrated in storage areas, although they are also scattered about the fortress, as might be expected. In contrast, the first set of plaster inscriptions (4.1–3) was found not far from Pithoi A and B, near the entrance to the fortress. This suggests, first, that the scribal exercises on Pithoi A and B might be related to the plaster wall inscriptions. Also of interest are the benches in the gate at the entrance where plaster inscriptions 4.1–3 were found. Such benches are unusual, but they do find a parallel in the room where the Deir ʿAlla plaster wall inscriptions were found (discussed above). Taken together, the physical context for plaster wall inscriptions also invites an interpretation relating to school curricula.

As mentioned above, the plaster texts are fragmentary and their reconstruction is quite tentative. Many of the plaster fragments have just a single letter or a couple partial letters. Still, it is worth presenting the more substantial fragments that contain translatable texts. The most substantial texts include KAI 4.1.1, 4.2. 4.3, 4.4.1, and 4.6.4.[70] I generally follow the reconstructions of the original publication, with minor differences based on other scholars' readings and my analysis of the published photographs, along with some original photographs (courtesy of West Semitic Research).[71] The inscriptions are too incomplete for many definitive improvements in the readings from the official edition. In any case, minor debates over the content and readings do not substantially change the question about whether these texts were intended for an advanced scribal curriculum. For these reasons, I do not wish to stray too far from the readings in the original publication in this context.

KAI 4.1.1 + 4.1.4, 4.1.3, 4.1.12 [for 4.1.4, 4.1.3, 4.1.12, see chapter 2]

0. [ ]*nʿry .⸢ś⸣rʿr*
1. [. . . *y*]*ʾrk.ymm.wyšbʿw*[. . . *w*]*ytnw.l*[*y*]*hwh*[.]*tymn.wlʿšrth*[. . .]
2. [. . . *k*]*y.hyṭb yhwh.hty*[*mn* . . .]*y hyṭb.ym*[*m* . . . *w*]*y⸢tnw⸣.y*[. . .]

0. [For] the Apprentices of the Commander of the Fortress[. . .]
1 [. . . May] he lengthen your days, and may they be full[. . . and] they shall give/recount to Yahweh of Têman and to his *ʾasherah*[72]
2. [. . . be]cause Yahweh of Tê[man] he has shown them favor [. . .] he has improved their day[s . . . and] they have given [. . .]

KAI 4.2

1. [. . .] *šnt* [. . .]
2. [. . .]*brʿš.wbzrḥ.ʾl.br*[*m.y*]*hw*[*h* . . .]
3. [. . .]*r.wymsn.hrm.wydkn.*[*g*]*bnm*[. . .]
4. [. . . h]*ʿrṣ.q*{*š*}*dš.ʿly.ʾlm*[. . .]
5. [. . .]*hkn* [*l*]*brk.bʿl.bym.mlḥmh*
6. [. . .]*l*[*brk.wlh*]*ll šm ʾl.bym.mlḥ*[*mh* . . .]

1. [. . .] years? [. . .]
2. [. . .]in the earthquake. And when El shines forth on the hei[ghts. Ya]hwe[h . . .]
3. [. . .]R. The mountains will melt, the hills will crush [. . .]
4. [. . . the] earth. The Holy One over the gods [. . .]
5. [. . .] prepare to bless Baʿal on the day of war [. . .]
6. [. . .] to [bless and pr]aise the name of ʾEl on the day of wa[r . . .]

KAI 4.3 (located in situ on the wall, 1.3 m above floor)
1. [. . .] *traces*
2. [. . .]*hly*[. . .]
3. [. . .]ʿ [. . .]*lyd*[.]*t*[. . .]*hn*[. . .]
4. [. . .]*yr hsq.b* ʾ[. . .]ʾ [. . .]*b*[. . .]
5. [. . .]*š*[. . .]*w*[. . .]*by*[. . .]
6. [. . .]*l*[. . .]*wy*[. . .]*k*[. . .]*ḥ*[. . .]*k* ʾ*d*[. . .]
7. [. . .]*n*[. . .]*nyw*[. . .]*šḥt qyn šdh wmrm h*[*rm* . . .]

7. [. . .] the Kênite destroyed a mountain and lofty mou[ntain range . . .]

KAI 4.4.1
1. [. . .] *traces*
2. [. . .]*p*ʿ*l.bq*[. . .][73]
3. [. . .]*hn.*ʾ*y*[. . .]

1. [. . .]
2. [. . .] made with [. . .]
3. [. . .]

KAI 4.6.4
1. [. . .] *traces*
2. [. . . *š*]*mm*[.*y*]*šm*ʿ*.kk*[*l* . . .]
3. [. . .]ʾ*mr.*ʾ*š/k/m.*ʾ*t.l*[. . .]
4. [. . .]ʾ*mr yš*ʾ*l*[. . .]
5. [. . .] *traces*

1. [. . .]
2. [. . . he]avens [shall] hear according to ever[ything . . .]
3. [. . .]said that you[. . .]
4. [. . .]said that he shall ask[. . .]
5. [. . .]

Let's be candid. Although the plaster inscriptions were quite extensive, there's not much left here, and much of it is tentative. Still, they will be important to our consideration of the advanced scribal curriculum. In chapter 2, I discussed the reconstructed title of the first inscription (line 0), "[For] the Apprentices of the Commander of the Fortress." This reconstruction is compelling and should shape our entire reading of the plaster inscriptions. Indeed the expression seems as though it would have little purpose in the poetry of the plaster fragments except as a title. This reconstruction then recasts the inscriptions in an entirely new light: they are educational; they are for the apprentices stationed at the fortress.

While the content of the study of these apprentices is fragmentary, some important themes may still be discerned as well as some literary techniques. The texts are clearly poetic and perhaps liturgical with religious themes. There is also a geographic dimension to the inscriptions that is appropriate to the location of this desert fortress. For example, they mention a more localized "Yahweh of Têman." In addition, the well-known Hebrew poetic technique of parallelism can be discerned in the fragments. For example, we find, "to bless Baal on the day of war, the name of El on the day of war" and "the mountains will melt, the hills will crush." Or "may He lengthen your days, may they be full" and "they shall give to Yahweh of Têman and to his *ʾasherah*." These are just the better-preserved examples of the parallelism that can be suggested throughout the plaster inscriptions (in spite of their fragmentary preservation). In this respect, the Kuntillet ʿAjrud poetry fits nicely with what is known from Ugaritic literature, Near Eastern poetry, and biblical poetry. Parallelism and word pairs are also hallmarks of oral composition and ready-made for memorization.[74] Moreover, poetic parallelism suggests that these texts came from a liturgy—which is one of the primary categories of an advanced cuneiform scribal curriculum.

Yahweh, El, and Baal are mentioned in the fragmentary texts. In KA 4.1, "Yahweh of Têman" or "Yahweh of the South" (*yhwh htymn*) is mentioned twice, along with the familiar concept of God blessing people and "lengthening their days" (*yʾrk ymm*). KA 4.2 seems to have a divine theophany where "El shines forth" (*wbzrḥ ʾl*); as a result, "the mountains melt" (*wymsn hrm*) and "the peaks are crushed" (*wydkn gbnm*). The reading "El shines forth" (*wb⌜z⌝rḥ ʾl*), is revised to "in the month of El" (*wb⌜y⌝rḥ ʾl*) in the Hebrew edition of the Kuntillet ʿAjrud inscriptions, but the epigraphic evidence is equivocal. The original reading remains more coherent, although admittedly tentative. The theophany is accompanied by the related and repeated concept of theomachy—"on the day of war" (*bym mlḥmh*). Theophany is, as mentioned in the context of Deir ʿAlla, a typical biblical topos, and these texts have specific parallels within biblical literature. So, for example, 1Sam 13:22, Hos 10:14, Amos 1:14, and Prov 21:31 all mention the "day of war." We witness the divine theophany accompanied by earthquakes especially in Psalm 18 as well as in Exodus 19. Earthquakes probably also generate the metaphor of "melting mountains" reflected in biblical poetry (e.g., Ps 97.4, Isa 34.3, Mic 1:4). And the divine theophany, *wbzrḥ.ʾl.br[m*, "and when El shines forth on the hei[ghts," resembles the imagery in Deut 33:2, "The LORD came from Sinai, and dawned from Seir upon us, he shone forth (*wzbḥ*) from Mount Paran." In both texts, the deity appears in a theophany in mountains. Military conflict or "a day of war," perhaps aided by the divine, is alluded to in a variety of texts. The plaster texts also seem to mention the Kenites, or perhaps the prediluvian villain Cain, in a military context (i.e., *šḥt*, "to destroy").

The geographic themes of the texts certainly are appropriate to its location. For example, the description of "Yahweh of Têman" locates the deity in a specific location, perhaps in the southern part of Edom or the Sinai. Given that Têman appears with the definite article (*yhwh htymn*), it should probably not be interpreted as a proper name. Rather, it is more likely a general term meaning "south." Perhaps it was originally a common noun and later developed into a proper name for the region. In any case, Têman or "the South" is more geographically appropriate to Kuntillet ʿAjrud's location than "Yahweh of Samaria." In Hab 3:3, we have the image *ʾlwh mtymn ybwʾ*, "Eloah comes (forth) from Têman." This metaphor of theophany is related to the sunrise, and it recalls the more vivid language in KA 4.2 line 2, *bzrḥ.ʾl*, "when El shines forth." The mention of a divine theophany is also accompanied by earthquake imagery, which is again appropriate to the region given its proximity to the Red Sea Geological Rift and its frequent earthquakes. The mention of the "day of war" recalls the theme of divine conflict, or theomachy, which is quite typical of Near Eastern mythology. The "day of war" also fits well with the interpretation of Kuntillet ʿAjrud as a military fortress sponsored by the state.[75] In general, the advanced scribal curriculum was more flexible, and thus it is appropriate that the themes of the Kuntillet ʿAjrud plaster texts seem especially appropriate to its local geographic, geologic, and functional context.

The theme of theomachy in the plaster texts is more generic. This kind of language appears in prominent texts like the Song of the Sea, the Ugaritic Baʿal Epic, and the Babylonian Creation Epic. In fact, all these literary texts could work perfectly as school texts; at the same time, this conjecture is based purely on the general context of the site and the other inscriptions. Such literary texts would be largely memorized and recited orally rather than copied as school exercises. It is for this reason that these literary texts were situated on the walls of the fortress rather than copied as exercises.

Biblical literary and ritual texts are deeply indebted to the religious, social, and political contexts of the ancient Near East. That is, they are a product of their times. Sometimes they appear to directly borrow and adapt Near Eastern antecedents. Examples of this are plentiful, including the *Instruction of Amenemope* in Proverbs, the *Hymn to Aten* in Psalm 104, and cuneiform legal and treaty traditions such as the *Vassal Treaty of Esarhaddon*.[76] In the Kuntillet ʿAjrud plaster texts, we seem to have religious and liturgical texts, albeit fragmentary, that would have worked well as an advanced curriculum. They would have essentially been like "library copies." The elegant paleography suggests they were written by master scribes. To repeat the words in the colophon of the Enuma Elish, "The master and the student should study them together, the teacher reads them and the pupil repeats them." The plaster texts would have been the kind of texts that students recited and memorized. The student learned them "by heart." In this respect, they would reflect an oral aspect of scribal education.

Epilogue

What have we accomplished here? First, this book has sketched out some of the historical context from which the early Israelite scribal curriculum emerged. In particular, we have seen that the early Israelite scribal curriculum began to develop in the transition from the Late Bronze Age to the early Iron Age, that is, between the twelfth and tenth centuries BCE. The alphabetic scribal culture of the early Levantine polities—particularly the Phoenician city-states and early Israel—owed a great deal to the demise of the great Egyptian empire of the New Kingdom.

As the New Kingdom receded, new polities emerged. These emerging kingdoms borrowed and adapted some of the Egyptian bureaucracy that was left behind as Egypt retreated to its confines along the Nile River Valley. This included, first of all, the technology of writing itself. The use of ink in early alphabetic inscriptions, for example, was an Egyptian legacy. Another significant contribution was the Egyptian accounting system, beginning with hieratic numerals but also including several loanwords pertaining to measurement and accounting. The Egyptian hieroglyphic writing system itself, however, was not part of the Egyptian legacy in the Levant. Rather, the Egyptians propagated the cuneiform writing system, which was already known and widely used throughout the Near East in the second millennium.

Second, this book has illustrated some of the tangible influence of the cuneiform school tradition in the development of an early alphabetic curriculum. This should not be surprising. There was no need to invent an alphabetic scribal curriculum from scratch. Almost the entire scope of the cuneiform elementary curriculum can be found in fragmentary inscriptions from the Levant dating to the Late Bronze Age. In other words, there was a local infrastructure for training scribes to read and write using the traditional cuneiform elementary education curriculum. This spread of the cuneiform scribal infrastructure to the periphery is specific to the second millennium BCE, and especially the Late Bronze Age. In contrast, there are no cuneiform school texts in Israel dating to the Iron Age (or later). This is an important observation when we consider the "vectors of transmission" for cuneiform scribal education and its influence on alphabetic writing. The Late Bronze–Iron Age transition became the critical moment for the formation of an early alphabetic scribal curriculum.

Third, I have offered examples of how the cuneiform scribal curriculum can be seen in early Hebrew inscriptions. This is evident, for example, with the Gezer Calendar, which looks like an adaptation of a Mesopotamian lexical tradition. More strikingly, I have shown that Kuntillet ʿAjrud inscriptions are a group of scribal exercises reflecting an array of the educational curricular categories that we know from the cuneiform tradition. It is hardly surprising that early alphabetic education would not have been invented de novo but rather adapted from previous models. For the emerging Israelite polity, the tradition at hand was the cuneiform tradition. This cuneiform scribal tradition disappeared in the Levant at the end of the Late Bronze Age—particularly with the retrenchment of the Egyptian Empire in the twelfth century BCE. This was the very period when alphabetic writing begins to emerge in the southern Levant. Thus there is no large gap between the demise of cuneiform culture and the emergence of early alphabetic culture, but rather a waning and waxing. Cuneiform was the writing system of the declining Egyptian administration in Canaan; the alphabet would be the writing system of the emerging polities. The change in writing systems should also be understood as a linguistic choice, with the cuneiform system being associated with the old colonial regime and the alphabetic system being adopted as a local innovation. There were likely elements of both utility and ideology intertwined in this shift.

Fourth, the elementary scribal curriculum is critical to understanding how education shaped what scribes composed and transmitted. The Hebrew Bible was influenced by the education of its scribes and, in particular, by their curriculum. This scribal education was quite conservative. It was passed along from generation to generation with little change. Major social upheavals, however, did profoundly shape innovation and changes. For ancient Israelite education, the first upheaval was the collapse of the Egyptian New Kingdom administration and the emergence of early Levantine polities (e.g., Phoenician city-states, Israel, and Judah). The next major upheaval was the rise of the Neo-Assyrian Empire, which would change the entire face of the ancient Near East for centuries. The Assyrians put an end to the Israelite states, and the Babylonians took over the Assyrian Empire and finally extinguished the Judean state. The destruction of Jerusalem and Judah resulted in the eclipse of the scribal infrastructure of the Hebrew alphabetic writing. The conditions during the Babylonian and early Persian periods were no longer conducive to the flourishing of Hebrew literature. A new scribal infrastructure would be built in the Persian period, but it was a new system complete with a different alphabet (borrowed from Aramaic) and presumably a new curriculum. Unlike the transition from the Late Bronze Age to the early Iron Age, the transition from the Iron Age to the Persian period was a break—not merely a waning and waxing.[1]

Finally, and most important, scribal creativity had its foundation in the building blocks of the educational curriculum. Adaptation was a literary tool in the formulation of biblical literature. These adaptations could be mundane but also quite profound. It started with using the alphabet as an organizing principle in literature and poetry. Furthermore, one of the more significant aspects of the curriculum was the making of lists, which began as a way for scribes to learn vocabulary. Copying lexical lists would also have been foundational for practicing penmanship as well as learning correct spelling—that is to say, paleography and orthography should be understood in the context of copying lexical lists. Making lists was one of the most important everyday tasks of the scribes, whether they were working for the palace, the temple, or the public market. Indeed 75 percent of Mesopotamian tablets are administrative and economic documents—variations of lists. As an abstraction, lists could be a way of organizing knowledge and the universe. Thus Solomon could learn to pontificate from lists about trees or animals as a reflection of his apparent study of lists that organized wisdom and knowledge (e.g., 1Kgs 4:33). But lists also had a more mundane purpose in the everyday life of a scribe. As Jack Goody points out, such lists, record keeping, and ledgers were central to the organization of complex societies.[2] And biblical literature incorporates a great variety of lists, including genealogies, tribute lists, receipts, accounting, administration, and itineraries, just to mention a few.[3] Ancient Israelite scribes adapted these lists for a variety of purposes in the composition of biblical literature.

One of the more productive adaptations in scribal education was letter writing. It has long been recognized that the genre of divine speech in prophetic writings owes much to the *Sitz im Leben* of sending messengers. This makes it seem as though divine speech had its origins strictly in an oral setting. Yet in the context of the Late Bronze and Iron Age, the sending of messengers was closely tied to the training of scribes. Letters were written and read. Scribes learned to write the forms and formulas. Although there was an oral performance by the messenger, the performance arose out of this scribal background. Letter writing was thus the basis for the divine messenger formulae of prophetic literature. But letter writing also influenced biblical narrative. Ever since the emergence of form criticism, oral storytelling has been a central part of our understanding of biblical narrative. And there is certainly an oral component to biblical narratives. At the same time, the use of messenger speech scenes as part of the literary style in biblical narrative owes a great deal to the forms of letter writing. Even one of the smallest aspects of the genre of letter writing—namely, the use of "and now" (ועתה) as a transitional phrase marking the break between a letter's formal introduction and the body of the letter—was adapted and used widely as a transitional marker in a variety of contexts in biblical literature. A scribe may have learned the expression while learning how to write letters, but it was adapted for a variety of other literary contexts in biblical literature. For a writing system like early Hebrew that did not have paragraph markers, it was a useful tool in the scribe's toolbox. And it illustrates how scribal education could influence biblical literature in ways both small and large.

Scribes also copied and memorized a variety of sayings. This practice is well attested in the cuneiform tradition. Now we have a glimpse of it in the Hebrew inscriptional corpus from Kuntillet ʿAjrud. As part of one of the practice letters, the writer included a traditional reciprocity formula (discussed in chapter 6). As we pointed out, the saying is strikingly similar to a verse in the Psalms (e.g., 20:3 [Eng. v. 2]), but also a variety of sayings in other biblical texts. Similar reciprocity formulas were pointed out in the Amarna letters as well as in Northwest Semitic inscriptions. Most noteworthy was the playful adaptation of the reciprocity formula in a practice letter from Ugarit (*KTU* 5.9). The long and conservative aspects of the educational curriculum were further suggested by the incorporation and adaptation of Psalm 20 by Papyrus Amherst 63, a fourth-century Aramaic text written with the Demotic writing system. This one example of a traditional saying in the student exercise from Kuntillet ʿAjrud inspires us to look for other vestiges of the scribal curriculum in biblical literature. One obvious example may be a proverb that is cited in two different biblical texts: "The parents eat sour grapes, and the children's teeth are set on edge" (Jer 31:29 and Ezek 18:2). We have good reason to believe that biblical wisdom literature and poetry incorporated sayings that were part of scribal education, even if their present form is an adaptation.

The part of scribal education that we know the least about is advanced education. There may be glimpses of an advanced curriculum in the plaster wall texts from Kuntillet ʿAjrud and Deir ʿAlla. Unfortunately, they are quite fragmentary, and their precise purpose remains uncertain. However, they seem to represent the genre of liturgical texts, which is one of the well-known categories of an advanced cuneiform scribal curriculum. It is also important to acknowledge that these plaster wall texts were not practice texts; they both give every indication of being written by an accomplished scribe. This actually accords well with an advanced cuneiform curriculum, which was often recited and memorized as opposed to being student practice texts. Scribes learned to write by practicing more elementary texts in the curriculum, including lexical lists, model texts (like letters), and sayings. The advanced curriculum was learned "by the heart," as the colophon to the Enuma Elish says. Likewise, the advanced learning of alphabetic scribes was through memorization and recitation. Biblical literature that might have been an advanced curriculum includes older songs such as Exodus 15. Indeed a liturgical text like Psalm 18, which is also integrated into a biblical narrative (2 Samuel 22), could have been part of a scribal curriculum. Liturgical texts like Psalm 100, which was widely borrowed, adapted, and interpreted by other biblical texts (e.g., Psalms 79, 95, and Ezekiel 34), might also have served as a scribal curriculum. Here, I am also reflecting on Seth Sanders's "rule of popularity," namely that "widely distributed material is more likely to be known."[4] In the same way, it seems likely that some biblical texts that were repeated, widely cited, adapted, and interpreted inner-biblically or extra-biblically may have originally had a role in the advanced scribal curriculum of ancient Israel and Judah.

Notes

Chapter 1

1. For robust reconstructions of ancient Israelite education, see André Lemaire, *Les écoles et la formation de la bible dans l'ancien Israël*, OBO 39 (Göttingen: Vandenhoek & Ruprecht, 1981), and Aaron Demsky, *Literacy in Ancient Israel* (Jerusalem: Bialik Institute, 2012) [Hebrew]. Erhard Blum has supported Lemaire's contention that the plaster texts from Deir 'Alla should be understood as more compelling evidence of an institutional school context than scholars have recognized; see Erhard Blum, "Dei altaramäischen Wandinscriften vom Tell Deir 'Alla und ihr Institutioneller Kontext," in *Materiale Textkulturen* (Berlin: de Gruyter, 2016), 36–40.
2. Karel Van der Toorn, *Scribal Culture and the Making of the Hebrew Bible* (Cambridge, MA: Harvard University Press, 2007), 97; for a similar assessment, see Nili Shupak, who writes, "No actual evidence for the existence of the institution of a school in Israel in the First Temple era has been found. Nor has any school literature, such as that discovered in Mesopotamia and Egypt, which sheds light on the school milieu, the material learned and the schooling methods, been uncovered" ("Learning Methods in Ancient Israel," *VT* 53 [2003]: 416).
3. See, for example, Christopher Rollston, "Scribal Curriculum during the First Temple Period: Epigraphic Hebrew and Biblical Evidence," in *Contextualizing Israel's Sacred Writings: Ancient Literacy, Orality, and Literary Production*, ed. Brian Schmidt (Atlanta, GA: Society of Biblical Literature, 2015), 71–102; also see Rollston's more general work, *Writing and Literacy in the World of Ancient Israel: Epigraphic Evidence from the Iron Age* (Atlanta, GA: Society of Biblical Literature, 2010).
4. David McLain Carr, *Writing on the Tablet of the Heart: Origins of Scripture and Literature* (Oxford: Oxford University Press, 2005), 156.
5. Proverbs is often cited as an example of a school curriculum, both in oral and written contexts, e.g., August Klostermann, *Schulwesen im alten Israel* (Leipzig: Georg Böhme, 1908); Gerhard von Rad, "Hiob XXXVIII Und Die Altägyptische Weisheit," in *Wisdom in Israel and in the Ancient Near East. Presented to Harold Henry Rowley by the Editorial Board of Vetus Testamentum in Celebration of His 65th Birthday, 24 March 1955*, ed. Martin Noth and D. Winton Thomas (SVT 3; Leiden: Brill, 1969). However, even this example is problematic; see now Jacqueline Vayntrub, "The Book of Proverbs and the Idea of Ancient Israelite Education," *ZAW* 128 (2016): 96–114.
6. Van der Toorn, *Scribal Culture*, 245.
7. *Enuma Elish* VII:145–46, 157–58 (as cited by van der Toorn, *Scribal Culture*, 245).

8. The term "school" can be problematic, as Christopher A. Rollston points out in "Scribal Education in Ancient Israel: The Old Hebrew Epigraphic Evidence," *BASOR* 344 (2006): 49–50.
9. See Yoram Cohen, *The Scribes and Scholars of the City of Emar in the Late Bronze Age* (Winona Lake, IN: Eisenbrauns, 2009).
10. See discussion by William Schniedewind, *A Social History of Hebrew: Its Origins through the Rabbinic Period* (New Haven, CT: Yale University Press, 2013), 59.
11. Schniedewind, *A Social History of Hebrew*, 57–59.
12. See Benjamin Sass, Yosef Garfinkel, Michael Hasel, and Martin Klingbeil, "The Lachish Jar Sherd: An Early Alphabetic Inscription Discovered in 2014," *BASOR* 374 (2015): 233–45. Also see André Lemaire, "Notes d'épigraphie sémitique," *Semitica* 58 (2016), 233–43. Also see my interpretation, "The Alphabetic 'Scribe' of the Lachish Jar Inscription and the Hieratic Tradition in the Early Iron Age," *BASOR* forthcoming.
13. A plausible alternative might be "PN *recorded* [. . .] 5 Hekat of wheat."
14. Sass et al., "The Lachish Jar Sherd," 243.
15. Georg Möller, *Hieratische Paläographie*, vol. 2 (Osnabrück: Otto Zeller, 1965), 50, no. 561.
16. The much later Palestinian hieratic system in Hebrew texts from the eighth and seventh centuries further simplified *ḥqꜣ.t* to a dot or a small, u-shaped, half circle; see Stefan Wimmer, *Palästinisches Hieratisch: Die Zahl- und Sonderzeichen in der althebräischen Schrift* (*ÄAT* 75; Wiesbaden: Harrassowitz, 2008), 262–67.
17. Wimmer, *Palästinisches Hieratisch*, 205.
18. Hana Vymazalová, "The Wooden Tablets from Cairo: The Use of the Grain Unit *hk3t* in Ancient Egypt," *Archiv Orientalia* 70 (2002): 27–42; also see Wolfgang Helck, "Maße und Gewichte," in *Lexikon der Ägyptologie*, vol. 3, ed. Wolfgang Helck and Wolfhart Westendorf (Wiesbaden: Harrassowtiz, 1980), 1199–209, esp. 1201–202.
19. According to Yosef Garfinkel (email communication), this storage jar would have held twenty to thirty liters.
20. David Jamieson-Drake, *Scribes and Schools in Monarchic Judah: A Socio-Archeological Approach* (Sheffield, England: Journal for the Study of the Old Testament, 1991); also see Schniedewind, *A Social History of Hebrew*, 60–61.
21. See Orly Goldwasser, "An Egyptian Scribe from Lachish and the Hieratic Tradition of the Hebrew Kingdoms," *Tel Aviv* 18 (1991): 248–53.
22. See Aaron Burke, "Left Behind: Egyptians in the Southern Levant after Empire," in *James K. Hoffmeier Festschrift*, ed. K. Lawson Younger (Winona Lake, IN: Eisenbrauns, forthcoming); also see Yuval Gadot, "Continuity and Change in the Late Bronze to Iron Age Transition in Israel's Coastal Palin: A Long Term Perspective," in *Bene Israel: Studies in the Archaeology of Israel and the Levant during the Bronze and Iron Ages in Honour of Israel Finkelstein*, ed. Alexander Fantalkin and Assaf Yasur-Landau (Leiden: Brill, 2008), 55–73.
23. See Schniedewind, *A Social History of Hebrew*, 56–60; also see Philip Zhakevich, "The Tools of an Israelite Scribe: A Semantic Study of the Terms Signifying the

Tools and Materials of Writing in Biblical Hebrew" (PhD diss., University of Texas at Austin, 2015).

24. See Schniedewind, *A Social History of Hebrew*, 56–60.
25. For a convenient English translation, see William Moran, *The Amarna Letters* (Baltimore, MD: Johns Hopkins University Press, 2000); for a critical edition of the cuneiform, see Anson F. Rainey, *The El-Amarna Correspondence: A New Edition of the Cuneiform Letters from the Site of El-Amarna Based on Collations of All Extant Tablets*, vol. 1, ed. William Schniedewind (HdO 110; Leiden: Brill, 2015).
26. Dominique Charpin, *Reading and Writing in Babylon*, trans. Jane Marie Todd (Cambridge, MA: Harvard University Press, 2010), 213.
27. Wayne Horowitz, Takayoshi Oshima, and Seth Sanders, *Cuneiform in Canaan: The Next Generation*, revised edition (Jerusalem: Israel Exploration Society, 2018), 5.
28. Charpin, *Reading and Writing in Babylon*, 214.
29. Horowitz, Oshima, and Sanders, *Cuneiform in Canaan*, 5.
30. On the basis of the fragmentary publication of these inscriptions, André Lemaire already recognized their importance for understanding of ancient Israelite education; see André Lemaire, 25–33.
31. See, for example, William Morrow, "Resistance and Hybridity in Late Bronze Age Canaan," *RB* 115 (2008): 322; Carr, *Writing on the Tablet of the Heart*; Eckart Otto, "Town and Rural Countryside in Ancient Israelite Law: Reception and Redaction in Cuneiform and Israelite Law," *JSOT* 57 (1993): 20–21; David Wright, *Inventing God's Law: How the Covenant Code of the Bible Used and Revised the Laws of Hammurabi* (New York: Oxford University Press, 2009); Shaun Zelig Aster, "Transmission of Neo-Assyrian Claims of Empire to Judah in the Late Eighth Century B.C.E.," *HUCA* 78 (2007): 1–44; Blum, "Dei altaramäischen Wandinscriften vom Tell Deir 'Alla und ihr Institutioneller Kontext," 21–52; Daniel Pioske "The Scribe of David: The Portrait of a Life," *MAARAV* 20 (2013): 163–88.
32. James Crenshaw, *Education in Ancient Israel: Across the Deadening Silence* (New York: Doubleday, 1998), 88.
33. See summary by David McLain Carr, *The Formation of the Hebrew Bible: A New Reconstruction* (Oxford: Oxford University Press, 2011), 356–60.
34. Entanglement is a particularly useful archaeological concept developed by Ian Hodder in *Entangled: An Archaeology of Relationships between Humans and Things* (Malden, MA: Wiley, 2012). This concept has been applied to the late second millennium Levant by Aaron Burke in two articles, "Left Behind" and "Entanglement, the Amorite *Koiné*, and Amorite Cultures in the Levant," *ARAM* 26 (2014): 357–73.
35. Morrow applies the scientific term "vector of transmission" to the question of concrete avenues and times when Near Eastern literature was supposedly borrowed by biblical authors ("Resistance and Hybridity in Late Bronze Age Canaan," 322). Also see Jeffrey Tigay, who uses the expression "channel of transmission," in "On Evaluating Claims of Literary Borrowing," in *The Tablet and the Scroll: Near Eastern Studies in Honor of William W. Hallo*, ed. Mark Cohen, Daniel Snell, and David Weisberg (Bethesda, MD: CDL, 1993), 255.

36. John A. Emerton, "The Teaching of Amenemope and Proverbs XXII 17–XXIV 22: Further Reflections on a Long-Standing Problem," *VT* 41 (2001): 431–65; Michael Fox, "From Amenemope to Proverbs: Editorial Art in Proverbs 22,17–23,11," *ZAW* 126 (2014): 76–91.
37. For example, Ryan Byrne, "The Refuge of Scribalism in Iron I Palestine," *BASOR* 345 (2007): 20; André Lemaire, "The Sage in School and Temple," in *The Sage in Israel and the Ancient Near East*, ed. John Gammie and Leo Perdue (Winona Lake, IN: Eisenbrauns, 1990), 165–81; Christopher Ansberry, *Be Wise, My Son, and Make My Heart Glad: An Exploration of the Courtly Nature of the Book of Proverbs* (BZAW, 422; Berlin: de Gruyter, 2011), 2–4. This position can be traced back as early as Klostermann, *Schulwesen im alten Israel*, 193–232.
38. For example, Niek Veldhuis, "Sumerian Proverbs in Their Curricular Context," *JAOS* 120 (2000): 383–99.
39. Wright, *Inventing God's Law*, 4–7.
40. See Melissa Ramos, "A Northwest Semitic Curse Formula: The Sefire Treaties and Deuteronomy 28," *ZAW* 128 (2016): 205–20; Carly Crouch, *Israel and the Assyrians: Deuteronomy, the Succession Treaty of Esarhaddon, and the Nature of Subversion* (Atlanta, GA: Society of Biblical Literature, 2014); Laura Quick, *Deuteronomy 28 and the Aramaic Curse Tradition* (Oxford: Oxford University Press, 2018).
41. Niek Veldhuis, *History of the Cuneiform Lexical Tradition* (GMTR 6; Münster: Ugarit-Verlag, 2014), 226.
42. My first realization of the importance of this approach came from Aaron Demsky's article, "The Education of Canaanite Scribes in the Mesopotamian Cuneiform Tradition," in *Bar Ilan Studies in Assyriology: Dedicated to Pinḥas Artzi*, ed. Jacob Klein and Aaron Skaist (Ramat Gan: Bar-Ilan University Press, 1990), 157–70. Also see Carr, *Writing on the Tablet of the Heart*, 17–46; van der Toorn, *Scribal Culture*, 51–74.
43. See especially Burke, "Left Behind."
44. Morrow, "Resistance and Hybridity in Late Bronze Age Canaan," 323.
45. See Burke, "Entanglement, the Amorite *Koiné*, and Amorite Cultures in the Levant."
46. See Robert Hawley, Dennis Pardee, and Carole Roche-Hawley, "The Scribal Culture of Ugarit," *JANES* 2 (2016): 229–67.
47. See Robert Hawley, "Studies in Ugaritic Epistolography" (PhD diss., University of Chicago, 2003); Robert Hawley, "On the Alphabetic Scribal Curriculum at Ugarit," in *51e Rencontre Assyriologique Internationale, Jul 2005*, ed. Martha T. Roth, Robert D. Biggs, and Jennie Myers (SAOC 62; Chicago: Oriental Institute, 2008), 57–67; Hawley, Pardee, and Roche-Hawley, "The Scribal Culture at Ugarit," 229–67.
48. Carr also focuses on literary borrowing; e.g., see *Writing on the Tablet of the Heart*, 157.
49. Morrow, "Resistance and Hybridity in Late Bronze Age Canaan," 324.
50. See Horowitz, Oshima, and Sanders, *Cuneiform in Canaan*, and Shlomo Izreʿel, *The Amarna Scholarly Tablets* (CM 9; Groningen: Styx, 1997).

51. See, for example, Stephanie Dalley, "The Influence of Mesopotamia upon Israel and the Bible," in *The Legacy of Mesopotamia*, ed. Stephanie Dalley (Oxford: Oxford University Press, 1998), 67.
52. See, for example, the classic work of Alexander Heidel, *The Babylonian Genesis: The Story of the Creation*, 2nd ed. (Chicago: University of Chicago Press, 1951).
53. Carr, *Writing on the Tablet of the Heart*, 157. Also see William Hallo, "Sumerian Literature: Background to the Bible," *BRev* 4 (1988): 38.
54. Niek Veldhuis, "Cuneiform Tablet as an Educational Tool," *Dutch Studies on Near Eastern Languages and Cultures* 2 (1996): 23.
55. These are published by Bordreuil, Pardee, and Hawley, *Une Bibliothèque Au Sud de La Ville: Textes 1994–2002 En Cunéiforme Alphabétique de La Maison d'Ourtenou* (RSOu 18; Paris: Maison de l'Orient et de la Méditerrané, 2012), 18, no. 81.
56. See, for example, the discussion in Richard Parkinson and Stephen Quirke, *Papyrus* (Austin: University of Texas Press, 1995), 47–48.
57. See Robert Hawley, "On the Alphabetic Scribal Curriculum at Ugarit," *Studies in Ancient Oriental Civilization* 62 (2005): 57–67.
58. See Hawley, Pardee, and Roche-Hawley, "The Scribal Culture of Ugarit," 232. More generally, Hawley has made the straightforward case that the Ugaritic scribal curriculum was adapted from Akkadian models; see Hawley, "On the Alphabetic Scribal Curriculum at Ugarit," 57–67.
59. See Wilfred Van Soldt, "The Written Sources: The Syllabic Akkadian Texts," in *Handbook of Ugaritic Studies*, ed. Wilfred Watson and Nicholas Wyatt (Leiden: Brill, 1999), 40–41; also see Wilfred Van Soldt, *Studies in the Akkadian of Ugarit: Dating and Grammar* (AOAT 40; Neukirchener: Neukirchen-Vluyn, 1991), 19–32.
60. See Olaf Pedersen, *Archives and Libraries of the Ancient Near East, 1500–300 B.C.* (Bethesda, MD: CDL Press, 1998), 68–80. Ugaritic School texts are published in *KTU* and the *Ugaritic Data Bank*, §§5.1–24.
61. Contra Hawley, "On the Alphabetic Scribal Curriculum at Ugarit," 57–67.
62. See Mark Smith, *The Ugaritic Baal Cycle: Volume I, Introduction with Text, Translation and Commentary of KTU 1.1–1.2* (VTSup 105; Leiden: Brill, 1994), 26–36.
63. Smith, The Ugaritic Baal Cycle, Volume I, 32.
64. See Horowitz, Oshima, and Sanders, *Cuneiform in Canaan*.
65. Niek Veldhuis, "Levels of Literacy," in *The Oxford Handbook of Cuneiform Culture*, ed. Karen Radner and Eleanor Robson (Oxford: Oxford University Press, 2011). Also see Niek Veldhuis, "Schools in Ancient Mesopotamia," *Oxford Bibliographies* (2015), doi: 10.1093/obo/9780195393361-0196. In addition, Stephen Tinney has a useful summary of Mesopotamian scribal education: "Texts, Tablets, and Teaching: Scribal Education in Nippur and Ur," *Expedition* 40 (1998): 40–50. I also profited from Stephen Tinney, "Education in Ancient Mesopotamia," paper presented at the Nangeroni Conference: Second Temple Jewish Paideia in Its Ancient Near Eastern and Hellenistic Contexts, Naples, Italy, June 30–July 4, 2015, which I served as a respondent.
66. Rollston, "Scribal Education," 60.
67. Veldhuis, "Cuneiform Tablet as an Educational Tool," 18.
68. See Veldhuis, *History of the Cuneiform Lexical Tradition*, 279–302.

69. See Veldhuis, *History of the Cuneiform Lexical Tradition*, 279–302.
70. Veldhuis, *History of the Cuneiform Lexical Tradition*, 357.
71. Veldhuis, *History of the Cuneiform Lexical Tradition*, 194–99.
72. See Horowitz, Oshima, and Sanders, *Cuneiform in Canaan*, 78–80, and the bibliography cited there.
73. See Eleanor Robson, "Mesopotamian Mathematics," in *The Mathematics of Egypt, Mesopotamia, China, India, and Islam: A Sourcebook*, ed. Victor Katz (Princeton, NJ: Princeton University Press, 2007), 57–186.
74. See Lemaire, *Les écoles*, 22–24; Shmuel Ahituv, *Echoes from the Past: Hebrew and Cognate Inscriptions from the Biblical Period* (Jerusalem: Carta, 2008), 207–13.
75. See Raz Kletter, *Economic Keystones: The Weight System of the Kingdom of Judah* (JSOTSup 276; Sheffield, England: Sheffield Academic Press, 1998).
76. Alice Mandell argued in "Contract, Scribal Exercise, or a Colossal Joke? Rethinking the MRZH. Tablet at Ugarit (RS 1957.702 = KTU 3.9 = TU 3.9)," paper presented at the Annual Meeting of the American Oriental Society, Los Angeles, March 17–20, 2017, that the Marzeaḥ Legal Tablet from Ugarit (*KTU* 3.9) is actually a school text. If she is correct (and I believe she is), this would be the lone alphabetic example of a practice school text in the legal genre.
77. Yuval Goren et al., "A Provenance Study of the Gilgamesh Fragment from Megiddo," *Archaeometry* 51 (2009): 763–73.
78. See, for example, Stephen Tinney's discussion of the cuneiform "Decad" in "On the Curricular Setting of Sumerian Literature," *Iraq* 61 (1999): 168–70.

Chapter 2

1. Note, for example, the publication in F. W. Dobbs-Allsopp et al., eds., *Hebrew Inscriptions: Texts from the Biblical Period of the Monarchy with Concordance* (New Haven, CT: Yale University Press, 2005), 277–98; Ahituv, *Echoes from the Past*, 313–29.
2. The inscriptions are now fully published in English; see Shmuel Ahituv, Esther Eshel, and Ze'ev Meshel, "The Inscriptions," in *Kuntillet ʿAjrud: An Iron Age II Religious Site on the Judah-Sinai Border*, ed. Ze'ev Meshel, Shmuel Ahituv, and Liora Freud (Jerusalem: Israel Exploration Society, 2012), 73–142. A new and updated Hebrew edition provides different, sometimes improved readings as well as a variety of different interpretations of the material culture. Unfortunately, it sometimes changes the numbering of the inscriptions. I will follow the numbering of the English edition. For the Hebrew edition, see Shmuel Ahituv and Esther Esther, ed., *To* YHWH *Teman and His* ashera: *The Inscriptions and Drawings from Kuntillet ʿAjrud ('Ḥorvat Tēman') in Sinai* (Jerusalem: Israel Exploration Society, 2015).
3. See the review by Demsky, *Literacy in Ancient Israel*, 171–94. Although Demsky provides a robust assessment of elementary and advanced education, his actual epigraphic examples are largely limited to abecedaries. Similarly, Rollston also surveys

the scribal curriculum, but his examples are restricted to abecedaries and hieratic numerals ("Scribal Curriculum," 84–90). The classic work on this would be Lemaire's *Les écoles*, 7–33, which may now be updated by his article, "The Kuntillet 'Ajrud Inscriptions Forty Years after Their Discovery," in *Alphabets, Texts and Artifacts in the Ancient Near East: Studies Presented to Benjamin Sass*, ed. Israel Finkelstein, Christian Robin, Thomas and Römer (Paris: Van Dieren Editeur, 2016), 196–208.

4. Lemaire, *Les écoles*, 7–33. There are also some examples of Ammonite (and perhaps Aramaic) seals that are abecedaries. They contain between four and eleven letters, and they were apparently used to practice the execution of seals; see Nahman Avigad and Benjamin Sass, *Corpus of West Semitic Stamp Seals* (Jerusalem: Israel Exploration Society, 1997), 366–71.
5. See Lemaire, *Les écoles*, 15–17.
6. See, for example, Jacqueline Vayntrub, "'Observe Due Measure': The Gezer Calendar and Dividing the Trip around the Sun," in *Epigraphy, Philology, and the Hebrew Bible: Methodological Perspectives on the Comparative Study of the Hebrew Bible in Honor of Jo Ann Hackett*, ed. Jeremy Hutton and Aaron Rubin (Atlanta, GA: Society of Biblical Literature, 2015), 191–207. In chapter 4, I show that the Gezer Calendar is a concrete adaptation of a Mesopotamian lexical list tradition.
7. Crenshaw, *Education in Ancient Israel*, 104. Also see interpretation, "The Gezer Calendar as an Adaptation of the Mesopotamian Lexical Tradition (Ura 1)," *Semitica* 61 (2019): 15–22.
8. More recently, scholars have questioned reading *ʾasherah* as a reference to a goddess and preferred reading it as a "sanctuary." See the summary of arguments and literature by Lemaire, "The Kuntillet ʿAjrud Inscriptions Forty Years after Their Discovery," 201–3. See further Jeremy Smoak and William Schniedewind, "Religion at Kuntillet ʿAjrud," *Religions* 10 (2019): 211; doi:10.3390/rel10030211.
9. Edward Palmer, *The Desert of the Exodus: Journeys on Foot in the Wilderness of the Forty Years' Wanderings* (London: Bell and Daldy, 1871),
10. On the excavations of Tel el-Kheleifeh and its identification, see Gary Pratico, *Nelson Glueck's 1938–40 Excavations at Tell el-Kheleifeh: A Reappraisal* (Atlanta, GA: Scholars Press, 1993). The problematic nature of the identification is also discussed by Ze'ev Meshel, "On the Problem of Tell el-Kheleifeh, Elath and Ezion-Geber," *EI: Archaeological, Historical and Geographical Studies* 12 (1975): 49–56.
11. The excavations are now published in Rudolph Cohen and Hannah Bernick-Greenberg, ed., *Excavations at Kadesh Barnea (Tell El-Qudeirat) 1976 1982* (Jerusalem: Israel Antiquities Authority, 2007).
12. Ze'ev Meshel, *Kuntillet ʿAjrud: An Iron Age II Religious Site on the Judah-Sinai Border* (Jerusalem: Israel Exploration Society, 2012), 3.
13. See the original publication of the drawings by Pirhiya Beck, "The Drawings from Ḥorvat Teiman (Kuntillet ʿAjrud)," *TA* 9 (1982): 3–68. Also see the discussion and bibliography in the site report, Meshel, *Kuntillet ʿAjrud: An Iron Age II Religious Site on the Judah-Sinai Border*, 358–64. A religious interpretation of the site was defended at length by Nadav Na'aman and Nurit Lissovsky, "Kuntillet ʿAjrud, Sacred Trees and the Asherah," *TA* 35 (2008): 186–208. See recent critiques by Lemaire,

"The Kuntillet ʿAjrud Inscriptions Forty Years after Their Discovery," 198–200; William Schniedewind, "Understanding Scribal Education in Ancient Israel: A View from Kuntillet ʿAjrud," *MAARV* 21 (2014): 272–75.

14. Tallay Ornan, "The Drawings from Kuntillet ʿAjrud," in *To* YHWH *Teman and His* ashera: *The Inscriptions and Drawings from Kuntillet ʿAjrud ('Ḥorvat Tēman') in Sinai*, ed. Shmuel Ahituv and Esther Eshel (Jerusalem: Yad Ben-Zvi, 2015), 44–68 [Hebrew]; also see Ornan, "Sketches and Final Works of Art: The Drawings and Wall Paintings of Kuntillet ʿAjrud Revisited," *TA* 43 (2016): 3–26.
15. See especially Judith Hadley, "Kuntillet ʿAjrud: Religious Centre or Desert Way Station?," *PEQ* 125 (1993): 115–24, and more recently Smoak and Schniedewind, "Religion at Kuntillet ʿAjrud."
16. The role of "scribes of the army" has been highlighted in an essay by Rollston, "Scribal Curriculum," 75–80, and the role of "military logistics" in the scribal profession has been highlighted by Demsky, *Literacy in Ancient Israel*, 201–3.
17. For the original drawing, see Shmuel Ahituv, Esther Eshel, and Ze'ev Meshel, "The Inscriptions," in *Kuntillet ʿAjrud: An Iron Age II Religious Site on the Judah-Sinai Border*, ed. Ze'ev Meshel, Shmuel Ahituv, and Liora Freud (Jerusalem: Israel Exploration Society, 2012), 92.
18. Michael Coogan, "Alphabets and Elements," *BASOR* 216 (1974): 61–63.
19. There are also distinct differences between the two inscriptions in black ink (3.11 and 3.13), which would make a total of three hands in just this section of six lines.
20. See Richard Parkinson, *Cracking Codes: The Rosetta Stone and Decipherment* (Berkeley: University of California Press, 1999), 143–61.
21. Parkinson and Quirke, *Papyrus*, 45.
22. An excellent example of this may be found in José Galán, "An Apprentice's Board from Dra Abu El-Naga," *JEA* 93 (2007): 95–116.
23. Dobbs-Allsop et al. suggests that the word *šmrn* "Shomron (i.e., Samaria)" is too faint to read (*Hebrew Inscriptions*, 295). However, the reading seems quite clear on the photographs in the final publication, and I accept their reading.
24. On polysemy in Hebrew, see Scott Noegel, "Polysemy," in *Encyclopedia of Hebrew Language and Linguistics*, volume 3, ed. Geoffrey Khan (Leiden: Brill, 2013), 178–96. Also see Joshua Blau's exhaustive treatment, "On Polyphony in Biblical Hebrew," in *Proceedings of the Israel Academy of Sciences and Humanities* 6/2 (Jerusalem: Israel Academy of Sciences and Humanities, 1982), 105–83.
25. Ahituv, Eshel, and Meshel, "The Inscriptions," 98.
26. Note that the word "barley" appears in Gezer Calendar (l.4) as well as the Samaria Ostraca (109:3). The hieratic for "barley" appears twice in Arad 25 (see Yohanon Aharoni and Joseph Naveh, *Arad Inscriptions* [Jerusalem: Israel Exploration Society, 1981], 50–51). Dobbs-Allsopp et al. also suggest the possible reading "hairs," which can be added to the list of possible meanings (*Hebrew Inscriptions*, 295).
27. Ahituv reads the word *ʾmn* as "Amen," which is possible (*Echoes from the Past*, 319). However, it is difficult to be certain without more context. Émile Puech suggests reading as a personal name, *ʾb̊ṣ̊r* "Abiṣur" ("Les Inscriptions Hébraïques de Kuntillet ʿAjrud [Sinaï]," *RB* 121 [2014]: 171).

28. Veldhuis, "Cuneiform Tablet as an Educational Tool," 18.
29. Veldhuis, *History of the Cuneiform Lexical Tradition*, 107–8.
30. See the general discussion of this aspect of the curriculum by Demsky, *Literacy in Ancient Israel*, 183–84. He points to scribal exercises in writing names at Ugarit (e.g., *KTU* 5.1, 5.7, 5.18, 5.22). For his interpretation of the Qeiyafa inscription, see Aaron Demsky, "An Iron Age IIA Writing Exercise from Khirbet Qeiyafa," *IEJ* 62 (2012): 186–99.
31. Ahituv, Meshel, and Eshel note that this is also attested as a personal name in a later Phoenician inscription ("The Inscriptions," 128); this is certainly possible, but a gentilic seems a more likely reading.
32. The sociolinguistic term for this is "iconization," a process of identity creation through an iconic visual or verbal discursive means; see Mark Sebba, "Iconisation, Attribution and Branding in Orthography," *Written Language and Literacy* 18 (2015): 208–27.
33. See the treatment of Kuntillet ʿAjrud in Israel Finkelstein, *The Forgotten Kingdom: The Archaeology and History of Northern Israel* (Atlanta, GA: Society of Biblical Literature, 2013), 138–39; and Israel Finkelstein, "The Historical Setting of Kuntillet ʿAjrud," *MAARAV* 20 (2013): 1–13.
34. Veldhuis, *History of the Cuneiform Lexical Tradition*, 107.
35. This is the opinion of Beck in the initial publication, "The Drawings from Ḥorvat Teiman (Kuntillet ʿAjrud)," 143. In contrast, Brian Schmidt has linked the artistic motifs and the texts, arguing that they complement each other; see his "The Iron Age Pithoi Drawings from Horvat Teman or Kuntillet ʿAjrud: Some New Proposals," *JANER* 2 (2002): 91–125. Even if this were accepted, I argue here that it is necessary to understand the purpose of the inscriptions in the context of scribal exercises; of course, scribal exercises may have religious content.
36. For example, Beck, "The Drawings and Decorative Designs," in *Kuntillet ʿAjrud*, 173–77.
37. Ornan, "The Drawings from Kuntillet ʿAjrud," 52–56. Othmar Keel and Christopher Uehlinger also see royal imagery in the iconography at Kuntillet ʿAjrud: *Gods, Goddesses, and Images of God* (Minneapolis, MN: Fortress, 1998), 245–46.
38. Veldhuis, "Cuneiform Tablet as an Educational Tool," 25.
39. See, for example, the article on *sap̱ar* in Johannes Botterweck, Helmut Ringgren, and Heinz-Josef Fabry, ed., *Theological Dictionary of the Old Testament*, volume 10,trans. D. Stott (Grand Rapids, MI: Eerdmans, 1999), 308. Also see the discussion by Demsky, *Literacy in Ancient Israel*, 188–89.
40. See Rollston, "Scribal Education," 66–67.
41. Wimmer does not present these typical Egyptian hieratic, but they are too obviously the numbers 5 and 6—that is, 5 strokes and 6 strokes—to be interpreted in any other way. And they are found in the Arad letters (e.g., the number 6 as six strokes in Arad 46:2). Wimmer, *Palästinisches Hieratisch*, 202–11. There is one instance of the number 7 being written with strokes instead of standard hieratic in an inscription from Jerusalem.
42. For the original drawing, see Ahituv, Eshel, and Meshel, "The Inscriptions," 87.

43. Ahituv, Eshel, and Meshel, "The Inscriptions," 87.
44. See Wimmer, *Palästinisches Hieratisch*, 216–17, 223, 225. Kuntillet ʿAjrud inscriptions are earlier than most of the hieratic numerals in our Hebrew epigraphic records, and this may explain why the forms are closer to the pristine Egyptian forms.
45. See Wimmer, *Palästinisches Hieratisch*, 93–115. Likewise the hieratic numerals on Arad 34 might also be understood as a scribal exercise (42–46). Aharoni and Naveh had suggested that Arad 34 was actually written by an Egyptian scribe (*Arad Inscriptions*, 63) but this seems unnecessary.
46. Lemaire already recognized these as letter templates in his early work on schools, and he provides a striking parallel with the Wadi Murabbaʿat papyrus (*Les écoles*, 58). The interpretation as a letter template is emphasized particularly by Ahituv and Eshel, who seem to be at odds with Meshel in their interpretation of the site and the inscriptions; see Ahituv, Eshel, and Meshel, "The Inscriptions," 134. Rollston also recognizes that "letter formulary" is a part of the scribal curriculum from the many examples but categorizes them with other texts for which we have no examples in the epigraphic record of school exercises like monumental inscriptions and legal texts; see Rollston, "Scribal Curriculum," 89–90; also Demsky, *Literacy in Ancient Israel*, 193–94. Most scholars do not seem to recognize these as epistolary exercises.
47. See Dennis Pardee and S. David Sperling, *Handbook of Ancient Hebrew Letters: A Study Edition* (Chico, CA: Scholars Press, 1982), 145.
48. Johannes Renz actually publishes the text together as two columns, lines 1–14; see his *Die Althebräischen Inschriften*, volume 1, in *Handbuch der Althebräischen Epigraphik*, ed. Johannes Renz and Wolfgang Röllig (Darmstadt: Wissenschaftliche Buchgesellschaft, 1995), 62–63.
49. Veldhuis, *The History of the Cuneiform Lexical Tradition*, 194–99.
50. Dobbs-Allsopp et al., *Hebrew Inscriptions*, 293.
51. Veldhuis, "Cuneiform Tablet as an Educational Tool," 23.
52. Ahituv, Eshel, and Meshel, "The Inscriptions," 76–77.
53. The importance of the Priestly Blessing as a potential scribal formula is described in Jeremy Smoak's recent book, *The Priestly Blessing in Inscription and Scripture: The Early History of Numbers 6:24–26* (New York: Oxford University Press, 2015). See also Jeremy Smoak, "Speaking with a Divine Voice: The Rhetoric of Epistolary Performance in Numbers 6:22–27," in *Text and Ritual in the Pentateuch*, ed. Christoph Nihan (forthcoming).
54. Ahituv, Eshel, and Meshel, "The Inscriptions," 98–100.
55. For an interdisciplinary account of impact of earthquakes, including an emphasis on the Middle East, see Amos Nur and Dawn Burgess, *Apocalypse: Earthquakes, Archaeology, and the Wrath of God* (Princeton, NJ: Princeton University Press, 2008).
56. In addition to Meshel, see Rollston, *Writing and Literacy*, 131. Rollston follows the general outline of priestly scribes suggested by van der Toorn, *Scribal Culture*, 75–108. See my review that critiques van der Toorn's projection of Second Temple priestly scribes back into the Iron Age (William Schniedewind, "Scribal Culture and the Making of the Hebrew Bible," *JHS* 10 [2010]: 29). André Lemaire, "Fragments from the Book of Balaam Found at Deir Alla," *BAR* 11 (2005): 39; and also André

Lemaire, "Remarques sur les inscriptions phéniciennes de Kuntillet ʿAjrud," *Sem* 55 (2013): 83–99. Brian Schmidt also compares Kuntillet ʿAjrud with Deir ʿAlla in "Memorializing Conflict: Toward an Iron Age 'Shadow' History of Israel's Earliest Literature," in *Contextualizing Israel's Sacred Writings: Ancient Literacy, Orality, and Literary Production*, ed. Brian Schmidt (Atlanta, GA: Society of Biblical Literature, 2015), 115–16).

57. See James Allen's introduction and translation, "The Craft of the Scribe," in *COS*, 3.2; and, Hans Fischer-Elfert, *Die satirische Streitschrift des Papyrus Anastasi I: Übersetzung und Kommentar* (ÄgAbh 44; Wiesbaden: Harrassowitz, 1986).
58. See Gregorio del Olmo Lete and J. Sanmartín, *A Dictionary of the Ugaritic Language in the Alphabetic Tradition*, 2nd ed. (Leiden: Brill, 2004), 536.
59. Allen, "The Craft of the Scribe," 3.2. Also see Fischer-Elfert, *Die satirische Streitscrift des Papyrus Anastasi I.*
60. Demsky, *Literacy in Ancient Israel*, 201–2.
61. This letter has been discussed by a variety of scholars. See, for example, Frank Moore Cross, "A Literate Soldier: Lachish Letter III," in *Biblical and Related Studies Presented to Samuel Iwry*, ed. Ann Kort and Scott Morschauser (Winona Lake, IN: Eisenbrauns, 1985), 41–47; and William Schniedewind, "Sociolinguistic Reflections on the Letter of a 'Literate' Soldier (Lachish 3)," *ZAH* 13 (2000), 157–67.
62. Rollston, "Scribal Curriculum," 78.
63. Translations taken from Allen, "The Craft of the Scribe," 3.2.
64. Ahituv, Eshel, and Meshel, "Inscriptions and Their Interpretation," in *To* YHWH *Teman and His* ashera: *The Inscriptions and Drawings from Kuntillet ʿAjrud ('Ḥorvat Tēman') in Sinai*, 113 [Hebrew]. The authors credit Erhard Blum with the reconstruction, and Professor Blum kindly shared his full reconstruction in email correspondence. The renumbering of the inscription as 4.2 seems to serve no purpose other than to create confusion since it remains part of the same inscription. I adhere to the original numbering of the English edition.
65. My reconstruction and drawing uses and adapts the published photos in the Hebrew edition of the Kuntillet ʿAjrud inscriptions; see Shmuel Ahituv, Esther Eshel, and Ze'ev Meshel, "Inscriptions and their Interpretation," in *To* YHWH *Teman and His* ashera: *The Inscriptions and Drawings from Kuntillet ʿAjrud ('Ḥorvat Tēman') in Sinai*, ed. Shmuel Ahituv and Esther Eshel (Jerusalem: Yad Ben-Zvi, 2015), 112–15. Their reconstruction relies on the work of Blum (see Erhard Blum, "Institutionelle und kulturelle Vorassetzungen der israelitischen Traditionsliteratur," in *Konstruktion, Transmission und Transformation von Tradition(en) im alten Israel*, ed. Ruth Ebach and Martin Leuenberger (Mohr Siebeck: Tübingen, 2018), 1–42). Another extensive reconstruction is offered by Puech, "Les Inscriptions Hébraïques de Kuntillet 'Ajrud (Sinaï)," 161–94. I find all these reconstructions to be speculative. Puech utilizes comparisons with the pithoi, which is a reasonable approach: "Comme plusieurs expressions sont identiques a celles des inscriptions dedicatoires des *pithoi* A et B, il est vraisemblable d'attendre sur ce pliitre une formulation tout au moins en partie comparable [As several expressions are identical to those of the dedicatory inscriptions of pithoi A and B, it is reasonable to expect on this plaster a formulation at least

partly comparable]" (175). But Puech's reconstructions are far too extensive to be convincing.

66. Compare the Hebrew and English editions. My thanks to Erhard Blum for supplying me with his reconstruction; see further Blum, "Institutionelle und kulturelle Voraussetzungen der israelitischen Traditionsliteratur," 26–27.
67. Author's translation. Original publication by Jacob Hoftijzer and Gerrit van der Kooij, *Aramaic Text from Deir 'Alla* (Leiden: Brill, 1976). Many reconstructions and translations are available, and the secondary literature is nicely summarized by Gareth Wearne, "The Plaster Texts from Kuntillet 'Ajrud and Deir 'Alla: An Inductive Approach to the Emergence of Northwest Semitic Literary Texts in the First Millennium B.C.E." (PhD diss., Macquarie University, 2011).
68. Dobbs-Allsop et al., catalogue four examples of *lśrʿr* in the Kuntillet ʿAjrud inscriptions (KAjr 5, 6, 7, and 8), which they translate "(belonging) to the Governor of the City" (*Hebrew Inscriptions*, 282–83). However, they mention that only one of these was published in a preliminary edition with a photo. In the official publication, there are only three published (Ahituv, Eshel, and Meshel, "The Inscriptions," 80–81).
69. Ahituv, Eshel, and Meshel, "The Inscriptions," 80–81. There is also some question about the missing definite article, especially in light of the new seal impression with this title (see my article, "The Commander of the Fortress: Understanding an Ancient Israelite Military Title," *BAR* 45/1 [2019]: 41–46). For example, Sarfatti argued that this may reflect pronunciation as with *Qere/Ketiv* variants of construct nouns ("Hebrew Inscriptions of the First Temple Period: A Survey and Some Linguistic Comments," MAARAV 3 [1982]: 71–73), but this is a poor comparison. *Qere/Ketiv* is a liturgical reading tradition. Rather, it reflects the history of the definite article, which was not used in early Hebrew (see Gogel, *A Grammar of Epigraphic Hebrew*, [Atlanta: Scholars Press, 1998] 61). Wearne also points to pronunciation, but this misses the point ("The Plaster Texts from Kuntillet ʿAjrud and Deir ʿAlla," 129–30).
70. Ahituv, Eshel, and Meshel, "The Inscriptions," 80.
71. See, for example, Dobbs-Allsop et al., *Hebrew Inscriptions*, 359.
72. See *HALOT*.
73. Tallay Ornan, Shlomit Weksler-Bdolah and Benjamin Sass, "A 'Governor of the City' Seal Impression from the Western Wall Plaza Excavations in Jerusalem," *Qadmaniot* 50 (2017): 100–103 [Hebrew].
74. Avigad and Sass, *Corpus of West Semitic Stamp Seals*, nos. 401 and 402. Several other unprovenanced seal impressions with the title *śrʿr* or *śr hʿr* have been published by Robert Deutsch in *Biblical Period Hebrew Bullae: The Josef Chaim Kaufman Collection* (Tel Aviv: Archaeological Center, 2003), 65–71. I am not convinced of their authenticity.
75. See Frank Frick, *The City in Ancient Israel* (SBLMS, 36; Missoula, MT: Scholars Press, 1977), 39.
76. See *HALOT*.
77. On the urbanization of the neo-Assyrian periphery, see Hans Kühne, "The Urbanization of the Assyrian Provinces," in *Nuove Fondazioni Nel Vincino Oriente*

Antico: Realtà E Ideologia, ed. Stefania Mazzoni (Piza: Giardini Editori e Stampatori, 1994), 55–84.

78. Seals from the early Iron Age were aniconic. The difference may be explained by the changing role of writing in Judah in the late Iron Age.
79. For a recent review of the *lmlk* seals, see Robb Andrew Young, *Hezekiah in History and Tradition* (SVT 155; Leiden: Brill, 2012), 50–58.
80. See, for example, *HALOT*, which translates *naʿar* as "1. lad, adolescent; 2. young man; and, 3. fellow, servant, attendant." For a thorough examination of the nuances of this term, see Carolyn Leeb, *Away from the Father's House: The Social Location of the Naʿar and Naʿarah in Ancient Israel* (Sheffield, England: Sheffield Academic Press, 2000); also see John MacDonald, "The Status and Role of the *Naʿar* in Israelite Society," *JNES* 35 (1976): 147–70.
81. See, for example, Aaron Demsky, "Researching Literacy in Ancient Israel—New Approaches and Recent Developments," in *See, I Will Bring a Scroll Recounting What Befell Me (Ps 40:8): Epigraphy and Daily Life from the Bible to the Talmud*, ed. Esther Eshel and Yigal Levin (Göttingen: Vandernhoeck & Ruprecht, 2014), 2n2.
82. James Hoch, *Semitic Words in Egyptian Texts of the New Kingdom and Third Intermediate Period* (Princeton, NJ: Princeton University Press, 1994), no. 245.
83. Hoch, *Semitic Words in Egyptian Texts of the New Kingdom and Third Intermediate Period*, no. 190.
84. See R. Mayer-Opificius and Walter Mayer, "Schlact bei Qadeš: Der Versuch einer neuen Rekonstrucktion," *UF* 26 (1994): 343–59.
85. Anson Rainey, "The Military Personnel of Ugarit," *JNES* 24 (1965): 21.
86. See, for example, Olmo Lete and Sanmartín, *A Dictionary of the Ugaritic Language*, 616; Leeb, *Away from the Father's House*, 173–82.
87. MacDonald, "The Status and Role of the *Naʿar*," 150.
88. Translations from Allen, "The Craft of the Scribe."
89. Blum is particularly critical of Lemaire's description of Kuntillet ʿAjrud as a school; see Lemaire, *Les écoles*, 25–32, and Blum, "Dei altaramäischen Wandinscriften vom Tell Deir ʿAlla und ihr Institutioneller Kontext," 22.

Chapter 3

1. Perhaps for this reason, scholars such as Ignace Jay Gelb described the early alphabet as a syllabic writing system; see his *A Study of Writing*, revised ed. (Chicago: University of Chicago, 1962). It is not. Similarly, William Hallo, "Isaiah 28:9–13 and the Ugaritic Abecedaries," *JBL* 77 (1958): 325.
2. A possible exception to this is the Korean script Hankul; see Ross King, "Korean Writing," in *The World's Writing Systems*, ed. Peter Daniels and William Bright (New York: Oxford University Press, 1996), 218–27. Many scholars believe that King Seycong borrowed the alphabetic concept from Indic writings systems, although the origins are still a matter of some debate (225).

3. "Phoenician" is an anachronistic term in this historical context. The term is a later (fifth-century BCE) Greek term for the early Canaanite coastal city-states of the eastern Mediterranean in the late second millennium.
4. Peter T. Daniels, "The Study of Writing Systems," in *The World's Writing Systems*, ed. Peter T. Daniels and William Bright (Oxford: Oxford University Press, 1996), 4.
5. Florian Coulmas, *Writing Systems: An Introduction to Their Linguistic Analysis* (Cambridge, England: Cambridge University Press, 2003), 113. Daniels view is specifically critiqued by Coulmas (see 113–15).
6. See Dennis Pardee, "The Ugaritic Alphabetic Cuneiform Writing System in the Context of Other Alphabetic Systems," in *Studies in Semitic and Afro-Asiatic Linguistics Presented to Gene B. Gragg*, ed. Cynthia Miller and Charles E. Jones (SAOC 60; Chicago: Oriental Institute of the University of Chicago, 2007), 181–200. Also see the general overview by Holger Gzella, "Abecedaries," in *Encyclopedia of Hebrew Language and Linguistics*, ed. Geoffrey Khan, et al. (Leiden: Brill, 2013), doi:http://dx.doi.org/10.1163/2212-4241_ehll_EHLL_COM_00000228.
7. Pierre Bordreuil and Dennis Pardee, "Textes alphabétiques en ougartique," in *Études ourgartiques*, volume 1: *Travux 1985–1995*, ed. Margerit Yon and Daniel Arnaud (*Ras Shamra-Ougarit* 24; Paris: Éditions Recherche sur les Civilisations, 2001), 341–48 (text 32).
8. See, for example, Frank Moore Cross, "Paleography and the Date of the Tell Faḫariyeh Bilingual Inscription," in *Solving Riddles and Untying Knots: Biblical, Epigraphic, and Semitic Studies in Honor of Jonas Greenfield*, ed. Ziony Zevit, Seymour Gitin, and Michael Sokoloff (Winona Lake, IN: Eisenbrauns, 1995), 393–409; and Jana Mynářova, "Tell Fekheriye Inscription: A Process of Authority on the Edge of the Assyrian Empire," in *The Process of Authority: The Dynamics in Transmission and Reception of Canonical Texts*, ed. Jan Dušek (DCLS 27; Boston: de Gruyter, 2016), 9–39.
9. See, for example, José Morais, "Constraints on the Development of Phonemic Awareness," in *Phonological Processes in Literacy: A Tribute to Isabelle Y. Liberman*, ed. Susan Brady and Donald Shankweiler (New York: Routledge, 2001), 5–28; Charles Read et al., "The Ability to Manipulate Speech Sounds Depends on Knowing Alphabetic Writing," *Cognition* 24 (1986): 31–44.
10. D. Gary Miller, *Ancient Scripts and Phonological Knowledge*, Current Issues in Linguistic Theory 116 (Philadelphia: John Benjamins, 1994), xiii.
11. William Albright, *City Invincible: A Symposium on Urbanization and Cultural Development in the Ancient Near East; Held at the Oriental Institute of the University of Chicago, December 4–7, 1958*, ed. Robert Martin Adams and Carl Hermann Kraeling (Chicago: University of Chicago Press, 1960), 123.
12. There is considerable debate about who invented the alphabet, but recent discoveries are making it increasingly clear that it was connected to ancient Egyptian military and trade. See the recent survey by Aaron Koller, "The Diffusion of the Alphabet in the Second Millennium BCE: On the Movements of Scribal Ideas from Egypt to the Levant, Mesopotamia, and Yemen," *Journal of Ancient Egyptian Interconnections* 20 (2018): 1–14.

13. See the classic study by William Albright, *The Proto-Sinaitic Inscriptions and Their Decipherment* (Cambridge, MA: Harvard University Press, 1966). The first inscription was actually found by Edward Palmer in the winter of 1868–69, but not published until 1904. The site itself was excavated by Sir Flinders Petrie in 1905. He discovered eleven inscriptions and suggested they were a linear alphabet.
14. The dating of the Wadi el-Ḥol and Serabit el-Khadim inscriptions is still the subject of debate. The original publications placed them in the Middle Kingdom period (nineteenth and eighteenth centuries BCE), whereas the new bilingual Theban Tomb 99 Ostracon is dated to the early New Kingdom (fifteenth century BCE). The dating criteria, however, are problematic. See, for example, Benjamin Sass, "The Genesis of the Alphabet and Its Development in the Second Millennium B.C. Twenty Years Later," *De Kêmi à Birīt Nāri* 2 (2005): 147–66.
15. Ben Haring, "*Halaḥam* on an Ostracon of the Early New Kingdom?," *JNES* 74 (2015): 189–96.
16. See especially Frank Kammerzell, "Die Entstehung der Alphabetreihe: Zum ägyptischen Ursprung der semitischen und westlichen Schriften," in *Hieroglyphen, Alphabete, Schriftreformen: Studien zu Multiliteralismus, Schriftwechsel und Orthographieneuregelungen*, ed. Dörte Borchers, Frank Kammerzell, and Stefan Weninger (Lingua Aegyptia 3; Göttingen: Seminar für Ägyptologie und Koptologie, 2001), 117–58.
17. Alan Gardiner, "The Egyptian Origin of the Semitic Alphabet," *JEA* 3 (1916): 1–16.
18. This is a topic of enormous scholarly debate. See, for example, Goldwasser, "On the Invention of the Alphabet," 124–40; Gordon Hamilton, *The Origins of the West Semitic Alphabet in Egyptian Scripts* (CBQMS 40; Washington, DC: Catholic Biblical Association, 2006); Frank Kammerzell, "Die Entstehung der Alphabetreihe," 117–58.
19. Alan Gardiner, *Ancient Egyptian Onomastica* (Oxford: Oxford University Press, 1947), 12; see further Haring, "*Halaḥam* on an Ostracon of the Early New Kingdom?," 191.
20. Contra Goldwasser, who imagines the alphabet as the work of a singular "genius" ("From the Iconic to the Linear," 118–60).
21. The origin of the alphabet is the topic of continuing debate; see, for example, the essays in Christophe Rico and Claudia Attucci, ed., *Origins of the Alphabet: Proceedings of the First Polis Institute Interdisciplinary Conference* (Cambridge, England: Cambridge Scholars Publishing, 2015).
22. Thomas Schneider, "A Double Abecedary? *Halaḥam* and *ʾAbgad* on the TT99 Ostracon," *BASOR* 379 (2018): 104–12.
23. In addition to Haring, see Schneider, "A Double Abecedary?," 103–11; and Hans Fischer-Elfert and Manfred Krebernick, "Zu den Buchstabennamen auf dem *Halaḥam*-Ostrakon aus TT99 (Grab des Senefri," *ZÄS* 143 (2016): 169–76.
24. Schneider, "A Double Abecedary?," 110. The reading of the obverse as a *halaḥam* abecedary seems certain; more uncertain, but also possible, is Schneider's reading of the reverse as an *ʾabgad* abecedary. If we accept Schneider's reading, then the two sides offer separate mnemonic devices for two different alphabetic traditions.

25. Frank Moore Cross and Thomas O. Lambdin suggested this in a classic article, "A Ugaritic Abecedary and the Origins of the Proto-Canaanite Alphabet," *BASOR* 160 (1960): 23.
26. Note, for example, the recently published *halaḥam* in South Semitic script, Ahmed Al-Jallad and Ali Al-Manaser, "A Thamudic B Abecedary in the South Semitic Letter Order," in *The Semitic Languages in Contact*, ed. Aaron Butts (Leiden: Brill, 2015), 1–15.
27. See discussion by Seth Sanders, *The Invention of Hebrew* (Urbana: University of Illinois Press, 2009), 90–96.
28. See Kammerzell, "Die Entstehung der Alphabetreihe," 131–51.
29. See Izreʿel, *The Amarna Scholarly Tablets*, 1–13; Rainey, *The El-Amarna Correspondence*, 1–35.
30. See Jana Mynářova, ed., *Handbook of Amarna Cuneiform Paleography* (Prague: Charles University, 2018).
31. I would agree with Rollston's general analysis that local alphabetic scripts begin to separate in the ninth or eighth century among the various Levantine polities (e.g., Phoenician city-states, Israel, and Judah); see his *Writing and Literacy*, 19–46.
32. See especially the seminal article by Byrne, "The Refuge of Scribalism in Iron I Palestine," 1–31.
33. I accept the recent scholarship that dates most Ugaritic texts to the late twelfth or early thirteenth century BCE, including the figure of the scribe Ilimilku; see Pardee, "Ugaritic Alphabetic Cuneiform in the Context of Other Alphabetic Systems," 189, and Joseph Lam and Dennis Pardee, "Diachrony in Ugaritic," in *Diachrony in Biblical Hebrew*, ed. Cynthia Miller-Naudé and Ziony Zevit (Winona Lake: Eisenbrauns, 2012), 407–32. However, it seems unlikely to me that the well-developed Ugaritic alphabet and its scribal apparatus just appeared overnight in the mid-thirteenth century BCE. It still makes sense to look for its creation in an earlier period and to see the end of the thirteenth century as its final, best attested, and most developed period. There is evidence, for example, of variations on the Ugaritic alphabet—both the shorter alphabet and the *halaḥam* alphabet—as well as paleographic and linguistic developments in the writing system (e.g., the paleographic evolution of the *g* and s as well as the linguistic merger of *s* and s_2) that seem to require a longer historical process.
34. For surveys of the epigraphic record relating to schools, see Lemaire, *Les écoles*, 7–33; Rollston, *Writing and Literacy*, 47–82; Sanders, *The Invention of Hebrew*, 90–96.
35. See, for example, Moshe Kochavi, "An Ostracon of the Period of the Judges from ʿIzbet Ṣarṭa," *TA* 4 (1977): 1–13; Aaron Demsky, "A Proto-Canaanite Abecedary Dating from the Period of the Judges and Its Implications for the History of the Alphabet," *TA* 4 (1977): 14–28; and Aaron Demsky, "The ʿIzbet Sartah Ostracon—Ten Years Later," in *ʿIzbet Sartah. An Early Iron Age Site Near Rosh Haʿayin, Israel*, ed. Israel Finkelstein and Vronwy Hankey (Oxford: Oxford University Press, 1986), 186–97.
36. See summaries by Aaron Demsky, "The Interface of Oral and Written Traditions in Ancient Israel: The Case of Abecedaries," in *Origins of the Alphabet: Proceedings of*

the First Polis Institute Interdisciplinary Conference, ed. Christophe Rico and Claudia Attucci (Newcastle upon Tyne, England: Cambridge Scholars Press, 2015), 23–31, and Demsky, *Literacy in Ancient Israel*, 171–82.

37. Stuart Weeks, *Early Israelite Wisdom* (Oxford: Oxford University Press, 2000), 133–56.
38. Demsky, "The Interface of Oral and Written Traditions in Ancient Israel," 23. Also see the many modern studies that emphasize the importance of learning letter names, e.g., Donna Raschke, Sandra Alper, and Elaine Eggers, "Recalling Alphabet Letter Names: A Mnemonic System to Facilitate Learning," *Preventing School Failure: Alternative Education for Children and Youth* 43 (1999): 80–83.
39. Irving Finkel, "A Babylonian ABC," *British Museum Magazine* 31 (1998): 20–22; Frank Cross and John Huehnergard, "The Alphabet on a Late Babylonian Cuneiform School Text," *Or* 72 (2003): 223–28.
40. See Horowitz, Oshima, and Sanders, *Cuneiform in Canaan*, 42–43 (Ashkelon 1).
41. Coulmas, *Writing* Systems, 113.
42. Menahem Haran, "Literacy and Schools in Ancient Israel," *SVT* 40 (1988): 81–95.
43. See, for example, Anthony Ceresko, "Endings and Beginnings: Alphabetic Thinking and the Shaping of Psalms 106 and 150," *CBQ* 68 (2006): 32–46.
44. Marshall McLuhan, *The Gutenberg Galaxy: The Making of the Typographic Man* (Toronto: University of Toronto Press, 1962).
45. The dating of these early inscriptions has been challenged; see Israel Finkelstein and Benjamin Sass, "The West Semitic Alphabetic Inscriptions, Late Bronze II to Iron IIA: Archeological Context, Distribution and Chronology," *HeBAI* 2 (2013): 149–220. But the evidence marshaled against the traditional dating remains weak.
46. See Hamilton, *The Origins of the West Semitic Alphabet in Egyptian Scripts.*
47. See Seth Sanders, "Writing and Early Iron Age Israel," in *Literate Culture and Tenth-Century Canaan*, ed. Ron Tappy and P. Kyle McCarter (Winona Lake, IN: Eisenbrauns, 2008), 102. The Izbet Ṣarta ostracon has one additional switch (*ḥet-zayin* instead of *zayin-ḥet*).
48. P. A. Munch, "Die alphabetische Akrostichie in der jüdischen Psalmendichtung," *ZDMG* 90 (1936): 708.
49. Munch, "Die alphabetische Akrostichie," 710.
50. Hermann Gunkel and Joachim Begrich, *Introduction to Psalms: The Genres of the Religious Lyric of Israel*, trans. James Nogalski (repr., Macon, GA: Mercer University Press, 1998), 64.
51. This explanation can already be found in the classic work of Robert Lowth, *Lectures on the Sacred Poetry of the Hebrews* (Boston: Andover, 1829), I, 57. See the general discussion by William Soll, "Babylonian and Biblical Acrostics," *Bib* 69 (1988): 320–22.
52. From *Merikarē* cited by Ronald Williams, "Scribal Training in Egypt," *JAOS* 92 (1972): 216.
53. Al Wolters, "Proverbs XXXI: 10–31 as Heroic Hymn: A Form-Critical Analysis," *VT* 38 (1988): 446–57.

54. Wilfred G. E. Watson, *Classical Hebrew Poetry: A Guide to Its Techniques. The Library of Hebrew Bible/Old Testament Studies* (JSOTSup 26; Sheffield, England: Sheffield Academic Press, 2009), 191.
55. Demsky, "Abecedaries," in *COS*, 1.107, 364.
56. See Wilfred G. Lambert, *Babylonian Wisdom Literature* (Oxford: Oxford University Press, 1960), 63.
57. My translation, adapted from B. Foster, emphasizes the repetition of the opening sign; see Foster, "The Babylonian Theodicy," in *COS*, 1:493–94, and Lambert, *Babylonian Wisdom Literature*, 76–79.
58. See Niek Veldhuis, "Elementary Education at Nippur: The Lists of Trees and Wooden Objects" (PhD diss., Rijksuniversiteit Groningen, 1997).
59. See Petra and Bonifatia Gesche's discussion of the two phases, elementary and advanced, of the Neo-Babylonian curriculum in *Schulunterricht in Babylonien: Im esrten Jahrtausend v. Chr.* (AOAT 275; Münster: Ugarit-Verlag, 2001). This distinction is also developed in Veldhuis, "Elementary Education at Nippur," and Niek Veldhuis, "On the Curriculum of the Neo-Babylonian School," *JAOS* 123 (2003): 27–33. The lexical lists are the first phase of education (i.e., elementary) and the *Babylonian Theodicy* belongs to the second phase.
60. Watson, *Classical Hebrew Poetry*, 196.
61. Kent Reynolds, *Torah as Teacher: The Exemplary Torah Student in Psalm 119* (Leiden: Brill, 2010), 16.
62. See William Soll, *Psalm 119: Matrix, Form, and Setting* (CBQMS 23; Washington, DC: Catholic Biblical Association, 1991), 52. Reynolds points out that this is not absolutely consistent (*Torah as Teacher*, 118), but there are so few exceptions that one must consider it a template from which the author was working even if attempts to reconstruct an original are not entirely convincing.
63. See Thomas Renz, "A Perfectly Broken Acrostic in Nahum 1?," *JHS* 9/23 (2010), doi: 10.5508/jhs.2009.v9.a23.
64. The deficiencies in the acrostic have caused some scholars to question whether Nah 1:2–8 is even an acrostic at all; e.g., Michael Floyd, "The Chimerical Acrostic of Nahum 1:2–10," *JBL* 113 (1994): 421–37. Yet it must be acknowledged that there is at least the remnant of an acrostic poem.
65. My organization of the acrostic follows S. de Vries, "The Acrostic of Nahum in the Jerusalem Liturgy," *VT* 16 (1966): 478. A similar reconstruction is offered by Renz, "A Perfectly Broken Acrostic in Nahum 1?," 9.
66. See observations by Coogan, "Alphabets and Elements," 61–63.
67. Some scholars (e.g., see the *Biblica Hebraica Stuttgardensia* note) suggest emending *gdwl kḥ* with *gdwl ḥsd*. The latter actually seems like a later version of this expression that gradually replaced *gdwl kḥ* (e.g., Neh 9:17; Ps 145:8; 2Chr 1:8).
68. See Anthony Ceresko, "The ABCs of Wisdom in Psalm XXXIV," *VT* 35 (1985): 99–104; and Ceresko, "Endings and Beginnings," 32–46. This is also developed by Avigdor Hurowitz, "Additional Elements of Alphabetical Thinking in Psalm XXXIV," *VT* 52 (2002): 326–33. This terminology relies on the theories of McLuhan, *The Gutenberg Galaxy*, that have been developed by a few of his students; e.g., Robert

Logan, *The Alphabet Effect: A Media Ecology Understanding of the Making of Western Civilization* (Cresskill, NJ: Hampton Press, 2004).

69. This has been pointed out by a variety of scholars; see especially Ceresko, "The ABCs of Wisdom in Psalm XXXIV," and Hurowitz, "Additional Elements of Alphabetical Thinking in Psalm XXXIV," 326–33. Some aspects are more convincing than others, and I present the most convincing observations here.
70. Michael Coogan, "'*LP*, 'To Be an Abecedarian,'" *BASOR* 110 (1990): 322.
71. In general, Hebrew prefers Verb-Subject-Object sentence structure, but a noted exception is sentences where God is the subject. This is likely a reflex of the emphatic importance of God in the sentence structure.
72. Mitchell Dahood, *Psalms I, 1–50* (AB 16; New York: Doubleday, 1995), 205.

Chapter 4

1. The most wide-ranging study of biblical lists is by Benjamin Scolnic, *Theme and Context in Biblical Lists* (Atlanta, GA: Scholars Press, 1995). A recent dissertation by Anat Mendel surveys and catalogues the various lists known in the biblical and epigraphic record as well as considering comparative examples: "Epigraphic Lists in Israel and Its Neighbors in the First Temple Period" (PhD diss., Hebrew University, 2014) [Hebrew]. Most of the attention to biblical lists has focused on genealogies, as in Robert Wilson's classic work, *Genealogy and History in the Biblical World* (YNER 7l; New Haven, CT: Yale University Press, 1977).
2. See Markus Hilgert, "Von 'Listenwissenschaft' und 'epistemischen Dingen': Konzeptuelle Annäherungen an altorientalische Wissenspraktiken," *Journal for General Philosophy of Science* 40 (2009): 277–309; Veldhuis, *History of the Cuneiform Lexical Tradition*, 22.
3. Wolfram von Soden, "Leistung und Grenze sumerische und babylonischer Wissenschaft," *Die Welt als Geschichte* 2 (1936): 411–64; Albrect Alt, "Die Weisheit Salomos," *TLZ* 76 (1951): 139–44.
4. Jack Goody, *Domestication of the Savage Mind*, Themes in the Social Sciences (Cambridge, England: Cambridge University Press, 1977), 80–81; also see, for example, Jean Bottero's description of lists in cuneiform, *Mesopotamia: Writing, Reasoning, and the Gods* (Chicago: University of Chicago Press, 1992), 29–31.
5. Scolnic, *Theme and Context in Biblical Lists*, 2.
6. Demsky assumes that lexical lists were part of scribal exercises in ancient Israel in his monograph, *Literacy in Ancient Israel*, 183–87.
7. A comprehensive history in cuneiform can be found in Veldhuis, *History of the Cuneiform Lexical Tradition*; also see the convenient analysis in Veldhuis, "Levels of Literacy." . On Egyptian onomastica, see Gardiner, *Ancient Egyptian Onomastica*.
8. Crenshaw, *Education in Ancient Israel*, 25–26.
9. Veldhuis, *History of the Cuneiform Lexical Tradition*, 226.
10. See Horowitz, Oshima, and Sanders, *Cuneiform in Canaan*.

11. See Tinney, "Texts, Tablets, and Teaching," 41–44. But the main source on lists is the magisterial work by Veldhuis, *History of the Cuneiform Lexical Tradition.*
12. A useful "crash course" in lexical lists is provided by Veldhuis, *History of the Cuneiform Lexical Tradition*, 6–13.
13. See, for example, Benno Landsberger, *The Series ḪAR-ra = Ḫubullu. Tablets I-IV* (MSL 5; Rome: Pontifical Biblical Institute, 1957).
14. Veldhuis, *History of the Cuneiform Lexical Tradition*, 149–50. Also see Veldhuis, "Elementary Education at Nippur."
15. Veldhuis, *History of the Cuneiform Lexical Tradition*, 357.
16. See Veldhuis, *History of the Cuneiform Lexical Tradition*, 279–302.
17. Cited by Carr, *Writing on the Tablet of the Heart*, 28, from Åke W. Sjöberg, "The Old Babylonian Edubba," in *Sumerological Studies in Honor of Thorkild Jacobsen on His Seventieth Birthday*, ed. Stephen Lieberman (AS 20; Chicago: University of Chicago Press, 1976), 163–64.
18. Veldhuis, *History of the Cuneiform Lexical Tradition*, 363–66.
19. My discussion is adapted from Veldhuis, who outlines changes in the lexical tradition resulting from "curricular setting, flexibility, and two-dimensionality" (*History of the Cuneiform Lexical Tradition*, 202). The two-dimensional situation reflects the cuneiform tradition of Sumerian and Akkadian in Mesopotamia proper, but the situation became multidimensional in peripheral locations like Ugarit, Emar, and the Levant in general.
20. See John Huehnergard, *Ugaritic Vocabulary in Syllabic Transcription* (HSS 34; Atlanta. GA: Scholars Press, 1987).
21. See Izre'el, *The Amarna Scholarly Tablets*; Veldhuis, *History of the Cuneiform Lexical Tradition*, 302–4.
22. The original publication was by Sydney Smith, C. J. Gadd, and T. Eric Peet, "A Cuneiform Vocabulary of Egyptian Words," *Journal of Egyptian Archaeology* 11 (1925): 230–40. Also see the publication by Izre'el, *The Amarna Scholarly Tablets*, 77–81.
23. This was already the conclusion of Smith, Gadd, and Peet, "A Cuneiform Vocabulary of Egyptian Words," 231.
24. See Carr, *Writing on the Tablet of the Heart*, 69–70 (see note 37 for bibliography).
25. As cited by Williams, "Scribal Training in Ancient Egypt," 219.
26. See Gerhard von Rad's originally published "Hiob xxxviii und die altägyptische Weisheit," *SVT* 1 (1955): 293–301 (translated as "Job XXXVIII and Ancient Egyptian Wisdom" and republished in *The Problem of the Hexateuch and Other Essays* [London: SCM Press, 1966], 281–91). Rad relies on Gardiner, *Ancient Egyptian Onomastica*. Tryggve Mettinger is also convinced of the influence of Egyptian onomastica in ancient Israel: *Solomonic State Officials: A Study of the Civil Government Officials of the Israelite Monarchy* (Lund: CWK Gleerups, 1971), 149–50. But the evidence cited is profoundly weak.
27. Michael Fox, "Egyptian Onomastica and Biblical Wisdom," *VT* 36 (1986): 304.
28. These are now comprehensively catalogued by Mendel, "Epigraphic Lists in Israel and Its Neighbors in the First Temple Period."

29. Lists of names and/or commodities can be found on the following ostraca: Arad 22, 23, 25, 27, 31, 33, 34, 35, 36, 37, 38, 39, 41, 42, 46, 47, 48, 49, 58, 59, 60, 65, 67, 69, 72, 76, and 81.
30. These are published in a variety of sources; see, for example, Ahituv, *Echoes of the Past*, 164–80. There are other, unprovenanced administrative ostraca that have been published, but we need to be cautious about their authenticity.
31. Lemaire seems to be the first scholar to describe the text as a list, saying that it was "essentiellement une liste de noms de mois" (*Les écoles*, 11). However, his discussion is quite brief, and his only support is that the Egyptian scholastic tradition also had these types of list (n. 23).
32. William F. Albright, "The Gezer Calendar," *BASOR* 92 (1943): 21.
33. For a summary of scholarly opinions, see the recent article by Vayntrub, "'Observe Due Measure,'" 191–93.
34. Johannes Renz, *Handbuch der Althebräischen Epigraphik*, vol. 3 (Darmstadt: Wissenschaftliche Buchgesellschaft, 1995), no. 1. Also see Dobbs-Allsop et al., *Hebrew Inscriptions*, 156. Kyle McCarter observes, "The limestone from which the small, hand-sized tablet is made is soft, and both surfaces show evidence of erasing and reuse. This suggests that it may have been a practice tablet and that its apparently formulaic inscription may have been a standard text used in scribal training" ("The Gezer Calendar," in *COS* 2.85).
35. See the review of literature by Vayntrub, "'Observe Due Measure,'" 191–207.
36. The handbook *Hebrew Inscriptions* also notes that its description as a "calendar" is "something of a misnomer" without explaining why (Dobbs-Allsop et al., *Hebrew Inscriptions*, 156). See especially Vayntrub, who discusses the problematic aspects of time measurement in the text ("'Observe Due Measure,'" 191–207).
37. See, for example, Oded Borowski, *Agriculture in Iron Age Israel* (Winona Lake, IN: Eisenbrauns, 1987), 32–38.
38. See the review of the literature in Dobbs-Allsop et al., *Hebrew Inscriptions*, 157–58. Another suggestion has been to see the so-called *waw* as the Egyptian hieratic number "2"; see J. B. Segal, "'Yrḥ' in the Gezer 'Calendar,'" *JSS* 7 (1962): 212–21. However, this is not supported by a close inspection of the hieratic tradition (see Wimmer, *Palästinisches Hieratisch*, 199–200). An alternative (and new) explanation concerning the *waw* appended to *yrḥ*, usually read as a plural/dual suffix, can be offered on the basis of the comparative lexical lists. It has been noted that the plural determinative MEŠ frequently—and arbitrarily—appears in the cuneiform lexical lists beginning in the Neo-Assyrian period. So, in Figure 2.2, we find GIŠ.MEŠ in three of the thirteen lines, and the plural determinative has no meaning in the lexical list. This is not an isolated example, and it must make us at least consider the possibility that the *waw* has no meaning at all other than affording scholars the opportunity to perform rather clever linguistic gymnastics. For me, however, the symmetry of a text with twelve months is too appealing to discard, and I prefer to see the *waw* as in some way intended to mark a dual.

39. Transcription and translation based Veldhuis, adapted to emphasize the repetition in the structure of the cuneiform text (*History of Cuneiform Lexical Tradition*, 412–13).
40. See Benno Landsberger, *Materialen zum sumerischen Lexicon V* (Rome: Pontifical Biblical Institute, 1957), 24–25.
41. Landsberger, *Materialen zum sumerischen Lexicon V*, 19.
42. Aaron Koller offers an ingenious philological explanation of *ʿṣd* in the Gezer Calendar, but it is much simpler to understand it as an adaptation of the cuneiform lexical tradition; see his *The Ancient Semantic Field of Cutting Tools in Biblical Hebrew: A Philological, Archaeological, and Semantic Study* (CBQMS 49; Washington, DC: Catholic Biblical Association, 2012), 75–128.
43. First, infinitives of the verb *eṣedu*, "to reap," cited above, and later infinitives *šurubum*, "to bring in (the harvest)" in lines 160–63.
44. John Huehnergard and Wilfred van Soldt, "A Cuneiform Lexical Text from Ashkelon with a Canaanite Column," *IEJ* 49 (1999): 191.
45. The original publication was by H. Misgave, Y. Garfinkel, and S. Ganor, "The Ostracon," in *Khirbet Qeiyafa Vol. 1: Excavation Report 2007–2008*, ed. Y. Garfinkel and S. Ganor (Jerusalem: Israel Exploration Society, 2009), 243–57. Some other publications include Gershon Galil, "The Hebrew Inscription from Khirbet Qeiyafa/Neta'im: Script, Language, Literature and History," *UF* 41 (2009): 193–242; Emile Puech, "L'ostracon de Khirbet Qeyafa et les débuts de la royauté en Israël," *RB* 117 (2010): 162–84; Alan Millard, "The Ostracon from the Days of David Found at Khirbet Qeiyafa," *TynBull* 62 (2011): 1–13; Christopher Rollston, "The Khirbet Qeiyafa Ostracon: Methodological Musings and Caveats," *TA* 38 (2011): 67–82; Aaron Demsky, "An Iron IIA Alphabetic Writing Exercise from Khirbet Qeiyafa," *IEJ* 62 (2012): 186–99; William Shea, "The Qeiyafa Ostracon: Separation of Powers in Ancient Israel," *Ugarit-Forschungen* 41 (2009): 601–10; Matthieu Richelle, "Quelques nouvelles lectures sur l'ostracon de Khirbet Qeiyafa," *Sem* 57 (2015): 147–62.
46. In addition to Demsky, Millard, and Richelle, Yardeni also considered the possibility that the text was merely a list of names; see "Further Observations on the Ostracon," in *Khirbet Qeiyafa, Volume 1. Excavation Report 2007–2008*, ed. Yosef Garfinkel and Saar Ganor (Jerusalem: Israel Exploration Society, 2008), 260.
47. My dating depends on the C14 along with paleographical considerations. For the material culture, see the discussion by its excavator, Yosef Garfinkel. Also see Lilly Singer-Avitz, "Khirbet Qeiyafa: Late Iron I in Spite of It All," *IEJ* 62 (2012): 177–85, and the literature cited there.
48. Galil suggests that the lines were written after the writing of the letters ("The Hebrew Inscription from Khirbet Qeiyafa/Neta'im," 194).
49. Demsky, "An Iron Age IIA Writing Exercise from Khirbet Qeiyafa," 192.
50. Compare, for example, the many administrative texts at Ugarit.
51. This classification borrows from Scolnic, *Theme and Context in Biblical Lists*, 14–18.
52. Dalley recognized the direct allusion to the cuneiform lexical tradition ("The Influence of Mesopotamia," 74).

53. For example, Alt, "Die Weisheit Salomos," 139–44; James Crenshaw, *Old Testament Wisdom: An Introduction* (Atlanta, GA: John Knox Press, 1981), 50–52.
54. John Gray, *I & II Kings* (OTL; Philadelphia: Westminster Press, 1963), 141.
55. John Day, "Foreign Semitic Influence on the Wisdom of Israel and Its Appropriation in the Book of Proverbs," in *Wisdom in Ancient Israel: Essays of J. A. Emerton*, ed. John Day, Robert P. Gordon, and Hugh Godfrey Maturin Williamson (Cambridge, England: Cambridge University Press, 1998), 61.
56. C. F. Burney, *Notes on the Hebrew Text of the Books of Kings: With an Introduction and Appendix* (Eugene: Wipf & Stock, 1903), 52; Veldhuis, *History of the Cuneiform Lexical Tradition*, 358.
57. Day, "Foreign Semitic Influence on the Wisdom of Israel and Its Appropriation in the Book of Proverbs," 62.
58. Veldhuis, *History of Cuneiform Lexical Tradition*, 201.
59. Veldhuis, *History of Cuneiform Lexical Tradition*, 201.
60. Veldhuis, *History of the Cuneiform Lexical Tradition*, 382–85.
61. See Alasdair Livingstone, "Ashurbanipal: Literate or Not?," *ZA* 97 (2007): 98–118.
62. Translation from Silvie Zamazalová, "The Education of Neo-Assyrian Princes," in *Oxford Handbook of Cuneiform Culture*, ed. Karen Radner and Eleanor Robson (Oxford: Oxford University Press, 2011).
63. Cited by Veldhuis, *History of the Cuneiform Lexical Tradition*, 384.
64. Note, for example, that Jeffrey H. Tigay corrects the JPS translation (*The JPS Torah Commentary, Deuteronomy* [Philadelphia: The Jewish Publication Society, 1996], 168). Tigay points out that the ancient commentator Philo argued that the king needed to write it himself because writing makes a more lasting impression than merely reading. The Qumran Temple Scroll, however, revises the Hebrew into a passive, so that "*they* copy the Torah for the king" (see 11QTemple 56:20–57:1).
65. The autonomous nature of the "Table of Nations" is also underscored by its presentation in the Leningrad Codex, where a blank line precedes and follows the genealogies in Genesis 10.
66. Baruch Levine, "The Descriptive Tabernacle Texts of the Pentateuch," *JAOS* 85 (1965): 307–18; also see Victor Hurowitz, "The Priestly Account of Building the Tabernacle," *JAOS* 105 (1985): 21–30.
67. Levine, "The Descriptive Tabernacle Texts of the Pentateuch," 316.
68. Scolnic, *Theme and Context in Biblical Lists*, 67–134.
69. Verses 3 and 5 should be understood as a *Wiederaufnahme*, repeating "And they set out from Rameses." The repetition frames additional editorial material that contextualizes the list within the broader narrative.
70. See Graham Davies, "The Wilderness Itineraries: A Comparative Study," *TynBull* 25 (1974): 57.
71. Example used by Davies, "The Wilderness Itineraries," 58. See updated edition of this text by Albert Kirk Grayson, *Assyrian Rulers of the Early First Millennium* BC *(1114–859)*, vol. 2 (Toronto: University of Toronto Press, 1991), 212–13 (*RIMA* 2.0.101.1, column iii, 5–7).

72. On the *Wiederaufnahme*, see H. Weiner, *The Composition of Judges II 11–1 Kings II 46* (Leipzig: J. C. Hinrichs, 1929), 2; see also C. Kuhl, "Die 'Wiederaufnahme'—ein literarisches Prinzip?" *ZAW* 64 (1952), 1–11; M. Fishbane, *Biblical Interpretation in Ancient Israel* (Oxford: Oxford University Press, 1985), 44–65;,Schniedewind, "Innerbiblical Exegesis," in *Dictionary of the Old Testament: Historical Books*, ed. Bill Arnold and Hugh Williamson (Downers Grove: Intervarsity, 2005), 502–509. In verses 1 and 2, we find the repetition, "These are the marches"; in verses 3 and 5, we have the repetition, "They set out from Rameses." The insertion in verses 1b–2a includes the expression "by the mouth of YHWH," which is fairly uncommon. The statement that "Moses recorded" seems to be a late ascription of Mosaic authorship just to this itinerary. This looks to me like a postexilic or P-ish expression, although it is impossible to be certain. In verse 3, the unique expression "they departed defiantly" (יצאו ביד רמה) clearly borrows from the narrative in Exod 14:8. And verse 4a contextualizes the itinerary list in a very broad narrative context.
73. Vayntrub, "'Observe Due Measure,'" 199–201.

Chapter 5

1. See *COS* 1.170. This text also has interesting parallels to Genesis 11 and the idea of "one language"; see Thorkild Jacobsen, *The Harps That Once* (New Haven, CT: Yale University Press, 1987), 275–319.
2. For a convenient translation, see Miriam Lichtheim, "The Report of Wenamun," in *COS*, 1.41.
3. For an exhaustive treatment, see Smith, *The Ugaritic Baal Cycle: Volume I* and Mark Smith and Wayne Pitard, *The Ugaritic Baal Cycle, Volume II, Introduction with Text, Translation and Commentary of KTU/CAT 1.3–1.4* (VTSup 114; Leiden: Brill, 2009).
4. See John Greene and Samuel Meier, *The Role of the Messenger and Message in the Ancient Near East* (BJS 169; Atlanta, GA: Scholars Press, 1989), 77–136; Dirk Schwiderski, *Handbuch des nordwestsemitischen Briefformulars: Ein Betrag zur Echtheitsfrage des aramäischen Briefe des Esrabuches* (BZAW 295; Berlin: de Gruyter, 2000), 323–27.
5. See Greene and Meier, *The Role of the Messenger and Message in the Ancient Near East*, 77–133. Also see examples in 2Kgs 5:5–7, 10:1–7, 19:14, 20:12; Jer 29:1–30; Esth 9:26–29; Ezra 4–7; Neh 2:8, 6:5; 2Chr 21:12.
6. See Pardee and Sperling, *Handbook*, 145-49; Hawley, "Studies in Ugaritic Epistolography."
7. First published in *Le Palais royal d'Ugarit* 2, no. 19. Recent discussions include Jonathan Yogev and Shamir Yona, "A Poetic Letter: The Ugaritic Tablet RS 16.265," *Studi Epigrafici e Linguistici* 31 (2014): 51–58; Juan-Pablo Vita, "The Scribal Exercise RS 16.265 from Ugarit in Its Near-Eastern Context," in *The Ancient Near East: A Life! Festscrift Karel Van Lerberghe*, ed. Tom Boiy, Joachim Bretschneider,

Anne Goddeeris, Hendrik Hameeuw, Greta Jans, and Jan Tavernier (OLA 220; Leuven: Peeters, 2012), 645–52.

8. The lines are numbered slightly differently in the original publication in *Le Palais royal d'Ugarit* 2 (no. 19), *KTU*, and by Pardee, "The Ugaritic Alphabetic Cuneiform Writing System in the Context of Other Alphabetic Systems," figure 12.5 (p. 192). Since I am utilizing Pardee's drawing, I follow Pardee's numbering as well.
9. This is noted by Hawley, "Studies in Ugaritic Epistolography," 214–15.
10. The line numbering differs among scholars because of the unusual arrangement of the columns, and I preserve the columns as labeled in *KTU* and tentatively prefer this line numbering as opposed to that suggested by Pardee.
11. Also see Bordreuil and Pardee, *Ras Shamra-Ougarit* 18, 205–6 (text no. 79).
12. For a full analysis of Ugaritic letters, see Hawley, "Studies in Ugaritic Epistolography." Hawley distinguishes two types of salutation formulas: the greeting formula, "May you be well," and the blessing formula, "May the gods guard you" (361–67).
13. Pardee actually translates this as though the scribe wrote the text correctly: "[Mess] age of ʾAbniya to ʾUrtēṯub: [I] fall" (see *COS* 3:115). However, his original publication of the text along with the drawing and photograph suggest that we have a student mistake here, see Pierre Bordreuil and Dennis Pardee, *Une bibliothèque au sud de la ville: Textes 1994–2002 en cunéiforme alphabétique de la Maison d'Ourtenou* (Paris: Maison de l'Orient et de la Méditerranée, 2012.
14. For an exhaustive study of Ugaritic letters, see Hawley, "Studies in Ugaritic Epistolography."
15. These are now published in the official version by Ahituv, Eshel, and Meshel, "The Inscriptions," 87, 95–97. For inscription 3.1, I follow Kyle McCarter, "Kuntillet ʿAjrud: Inscribed Pithos 1 (2.47A)," in *COS*, 2:171. McCarter points out that the reign of Joash in Israel (ca. 802–787 BCE) corresponds with the dating of the Kuntillet ʿAjrud inscriptions. Ahituv, Eshel, and Meshel are more reserved in the official publication and do not offer a reconstruction ("The Inscriptions," 89–90). McCarter's reconstruction is hypothetical, but it fits with the content of the practice introduction that suggests it is from a superior to an inferior.
16. See EA 342–44 discussed by Izre'el, *Amarna Scholarly Tablets*, 20–23.
17. See my comments on this in "Scripturalization in Ancient Israel," 314–18.
18. The reconstruction is developed on the basis of the official publication and photos by Ahituv, Eshel, and Meshel, "The Inscriptions," A more elaborate reconstruction is offered by Émile Puech, but he offers no evidence of different or better photographs upon which he bases his readings, so it is difficult to have any confidence in his readings ("Les Inscriptions Hébraïques de Kuntillet ʿAjrud [Sinaï]," 172).
19. The interpretation of the Hebrew *ʾšrh*, which is here translated as a proper noun, is debated. Many scholars point out that a proper noun in Hebrew normally does not take a pronominal suffix, as in "his Asherah." This is true in biblical Hebrew, but a proper noun also does not take a definite article, as in "the Teman," which we also have here. Some scholars would therefore argue that these are not proper nouns. However, the grammar of vernacular Israelite Hebrew of the early Iron Age should not be completely restricted by the grammar of biblical Hebrew or even Judean

Hebrew of the late Iron Age. See, for example, discussion by Ahituv, *Echoes from the Past*, 221–24, 319; Mark Smith, *The Early History of God: Yahweh and the Other Deities in Ancient Israel*, 2nd ed. (Grand Rapids, MI: Eerdmans, 2002), 108–47; Paolo Xella, "Le deiu et 'sa' déesse: L'utilisation des suffixes pronominaux avec des théonymes d'Ebla à Ugarit et à Kuntillet 'Ajrud," *UF* 27 (1995): 599–610; Steve Wiggins, *A Reassessment of Asherah: With Further Considerations of the Goddess* (Piscataway, NJ: Gorgias Press, 2007), 197–208; Benjamin Sass, "On Epigraphic Hebrew ʾŠR and *ʾŠRH, and on Biblical Asherah*," *Bible et Proche-Orient: Mélanges André Lemaire. Transeuphratène* 46 (2014): 50–60. Puech reads line 1 as *hmlk.ʾšyw.ʾmr.brkt.ʾtkm. lyhwh.htmn.wʾšrth* ("Les Inscriptions Hébraïques de Kuntillet ʿAjrud [Sinaï]," 172–74), but he does not give any substantive evidence for these readings, nor does he see this as a practice letter (even though his reading would fit such an interpretation).

20. This is partially recognized in the treatment by Dobbs-Allsop et al., where they call it a "blessing formula" but not a practice letter (*Hebrew Inscriptions*, 296). It is not observed in the official publication by Ahituv, Eshel, and Meshel, "The Inscriptions," 98–100, nor in the inscription handbook by Ahituv, *Echoes of the Past*, 318–19.
21. A convenient translation may be found by Dennis Pardee in *COS*, 3:115.
22. This pattern actually follows the large corpus of the Mari letters, which also have just the abbreviated address without all the additional formalities; see Wolfgang Heimpel, *Letters to the King of Mari: A New Translation, with Historical Introduction, Notes, and Commentary* (Winona Lake, IN: Eisenbrauns, 2003).
23. Alternatively, the sender may wish that "Yahweh cause you to see peace" (e.g., Lach 6:1–2).
24. See Jesús-Luis Cunchillos, "The Ugaritic Letters," in *Handbook of Ugaritic Studies*, ed. Wilfred G. E. Watson and Nicholas Wyatt (Leiden: Brill, 1999), 359–74; Hawley, "Studies in Ugaritic Epistolography"; Pardee and Sperling, *Handbook*.
25. Always in the *Hiphil* conjugation, for example, *lhgd* */lehaggīd/, "to report," in Lachish 3:1–2.
26. Formally, the expression *lʾmr*, "saying," parallels the use of the imperative verb *rgm*, "speak thus," which introduces direct speech in Ugaritic letters. For example, *KTU* 2.16 begins, "Message of Talmiyanu: To Ṯarriyell, my mother, *speak* (*rgm*): 'May it be well.'" Other parallels may be found in Mesopotamian letters such as the Mari corpus, where we find *qibima umma*, "speak, thus."
27. The typical spelling in Epigraphic Hebrew is the shorted form *wʿt*, while the longer (*plene*) spelling *wʿth* is found in Standard Biblical Hebrew. The orthography has been the subject of some discussion. Dennis Pardee rightly rejected D. N. Freedman's suggestion that the defective spelling in inscriptions "indicates a pronunciation of *ʿat* or *ʿēt*." David Noel Freedman, "The Orthography of the Arad Ostraca," *IEJ* 19 (1969): 52; Dennis Pardee, "Letters from Tel Arad," *UF* 10 (1978): 292. Pardee favors Aharoni's vocalization, *ʿattā*, which was based on the variation in the spelling of 2ms verbal forms (e.g., *ydʿth*, Arad 40:9; see Aharoni and Naveh *Arad Inscriptions*, 12). Freedman's suggestion makes it difficult to account for the Standard Biblical Hebrew orthography. As Pardee had noted, the vocalization of *wʿt* is uncertain, and it is difficult to know whether its status in Epigraphic Hebrew as a homograph with *ʿēt*,

"time," might have influenced the biblical orthography or whether its orthography was simply the reflection of a phonological development.

28. The transitional particle *wʿt* was identified by Pardee in an article ("Letters from Tel *Arad*") as well as Pardee and Sperling, *Handbook.* He notes that although he translates *wʿt* literally, "it corresponds more nearly to a paragraph division in English usage" ("Letters from Tel Arad," 292). For a more complete discussion of this marker in Northwest Semitic texts, see my contribution to the Pardee *Festschrift*, " 'And Now' *wʿt(h)*: A Transition Particle in Ancient Hebrew," in *"Like ʾIlu Are You Wise": Studies in Northwest Semitic Languages and Literatures in Honor of Dennis G. Pardee*, ed. H. H. Hardy, Joseph Lam, and Eric D. Reymond (Chicago: Oriental Institute) forthcoming.
29. For a general overview of the history and function of the space in writing, see Paul Saenger, *Space between Words: The Origins of Silent Reading* (Figurae Reading Medieval Culture; Palo Alto, CA: Stanford University Press, 1997).
30. See Frederick James Mabie, "Ancient Near Eastern Scribes and the Mark(s) They Left: A Catalog and Analysis of Scribal Auxiliary Marks in the Amarna Corpus and in the Cuneiform Alphabetic Texts of Ugarit and Ras Ibn Hani" (PhD diss., University of California Los Angeles, 2004).
31. Some of the unprovenanced texts like the Moussaieff Ostracon or the "Silver, Pistachio and Grain" Ostracon must be treated with some skepticism (see Dobbs-Allsopp et al., *Hebrew Inscriptions*, 570–71, and Ahituv, *Echoes from the Past*, 199–202). The latter, for example, has the incorrect epigraphic spelling *wʿth* (as in Standard Biblical Hebrew, but not Epigraphic Hebrew), which makes it even more suspect as a forgery.
32. On Horvat ʿUza, see Bruce Cresson and Izhaq Beit-Arieh, "An Edomite Ostracon from Ḥorvat ʿUza," *TA* 12 (1985): 97–98; on Tell el-Mazār letter, see Khair Yassine and Javier Teixidor, "Ammonite and Aramaic Inscriptions from Tel l-Mazār in Jordan," *BASOR* 264 (1986): 47. Also see Schwiderski, *Handbuch des nordwestsemitischen Briefformulars*, 55–61.
33. Metapragmatics is the linguistic anthropology category that studies how language characterizes speech awareness, functions, and reference. In the present case, metapragmatics seems like a useful theoretical category for *wʿt* inasmuch as it marks an awareness in the shift of the function of language and speakers. On metapragmatics, see Michael Silverstein, "The Limits of Awareness," in *Linguistic Anthropology: A Reader*, ed. Alessandro Duranti (Malden, MA: Blackwell, 2001), 382–401, as well as John Lucy, *Reflexive Language: Reported Speech and Metapragmatics* (Cambridge, England: Cambridge University, 2004), for its role in reported speech.
34. See James Lindenberger, *Ancient Aramaic and Hebrew Letters* (Atlanta, GA: Scholars Press, 1994). Also see Schwiderski, *Handbuch des nordwestsemitischen Briefformulars*, 164–73.
35. The pronoun/conjugation *š* fills the semantic function in the Bar-Kokhba Hebrew letters, while its semantic cognate *d(y)* was used in Aramaic (Pardee and Sperling, *Handbook*, 149–50).

36. The standard Hebrew dictionary of Koehler and Baumgartner suggests that 241 out of 273 occurrences introduce a new section, while 24 times it may be translated "but now." A few of these adversarial examples are actually suspect (e.g., Gen 32:11; Deut 10:22), while the remainder are concentrated in later Biblical Hebrew (e.g., Isa 43:1, 44:1, 47:8, 48:16, 49:5, 64:7; Hag 2:4; Ezr 9:8).
37. H. A. Brongers writes, "Zum Schluss muss nochmals darauf hingewiesen werden, dass *w*[e]*ʿattāh* niemals am Anfang einer Ansprache erscheint": "Bemerkungen zum Gebrauch des adverbialen *weʿattāh* im Alten Testament (Ein Lexikologischer Beitrag)," *VT* 15 (1965): 298.
38. Pardee, "Letters from Tel Arad," 292.
39. Examples of the expression *wʿth šmʿ* (or variations thereof) include Gen 27:8, 42; Ex 19:5; Deut 4:1; 1Sam 8:9, 15:1, 25:7, 26:19; Isa 44:1, 47:8; Jer 37:20, 42:18; Amos 7:16; Prov 5:7.
40. See Ludwig Köhler, *Deuterojesaja (Jesaja 40–55) stilkritisch undersucht* (BZAW, 37; Giessen: Töpelmann, 1923). Also see Claus Westermann, *Basic Forms of Prophetic Speech*, trans. Hugh Clayton White (Louisville, KY: Westminster John Knox Press, 1991), 98–128; and James Ross, "The Prophet as Yahweh's Messenger," in *Israel's Prophetic Heritage: Essays in Honor of James Muilenberg*, ed. Benedict Anderson and Walter Harrelson (New York: Harper, 1962), 98–107.
41. This point is made in a classic article by Sigmund Mowinckel, "'The Sprit' and the 'Word' in the Pre-Exilic Reforming Prophets," *JBL* 53 (1934): 199–227.
42. Occasionally, this expression will be used for someone not normally considered a prophet; e.g., Abram in a vision (Gen 15:1), Solomon (1Kgs 6:11). These are exceptions.
43. William Schniedewind, *The Word of God in Transition: From Prophet to Exegete in the Second Temple Period* (JSOTSS, 197; Sheffield, England: Sheffield Academic Press, 1995), 130–62. Also see William Schniedewind, "Scripturalization in Ancient Judah," in *Contextualizing Israel's Sacred Writings: Ancient Literacy, Orality, and Literary Production*, ed. Brian Schmidt (Atlanta, GA: SBL Press, 2015), 305–21.
44. See my comments in "Scripturalization in Ancient Judah," 314–15.
45. John Holladay, "Assyrian Statecraft and the Prophets of Israel," in *Prophecy in Israel: Search for Identity*, ed. David Petersen (Philadelphia: Fortress Press, 1987), 130.
46. Holladay, "Assyrian Statecraft and the Prophets of Israel," 123. Also see Jack Lindblom, "Die prophetische Orakelformel," in *Die literarische Gattung der prophetischen Literatur* (Uppsala: A-B Lundequistska Bokhandeln, 1924), appendix; Westermann, *Forms of Prophetic Speech*, 35–36.
47. Lindblom, "Die prophetische Orakelformel," appendix; Westermann, *Forms of Prophetic Speech*, 35–36. See especially the Mari letters in Heimpel, *Letters to the King of Mari*.
48. In this example, the personal name is Nabû-duru-uṣur (SAA 1:10:1). See Simon Parpola, *The Correspondence of Sargon II, Part I: Letters from Assyria and the West* (SAA 1; Helsinki: Helsinki University Press, 1987), 12.

49. In Marc Brettler's study, *God Is King: Understanding an Israelite Metaphor* (JSOTSS 76; Sheffield, England: Sheffield Academic Press, 1989), he discusses the many parallels between divine kingship and human kingship, including a brief discussion of prophetic speech (see p. 108).
50. Meindert Dijkstra, "Prophecy by Letter (Jeremiah XXIX 24–32)," *VT* 33 (1983): 319–22.

Chapter 6

1. Veldhuis, "Elementary Education at Nippur," 62.
2. Veldhuis, "Elementary Education at Nippur," 63.
3. William Albright, "An Archaic Hebrew Proverb in an Amarna Letter from Central Palestine," *BASOR* 89 (1943): 29–32.
4. See Katherine Dell, *The Book of Proverbs in Social and Theological Context* (Cambridge, England: Cambridge University Press, 2006), 57.
5. The language of the psalm as a whole is not demonstrably northern; see Gary Rendsburg, *Linguistic Evidence for the Northern Origin of Selected Psalms* (SBLMS 43; Atlanta, GA: Scholars, 1990). If it were originally northern, then we must hypothesize that it was redacted and adapted in Jerusalem leaving only "the God of Jacob" as a trace of its origins.
6. See Anton Jirku, "Kana'anäische Psalmenfragmente in der vorisraelitischen Zeit Palästinas und Syriens," *JBL* 52 (1933): 108–20. More recently, these are developed by Richard Hess, "Hebrew Psalms and Amarna Correspondence from Jerusalem," *ZAW* 101 (1989): 249–65 and Avi Shveka, "A Trace of the Tradition of Diplomatic Correspondence in Royal Psalms," *JSS* 100 (2005): 297–320.
7. The translation is my own, and I use the transcription from the new edition by A. F. Rainey, *The El-Amarna Correspondence*, 92–93.
8. Shveka, "A Trace of the Tradition of Diplomatic Correspondence," 298–99.
9. The word may also appear in Ps 61:6, but there it is spelled יְרֻשַּׁת, which seems to be a corrupted form of the original root ʾ*rš*, see *HALOT*.
10. Cited from Shveka, "A Trace of the Tradition of Diplomatic Correspondence," 301.
11. See Moshe Weinfeld, "The Significance of the Political 'Brotherhood Covenant' in Israel and in the Ancient Near East," in *Homage to Shmuel: Studies in the World of the Bible*, ed. Zipora Talshir, Shamir Yona, and Daniel Sivan (Jerusalem: Bialik Institute, 2001), 178–83 [Hebrew].
12. Now published in a new edition by Karel van der Toorn, *Papyrus Amherst 63* (AOAT, 448; Münster: Ugarit-Verlag, 2018). Van der Toorn's work relies upon the groundbreaking work of Richard Steiner and Charles Nims, which is published in an online preliminary edition, "The Aramaic Text in Demotic Script: Text, Translation, and Notes" (available on Steiner's academia.edu page with a copyright of 2017).
13. Raik Heckl, "Inside the Canon and Out: The Relationship between Psalm 20 and Papyrus Amherst 63," *Sem* 56 (2014): 362.

14. See Karel van der Toorn, "Celebrating the New Year with the Israelites: Three Extrabiblical Psalms from Papyrus Amherst 63," *JBL* 136 (2017): 633–49; and Karel van der Toorn, "Psalm 20 and Amherst Papyrus 63, XII, 11–19: A Case Study of a Text in Transit," in *Le-ma'an Ziony: Essays in Honor of Ziony Zevit*, ed. Frederick Greenspahn and Gary Rendsburg (Eugene, OR: Cascade Books, 2017), 244–62.
15. This parallel follows the layout by Karel van der Toorn, "Egyptian Papyrus Shed New Light on Jewish History," *BAR* 44/4 (2018): 37; also see his critical edition, *Papyrus Amherst 63*, 165–69.
16. See Moshe Weinfield, "The Pagan Version of Psalm 20:2–6: Vicissitudes of a Psalmodic Creation in Israel and Its Neighbors," *EI* 18 (1985): 130–40 [Hebrew], 70*. He writes, "It is well known that in Deuteronomy, we find in the days of Josiah many northern elements. The explanation for this is that after the destruction of Samaria, writers and a cultural elite descended from Samaria to Jerusalem, bringing with them a rich literary heritage. In the opinion of H. L. Ginsberg this teaches us that Proverbs 25, in the days of Hezekiah, dealt in Judea with a supplementary assembly that came from the north, and if so, a psalm, and also other northern chants, were formulated and processed in Jerusalem at that time" (138).
17. Shveka, for example, prefers to see the political context as original; also see Shveka for the history of scholarship, "A Trace of the Tradition of Diplomatic Correspondence."
18. Hess, "Hebrew Psalms and Amarna Correspondence from Jerusalem," 250.
19. Hess, "Hebrew Psalms and Amarna Correspondence from Jerusalem," 251.
20. For a convenient English translation of the *Instruction of Amenemopet*, see Miriam Lichtheim, "Instruction of Amenemope," in *COS*, 1.47.
21. John Ray, "Egyptian Wisdom Literature," in *Wisdom in Ancient Israel: Essays in Honour of J. A. Emerton*, ed. John Day, Robert Gordon, and Hugh Williamson (Cambridge, England: Cambridge University Press, 1998), 24.
22. See Vincent P.-M. Laisney, *L'Enseignement d'Aménémopé* (StPohl Series Major 19; Rome: Pontifical Biblical Institute, 2007).
23. Compare, for example, the analysis of John Ruffle, "The Teaching of Amenemopet and Its Connection with the Book of Proverbs," *TynBul* 28 (1977): 29–68; Emerton, "The Teaching of Amenemope and Proverbs XXI 17–XXIV 22," 431–65; Fox, "From Amenemope to Proverbs," 76–91. Fox imagines an Aramaic version of *Amenemope* (although there is no evidence that such a translation was ever made and no reason to suppose it would have been made). In this he is influenced by Bernd U. Schipper, who argues that the Egyptian-Hebrew influences should be dated to the seventh century BCE: "Egyptian Imperialism after the New Kingdom: The 26th Dynasty and the Southern Levant," in *Egypt, Canaan and Israel: History, Imperialism, Ideology and Literature. Proceedings of a Conference at the University of Haifa, 3–7 May 2009*, ed. Shay Bar, D. Khan, and J. J. Shirley (Leiden: Brill, 2011), 269–90. However, the hieratic numerals that this study has identified from Kuntillet ʿAjrud date to 800 BCE, and therefore the contacts must precede the mid- to late seventh century. As discussed in the introduction, the archaeology of the New Kingdom in the Levant has shown that the Egyptian presence in the Levant lasted until the end of the twelfth

century. This is still the only ancient historical period with a direct and extended Egyptian presence in the southern Levant.

24. Fox assumes that there must have been an Aramaic translation that a Hebrew scribe was working from during the seventh century BCE ("From Amenemope to Proverbs," 77). This hypothesis just adds layers of problems to the transmission mechanism.
25. Fox, "From Amenemope to Proverbs," 80–81.
26. Fox offers a fanciful explanation to account for the problematic relationship between the organization of Proverbs and Amenemopet. He posits that a scribe was reading through a scroll several times and gathered material each time, hence the difficult relationship between the structure of Proverbs and the material in Amenemopet. However, the overly textual model does not explain the very loose textual relationship between the actual wording in Proverbs and Amenemopet. The traditional oral approach still accounts much better for the loose textual relationship.
27. See Bernd Schipper, "Die Lehre des Amenemope und Prov 22,17–24,22," *ZAW* 117 (2005): 53–72, 232–48; Carr, *Writing on the Tablet of the Heart*, 126–28.
28. See Emerton's careful approach to the problem, "The Teaching of Amenemope and Proverbs XXII 17–XXIV 22," 432.
29. Emerton, "The Teaching of Amenemope and Proverbs XXII 17–XXIV 22."
30. See the overview of the translation problem by Gary Rendsburg, "Hebrew Philological Notes (II)," *HS* 42 (2001): 192–95.
31. Gesenius's classic grammar struggles with this expression but seems to suggest that it is acceptable Hebrew grammar although likely corrupt (*GKC* §135e). The suggestion that it is corrupt likely stems from the use of the *Hiph'il* verb, which is unparalleled.
32. Note that the spelling *Amenemopet* with the final *t* is a well-attested alternate spelling in the New Kingdom period. The emendation proposed here is found in the New American Bible translation (1970). It is defended at length by Gary Rendsburg, "Literary and Linguistics Matters in Proverbs," in *Perspectives on Israelite Wisdom: Proceedings of the Oxford Old Testament Seminar* (London: T & T Clark, 2016), 127–29, and Rendsburg, "Hebrew Philological Notes (II)," 192–95.
33. Translation of *The Instruction of Amenemope* by Lichtheim in *COS* 1.47.
34. Fox ("From Amenemope to Proverbs," 82) seems to imply that the term *mhr* is written in the text of the *Instructions of Amenemope* (perhaps based on a misreading of Lichtheim's translation in *COS*). However, the recent publication of the *Instructions of Amenemope* manuscripts by Laisney (*L'Enseignement de'Aménémope*, 363) does not use the West Semitic loanword *mhr* in the Egyptian text. The text only uses the usual Egyptian word for "scribe," *sš*.
35. The discussion here follows the introduction and translation by Allen, "The Craft of the Scribe," 3.2.
36. A similar corruption is found with the Egyptian term *sš* "scribe," in the Hebrew Bible. The Hebrew Bible forgets this Egyptian word in two separate passages, misunderstanding it as some form of a personal name Shisha or Sheva; see 2Sam 20:25; 1Kgs 4:3, and discussions by Mettinger, *Solomonic State Officials*, 25–26; Schniedewind, *A Social History of Hebrew*, 59.

37. Jeffrey Zorn suggests that the *mahir* may be referred to by the Akkadian term *rābiṣu* (MÁŠKIM), "commissioner," in the Amarna letters: "LÚ.pa-ma-ḫa in EA 162:74 and the Role of the *MHR* in Egypt and Ugarit," *JNES* 50 (1991): 129–38.
38. See Luis Siddall, "The Amarna Letters from Tyre as a Source for Understanding Atenism and Imperial Administration," *Journal of Ancient Egyptian Interconnections* 2 (2010): 24–35. In a classic article, William Albright points to Egyptian vocabulary and idioms; on this basis, he argues that the scribe at Tyre was a native Egyptian: "The Egyptian Correspondence of Abimilki, Prince of Tyre," *JEA* 23 (1937): 190–203.
39. Transcriptions and translations follow Rainey, *The El-Amarna Correspondence*.
40. Zorn, "LÚ. Pa-Ma-Ḫa-a in EA 162:74 and the Role of the *MHR* in Egypt and Ugarit," 133.
41. Some lexicons will list four occurrences, including Isaiah 16:5. However, in Isaiah 16:5, it is spelled defectively (*mhr* instead of *mhyr*), and its meaning does not seem to relate directly to the scribal or administrative profession (see *HALOT*).
42. The author later addresses the students, "O *tjupir yadiʿa*," which is understood as a Semitic phrase that should be translated "learned scribe"; then it uses the Egyptian equivalent, *zẖʾw sšʾw*, later in the same context. See Allen, "The Craft of the Scribe," note 29.
43. See especially Edward Ullendorff, "The Contribution of South Semitics to Hebrew Lexicography," *VT* 6 (1956): 195; James Barr, *Comparative Philology and the Text of the Old Testament* (Winona Lake, IN: Eisenbrauns, 1987), 295.
44. See Barr, *Comparative Philology and the Text of the Old Testament*, 295.
45. Olmo Lete and Sanmartín, *A Dictionary of the Ugaritic Language in the Alphabetic Tradition*, 2:536–37.
46. These are collected by Bendt Alster, *Proverbs of Ancient Sumer*, 2 volumes (Bethesda, MD: CDL Press, 1997); also see the classic work of Lambert, *Babylonian Wisdom Literature*.
47. See Wolfgang Roth, *Numerical Sayings in the Old Testament: A Form-Critical Study* (SVT, 13; Leiden: Brill, 1965).
48. Also see Prov 30:18, 21, 24, 29.
49. From the new edition by Smith and Pitard, *The Ugaritic Baal Cycle: Volume II*, 78.
50. See, for example, discussions by Edward L. Greenstein, "Wisdom in Ugaritic," *Beit Mikra: Journal for the Study of the Bible and Its World* 57 (2012): 72–73 [Hebrew]; Anton Schoors, "Literary Phrases," in *Ras Shamra Parallels: The Texts from Ugarit and the Hebrew Bible*, vol. 1, ed. Loren Fisher (AnOr 49; Rome: Pontifical Biblical Institute, 1972), 20; Joseph Blenkinsopp, *Wisdom and Law in the Old Testament: The Ordering of Life in Israel and Early Judaism*, rev. ed. (Oxford: Oxford University Press, 1995), 35–38.
51. For example, in *Numerical Sayings in the Old Testament*, Wolfgang Roth cites comparisons with Greek and even Indian literature in addition to numerous postbiblical rabbinic examples.
52. See the convenient edition Benjamin Franklin, *Poor Richard's Almanack*, ed. Andrew S. Trees (repr. New York: Barnes & Noble, 2004), originally published 1733–58.

Also see William Pencak, "Politics and Ideology in 'Poor Richard's Almanack,'" *Pennsylvania Magazine of History and Biography* 116 (1992): 183–211.

53. Daniel Pioske, "Prose Writing in an Age of Orality: A Study of 2 Sam 5:6–9," *VT* 66 (2016): 263.
54. Dell, *Proverbs*, 161; also see Vayntrub, "The Book of Proverbs and the Idea of Ancient Israelite Education," 96–114.
55. Carr, *The Formation of the Hebrew Bible*, 408–31.
56. See Dell, *Proverbs*, 15; also see J. William Whedbee, *Isaiah and Wisdom* (New York: Abingdon, 1971).
57. See the sage observations by Lemaire, "The Sage in School and Temple," 165–81.
58. See already William Albright, "Some Canaanite-Phoenician Sources of Hebrew Wisdom," in *Wisdom in Israel and in the Ancient Near East*, ed. M. Noth and D. W. Thomas (SVT 3; Leiden: Brill, 1955), 1–15; Harold Ginsberg, *The Israelian Heritage of Judaism* (New York: Ktav, 1982), 34–38; Rendsburg, "Literary and Linguistic Matters in the Book of Proverbs," 111–47.
59. Rendsburg borrows the language of Prov 25:1 here ("Literary and Linguistic Matters in the Book of Proverbs," 112–13).
60. See Michael Fishbane, *Biblical Interpretation in Ancient Israel* (Oxford: Oxford University Press, 1985).
61. See Weinfeld, *Deuteronomy and the Deuteronomic School* (Winona Lake: Eisenbrauns, 1992), 244–81.
62. Carr, *The Formation of the Hebrew Bible*, 416.
63. Carr, *The Formation of the Hebrew Bible*, 417–25.

Chapter 7

1. See Seth Sanders, *From Adapa to Enoch: Scribal Culture and Religious Vision in Judea and Babylon* (TSAJ 167; Tübingen: Mohr Siebeck, 2017).
2. Sanders, *From Adapa to Enoch*, 228.
3. Sanders, *From Adapa to Enoch*, 228.
4. Sanders, *From Adapa to Enoch*, 228.
5. Sanders, *From Adapa to Enoch*, 233.
6. See Sara J. Milstein, "The Origins of Adapa," *ZA* 104 (2015): 31; Sanders, *Adapa to Enoch*, 178.
7. Martha T. Roth, "Mesopotamian Legal Traditions and the Laws of Hammurabi," *Chicago Kent Law Review* 71 (1995): 13–40; Victor Hurowitz, "Hammurabi in Mesopotamian Tradition," in *"An Experienced Scribe Who Neglects Nothing": Ancient Near Eastern Studies in Honor of Jacob Klein*, ed. Y. Sefati et al. (Bethseda, MD: CDL Press, 2005), 497–532.
8. Van der Toorn, *Scribal Culture*, 245.
9. The complex relationship between memorization and copying is summarized and developed by Carr, *The Formation of the Hebrew Bible*, 13–36.

10. See Morrow, "Resistance and Hybridity in Late Bronze Age Canaan," 327.
11. See Daniel Arnaud, *Corpus des textes de bibliothèque de Ras Shamra-Ougarit 1936–2000) en sumérien, babylonien et assyrien* (*AuOr* 23; Sabadella: Ed. Ausa, 2007), no. 42, pp. 130–34 and pls. 19–20; Andrew George, "The Gilgameš Epic at Ugarit," *AuOr* 25 (2007): 237–54; and Sara J. Milstein, *Tracking the Master Scribe: Revision through Introduction in Biblical and Mesopotamian Literature* (Oxford: Oxford University Press, 2016), 110–46.
12. George, "The Gilgameš Epic at Ugarit," 237.
13. Andrew George, *The Babylonian Gilgamesh Epic: Introduction, Critical Edition and Cuneiform Texts*, vol. 1 (Oxford: Oxford University Press, 2003), 33–39.
14. Tinney, "Education in Ancient Mesopotamia."
15. Eleanor Robson, "The Tablet House: A Scribal School in Old Babylonian Nippur," *RA* 93 (2001): 53–54.
16. See George, *The Babylonian Gilgamesh Epic,* 342–47; also see Andrew George, *The Epic of Gilgamesh* (London: Penguin Books, 1999), 138–39.
17. These were originally published by Arnaud in *Corpus des textes de bibliothèque de Ras Shamra-Ougarit (1936–2000)*, nos. 42–45.
18. George, "The Gilgameš Epic at Ugarit," 246.
19. Milstein, *Tracking the Master Scribe*, 124–30.
20. See, for example, George, *The Babylonian Gilgamesh Epic*, 54–70; Tikva Frymer-Kensky, "The Atrahasis Epic and Its Significance for Our Understanding of Genesis 1–9," *BA* 40 (1977): 147–55; Esther Hamori, "Echoes of Gilgamesh in the Jacob Story," *JBL* 130 (2011): 625–42; Matthew J. Suriano, "Kingship and *Carpe Diem*, between Gilgamesh and Qoheleth," *VT* 67 (2017): 285–306.
21. Sanders, *From Adapa to Enoch*, 163.
22. The latter would be the solution preferred by Morrow, "Resistance and Hybridity," but we can't discount the legacy of oral tradition for texts like Qohelet and the Jacob Cycle, given the very general nature of the influence.
23. See Józef Milik, ed., *The Books of Enoch: Aramaic Fragments of Qumran Cave 4* (Oxford: Clarendon Press, 1976), 313; Klaus Beyer, *Die aramäische Texte vom Toten Meer, Ergänzungsband* (Göttingen: Vanderhoeck & Ruprecht, 1994), 119–21. Also see Loren Stuckenbruck, *The Book of Giants from Qumran: Texts, Translation, and Commentary* (TSAJ 63; Tübingen: Mohr Siebeck, 1997), and Émile Puech, *Qumrân Grotte 4: Textes arameens, première partie* (DJD 31; Oxford: Oxford University Press, 2001), 28–38, 74–78 (4Q530 frags. 2–12, 4Q531 frag. 22); Matthew Goff, "Gilgamesh the Giant: The Qumran *Book of Giants'* Appropriation of *Gilgamesh* Motifs," *Dead Sea Discoveries* 16 (2009): 221–53.
24. Dalley, "The Influence of Mesopotamia," 43.
25. See Dalley, "The Influence of Mesopotamia," 74; Jeffrey Tigay, *The Evolution of the Gilgamesh Epic* (Philadelphia: University of Pennsylvania Press, 1982), 167–68; Gerda de Villiers, "The *Epic of Gilgamesh* and the Old Testament: Parallels beyond the Deluge," *Old Testament Essays* 19 (2006): 26–34.
26. Robert Gordis, *Koheleth the Man and His World: A Study of Ecclesiastes*, 3rd ed. (New York: Schocken, 1968), 303–4.

27. Shawna Dolansky, "Gilgamesh and the Bible," *Bible Odyssey*, online: https://www.bibleodyssey.org:443/places/related-articles/gilgamesh-and-the-bible.
28. This idea was first proposed by André Lemaire; see especially "Les inscriptions sur plâtre de Deir 'Alla et leur signification historique et culturelle," in *The Balaam Text from Deir 'Alla Re-evaluated: Proceedings of the International Symposium Held at Leiden 21–24 August 1989* (Leiden: Brill, 1991), 54–55. It is has been recently advanced further by Blum, "Die Wandinschriften 4.2 Und 4.6 Sowie Die Pithos-Inschrift 3.9 Aus Kuntillet ʿAğrūd," 36–38.
29. See the summary by Wearne, "The Plaster Texts from Kuntillet ʿAjrud and Deir ʿAlla," 253–454. He seems to prefer the dream incubation interpretation, which is based on his interpretation of the content of the texts.
30. Wearne, "The Plaster Texts from Kuntillet ʿAjrud and Deir ʿAlla," 450.
31. See especially Lemaire, "Fragments from the Book of Balaam Found at Deir 'Alla,", and "Les inscriptions sur plâtre de Deir ʿAlla et leur signification historique et culturelle," 35–57.
32. The *aleph* has an unusual bent beak shape. The *beth* is formed by making a triangle and adding a leg (much like some student writing at Kuntillet ʿAjrud). The *gimel* has an unusual extension on the top of its angular shape. And the *dalet* is altogether anomalous in its form.
33. Jo Ann Hackett, *The Balaam Text from Deir ʿAllā* (HSM 31; Chico, CA: Scholars Press, 1984), 34.
34. A convenient discussion and translation by Baruch Levine may be found in *COS*, 2.27.
35. The two major parts of the plaster texts were originally numbered Combination I and II, as if they were two columns; however, it seems more likely that they are part of a single column and hence are more appropriately numbered A and B; see Blum, "Die altaramäischen Wandinschriften vom Tell Deir ʿAlla und ihr institutioneller Kontext," 24n17. On the education rubrics, also see Gareth Wearne, "'Guard It on Your Tongue!': The Second Rubric in the Deir ʿAlla Plaster Texts as an Instruction for the Oral Performance of the Narrative," in *Registers and Modes of Communication in the Ancient Near East: Getting the Message Across*, ed. K. Keimer and G. Davis (London: Routledge, 2018), 125–42.
36. I follow the reconstruction of Blum, "Die altaramäischen Wandinschriften vom Tell Deir ʿAlla und ihr institutioneller Kontext," 29, 44.
37. My reading is especially informed by Blum and Wearne; see Blum, "Die altaramäischen Wandinschriften vom Tell Deir ʿAlla und ihr institutioneller Kontext," 38–39, and Wearne, "'Guard It on Your Tongue!,'" 128.
38. Blum, "Die altaramäischen Wandinschriften vom Tell Deir ʿAlla und ihr institutioneller Kontext," 46.
39. Frank Polak, "Divine Names, Sociolinguistics, and the Pragmatics of Pentateuchal Narrative," in *Words, Ideas, Worlds: Biblical Essays in Honour of Yairah Amit*, ed. Athalia Brenner and Frank Polak (Sheffield, England: Sheffield Phoenix Press, 2012), 174; and Frank Polak, "Syntactic-Stylistic Aspects of the So-Called 'Priestly' Work in the *Torah*," in *Le-ma'an Ziony: Essays in Honor of Ziony Zevit*,

ed. Frederick Greenspahn and Gary Rendsburg (Eugene, OR: Cascade Books, 2017), 357.

40. See P. Schmidt and N. Nel, "Theophany as Type-Scene in the Hebrew Bible," *JSS* 11 (2002): 256–81; George Savran, "Theophany as Type Scene," *Prooftexts* 23 (2003): 11949.
41. Robson, "The Tablet House," 39–66.
42. See Ignacio Márquez Rowe, "The Legal Texts from Ugarit," in *Handbook of Ugaritic Studies*, ed. Wilfred G. E. Watson and Nicholas Wyatt (Leiden: Brill, 1995), 390–422.
43. See, for example, Wright's *Inventing God's Law*; Bruce Wells, "The Covenant Code and Near Eastern Legal Traditions: A Response to David P. Wright," *MAARAV* 13 (2006): 85–118.
44. Note the discussion of this topic as part of the huge tome byJan Gertz et al., *The Formation of the Pentateuch: Bridging the Academic Cultures of Europe, Israel, and North America*(FAT 111; Tübingen: Mohr Siebeck, 2016).
45. Stephanie Dalley, "Occasions and Opportunities: 1. To the Persian Conquest," in *The Legacy of Mesopotamia*, ed. Stephanie Dalley (Oxford: Oxford University Press, 1998), 19.
46. Martha Roth, *Law Collections from Mesopotamia and Asia Minor*, 2nd ed. (WAW 6; Atlanta, GA: Society of Biblical Literature, 1997), 2.
47. Roth, *Law Collections from Mesopotamia*, 2.
48. See also the outline by Tinney, "On the Curricular Setting of Sumerian Literature," 159–72.
49. Roth, *Law Collections from Mesopotamia*, 5.
50. As illustrated by Hurowitz, "Hammurabi in Mesopotamian Tradition," 497–532.
51. See, for example, Bernard Levinson, *Deuteronomy and the Hermeneutics of Legal Innovation* (New York: Oxford University Press, 1997).
52. Most notably, John Van Seters, *A Law Book for the Diaspora: Revision in the Study of the Covenant Code* (Oxford: Oxford University Press, 2002).
53. Carr, *The Formation of the Hebrew Bible*, 471–72; also see Wells, "The Covenant Code and Near Eastern Legal Traditions: A Response to David P. Wright," 85–118.
54. My discussion as well as my transcriptions and translations are based on the edition by Wayne Horowitz, Takayoshi Oshima, and Filip Vukosavović, "Hazor 18: Fragments of a Cuneiform Law Collection from Hazor," *IEJ* 62 (2012): 158–76.
55. Gary Knoppers and Paul Harvey, "The Pentateuch in Ancient Mediterranean Context: The Publication of Local Lawcodes," in *The Pentateuch as Torah: New Models for Understanding Its Promulgation and Acceptance*, ed. G. Knoppers and Bernard Levinson (Winona Lake, IN: Eisenbrauns, 2007), 105–41.
56. Filip Vukosavović, "The Laws of Hazor and the ANE Parallels," *RA* 108 (2014): 41–44.
57. Wright, *Inventing God's Law*, 5.
58. Wright, *Inventing God's Law*, 3.
59. Wright argues that the Code of Hammurabi was "canonical" in the Neo-Assyrian period (*Inventing God's Law*, 107). While it is true that it was included in Neo-Assyrian libraries and archives, there is no evidence that it was part of a regular school curriculum. I prefer to follow Roth's suggestion that the Code of Hammurabi

was studied only by "rare and fortunate scribes" (*Law Collections from Mesopotamia and Asia Minor*, 2).

60. Bob Becking suggests that Akkadian may have been known in Samaria by émigrés; see *The Fall of Samaria: An Historical and Archaeological Study* (Leiden: Brill, 1992), 114. Even if this were true, it is a very long way from some émigrés in Samaria knowing some Akkadian to an intimate textual knowledge of the Code of Hammurabi.
61. See Van Seters, *A Law Book for the Diaspora*; William Morrow, "Cuneiform Literacy and Deuteronomic Composition," *BO* 62 (2005): 204–13.
62. My analysis here is dependent on the papers and dissertation of Timothy Hogue; see, for example, "The Monumentality of the Sinaitic Decalogue: Reading Exodus 20 in Light of Northwest Semitic Monument-Making Practices," *JBL* 138 (2019): 79–99.
63. See Tinney, "On the Curricular Setting of Sumerian Literature," 159–72; Robson, "The Tablet House," 39–66.
64. For an exhaustive review of the secondary literature, see Wearne, "The Plaster Texts from Kuntillet ʿAjrud and Deir ʿAlla," 79–122.
65. Lemaire, *Les écoles*, 25–30.
66. Tinney, "On the Curricular Setting of Sumerian Literature," 159–72; Robson, "The Tablet House," 52–53.
67. For an extensive critique of the interpretation of the Kuntillet ʿAjrud site and inscriptions as "religious," see Jeremy Smoak and William Schniedewind, "Religion at Kuntillet ʿAjrud," *Religions* 10 (2019): doi:10.3390/rel10030211.
68. See Ahituv, Eshel, and Meshel, "The Inscriptions," 105–22. New (and improved?) readings are found in the later Hebrew edition by Ahituv, Eshel, and Meshel, "The Inscriptions and Their Interpretation," 73–121 [Hebrew]. Also see Lemaire, "Remarques sur les inscriptions phéniciennes de Kuntillet ʿAjrud," 83–99; Blum, "Die Wandinschriften 4.2 und 4.6 sowie die Pithos-Inschrift 3.9 aus Kuntillet ʿAğrud," *ZDPV* 129 (2013): 21–54; Puech, "Les Inscriptions Hébraïques de Kuntillet ʿAjrud (Sinaï)," 161–94.
69. See Na'ama Pat-El, "Israelian Hebrew: A Re-evaluation," *VT* 67 (2017): 243–45.
70. These are the numbers from the English edition; some of these are renumbered in the Hebrew edition.
71. Puech offers much more complete reconstructions than the official edition, but his reconstructions are based on the same photos as the original edition. It is not at all clear where his reconstructions might be superior; see Puech, "Les Inscriptions Hébraïques de Kuntillet ʿAjrud (Sinaï)," 161–94. Also see the extensive discussions of various readings and proposals by Wearne in his dissertation, "The Plaster Texts from Kuntillet ʿAjrud and Deir ʿAlla," 79–122; Lemaire, "Remarques sur les inscriptions phéniciennes de Kuntillet ʿAjrud," 83–99; Nadav Na'aman, "A New Outlook at Kuntillet ʿAjrud and Its Inscriptions," *Maarav* 20 (2013): 39–51; Blum, "Die Wandinschriften 4.2 und 4.6 sowie die Pithos-Inschrift 3.9 aus Kuntillet ʿAğrud," 21–54.
72. Benjamin Sass has proposed reading *ʾasherah* as meaning "shrine, sanctuary" instead of referring to the Canaanite deity or more generally "goddess"; see "On Epigraphic

Hebrew ʾŠR and ʾŠRH, and on Biblical Asherah," in *Bible et Proche-Orient: Mélanges André Lemaire III*, vol. 3, ed. Josette Elayi and Jean-Marie Durand (*Transeu* 46; Paris: Gabalda, 2014), 47–66. I do not find this interpretation convincing; see Smoak and Schniedewind, "Religion at Kuntillet ʿAjrud."

73. Based on the Hebrew edition by Ahituv, Eshel, and Meshel, "Inscriptions and Their Interpretation," 117. In the English *editio princeps*, Meshel, Ahituv, and Eshel suggested reconstructing this as [*wrʿm*] *bʿl bql*[*h*] "Baʾal [thundered] with [his] voice" ("The Inscriptions," 117). The theme of divine theophany would be evident in this reading, but the reading in the Hebrew edition seems preferable.
74. See Watson, *Classical Hebrew Poetry*, 136–42.
75. See Tallay Ornan's chapter on the drawings in the Hebrew edition, "The Drawings from Kuntillet ʿAjrud," 43–68.
76. Examples are conveniently collected and summarized in Kenton Sparks, *Ancient Texts for the Study of the Hebrew Bible: A Guide to the Background Literature* (Peabody, MA: Hendrickson, 2005).

Epilogue

1. See my article, "Aramaic, the Death of Written Hebrew, and Language Shift in the Persian Period," in *Margins of Writing: Origins of Cultures*, ed. Seth Sanders (Oriental Institute Seminars 2; Chicago, 2006), 135–52; and Schniedewind, *A Social History of Hebrew*, 126–63.
2. Jack Goody, *The Logic of Writing and the Organization of Society* (Cambridge, England: Cambridge University Press, 1986).
3. This is a topic that deserves further systematic and synthetic treatment. The best summary is Scolnic's revised dissertation, *Theme and Context in Biblical Lists*, 1–25. In spite of their importance, lists do not receive much attention.
4. Sanders, *From Adapa to Enoch*, 233.

Bibliography

Aharoni, Yohanon, and Joseph Naveh. *Arad Inscriptions*. Jerusalem: Israel Exploration Society, 1981.

Ahituv, Shmuel. *Echoes from the Past: Hebrew and Cognate Inscriptions from the Biblical Period*. Jerusalem: Carta, 2008.

Ahituv, Shmuel, Esther Eshel, and Zeev Meshel. "The Inscriptions." Pages 73–142 in *Kuntillet ʿAjrud: An Iron Age II Religious Site on the Judah-Sinai Border*. Edited by Zeev Meshel, Shmuel Ahituv, and Liora Freud. Jerusalem: Israel Exploration Society, 2012.

Albright, William Foxwell. "The Egyptian Correspondence of Abimilki, Prince of Tyre." *JEA* 23 (1937): 190–203.

Albright, William Foxwell. *City Invincible: A Symposium on Urbanization and Cultural Development in the Ancient Near East; Held at the Oriental Institute of the University of Chicago, December 4–7, 1958*. Edited by Robert Martin Adams and Carl Hermann Kraeling. Chicago: University of Chicago Press, 1960.

Albright, William Foxwell. *The Proto-Sinaitic Inscriptions and Their Decipherment*. Cambridge, MA: Harvard University Press, 1969.

Al-Jallad, Ahmed, and Ali Al-Manaser. "A Thamudic B Abecedary in the South Semitic Letter Order." Pages 1–15 in *The Semitic Languages in Contact*. Edited by Aaron Butts. Leiden: Brill, 2015.

Alster, Bendt. *Proverbs of Ancient Sumer: The World's Earliest Proverb Collections*. Bethesda, MD: CDL Press, 1997.

Alt, Albrecht. "Die Weisheit Salomos." *TLZ* 76 (1951): 139–44.

Arnaud, Daniel. *Corpus Des Textes de Bibliothèque de Ras Shamra-Ougarit: (1936–2000); En Sumérien, Babylonien et Assyrien*. AuOr 23. Sabadella: Ed. Ausa, 2007.

Aster, Shawn Zelig. "Transmission of Neo-Assyrian Claims of Empire to Judah in the Late Eighth Century B.C.E." *HUCA* 78 (2007): 1–44.

Avigad, Nahman, and Benjamin Sass. *Corpus of West Semitic Stamp Seals*. Jerusalem: Israel Exploration Society, 1997.

Beck, Pirhiya. "The Drawings from Horvat Teiman (Kuntillet 'Ajrud)." *TA* 9 (1982): 3–68.

Becking, Bob. *The Fall of Samaria: An Historical and Archaeological Study*. Leiden: E. J. Brill, 1992.

Beyer, Klaus. *Die Aramäische Texte Vom Toten Meer, Ergänzungsband*. Göttingen: Vandenhoeck & Ruprecht, 1994.

Blenkinsopp, Joseph. *Wisdom and Law in the Old Testament: The Ordering of Life in Israel and Early Judaism*. Rev. ed. Oxford: Oxford University Press, 1995.

Blum, Erhard. "Die Wandinschriften 4.2 Und 4.6 Sowie Die Pithos-Inschrift 3.9 Aus Kuntillet ʿAǧrūd." *ZDPV* 129 (2013): 21–54.

Blum, Erhard. "Die altaramäischen Wandinschriften vom Tell Deir ʿAlla und ihr institutioneller Kontext." Pages 21–52 in *Materiale Textkulturen*. Volume 15. Edited by Ludger Lieb. Berlin: de Gruyter, 2016.

Blum, Erhard. "Institutionelle und kulturelle Vorassetzungen der israelitischen Traditionsliteratur." Pages 1–42 in *Konstruktion, Transmission und Transformation von Tradition(en) im alten Israel*, edited by Ruth Ebach and Martin Leuenberger. Mohr Siebeck: Tübingen, 2018.

Bordreuil, Pierre, and Dennis Pardee. *A Manual of Ugaritic*. Winona Lake, IN: Eisenbrauns, 2009.

Bordreuil, Pierre, and Dennis Pardee. *Une Bibliothèque Au Sud de La Ville: Textes 1994–2002 En Cunéiforme Alphabétique de La Maison d'Ourtenou*. RSou 18. Paris: Maison de l'Orient et de la Méditerranée, 2012.

Borowski, Oded. *Agriculture in Iron Age Israel*. Winona Lake, IN: Eisenbrauns, 1987.

Bottéro, Jean. *Mesopotamia: Writing, Reasoning, and the Gods*. Translated by Zainab Bahrani and Marc Van De Mieropp. Chicago: University of Chicago Press, 1992.

Botterweck, Johannes, Helmer Ringgren, and Heinz-Josef Fabry, eds. *Theological Dictionary of the Old Testament*. Translated by D. Stott. Grand Rapids, MI: Eerdmans, 1998.

Brettler, Marc Zvi. *God Is King: Understanding an Israelite Metaphor*. JSOTSup 76. Sheffield, England: Sheffield Academic Press, 1989.

Brongers, H. A. "Bemerkungen Zum Gebrauch Des Adverbialen We'attāh Im Alten Testament (Ein Lexikologischer Beitrag)." *VT* 15 (1965): 289–99.

Burke, Aaron. "Entanglement, the Amorite Koiné, and Amorite Cultures in the Levant." *ARAM* 26 (2014): 357–73.

Burke, Aaron. "Left Behind: Egyptian in the Southern Levant after Empire." In *James K. Hoffmeier Festschrift*. Winona Lake, IN: Eisenbrauns, forthcoming.

Burney, C. F. *Notes on the Hebrew Text of the Books of Kings: With an Introduction and Appendix*. Eugene: Wipf & Stock, 1903.

Byrne, Ryan. "The Refuge of Scribalism in Iron I Palestine." *BASOR* 345 (2007): 1–31.

Carr, David McLain. *Writing on the Tablet of the Heart: Origins of Scripture and Literature*. Oxford: Oxford University Press, 2005.

Carr, David McLain. *The Formation of the Hebrew Bible: A New Reconstruction*. Oxford: Oxford University Press, 2011.

Ceresko, Anthony R. "The ABCs of Wisdom in Psalm XXXIV." *VT* 35 (1985): 99–104.

Ceresko, Anthony R. "Endings and Beginnings: Alphabetic Thinking and the Shaping of Psalms 106 and 150." *CBQ* 68 (2006): 32–46.

Charpin, Dominique. *Reading and Writing in Babylon*. Translated by Jane Marie Todd. Cambridge, MA: Harvard University Press, 2010.

Cohen, Rudolph, and Hannah Bernick-Greenberg, eds. *Excavations at Kadesh Barnea (Tell El-Qudeirat) 1976–1982*. Jerusalem: Israel Antiquities Authority, 2007.

Coulmas, Florian. *Writing Systems: An Introduction to Their Linguistic Analysis*. Cambridge, England: Cambridge University Press, 2003.

Crenshaw, James L. *Old Testament Wisdom: An Introduction*. Atlanta, GA: John Knox Press, 1981.

Crenshaw, James L. *Education in Ancient Israel: Across the Deadening Silence*. New York: Doubleday, 1998.

Cresson, Bruce, and Itzhaq Beit-Arieh. "An Edomite Ostracon from Horvat 'Uza." *TA* 12 (1985): 96–101.

Cross, Frank Moore. "A Literate Soldier: Lachish Letter III." Pages 41–47 in *Biblical and Related Studies Presented to Samuel Iwry*. Edited by Ann Kort and Scott Morschauser. Winona Lake, IN: Eisenbrauns, 1985.

Cross, Frank Moore. "Paleography and the Date of the Tell Fahariyeh Bilingual Inscription." Pages 393–409 in *Solving Riddles and Untying Knots: Biblical, Epigraphic, and Semitic Studies in Honor of Jonas C. Greenfield*. Edited by Ziony Zevit, Seymour Gitin, and Sokoloff Michael. Winona Lake, IN: Eisenbrauns, 1995.

Cross, Frank Moore, and John Huehnergard. "The Alphabet on a Late Babylonian Cuneiform School Tablet." *Or* 72 (2003): 223–28.

Cross, Frank Moore, and Thomas O. Lambdin. "A Ugaritic Abecedary and the Origins of the Proto-Canaanite Alphabet." *BASOR* 160 (1960): 21–26.

Crouch, Carly L. *Israel and the Assyrians: Deuteronomy, the Succession Treaty of Esarhaddon, and the Nature of Subversion*. Atlanta, GA: Society of Biblical Literature, 2014.

Cunchillos, Jesús-Luis. "The Ugaritic Letters." Pages 359–74 in *Handbook of Ugaritic Studies*. Edited by Wilfred G. E. Watson and Nicholas Wyatt. Leiden: Brill, 1999.

Cunchillos, Jesús-Luis, J. P. Vita, and José-Ángel Zamora, eds. *Ugaritic Data Bank*. Translated by Alfonso Lacadena and Alberto Castro. Madrid: Laboratorio de Hermeneumatic, 2003.

Dahood, Mitchell J. *Psalms I, 1–50*. AB 16. New Haven, CT: Yale University Press, 1995.

Dalley, Stephanie. "Occasions and Opportunities: 1. To the Persian Conquest." Pages 9–34 in *The Legacy of Mesopotamia*. Edited by Stephanie Dalley. Oxford: Oxford University Press, 1998.

Dalley, Stephanie. "The Influence of Mesopotamia upon Israel and the Bible." Pages 57–84 in *The Legacy of Mesopotamia*. Edited by Stephanie Dalley. Oxford: Oxford University Press, 1998.

Daniels, Peter T. "The Study of Writing Systems." Pages 3–17 in *The World's Writing Systems*. Edited by Peter T. Daniels and William Bright. Oxford: Oxford University Press, 1996.

Day, John. "Foreign Semitic Influence on the Wisdom of Israel and Its Appropriation in the Book of Proverbs." Pages 55–70 in *Wisdom in Ancient Israel: Essays of J. A. Emerton*. Edited by John Day, Robert P. Gordon, and Hugh Godfrey Maturin Williamson. Cambridge, England: Cambridge University Press, 1998.

Demsky, Aaron. "A Proto-Canaanite Abecedary Dating from the Period of the Judges and Its Implications for the History of the Alphabet." *TA* 4 (1977): 14–27.

Demsky, Aaron. "The 'Izbet Sartah Ostracon—Ten Years Later." Pages 186–97 in *Izbet Ṣarṭah: An Early Iron Age Site Near Rosh Ha'ayin, Israel*. Edited by Israel Finkelstein and Vronwy Hankey. Oxford: Oxford University Press, 1986.

Demsky, Aaron. "The Education of Canaanite Scribes in the Mesopotamian Cuneiform Tradition." Pages 157–70 in *Bar-Ilan Studies in Assyriology: Dedicated to Pinḥas Artzi*. Edited by Jacob Klein and Aaron Skaist. Ramat-Gan: Bar-Ilan University Press, 1990.

Demsky, Aaron. "An Iron Age IIA Alphabetic Writing Exercise from Khirbet Qeiyafa." *IEJ* 62 (2012): 186–99.

Demsky, Aaron. *Literacy in Ancient Israel*. Jerusalem: Bialik Institute, 2012. [Hebrew]

Demsky, Aaron. "Researching Literacy in Ancient Israel—New Approaches and Recent Developments." Pages 89–104 in *See, I Will Bring a Scroll Recounting What Befell Me (Ps 40:8): Epigraphy and Daily Life from the Bible to the Talmud*. Edited by Esther Eshel and Yigal Levin. Göttingen: Vandenhoeck & Ruprecht, 2014.

Demsky, Aaron. "The Interface of Oral and Written Traditions in Ancient Israel: The Case of Abecedaries." Pages 23–31 in *Origins of the Alphabet: Proceedings of the First Polis Institute Interdisciplinary Conference*. Edited by Christophe Rico and Claudia Attucci. Newcastle upon Tyne, England: Cambridge Scholars Press, 2015.

Dijkstra, Meindert. "Prophecy by Letter (Jeremiah XXIX 24–32)." *VT* 33 (1983): 319–22.

Dobbs-Allsopp, F., J. M. Roberts, Choon Seow, and Robert Whitaker, eds. *Hebrew Inscriptions: Texts from the Biblical Period of the Monarchy with Concordance*. New Haven, CT: Yale University Press, 2005.

Dolansky, Shawna, "Gilgamesh and the Bible." *Bible Odyssey*. Online: https://www.bibleodyssey.org:443/places/related-articles/gilgamesh-and-the-bible.

Emerton, John A. "The Teaching of Amenemope and Proverbs XXII 17–XXIV 22: Further Reflections on a Long-Standing Problem." *VT* 51 (2001): 431–65.

Finkel, Irving. "A Babylonian ABC." *British Museum Magazine* 31 (1998): 20–22.

Finkelstein, Israel. *The Forgotten Kingdom: The Archaeology and History of Northern Israel*. Atlanta, GA: Society of Biblical Literature, 2013.

Finkelstein, Israel. "The Historical Setting of Kuntillet ʿAjrud." *MAARAV* 20 (2013): 27–38.

Finkelstein, Israel, and Benjamin Sass. "The West Semitic Alphabetic Inscriptions, Late Bronze II to Iron IIA: Archeological Context, Distribution and Chronology." *HBAI* 2 (2013): 149–220.

Fischer-Elfert, Hans W. *Die Satirische Streitschrift Des Papyrus Anastasi I: Übersetzung Und Kommentar*. ÄgAbh 44. Wiesbaden: Harrassowitz, 1986.

Fischer-Elfert, Hans W., and Manfred Krebernik. "Zu Den Buchstabennamen Auf Dem Halaḥam-Ostrakon Aus TT 99 (Grab Des Sennefri)." *ZÄS* 143 (2016): 169–76.

Fishbane, Michael. *Biblical Interpretation in Ancient Israel*. Oxford: Oxford University Press, 1985.

Fox, Michael V. "Egyptian Onomastica and Biblical Wisdom." *VT* 36 (1986): 302–10.

Fox, Michael V. "From Amenemope to Proverbs: Editorial Art in Proverbs 22,17–23,11." *ZAW* 126 (2014): 76–91.

Franken, H. J. "Introduction." In *The Balaam Text from Deir ʿAlla Re-Evaluated: Proceedings of the International Symposium Held at Leiden, 21–24 August 1989*. Edited by Jacob Hoftijzer and Gerrit Van der Kooij. Leiden: Brill, 1991.

Franklin, Benjamin. *Poor Richard's Almanack*. Edited by Andrew S. Trees. 1733–58. Repr. New York: Barnes & Nobles, 2004.

Freedman, David Noel. "The Orthography of the Arad Ostraca." *IEJ* 19 (1969): 52–56.

Frick, Frank. *The City in Ancient Israel*. SBLMS 36. Missoula, MT: Scholars Press, 1977.

Frymer-Kensky, Tikva. "The Atrahasis Epic and Its Significance for Our Understanding of Genesis 1–9." *BA* 40 (1977): 147–55.

Galán, José M. "An Apprentice's Board from Dra Abu El-Naga." *JEA* 93 (2007): 95–116.

Galil, Gershon. "The Hebrew Inscription from Khirbet Qeiyafa/Neta'im: Script, Language, Literature and History." *UF* 41 (2009): 193–242.

Gardiner, Alan H. "The Egyptian Origin of the Semitic Alphabet." *JEA* 3 (1916): 1–16.

Gardiner, Alan H. *Ancient Egyptian Onomastica*. Oxford: Oxford University Press, 1947.

Garfinkel, Yosef, and Saar Ganor, eds. *Khirbet Qeiyafa: Excavation Report 2007–2008*. Vol. 1. Jerusalem: Israel Exploration Society, 2009.

Gelb, Ignace Jay. *A Study of Writing*. Revised ed. Chicago: University of Chicago Press, 1962.

George, Andrew. *The Epic of Gilgamesh*. London: Penguin Books, 1999.

George, Andrew. *The Babylonian Gilgamesh Epic: Introduction, Critical Edition and Cuneiform Texts*. 2 vols. Oxford: Oxford University Press, 2003.

George, Andrew. "The Gilgameš Epic at Ugarit." *AuOr* 25 (2007): 237–54.

Gertz, Jan Christian, Bernard M Levinson, Dalit Rom-Shiloni, and Konrad Schmid, eds. *The Formation of the Pentateuch: Bridging the Academic Cultures of Europe, Israel, and North America*. FAT 111. Tübingen: Mohr Siebeck, 2016.

Gesche, Petra D., and Bonifatia Gesche. *Schulunterricht in Babylonien: Im Ersten Jahrtausend V. Chr.* AOAT 275. Münster: Ugarit-Verlag, 2000.

Gesenius, Wilhelm, and Emil Kautzsch. *Gesenius' Hebrew Grammar*. 2nd ed. Oxford: Clarendon Press, 1910.

Goldwasser, Orly. "On the Invention of the Alphabet: On 'Lost Papyri' and the Egyptian Alphabet." Pages 124–40 in *Origins of the Alphabet: Proceedings of the First Polis Institute Interdisciplinary Conference*. Edited by Christophe Rico and Claudia Attucci. Newcastle upon Tyne, England: Cambridge Scholars Press, 2015.

Goldwasser, Orly. "From the Iconic to the Linear—The Egyptian Scribes of Lachish and the Modification of the Early Alphabet in the Late Bronze Age." Pages 118–60 in *Alphabets, Texts and Artifacts in the Ancient Near East: Studies Presented to Benjamin Sass*. Edited by Israel Finkelstein, Thomas Römer, and Christian Robin. Paris: Van Dieren Editeur, 2016.

Goody, Jack. *Domestication of the Savage Mind*. Themes in the Social Sciences. Cambridge, England: Cambridge University Press, 1977.

Gordis, Robert. *Koheleth the Man and His World: A Study of Ecclesiastes*. 3rd ed. New York: Schocken, 1968.

Goren, Yuval, Hans Mommsen, Israel Finkelstein, and Nadav Na'aman. "A Provenance Study of the Gilgamesh Fragment from Megiddo." *Archaeometry* 51 (2009): 763–73.

Graham Davies. "The Wilderness Itineraries: A Comparative Study." *TynBul* 25 (1974): 46–81.

Gray, John. *I & II Kings*. OTL. Philadelphia: Westminster Press, 1963.

Grayson, Albert Kirk. *Assyrian Rulers of the Early First Millennium BC (1114–859)*. Vol. 2. RIM. Toronto: University of Toronto Press, 1991.

Greene, John T., and Samuel Meier. *The Role of the Messenger and Message in the Ancient Near East*. BJS 169. Atlanta, GA: Scholars Press, 1989.

Greenstein, Edward L. "Wisdom Written in Ugaritic." *Beit Mikra: Journal for the Study of the Bible and Its World* 57 (2012): 91–72. [Hebrew]

Gunkel, Hermann, and Joachim Begrich. *Introduction to Psalms: The Genres of the Religious Lyric of Israel*. Translated by James Nogalski. 1933. Repr., Macon, GA: Mercer University Press, 1998.

Gzella, Holger. "Abecedaries." In *Encyclopedia of Hebrew Language and Linguistics*. Edited by Geoffrey Khan, Shmuel Bolozky, Steven Fassberg, Gary Rendsburg, Aaron Rubin, Ora Schwarzwald, and Tamar Zewi. Leiden: Brill, 2013. [Online: doi:http://dx.doi.org/10.1163/2212-4241_ehll_EHLL_COM_00000228]

Hadley, Judith M. "Kuntillet Ajrud: Religious Centre or Desert Way Station?" *PEQ* 125 (1993): 115–24.

Hallo, William W. "Isaiah 28:9–13 and the Ugaritic Abecedaries." *JBL* 77 (1958): 324–38.

Hallo, William W. "Sumerian Literature: Background to the Bible." *BRev* 4 (1988): 28–38.

Hamilton, Gordon J. *The Origins of the West Semitic Alphabet in Egyptian Scripts*. CBQMS 40. Washington, DC: Catholic Biblical Association, 2006.

Hamori, Esther. "Echoes of Gilgamesh in the Jacob Story." *JBL* 130 (2011): 625–42.

Haran, Menahem. "On the Diffusion of Literacy and Schools in Ancient Israel." Pages 81–95 in *Congress Volume Jerusalem 1986*. Edited by John A. Emerton. Leiden: Brill, 1988.

Haring, Ben. "*Halaḥam* on an Ostracon of the Early New Kingdom?" *JNES* 74 (2015): 189–96.

Hawley, Robert. "Studies in Ugaritic Epistolography." PhD diss., University of Chicago, 2003.

Hawley, Robert. "On the Alphabetic Scribal Curriculum at Ugarit." *Studies in Ancient Oriental Civilization* 62 (2005): 57–67.

Hawley, Robert, Dennis Pardee, and Carole Roche-Hawley. "The Scribal Culture of Ugarit." *JANES* 2 (2016): 229–67.

Heckl, Raik. "Inside the Canon and Out: The Relationship between Psalm 20 and Papyrus Amherst 63." *Sem* 56 (2014): 359–79.

Heidel, Alexander. *The Babylonian Genesis: The Story of the Creation*. 2nd ed. Chicago: University of Chicago Press, 1951.

Heimpel, Wolfgang. *Letters to the King of Mari: A New Translation, with Historical Introduction, Notes, and Commentary*. Winona Lake, IN: Eisenbrauns, 2003.

Hess, Richard S. "Hebrew Psalms and Amarna Correspondence from Jerusalem: Some Comparisons and Implications" *ZAW* 101 (1989): 249–65.

Hilgert, Markus. "Von 'Listenwissenschaft' Und 'epistemischen Dingen': Konzeptuelle Annäherungen an Altorientalische Wissenspraktiken." *Journal for General Philosophy of Science* 40, no. 2 (2009): 277–309.

Hoch, James E. *Semitic Words in Egyptian Texts of the New Kingdom and Third Intermediate Period*. Princeton, NJ: Princeton University Press, 1994.

Hodder, Ian. *Entangled: An Archaeology of the Relationships between Humans and Things*. Malden, MA: Wiley-Blackwell, 2012.

Hogue, Timothy. "The Monumentality of the Sinaitic Decalogue: Reading Exodus 20 in Light of Northwest Semitic Monument-Making Practices," *JBL* 138 (2019): 79–99.

Holladay, John. "Assyrian Statecraft and the Prophets of Israel." Pages 122–43 in *Prophecy in Israel: Search for Identity*. Edited by David Petersen. IRT 10. Philadelphia: Fortress Press, 1987.

Horowitz, Wayne, Takayoshi Oshima, and Seth Sanders. *Cuneiform in Canaan: The Next Generation. Revised Edition*. Jerusalem: Israel Exploration Society, 2018.

Horowitz, Wayne, Takayoshi Oshima, and Filip Vukosavović. "Hazor 18: Fragments of a Cuneiform Law Collection from Hazor." *IEJ* 62 (2012): 158–76.

Huehnergard, John. *Ugaritic Vocabulary in Syllabic Transcription*. HSS 32. Atlanta, GA: Scholars Press, 1987.

Huehnergard, John, and Wilfred van Soldt. "A Cuneiform Lexical Text from Ashkelon with a Canaanite Column." *IEJ* 49 (1999): 184–92.

Hurowitz, Victor Avigdor. "The Priestly Account of Building the Tabernacle." *JAOS* 105 (1985): 21–30.

Hurowitz, Victor Avigdor. "Additional Elements of Alphabetical Thinking in Psalm XXXIV." *VT* 52 (2002): 326–33.

Izreʿel, Shlomo. *The Amarna Scholarly Tablets*. CM 9. Göttingen: Styx, 1997.

Jacobsen, Thorkild. *The Harps That Once*. New Haven, CT: Yale University Press, 1987.

Jamieson-Drake, David W. *Scribes and Schools in Monarchic Judah: A Socio-Archeological Approach*. Sheffield, England: Journal for the Study of the Old Testament, 1991.

Jirku, Anton. "Kana'anäische Psalmenfragmente in Der Vorisraelitischen Zeit Palästinas Und Syriens." *JBL* 53 (1933): 108–20.

Kammerzell, Frank. "Die Entstehung Der Alphabetreihe: Zum Ägyptischen Ursprung Der Semitischen Und Westlichen Schriften." Pages 117–58 in *Hieroglyphen, Alphabete, Schriftreformen: Studien Zu Multiliteralismus, Schriftwechsel Und Orthographieneuregelungen*. Edited by Dörte Borchers, Stefan Weninger, and Frank Kammerzell. Lingua Aegyptia 3. Göttingen: Seminar für Ägyptologie und Koptologie, 2011.

Keel, Othmar, and Christopher Uehlinger. *Gods, Goddesses, and Images of God*. Minneapolis, MN: Fortress Press, 1998.

King, Ross. "Korean Writing." Pages 218–25 in *The World's Writing Systems*. Edited by Peter T. Daniels and William Bright. Oxford: Oxford University Press, 1996.

Kletter, Raz. *Economic Keystones: The Weight System of the Kingdom of Judah*. JSOTSup 276. Sheffield, England: Sheffield Academic Press, 1998.

Klostermann, August. *Schulwesen Im Alten Israel*. Leipzig: Georg Böhme, 1908.

Kochavi, Moshe. "An Ostracon of the Period of the Judges from 'Izbet Sartah." *TA* 4 (1977): 1–13.

Koehler, Ludwig, Walter Baumgartner, and Johann J. Stamm, eds. *The Hebrew and Aramaic Lexicon of the Old Testament*. Translated and edited by Marilyn E. Richardson. 3rd ed. 2 vols. Leiden: Brill, 1994–99.

Köhler, Ludwig. *Deuterojesaja (Jesaja 40–55) Stilkritisch Undersucht*. BZAW 37. Giessen: Töpelmann, 1923.

Laisney, Vincent Pierre-Michel. *L'Enseignement d'Aménémopé*. StPohl Series Maior 19. Rome: Pontifical Biblical Institute, 2007.

Lambert, Wilfred G. *Babylonian Wisdom Literature*. Oxford: Oxford University Press, 1960.

Landsberger, Benno. *Materialen Zum Sumerischen Lexicon V*. Rome: Pontifical Biblical Institute, 1957.

Landsberger, Benno. *The Series ḪAR-Ra = Ḫubullu. Tablets I–IV.* MSL 5. Rome: Pontifical Biblical Institute, 1957.

Leeb, Carolyn S. *Away from the Father's House: The Social Location of the Na'ar and Na'arah in Ancient Israel.* Sheffield, England: Sheffield Academic Press, 2000.

Lemaire, André. *Les écoles et la formation de la bible dans l'ancien Israël.* OBO 39. Göttingen: Vandenhoek & Ruprecht, 1981.

Lemaire, André. "Fragments from the Book of Balaam Found at Deir Alla." *BAR* 11 (2005): 27–39.

Lemaire, André. "Remarques Sur Les Inscriptions Phéniciennes de Kuntillet ʿAjrud." *Sem* 55 (2013): 83–99.

Lemaire, André. "The Kuntillet 'Ajrud Inscriptions Forty Years after Their Discovery." Pages 196–208 in *Alphabets, Texts and Artifacts in the Ancient Near East: Studies Presented to Benjamin Sass.* Edited by Israel Finkelstein, Christian Robin, and Thomas Römer. Paris: Van Dieren Editeur, 2016.

Lemaire, André. "Notes d'épigraphie sémitique," *Semitica* 58 (2016), 237–246.

Levine, Baruch A. "The Descriptive Tabernacle Texts of the Pentateuch." *JAOS* 85 (1965): 307–18.

Lindblom. "Die Prophetische Orakelformel." In *Die Literarische Gattung Der Prophetischen Literatur.* Uppsala: A-B Lundequistska Bokhandeln, 1924.

Lindenberger, James. *Ancient Aramaic and Hebrew Letters.* Atlanta, GA: Scholars Press, 1994.

Livingstone, Alasdair. "Ashurbanipal: Literate or Not?" *ZA* 97 (2007): 98–118.

Logan, Robert K. *The Alphabet Effect: A Media Ecology Understanding of the Making of Western Civilization.* Cresskill, NJ: Hampton Press, 2004.

Lowth, Robert. *Lectures on the Sacred Poetry of the Hebrews.* Boston: Andover, 1829.

Lucy, John. *Reflexive Language: Reported Speech and Metapragmatics.* Cambridge, England: Cambridge University Press, 2004.

Mabie, Frederick James. "Ancient Near Eastern Scribes and the Mark(s) They Left: A Catalog and Analysis of Scribal Auxiliary Marks in the Amarna Corpus and in the Cuneiform Alphabetic Texts of Ugarit and Ras Ibn Hani." PhD diss., University of California Los Angeles, 2004.

MacDonald, John. "The Status and Role of the *Naʿar* in Israelite Society." *JNES* 35 (1976): 147–70.

Mandell, Alice. "Contract, Scribal Exercise, or a Colossal Joke? Rethinking the MRZH. Tablet at Ugarit (RS 1957.702 = KTU 3.9 = TU 3.9)." Paper presented at the Annual Meeting of the American Oriental Society. Los Angeles, March 17–20, 2017.

Manfried, Dietrich, Oswald Loretz, and Joaquín Sanmartín, eds. *The Cuneiform Alphabetic Texts from Ugarit, Ras Ibn Hani and Other Places.* Münster: Ugarit-Verlag, 1995.

Mayer-Opificius, R., and Walter Mayer. "Schlact Bei Qadeš: Der Versuch Einer Neuen Rekonstrucktion." *UF* 26 (1994): 321–68.

McLuhan, Marshall. *The Gutenberg Galaxy: The Making of Typographic Man.* Toronto: University of Toronto Press, 1962.

Mendel, Anat. "Epigraphic Lists in Israel and Its Neighbors in the First Temple Period." PhD diss., Hebrew University, 2014. [Hebrew]

Meshel, Zeev. "On the Problem of Tell el-Kheleifeh, Elath and Ezion-Geber." *EI: Archaeological, Historical and Geographical Studies* 12 (1975): 49–56.

Meshel, Zeev. *Kuntillet ʿAjrud: An Iron Age II Religious Site on the Judah-Sinai Border*. Jerusalem: Israel Exploration Society, 2012.

Mettinger, Tryggve N. D. *Solomonic State Officials: A Study of the Civil Government Officials of the Israelite Monarchy*. Lund: CWK Gleerups, 1971.

Milik, Józef Tadeusz, ed. *The Books of Enoch: Aramaic Fragments of Qumran Cave 4*. Oxford: Clarendon Press, 1976.

Millard, Alan R. "The Ostracon from the Days of David Found at Khirbet Qeiyafa." *TynBul* 62 (2011): 1–13.

Miller, D. Gary. *Ancient Scripts and Phonological Knowledge*. Current Issues in Linguistic Theory 116. Philadelphia: John Benjamins Publishing, 1994.

Milstein, Sara J. "The Origins of Adapa." *ZA* 105 (2015): 30–41.

Milstein, Sara J. *Tracking the Master Scribe: Revision through Introduction in Biblical and Mesopotamian Literature*. Oxford: Oxford University Press, 2016.

Morais, José. "Constraints on the Development of Phonemic Awareness." Pages 5–28 in *Phonological Processes in Literacy: A Tribute to Isabelle Y. Liberman*. Edited by Donald P. Shankweiler and Susan Brady. New York: Routledge, 2001.

Morrow, William S. "Cuneiform Literacy and Deuteronomic Composition." *BO* 62 (2005): 204–13.

Morrow, William S. "Resistance and Hybridity in Late Bronze Age Canaan." *RB* 115 (2008): 321–39.

Mowinckel, Sigmund. "'The Spirit' and the 'Word' in the Pre-Exilic Reforming Prophets." *JBL* 53 (1934): 199–227.

Munch, P. A. "Die Alphabetische Akrostichie in Der Jüdischen Psalmendichtung." *ZDMG* 90 (1936): 703–10.

Mynářova, Jana. "Tell Fekheriye Inscription: A Process of Authority on the Edge of the Assyrian Empire." Pages 9–40 in *The Process of Authority: The Dynamics in Transmission and Reception of Canonical Texts*. Edited by Jan Dušek. DCLS 27. Boston: de Gruyter, 2016.

Mynářova, Jana, ed. *Handbook of Amarna Cuneiform Paleography*. Prague: Charles University Press, 2018.

Na'aman, Nadav. "A New Outlook at Kuntillet ʿAjrud and Its Inscriptions." *MAARAV* 20 (2015): 39–51.

Na'aman, Nadav, and Nurit Lissovsky. "Kuntillet 'Ajrud, Sacred Trees and the Asherah." *TA* 35 (2008): 186–208.

Nur, Amos, and Dawn Burgess. *Apocalypse: Earthquakes, Archaeology, and the Wrath of God*. Princeton, NJ: Princeton University Press, 2008.

Olmo Lete, Gregorio del, and J. Sanmartín. *A Dictionary of the Ugaritic Language in the Alphabetic Tradition*. 2nd ed. Leiden: Brill, 2004.

Ornan, Tallay. "The Drawings from Kuntillet ʿAjrud," Pages 44–68 in *To* YHWH *Teman and His* ashera: *The Inscriptions and Drawings from Kuntillet ʿAjrud ('Ḥorvat Tēman') in Sinai*. Edited by Shmuel Ahituv and Esther Eshel. Jerusalem: Yad Ben-Zvi, 2015. [Hebrew]

Ornan, Tallay. "Sketches and Final Works of Art: The Drawings and Wall Paintings of Kuntillet 'Ajrud Revisited," *TA* 43 (2016): 3–26.

Ornan, Tallay, Shlomit Weksler-Bdolah, and Benjamin Sass. "A 'Governor of the City' Seal Impression from the Western Wall Plaza Excavations in Jerusalem." *Qadmaniot* 50 (2017): 100–103. [Hebrew]

Otto, Eckart. "Town and Rural Countryside in Ancient Israelite Law: Reception and Redaction in Cuneiform and Israelite Law." *JSOT* 57 (1993): 3–22.

Palmer, Edward H. *The Desert of the Exodus: Journeys on Foot in the Wilderness of the Forty Years' Wanderings*. London: Bell and Daldy, 1871.

Pardee, Dennis. "Letters from Tel Arad." *UF* 10 (1978): 289–336.

Pardee, Dennis. "The Ugaritic Alphabetic Cuneiform Writing System in the Context of Other Alphabetic Systems." Pages 181–200 in *Studies in Semitic and Afro-Asiatic Linguistics Presented to Gene B. Gragg*. Edited by Cynthia L. Miller and Charles E. Jones. SAOC 60. Chicago: Oriental Institute of the University of Chicago, 2007.

Pardee, Dennis, and S. David Sperling. *Handbook of Ancient Hebrew Letters: A Study Edition*. Vol. 15. SBLSBS. Chico, CA: Scholars Press, 1982.

Parkinson, Richard. *Cracking Codes: The Rosetta Stone and Decipherment*. Berkeley: University of California Press, 1999.

Parkinson, Richard, and Stephen Quirke. *Papyrus*. Austin: University of Texas Press, 1995.

Parpola, Simo. *The Correspondence of Sargon II, Part I: Letters from Assyria and the West*. SAA 1. Helsinki: Helsinki University Press, 1987.

Pedersen, Olof. *Archives and Libraries in the Ancient Near East, 1500–300 B.C.* Bethesda, MD: CDL Press, 1998.

Pencak, William. "Politics and Ideology in 'Poor Richard's Almanack.'" *Pennsylvania Magazine of History and Biography* 116 (1992): 183–211.

Pioske, Daniel. "The Scribe of David: A Portrait of a Life." *MAARAV* 20 (2013): 163–88.

Pioske, Daniel. "Prose Writing in an Age of Orality: A Study of 2 Sam 5:6–9." *VT* 66 (2016): 261–79.

Pratico, Gary. *Nelson Glueck's 1938–40 Excavations at Tell El-Kheleifeh: A Reappraisal*. Atlanta, GA: Scholars Press, 1993.

Puech, Émile. *Qumrân Grotte 4: Textes arameens, première partie*. DJD 31. Oxford: Clarendon Press, 2001.

Puech, Émile. "'L'ostracon de Khirbet Qeyafa et les débuts de la royauté en Israël.'" *RB* 117 (2010): 162–84.

Puech, Émile. "Les Inscriptions Hébraïques de Kuntillet 'Ajrud (Sinaï)." *RB* 121 (2014): 161–94.

Quick, Laura. "Job 38 and Ancient Egyptian Wisdom." Pages 281–91 in *The Problem of the Hexateuch and Other Essays*. Translated by E. W. Trueman Dicken. New York: McGraw-Hill, 1966.

Quick, Laura. *Wisdom in Israel*. Translated by James D. Martin. London: S.C.M Press, 1972.

Quick, Laura. *Deuteronomy 28 and the Aramaic Curse Tradition*. New York: Oxford University Press, 2018.

Rad, Gerhard von. "Hiob XXXVIII Und Die Altägyptische Weisheit." Pages 293–301 in *Wisdom in Israel and in the Ancient Near East: Presented to Harold Henry Rowley by the Editorial Board of Vetus Testamentum in Celebration of His 65th Birthday, 24 March 1955*. Edited by Martin Noth and D. Winton Thomas. SVT 3. Leiden: Brill, 1969.

Rad, Gerhard von. "Job XXXVIII and Ancient Egyptian Wisdom." Pages 281–91 in *The Problem of the Hexateuch and Other Essays*. London: SCM Press, 1966.

Rainey, Anson F. "The Military Personnel of Ugarit." *JNES* 24 (1965): 17–27.

Rainey, Anson F. *The El-Amarna Correspondence: A New Edition of the Cuneiform Letters from the Site of El-Amarna Based on Collations of All Extant Tablets*. Edited by William Schniedewind. Vol. 1. HdO 110. Leiden: Brill, 2015.

Ramos, Melissa. "A Northwest Semitic Curse Formula: The Sefire Treaty and Deuteronomy 28." *ZAW* 128 (2016): 205–20.

Raschke, Donna, Sandra Alper, and Elaine Eggers. "Recalling Alphabet Letter Names: A Mnemonic System to Facilitate Learning." *Preventing School Failure: Alternative Education for Children and Youth* 43(1999): 80–83.

Ray, John. "Egyptian Wisdom Literature." Pages 17–29 in *Wisdom in Ancient Israel: Essays of J. A. Emerton*. Edited by John Day, Robert P. Gordon, and Hugh Godfrey Maturin Williamson. Cambridge, England: Cambridge University Press, 1998.

Read, Charles, Zhang Yun-Fei, Nie Hong-Yin, and Ding Bao-Qing. "The Ability to Manipulate Speech Sounds Depends on Knowing Alphabetic Writing." *Cognition* 24 (1986): 31–44.

Rendsburg, Gary. *Linguistic Evidence for the Northern Origin of Selected Psalms*. SBLMS 43. Atlanta, GA: Scholars Press, 1990.

Rendsburg, Gary. "Hebrew Philological Notes (II)." *HS* 42 (2001): 187–95.

Rendsburg, Gary. "Literary and Linguistic Matters in the Book of Proverbs." Pages 111–47 in *Perspectives on Israelite Wisdom: Proceedings of the Oxford Old Testament Seminar*. Edited by John Jarick. London: T&T Clark, 2016.

Renz, Johannes, and Wolfgang Röllig. *Handbuch der Althebräischen Epigraphik*. Vol. 1. Darmstadt: Wissenschaftliche Buchgesellschaft, 1995.

Reynolds, Kent. *Torah as Teacher: The Exemplary Torah Student in Psalm 119*. Leiden: Brill, 2010.

Richelle, Matthieu. "Quelques nouvelles lectures sur l'ostracon de Khirbet Qeiyafa." *Sem* 57 (2015): 147–62.

Rico, Christophe, and Claudia Attucci, eds. *Origins of the Alphabet: Proceedings of the First Polis Institute Interdisciplinary Conference*. Cambridge, England: Cambridge Scholars Publishing, 2015.

Robson, Eleanor. "The Tablet House: A Scribal School in Old Babylonian Nippur." *RA* 93 (2001): 39–66.

Robson, Eleanor. "Mesopotamian Mathematics." Pages 57–186 in *The Mathematics of Egypt, Mesopotamia, China, India, and Islam: A Sourcebook*. Edited by Victor J. Katz. Princeton, NJ: Princeton University Press, 2007.

Robson, Eleanor. "The Production and Dissemination of Scholarly Knowledge." Pages 557–76 in *The Oxford Handbook of Cuneiform Culture*. Edited by Karen Radner and Eleanor Robson. Oxford: Oxford University Press, 2011.

Rollston, Christopher A. "Scribal Education in Ancient Israel: The Old Hebrew Epigraphic Evidence." *BASOR* 344 (2006): 47–74.

Rollston, Christopher A. *Writing and Literacy in the World of Ancient Israel: Epigraphic Evidence from the Iron Age*. Atlanta: SBL Press, 2010.

Rollston, Christopher A. "The Khirbet Qeiyafa Ostracon: Methodological Musings and Caveats." *TA* 38 (2011): 67–82.

Rollston, Christopher A. "Scribal Curriculum during the First Temple Period: Epigraphic Hebrew and Biblical Evidence." Pages 71–102 in *Contextualizing Israel's Sacred Writings: Ancient Literacy, Orality, and Literary Production*. Edited by Brian B Schmidt. Atlanta, GA: Society of Biblical Literature, 2015.

Ross, James. "The Prophet as Yahweh's Messenger." Pages 98–107 in *Israel's Prophetic Heritage: Essays in Honor of James Muilenburg*. Edited by Bernhard Anderson and Walter Harrelson. New York: Harper, 1962.

Roth, Martha T. *Law Collections from Mesopotamia and Asia Minor*. 2nd ed. WAW 6. Atlanta, GA: Society of Biblical Literature, 1997.

Roth, Wolfgang. *Numerical Sayings in the Old Testament: A Form-Critical Study*. SVT 13. Leiden: Brill, 1965.

Rowe, Ignacio Márquez. "The Legal Texts from Ugarit." Pages 390–422 in *Handbook of Ugaritic Studies*. Edited by Wilfred G. E. Watson and Nicholas Wyatt. Leiden: Brill, 1999.

Ruffle, John. "The Teaching of Amenemope and Its Connection with the Book of Proverbs." *TynBul* 8 (1977): 29–78.

Saenger, Paul. *Space between Words: The Origins of Silent Reading*. Figurae Reading Medieval Culture. Palo Alto, CA: Stanford University Press, 1997.

Sanders, Seth. "Writing and Early Iron Age Israel." Pages 97–112 in *Literate Culture and Tenth-Century Canaan*. Edited by Ron Tappy and P. Kyle McCarter. Winona Lake, IN: Eisenbrauns, 2008.

Sanders, Seth. *The Invention of Hebrew*. Chicago: University of Illinois Press, 2009.

Sanders, Seth. *From Adapa to Enoch: Scribal Culture and Religious Vision in Judea and Babylon*. TSAJ 167. Tübingen: Mohr Siebeck, 2017.

Sass, Benjamin. "The Genesis of the Alphabet and Its Development in the Second Millennium B.C.—Twenty Years Later." *De Kemi à Birit Nari* 2 (2005): 147–66.

Sass, Benjamin. "On Epigraphic Hebrew 'ŠR and *'ŠRH, and on Biblical Asherah." *Bible et Proche-Orient: Mélanges André Lemaire. Transeuphratène* 46 (2014): 47–66.

Schipper, Bernd U. "Egyptian Imperialism after the New Kingdom: The 26th Dynasty and the Southern Levant." Pages 269–90 in *Egypt, Canaan and Israel: History, Imperialism, Ideology and Literature. Proceedings of a Conference at the University of Haifa, 3–7 May 2009*. Edited by Shay Bar, D. Kahn, and J. J. Shirley. Leiden: Brill, 2011.

Schipper, Bernd Ulrich. "Die Lehre Des Amenemope Und Prov 22,17–24,22: Eine Neubestimmung Des Literarischen Verhältnisses (Teil 1)." *ZAW* 117 (2005): 53–72.

Schmidt, Brian B. "The Iron Age Pithoi Drawings from Horvat Teman or Kuntillet'Ajrud: Some New Proposals." *JANER* 2 (2002): 91–125.

Schmidt, Brian B. "Memorializing Conflict: Toward an Iron Age 'Shadow' History of Israel's Earliest Literature." Pages 103–32 in *Contextualizing Israel's Sacred*

Writings: Ancient Literacy, Orality, and Literary Production. Edited by Brian B. Schmidt. Atlanta, GA: Society of Biblical Literature, 2015.

Schneider, Thomas. "A Double Abecedary? *Halaḥam* and *ʾAbgad* on the TT99 Ostracon." *BASOR* 379 (2018): 103–12.

Schniedewind, William. "Sociolinguistic Reflections on the Letter of a 'Literate' Soldier (Lachish 3)." *ZAH* 13 (2000): 157–67.

Schniedewind, William. "Scribal Culture and the Making of the Hebrew Bible." *JHS* 10 (2010): 29.

Schniedewind, William. *A Social History of Hebrew: Its Origins through the Rabbinic Period*. New Haven, CT: Yale University Press, 2014.

Schniedewind, William. "Understanding Scribal Education in Ancient Israel: A View from Kuntillet ʿAjrud." *MAARV* 21 (2014): 271–93.

Schniedewind, William. "Scripturalization in Ancient Israel." Pages 305–21 in *Contextualizing Israel's Sacred Writings: Ancient Literacy, Orality, and Literary Production*. Edited by Brian B Schmidt. Atlanta, GA: SBL Press, 2015.

Schniedewind, William. "An Early Iron Age Phase to Kuntillet ʿAjrud." Pages 134–48 in *Le-Maʿan Ziony: Essays in Honor of Ziony Zevit*. Edited by Gary Rendsburg and Frederick Greenspahn. Eugene, OR: Cascade Books, 2017.

Schniedewind, William. "Education in Ancient Israel and Judah into the Persian Period." Pages 11–28 in *Second Temple Jewish Paideia in Context*. Edited by G. Boccaccini and J. Zurawski. BZNW. Berlin: de Gruyter, 2017.

Schniedewind, William. "'And Now' *wʿt(h)*: A Transition Particle in Ancient Hebrew." Forthcoming in *"Like ʾIlu Are You Wise": Studies in Northwest Semitic Languages and Literatures in Honor of Dennis G. Pardee*. Edited by H. H. Hardy, Joseph Lam, and Eric D. Reymond. Chicago: Oriental Institute.

Schoors, Anton. "Literary Phrases." Pages 3–70 in *Ras Shamra Parallels: The Texts from Ugarit and the Hebrew Bible*. Vol 1. Edited by Loren R. Fisher. AnOr 49. Rome: Pontifical Biblical Institute, 1972.

Schwiderski, Dirk. *Handbuch Des Nordwestsemitischen Briefformulars: Ein Betrag Zur Echtheitsfrage Des Aramäischen Briefe Des Esrabuches*. BZAW 295. Berlin: de Gruyter, 2000.

Scolnic, Benjamin Edidin. *Theme and Context in Biblical Lists*. Atlanta, GA: Scholars Press, 1995.

Scott, R. B. Y. "Solomon and the Beginnings of Wisdom." Pages 262–79 in *Wisdom in Israel and in the Ancient Near East: Presented to Harold Henry Rowley by the Editorial Board of Vetus Testamentum in Celebration of His 65th Birthday, 24 March 1955*. Edited by Martin Noth and D. Winton Thomas. SVT 3. Leiden: Brill, 1969.

Sebba, Mark. "Iconisation, Attribution and Branding in Orthography." *Written Language and Literacy* 18 (2015): 208–27.

Segal, J. B. "'YRH' in the Gezer 'Calendar.'" *JSS* 7 (1962): 212–21.

Shea, William. "The Qeiyafa Ostracon: Separation of Powers in Ancient Israel." *UF* 41 (2009): 601–10.

Shupak, Nili. "Learning Methods in Ancient Israel." *VT* 53 (2003): 416–26.

Shveka, Avi. "A Trace of the Tradition of Diplomatic Correspondence in Royal Psalms." *JSS* 100 (2005): 297–320.

Siddall, Luis Robert. "The Amarna Letters from Tyre as a Source for Understanding Atenism and Imperial Administration." *Journal of Ancient Egyptian Interconnections* 2 (2010): 24–35.

Silverstein, Michael. "The Limits of Awareness." Pages 382–401 in *Linguistic Anthropology: A Reader*. Edited by Alessandro Duranti. Malden, MA: Blackwell, 2001.

Singer-Avitz, Lily. "Khirbet Qeiyafa: Late Iron Age I in Spite of It All." *IEJ* 62 (2012): 177–85.

Sjöberg, Åke W. "The Old Babylonian Eduba." Pages 159–80 in *Sumerological Studies in Honor of Thorkild Jacobsen on His Seventieth Birthday*. Edited by Stephen Lieberman. AS 20. Chicago: University of Chicago Press, 1976.

Smith, Mark S. *The Ugaritic Baal Cycle: Volume I, Introduction with Text, Translation and Commentary of KTU 1.1–1.2*. VTSup 105. Leiden: Brill, 1994.

Smith, Mark S. *The Early History of God: Yahweh and the Other Deities in Ancient Israel*. 2nd ed. Grand Rapids, MI: Eerdmans, 2002.

Smith, Mark S., and Wayne Pitard. *The Ugaritic Baal Cycle: Volume II, Introduction with Text, Translation and Commentary of KTU/CAT 1.3–1.4*. VTSup 114. Leiden: Brill, 2008.

Smoak, Jeremy. *The Priestly Blessing in Inscription and Scripture: The Early History of Numbers 6:24–26*. New York: Oxford University Press, 2015.

Smoak, Jeremy, and William Schniedewind. "Religion at Kuntillet ʿAjrud." *Religions* 10 (2019): doi:10.3390/rel10030211.

Soden, Wolfram von. "Leistung Und Grenze Sumerische Und Babylonischer Wissenschaf." *Die Welt Als Geschichte* 2 (1936): 411–64.

Soll, William Michael. "Babylonian and Biblical Acrostics." *Bib* 69 (1988): 305–23.

Soll, William Michael. *Psalm 119: Matrix, Form, and Setting*. CBQMS 23. Washington, DC: Catholic Biblical Association of America, 1991.

Sparks, Kenton. *Ancient Texts for the Study of the Hebrew Bible: A Guide to the Background Literature*. Peabody, MA: Hendrickson Publishers, 2005.

Steiner, Richard, and Charles Nims. "The Aramaic Text in Demotic Script: Text, Translation, and Notes." Online self-publication, 2017.

Stuckenbruck, Loren. *The Book of Giants from Qumran: Texts, Translation, and Commentary*. TSAJ 63. Tübingen: Mohr Siebeck, 1997.

Suriano, Matthew J. "Kingship and *Carpe Diem* between Gilgamesh and Qoheleth." *VT* 67 (2017): 285–306.

Tigay, Jeffrey H. "On Evaluating Claims of Literary Borrowing." Pages 250–55 in *The Tablet and the Scroll: Near Eastern Studies in Honor of William W. Hallo*. Edited by Mark E Cohen, Daniel C. Snell, and David B. Weisberg. Bethesda, MD: CDL Press, 1993.

Tigay, Jeffrey H. *The JPS Torah Commentary, Deuteronomy*. Philadelphia: The Jewish Publication Society, 1996.

Tigay, Jeffrey H. *The Evolution of the Gilgamesh Epic*. Philadelphia: University of Pennsylvania Press,1982.

Tinney, Stephen. "Texts, Tablets, and Teaching: Scribal Education in Nippur and Ur." *Expedition* 40 (1998): 40–50.

Tinney, Stephen. "On the Curricular Setting of Sumerian Literature." *Iraq* 61 (1999): 159–72.

Tinney, Stephen. "Education in Ancient Mesopotamia." Paper presented at the Nangeroni Conference: Second Temple Jewish Paideia in Its Ancient Near Eastern and Hellenistic Contexts. Naples, Italy, June 30–July 4, 2015.

Toorn, Karel van der. *Scribal Culture and the Making of the Hebrew Bible*. Cambridge, MA: Harvard University Press, 2007.

Toorn, Karel van der. "Celebrating the New Year with the Israelites: Three Extrabiblical Psalms from Papyrus Amherst 63." *JBL* 136 (2017): 633–49.

Toorn, Karel van der. *Papyrus Amherst 63*. AOAT 448. Münster: Ugarit-Verlag, 2018.

Ullendorff, Edward. "The Contribution of South Semitics to Hebrew Lexicography." *VT* 6 (1956): 190–98.

Van Seters, John. *A Law Book for the Diaspora: Revision in the Study of the Covenant Code*. Oxford: Oxford University Press, 2002.

Van Soldt, Wilfred. *Studies in the Akkadian of Ugarit: Dating and Grammar*. AOAT 40. Neukirchener: Neukirchen-Vluyn, 1991.

Van Soldt, Wilfred. "The Written Sources: The Syllabic Akkadian Texts." Pages 28–45 in *Handbook of Ugaritic Studies*. Edited by Wilfred G. E. Watson and Nicolas Wyatt. Leiden: Brill, 1999.

Vanstiphout, H. L. J. "How Did They Learn Sumerian?" *JCS* 31 (1979): 118–26.

Vayntrub, Jacqueline. "'Observe Due Measure': The Gezer Calendar and Dividing the Trip around the Sun." Pages 191–207 in *Epigraphy, Philology, and the Hebrew Bible: Methodological Perspectives on the Comparative Study of the Hebrew Bible in Honor of Jo Ann Hackett*. Edited by Jeremy Michael Hutton and Aaron D. Rubin. Atlanta, GA: Society of Biblical Literature, 2015.

Vayntrub, Jacqueline. "The Book of Proverbs and the Idea of Ancient Israelite Education." *ZAW* 128 (2016): 96–114.

Veldhuis, Niek. "Cuneiform Tablet as an Educational Tool." *Dutch Studies on Near Eastern Languages and Cultures* 2 (1996): 11–26.

Veldhuis, Niek. "Elementary Education at Nippur: The Lists of Trees and Wooden Objects." PhD diss., Rijksuniversiteit Groningen, 1997.

Veldhuis, Niek. "On the Curriculum of the Neo-Babylonian School." *JAOS* 123 (2003): 627–33.

Veldhuis, Niek. "Levels of Literacy." Pages 68–89 in *The Oxford Handbook of Cuneiform Culture*. Edited by Karen Radner and Eleanor Robson. Oxford: Oxford University Press, 2011.

Veldhuis, Niek. *History of the Cuneiform Lexical Tradition*. GMTR 7. Münster: Ugarit-Verlag, 2016.

Veldhuis, Niek. "Schools in Ancient Mesopotamia." *Oxford Bibliographies* (2015). doi: 10.1093/obo/9780195393361-0196

Vita, Juan-Pablo. "The Scribal Exercise RS 16.265 from Ugarit in Its Near-Eastern Context." Pages 645–52 in *The Ancient Near East: A Life! Festscrift Karel Van Lerberghe*. Edited by Tom Boiy, Joachim Bretschneider, Anne Goddeeris, Hendrik Hameeuw, Greta Jans, and Jan Tavernier. OLA 220. Leuven: Peeters, 2012.

Vukosavović, Filip. "The Laws of Hazor and the ANE Parallels." *RA* 108 (2014): 41–44.

Watson, Wilfred G. E. *Classical Hebrew Poetry: A Guide to Its Techniques*. The Library of Hebrew Bible/Old Testament Studies. JSOTSup 26. Sheffield, England: Sheffield Academic Press, 2009.

Wearne, Gareth. "The Plaster Texts from Kuntillet ʿAjrud and Deir ʿAlla: An Inductive Approach to the Emergence of Northwest Semitic Literary Texts in the First Millennium B.C.E." PhD diss., Macquarie University, 2015.

Weeks, Stuart. *Early Israelite Wisdom*. Oxford: Oxford University Press, 2000.

Weinfeld, Moshe. "The Pagan Version of Psalm 20:2–6: Vicissitudes of a Psalmodic Creation in Israel and Its Neighbors." *EI* 18 (1985): 130–40. [Hebrew]

Weinfeld, Moshe. "The Significance of the Political 'Brotherhood Covenant' in Israel and in the Ancient Near East." Pages 178–83 in *Homage to Shmuel: Studies in the World of the Bible*. Edited by Zipora Talshir, Shamir Yona, and Daniel Sivan. Jerusalem: Bialik Institute, 2001. [Hebrew]

Wells, Bruce. "The Covenant Code and Near Eastern Legal Traditions: A Response to David P. Wright." *MAARAV* 13 (2006): 85–118.

Westermann, Claus. *Basic Forms of Prophetic Speech*. Translated by Hugh Clayton White. Louisville, KY: Westminster John Knox Press, 1991.

Whybray, Roger. *The Composition of the Book of Proverbs*. JSOTSup 168. Sheffield, England: Sheffield Academic Press, 1994.

Wiggins, Steve. *A Reassessment of Asherah: With Further Considerations of the Goddess*. Piscataway, NJ: Gorgias Press, 2007.

Williams, Ronald J. "Scribal Training in Ancient Egypt." *JAOS* 92 (1972): 214–21.

Wilson, Robert R. *Genealogy and History in the Biblical World*. YNER 7. New Haven, CT: Yale University Press, 1977.

Wimmer, Stefan. *Palästinisches Hieratisch: Die Zahl- Und Sonderzeichen in Der Althebräischen Schrift*. ÄAT 75. Wiesbaden: Harrassowitz, 2008.

Wright, David P. *Inventing God's Law: How the Covenant Code of the Bible Used and Revised the Laws of Hammurabi*. New York: Oxford University Press, 2009.

Yassine, Khair, and Javier Teixidor. "Ammonite and Aramaic Inscriptions from Tell El-Mazār in Jordan." *BASOR* 264 (1986): 45–50.

Yogev, Jonathan, and Shamir Yona. "A Poetic Letter: The Ugaritic Tablet RS 16.265." *SEL* 31 (2014): 51–58.

Young, Robb Andrew. *Hezekiah in History and Tradition*. SVT 155. Leiden: Brill, 2012.

Younger, K. Lawson, and William W. Hallo, eds. *Archival Documents from the Biblical World*. Vol. 3 of *The Context of Scripture*. Leiden: Brill, 2003.

Younger, K. Lawson, and William W. Hallo, eds. *Canonical Compositions from the Biblical World*. Vol. 1 of *The Context of Scripture*. Leiden: Brill, 2003.

Younger, K. Lawson, and William W. Hallo, eds. *Monumental Inscriptions from the Biblical World*. Vol. 2 of *The Context of Scripture*. Leiden: Brill, 2003.

Zamazalová, Silvie. "The Education of Neo-Assyrian Princes." Pages 313–34 in *Oxford Handbook of Cuneiform Culture*. Edited by Karen Radner and Eleanor Robson. Oxford: Oxford University Press, 2011.

Zhakevich, Phillip. "The Tools of an Israelite Scribe: A Semantic Study of the Terms Signifying the Tools and Materials of Writing in Biblical Hebrew." PhD diss., University of Texas at Austin, 2015.

Zorn, Jeffrey. "LÚ. Pa-Ma-Ḫa-a in EA 162:74 and the Role of the MHR in Egypt and Ugarit." *JNES* 50 (1991): 129–38.

Index of Citations of Primary Texts

Index Term List